Achievements and Challenges of Fiscal Decentralization

Lessons from Mexico

Edited by
Marcelo M. Giugale and
Steven B. Webb

THE WORLD BANK
WASHINGTON, D.C.

©2000 The International Bank for Reconstuction
and Development/THE WORLD BANK
1818 H Street N.W.
Washington, D.C. 20433

The cover illustration is *Pareja* (1990) by Rodrigo Pimentel, reproduced courtesy of the artist and Chac-Mool Gallery, Los Angeles. Photograph by Javier Hinojosa.

Library of Congress Cataloging-in-Publication data has been applied for.

Contents

List of Tables

List of Figures

List of Boxes

Acknowledgements

THIS VOLUME IS THE RESULT of a team effort and, as such, it has benefited from an array of invaluable contributions. Our thanks are therefore due to a large number of people. First, the chapters' authors, who have provided not just material of outstanding technical quality but a remarkable commitment to enriching the debate about decentralization in Mexico. We consider ourselves fortunate to share this book with Enrique Cabrero Mendoza, Thomas Courchene, Alberto Díaz-Cayeros, Fausto Hernández Trillo, Jorge Martinez-Vazquez, Charles E. McLure, Jr., Vinh Nguyen, João C. Oliveira, and Fernando Rojas.

While this book reflects the authors' own views (and not necessarily the views of the World Bank, its Board of Executive Directors or its member countries), its production was institutionally housed at the World Bank. We thus benefited enormously from the general guidance of Olivier Lafourcade (Director of the Mexico Country Department) and Guillermo Perry (Chief Economist for the Latin America and Caribbean Region), and from the auspices of the office of David de Ferranti (Vice-President for Latin America and the Caribbean Region).

We are also thankful to Adolfo Brizzi, Richard Clifford, Julio Cordoba, Jozef Draaisma, Stephen Everhart, Fernando Montes-Negret and Eduardo Velez for their illuminating comments on earlier versions of the various chapters, and to Robert Duval-Hernandez and Eric Zuckerman, for their quantitative and analytical assistance.

Finally, we are especially grateful to Michael Geller, who superbly managed the production and support team. This team included: Peggy O'Donnell, our planning and budget advisor; Elizabeth Forsythe and Diane Stamm, the principal language editors; Maria del Carmen Navarrete Angeles, who contributed to the Spanish translation of the overview; Christopher Neal and Lee Morrison who, together with Paola Scalabrin and Jeong Hyun You, spearheaded the publicity and printing efforts; Cynthia Masson-Barrero and Liliana Wiesner who helped shepherd the project along at various stages; and Esthella Provas at Chac-Mool Gallery in Los Angeles who identified the art of Rodrigo Pimentel for use on the cover of this volume. Our thanks to all of them.

Marcelo M. Giugale and Steven B. Webb
Washington D.C. and Mexico City
April 17, 2000

Acronyms

CAPFCE	Comité Administrador del Programa Federal de Construcción de Escuelas
CEDEMUN	Centro de Desarrollo Municipal
CGC	Commonwealth Grants Commission
CIDAC	Centro de Investigación para el Desarrollo, A.C.
CNA	Comisión Nacional del Agua
CNS	Consejo Nacional de Salud
CONAFE	Consejo Nacional de Fomento Educativo
COPLADE	Comités de Planeación para el Desarrollo del Estado
COPLADEMUN	Comités de Planeación para el Desarrollo Municipal
COPRE	Comisión Presidencial para la Reforma del Estado
CVAT	Compensating value added tax
DIF	Desarrollo Integral de la Familia
EDUCO	Educación con Participación de la Communidad
FAEA	Fondo de Aportaciones para la Educación de los Adultos
FAEB	Fondo de Aportaciones para la Educación Básica y Normal
FAETA	Fondo de Aportaciones para la Educación Tecnológica y de los Adultos
FAFM	Fondo de Aportaciones para el Fortalecimiento de los Municipios
FAISE	Fondo de Infraestructura Social Estatal
FAISM	Fondo de Aportaciones para Infraestructura Social Municipal
FAM	Fondo de Aportaciones Múltiples
FASP	Fondo de Aportaciones para la Seguridad Pública
FASSA	Fondo de Aportaciones para los Servicios de Salud
FFM	Fideicomiso de Fomento Minero
FGP	Fondo General de Participaciones
FISM	Fondo para la Infraestructura Social Municipal

GDP	Gross domestic product
IEPS	Impueso Especial sobre Producción y Servicio
IMF	International Monetary Fund
IMSS-	Instituto Mexicano del Seguro Social
COPLAMAR	Coordinación General del Plan Nacional de Zonas Deprimidas y Grupos Marginados
INDETEC	Instituto para el Desarrollo Técnico de las Haciendas Públicas
INE	Instituto Nacional de Ecología
INEA	Instituto Nacional para la Educación de los Adultos
INEGI	Instituto Nacional de Estadística Geografía e Informática
IPF	Inversión Pública Federal Instituto Nacional de Estadísticas Geografia y Investigaci
ISAN	Impuesto Sobre Automóbiles Nuevos
ISIM	Impuesto Sobre Ingresos Mercantiles
ISSSTE	Instituto de Seguridad y Servicios Sociales de los Trabajadores del Estado
IVA	Impuesto al Valor Agregado (Value Added Tax)
MARINA	Secretaría de Marina
NAFTA	North American Free Trade Agreement
NEP	Nueva Estrategia de Programción
OCDE	Organización para la Cooperación y el Desarrollo Económico
OECD	Organization for Economic Cooperation and Development
OPD	Organismos públicos de descentralización
PAN	Partido Acción Nacional
PAO	Planes operativos anuales
PARE	Programa para Abatir el Rezago Educativo
PEMEX	Mexico's nationalized oil company
PRD	Partido de la Revolución Democrática
PRI	Partido Revoluciónario Institucional
PROCAMPO	Programa de Apoyos Directos al Campo
PRODEI	Programa para el Desarrollo de la Educación Inicial
PROGRESA	Programa de Educación, Salud y Alimentación
PROMAP	Programa de Mejoramiento de la Administración Pública
PRONASOL	Programa Nacional de Solidaridad
RFP	Recaudación Federal Participable
RST	Retail sales tax
SECODAM	Secretaría de Controlaría y Desarrollo Administrativo

SEDENA	Secretaría de la Defense Nacional
SEDESOL	Secretariat de Desarrollo Social
SHCP	Secretaría de Hacienda y Crédito Público
SNCF	Sistema Nacional de Coordinación Fiscal (Pacto Fiscal)
SSA	Secretaría de Salud
VAT	Value Added Tax

BK Title: # Preface *NA*

Olivier Lafourcade*

DEMOCRATIZATION, DECENTRALIZATION, DEVELOPMENT. These three sequential forces have swept the world over the last decade and have redrawn the maps of politics, power, and prosperity. Undoubtedly, they have been fostered and accelerated by globalization (financial and commercial) and by the information technology revolution. Understanding those forces of change (despite their speed and complexity) is of the utmost importance for, in the end, their value will be measured by one simple yardstick—their impact on people's quality of life, especially among the poor.

Modern Mexico has been fully engaged in, and is thus a rich case study of, the democratization, decentralization, and development trio. In recent years, enhanced political competition has redistributed decision-making across the three levels of government (federal, state, and municipal) and has made it more accountable to the average citizen. It has also given subnational governments a renewed role as economic agents. The taxation, spending, borrowing, and institutions of Mexican states and municipalities are now increasingly (albeit unevenly) under the rigor of market discipline. The combined, closer scrutiny of voters and financiers is creating a new incentive framework for policymakers—a framework where necessary reforms become both inescapable and, more importantly, a perceived source of potential reward.

This book is the product of the analytical work of a large number of experts, Mexican and foreign. They here document Mexico's decentralization experience; conceptualize its main trends, policies, and options; and bring it into the light of international comparison. They distill critical

* Director, Mexico Country Department, the World Bank. As with other chapters in this book, the opinions expressed here are the author's own, and do not necessarily reflect the views of the World Bank, its Board of Executive Directors, or its member countries.

lessons and challenges that are of relevance for Mexico, for Latin America and, generally, for countries that are embarking on far reaching decentralization efforts. This renders the volume a major contribution to our knowledge and thinking in this area. And a timely one: for decentralization is an irreversible process that is likely to continue occupying policymakers for years to come.

βh Title: Overview

Marcelo Giugale, Vinh Nguyen, Fernando Rojas, and
Steven B. Webb

ALTHOUGH THE PHENOMENON OF "DECENTRALIZATION" is worldwide and its meaning, implementation, and effects vary from country to country, the experiences point to three lessons applicable anywhere.

First, decentralization often has major effects on concerns ranging from macroeconomic stability to poverty alleviation, the provision of social services, and the quality of governance (Burki, Dillinger, and Perry 1999). For this reason, a country decentralizing its public sector needs to develop a coherent *decentralization strategy*. Decentralization, properly done, can have many economic benefits as well, producing greater efficiency, responsiveness, and accountability in the delivery of services desired by the local population. Improperly done, decentralization can have undesirable consequences, leading to macroeconomic disequilibrium, exacerbating regional differences and conflicts, or reducing the quality and quantity of public services. Paying adequate attention to the interactions of various policy areas can avert many problems with decentralization. Although there is no one right path to decentralization, and determining the appropriate extent and nature of decentralization is a political decision for the country, a number of common mistakes can be avoided. For example, it is always a mistake to decentralize revenues without decentralizing a corresponding set of responsibilities, and it is usually wrong to give exactly the same revenue and responsibilities to small and large municipal governments.

Second, because decentralization everywhere is an ongoing, evolving activity, a successful strategy requires *adequate institutional infrastructure* to develop, monitor, and implement the decentralization policy. The necessary infrastructure includes legal and regulatory frameworks, organizations for coordination, and capacity-building programs. Even the best-planned strategies do not sustain themselves without such institutional support. In particular, experience everywhere shows the need to develop and publicize accurate, complete, and trustworthy information on all aspects of the

1

decentralization process. This reduces the confusion and political and bureaucratic conflicts that invariably accompany any major change.

Third, the Latin American experience with decentralization shows that abrupt, across-the-board efforts have generally failed. Countries have had to go back to incremental decentralization, with differentiated rules according to different management capacity of territorial units. This was the experience with the Colombian laws of 1986, the Brazilian constitution of 1988, the Venezuelan Organic Law of Decentralization in 1988, and the Bolivian Popular Participation and Decentralization laws of 1994 and 1996.

These lessons apply to Mexico. The country is progressing toward more autonomy, fiscal responsibility, and accountability at subnational levels of government. States now spend close to half as much as the federal government (see table O.1). The municipal share of public spending has also grown, although this trend is not as fully documented. This process is being driven by heightened political competition at all levels of government and by the desire of the federal government to include decentralization in its program for broadening political participation.

Each country must, however, develop its own strategy of decentralization and its own particular institutional infrastructure in accordance with its history, its objectives, and the constraints it faces. The models of decentralization found in the world range along a spectrum. One end, exemplified in Canada, may be labeled full legislative federalism in the sense that the main source of funds for subnational governments is their own taxes, and they have almost complete autonomy as to how they spend them. Canada carries provincial autonomy so far as to have no federal constraints

Table O.1. Fiscal Magnitudes: Federal and State Governments, 1997

	Percent of GDP	
	Federal	States*
Own spending	11.5	4.9
1991	8.4	3.0
1996	7.7	4.9
Own revenue	15.8	1.0
Disposable revenue	13.2	5.4
Primary balance	−1.3	0.0
Overall balance	−4.9	−0.1
Debt service	18.4	0.3
Debt stock	31.0	1.5

* Tabasco and Tamaulipuas not included; no data.
Source: SHCP and authors' estimates.

at all on provincial borrowing, leaving the regulatory task entirely to the capital market, although the provinces impose strict controls on municipal borrowing. The regional inequalities arising from differences in the tax base in Canada are partly equalized through federal transfers. Switzerland and the United States follow variants of this model, though with less equalization (none in the United States), less uniform state tax policies, and more detailed federal attempts to influence state spending. In Latin America, Brazil's decentralization is closest to this end of the spectrum, with the larger states raising much of their own revenue and designing their own social sector programs. But the federal government in Brazil has frequently gotten involved, often disruptively, in the personnel policies and debt management of the states.

The model at the other end of the spectrum—administrative federalism—is found in Germany and Australia. Transfers are the major source of states' revenue, and federal (or joint) policies guide most subnational expenditures. Regional equalization policies, largely implemented through transfers, are very strong. Moreover, tight central controls are imposed on subnational borrowing. Colombia and Venezuela follow this model in Latin America, although the equalization component is largely absent.

Varying combinations of the features mentioned—revenue independence, expenditure autonomy, debt autonomy, and equalization—may be found in other countries. In Argentina, for example, transfers are more important than in Brazil, but states have more autonomy in controlling personnel costs and the market plays a larger role in debt management.

Mexico could, in principle, mix and match these characteristics as it wishes. Given that Mexico has already made the major decisions about decentralization of spending responsibility and subnational borrowing, the next critical decision concerns the importance of transfers and the extent to which the tax system should be decentralized. This will go hand in hand with the decision about the degree to which federal transfers will compensate for the regional disparities that would otherwise follow from tax decentralization. Another important decision, which may require revision as the transfer system evolves, is the extent to which the center will guide, monitor, or control the details of expenditures (for example, through financial market regulations or conditions of transfer). The institutional structures mentioned earlier will be needed to attain consensus on these policy objectives and to implement and sustain them.

Mexico has already started down the road to decentralization, with its own model being constructed in Mexico, as it must be. Some actions already taken seem desirable and should be sustained and strengthened, such as the end of discretionary transfers and support for more uniform and comprehensible state accounting and public reporting. Others seem less desirable. This book is a collection of papers that draws on worldwide experiences with decentralization in order to focus on what is needed to develop a coherent and sustainable decentralization strategy in Mexico, and the necessary institutional underpinnings for it.

In this overview, we distill the main messages that the authors deliver in those papers. The discussion here is organized around five themes: (1) institutions for decentralization, (2) spending and service delivery, (3) subnational taxes and revenue, (4) intergovernmental transfers, and (5) subnational borrowing and debt management. A vision of Mexico's path and options in decentralization then emerges and is articulated for the short, medium, and long term.

Institutions for Decentralization

The key institutional issues in decentralization are reinforcing confidence in decentralization among key stakeholders, improving intergovernmental coordination and conflict resolution, strengthening and democratizing the process for control and accountability, coordinating the multilevel budget process, regularizing the distinctions between municipalities with different administrative capacities, implementing cooperative capacity building, and dealing with the peculiarities of the Federal District's relationship with its neighbors and the federal government.

Intergovernmental Coordination

International experience shows the importance, and the difficulties, of collective institutions that steer the decentralization process and serve as forums for negotiations and preemptive conflict resolution (see box O.1). Developing such institutions is particularly challenging for Mexico, because of its trial-and-error approach to decentralization and the resultant political, regional, intersectoral, and even intrasectoral fragmentation. Thus far Mexico has improved its intergovernmental and intersectoral coordination largely through top-down mechanisms, such as conditional transfers and federal monitoring. Now it is necessary to create a consensus-building mechanism that is trusted by all parties and that takes care of the following critical tasks:

- Proposing a long-term view of decentralization, intermediate goals, and ongoing adjustments;
- Promoting forums for discussing and negotiating intergovernmental fiscal arrangements and preventing interjurisdictional conflict;
- Producing an annual report on progress and current issues in decentralization, keeping federal agencies and subnational governments alerted to their responsibilities within the decentralization process;

Box O.1. Coordination of Decentralization: Lessons in Latin America

The Latin American experience with coordination of the decentralization process indicates the following lessons:

1. Horizontal, intersecretary agreements (national level) or conferences of governors, mayors, or finance secretaries (subnational level) have had only modest effects, generally restricted to a few specific policies. Broader scope agreements seem to require presidential support and definite commitment from the Ministry of Finance.
2. Presidential Commissions may be more effective, but their sustainability depends on the continuity of presidential support, as indicated by the Comisión Presidencial para la Reforma del Estado (COPRE) experience in Venezuela.
3. Presidential support for a lower-level agency, such as the Bolivian experience with the *Sub-secretaría de Participación Popular,* is usually short-lived; in Bolivia it lasted only while it had unrestricted presidential backing.
4. A single agency at the ministerial level, like the Ministry of Government or the Interior, or the Ministry of the Presidency, has usually failed, as the Ministry of Finance or the planning agency became pivotal for the advance of decentralization.
5. A special unit at the presidential level, like the *Secretaría de la Presidencia,* usually lacks effective coordination capacity vis-à-vis sector ministries, and especially the Ministry of Finance.
6. Experiences where no agency is primarily responsible, as in Chile and Colombia, illustrate that the Ministry of Finance or the national planning office usually takes over when the process of decentralization is not clearly headed by another agency.

- Providing reliable information for the public discussion of federal, state, and local fiscal and financial policy, and evaluating the design and exchange of information;
- Designing, collecting, and disseminating key indicators for the implementation of decentralization, monitoring the changes of revenue and expenditure responsibilities, and evaluating the capacity of subnational governments to assume new responsibilities.

To help address these needs, in early 2000 the Mexican federal government established a Decentralization Committee within the *Secretaría de Hacienda y Crédito Público* (SHCP), with a Technical Secretariat, and chaired on a rotating basis by the three undersecretaries—*Ingresos, Egresos, and Credito Publico*. This interagency committee will play an important role in coordinating intergovernmental fiscal relations and preparing a revision of the fiscal pact and a new *Ley de Coordinación Hacendaria* (dealing with revenues, transfers, and responsibilities at all levels of government). The Secretariat will be responsible for technical analysis of the evolution of the decentralization process in order to guide federal policy on the matter. The unit will design and test indicators for monitoring intergovernmental fiscal relations and decentralization as a whole; collect and publish subnational fiscal statistics; and disseminate periodic analysis, promote public debate, and maintain communication with congresses, their accounting offices (*Contaduría Mayor de Hacienda de la Honorable Camara de Diputados*), and the *Secretaría de Controlaría y Desarrollo Administrativo* (SECODAM). The committee will put together and coordinate the decentralization efforts currently developed by each of the three undersecretaries, and coordinate the various technical assistance and subnational strengthening programs offered by SHCP, Banobras, and other federal institutions. The committee will not be formally institutionalized during the Zedillo administration, leaving it to the next administration to decide whether and how to do this.

Prevention and Resolution of Conflicts

Sound intergovernmental coordination will require specific institutions for negotiations and conflict resolution, because effective decentralization requires more than the design of revenues, transfers, borrowing, and responsibilities. No system can foresee and specify everything in advance. Issues and disputes arise that need to be settled, and the method for doing this has important incentive effects for how the system actually works.

Like other decentralizing countries, Mexico has a growing number of interjurisdictional conflicts. The courts need to strengthen their capacity to handle constitutional and administrative disputes that arise in connection with decentralization. The country could also develop alternative means for resolving disputes, because court procedures tend to be expensive, time-consuming, and often unnecessary. Some conflicts are being averted or resolved through informal negotiations and willingness to compromise. The lack of institutionalized alternate channels for resolving disputes often makes the outcome a question of which side has greater political power, and this undermines the credibility of the rules. It would help if the non-judicial means to resolve interjurisdictional conflicts were institutionalized and if conciliatory experts and judges were trained in the principles and operating rules of decentralization. In the health sector, the National Health Council (*Consejo Nacional de Salud*) resolves many disputes, and this institution could be a model for other sectors with major decentralization issues, such as education, water, road transport, and environment.

Democratic Accountability and Control

Effective controls are both a prerequisite and an essential component of strengthening management capacity, autonomy, and accountability at subnational levels. Because the impetus for decentralization in Mexico has come not only from the federal government, but also from democratic competition in Congress and subnational governments, it is important to have systematic public disclosure of all government accounts, opening the potential for decentralized democratic control.

In a decentralized Mexico, institutional development toward effective controls should capitalize on the strengths of the existing mechanisms. Mexico has accumulated significant experience and technical expertise at SECODAM and some of the state comptrollers (in the executive branch). The congressional accounting offices, independent units of increasingly pluralist congresses, are emerging as some of the more trusted institutions in the country. The *Homologación* Program of SHCP also tries to standardize the states' financial reporting. Besides these official institutions, some states and federal agencies now conduct external audits through specialized firms.

In the Mexican model, controls are a matter of intergovernmental coordination. The congressional accounting office dictates guidelines for the accounting offices of state legislatures to follow. To strengthen the political autonomy and credibility of these institutions, Mexico might consider the models of the U.S. General Accounting Office, which Congress endows with considerable autonomous investigative authority, or the parliamentary finance committees in some British commonwealth countries, which the Constitution establishes under the chairmanship of the opposition party. On the executive side in Mexico, SECODAM coordinates with state comptrollers and assists them with knowledge-management programs. The states are legally responsible for fiscal control of municipalities. Although in principle each level of government should have its own independent controls, the federal level has organized arrangements that provide the basis for strengthening controls at all levels during the transition to a more decentralized system.

Budget Coordination

At present, budget coordination in Mexico involves primarily the harmonization of spending priorities at different levels of government. Mechanisms are different for federal–state budget coordination and for state–municipal coordination, and for federal–municipal coordination.

Federal–state budget coordination operates through the federal budget process and other mechanisms. States used to submit annual sectoral operating plans (*planes operativos anuales*, POAs) that were then adjusted and incorporated into the federal sectoral plan submitted to SHCP. This process was partially replaced in the Fiscal Coordination Law by automatic formula mechanisms, but the federal ministries of education and health still require states to prepare some sort of POAs for the sector budget. Once the plan has been submitted, SHCP further filters the sector POAs and submits the budget bill to Congress. Although the present budget preparation mechanism ensures some exchange of information and opportunities for reconciliation of federal and state priorities, it still falls short of explicit and transparent criteria for allocating federal resources across the states.

Besides preparation of the federal budget, the regular federal–state coordinating meetings (the quarterly meetings between SHCP, both the Income and Expense departments, and the finance ministries of the states) and the federal Fiscal Pact are also contexts for coordinating the budget. Revenue coordination and tax harmonization between the federal level and the states are achieved mainly through the Fiscal Pact and the corresponding general revenue transfer of nearly 22 percent of the *recaudación federal participable* (the *participaciones*).[1] However, since the fiscal year is the calendar year for all levels of government, the federal budget data go to states and municipalities only at the very end of the previous fiscal year or the beginning of the new year, which makes subnational budgeting increasingly difficult because federal budgets and transfers are less predictable and are approved later in December.

Further budget coordination takes place through the growing number of pari-passu programs, agreements for sector matching grants, and earmarked transfers for sector decentralization, such as the Educational Federalization Program, now the first and largest fund of Ramo 33.[2] Extraordinary transfers for specific investment purposes may also be seen as coordination mechanisms.[3] In fact, extraordinary transfers have stimulated the agreements for uniform accounting and reporting between the federal government and the states (the *Homologación* Program).

State–municipal budget coordination involves state-level approval of municipal budgets and borrowing.[4] In theory, municipal budgets have to conform with the state development plan, primarily for investment, but this is rarely practiced. Special agreements between states and municipalities can provide an additional opportunity to reconcile the spending priorities of these two levels and to coordinate revenue-raising goals and instruments.[5]

Federal–municipal budget coordination, even federal–state–municipal coordination, is also pursued through the transformation of Ramo 26 (budget category 26) into Ramo 33. Formulas already specify most of the allocation of the special funds of Ramo 33—primarily, but not exclusively, sector funds. Therefore, Ramo 33 is in practice a mechanism by which the federal level (Congress and executive branch) guarantees the territorial allocation of resources according to federal priorities. Accounting and reporting for Ramo 33 resources are still deficient, however, and neither stimulates intergovernmental trust nor allows for monitoring or impact evaluation.[6]

The current mechanisms for budget coordination—mostly spending—hinder subnational autonomy and initiative. Rather than stimulating more efficient allocation of resources in the territories, they tend to increase federal control of the allocation of resources, even as states are granted more political responsibility for them. As a result, these mechanisms confuse the distribution of responsibilities among levels of government and reduce the accountability of each level. In addition, these mechanisms do not help true bilateral spending coordination because they are mainly formal budget and planning tools.[7]

Categorizing Municipalities

The diversity of state and local governments needs to be matched with differentiated federal rules toward local governments (see box O.2 for international experience). There is wide variation in the scale, administrative capacity, tax bases, and poverty levels of states and municipalities in Mexico, but the legal framework for decentralization does not recognize these differences. At present, federal rules do not categorize municipalities by size and capacity to determine differential spending authority, tax authority, borrowing authority, reporting requirements, or eligibility for technical assistance. The details of the problem and the appropriate solution may be different for municipalities and for states.

Box O.2 International Experience with Differential Treatment of Municipalities

Experience in Latin America shows that, when responsibilities of subnational units are not explicitly differentiated according to effective fiscal and/or management capacity, de facto differentiation takes place, often in ad hoc, chaotic ways. It is therefore advisable to explicitly differentiate among subnational units while at the same time establishing the standards to move from one category to another. The Colombian process of certification is an example of flexible categorization that stimulates regional and local governments to qualify themselves to assume responsibilities in education and health. To be certified, departments have to demonstrate to the national government that they can assume the new responsibilities in health and education—that they have developed the required planning, financing, monitoring, and reporting capacity. After a department has been certified, its municipalities may apply to the department for certification. In another example of categorization and upgrading, Spain has gradually increased the number and responsibilities of the autonomías—areas like Catalonia with special status—and expanded their responsibilities.

Mexico has over 2,400 municipalities, spanning a wide range, from cities with several million inhabitants, policymakers with high levels of formal education, and computerized fiscal accounts, to small towns with populations under 5,000, leaders with little formal education, and informal accounting practices at best. Only 25 to 40 percent of the municipalities measure up to standard indicators of capacity: having a budget planning unit, an evaluation unit, and computerized accounts; having and using an internal administrative code; having regulations for the *cadastre*;[8] and raising more than half of their own resources. It seems unrealistic to have the same rules for all municipalities. In practice, states often demand less than the legal requirement from small and poor municipalities. Still, small municipalities doing an appropriate amount of reporting for their size should not be in a state of noncompliance. Large municipalities frequently do more than the minimum to satisfy the requirements of their own management or of their private sector creditors. Still, some larger cities have inadequate administration, even though they meet the letter of the law.

The fiscal and administrative capacity of Mexico's 32 states also varies widely. For example, as of 1997, only three states had a fiscal coordination law, a budget, accounting, and public spending law, and a public debt law; seven states had none of these laws. All states now have these laws, although their effectiveness varies in part because of their newness. Targeted transfers for capacity-building programs, such as those in the 2000 budget, could help to bring states up to a uniform standard. As state and municipal governments become more democratic and more accountable, citizens will demand better reporting from their governments.

Capacity Building

All stakeholders agree on the need to improve the technical and administrative capacity of subnational governments. For example, technical shortcomings deter proper accounting and reporting of the Ramo 33 transfers, particularly in municipalities with low fiscal and management capacity. There is less agreement, however, on the best way to strengthen subnational capacity. Federally run programs for strengthening subnational administrative capacity, such as the *Homologación* Program, have had limited impact. Some federal funds for institutional development at the municipal level come from the option each municipality has of using 2 percent of one Ramo 33 fund (municipal infrastructure) for this purpose. For small municipalities, however, which need capacity building the most, the amount comes to only a few hundred pesos—too little and too scattered for Mexico's 2,400 municipalities. The state of Puebla has developed a series of agreements with its municipalities to concentrate and augment these resources at the state level and to provide a program of capacity building, based on a survey of local needs. The federal government is also planning new programs for supporting capacity building at state and local levels. There will be pressure on these governments in order to improve their access to credit markets when these are reformed as described below.

Civil service reform at subnational levels is needed and perhaps inevitable, but it will have limited success or impact while the old incentives remain in place. State and local government officials, like federal government officials, respond to the incentives with which they are faced. If those incentives discourage initiative and reward inefficiency, it should come as no surprise to find unaccountable and inefficient subnational administrations. Solving the problem of limited administrative capacity in some jurisdictions will require altering the federally controlled personnel incentive system to allow honest, well-trained people to pursue an attractive career in subnational government.

Federal District Relations

The Federal District faces particular challenges in its relationship with the federal government and with the neighboring states. For example, the Federal District has to have its budget and borrowing limits approved annually in the federal Congress; it does not get some of the Ramo 33 funds; nor is it responsible for basic education. The Federal District believes that it subsidizes its neighbors via support for the metro train system, while its neighbors feel that they subsidize the Federal District via water sector investments. The rapid transformation of the political and fiscal status of the Federal District, and the possible creation of municipalities within it, have made a review and reform of its vertical and horizontal intergovernmental relations necessary. International experience, such as from the São Paulo metropolitan area in Brazil, may help to elucidate the range of options.

Spending and Service Delivery

Decentralization is expected to provide many economic benefits in the areas of spending and service delivery. These benefits include choosing the mix of public sector activities that best suit the taste and needs of citizens in a local area, providing the services in a more cost-effective way by adapting the method of delivery to local circumstances, and allowing citizens to express more directly their concerns about service provision. The benefits will also depend on strengthening the link between subnational spending choices and self-taxing decisions. Realizing these benefits in Mexico will depend on the actions of local authorities and citizens, but the federal government can help by creating an environment that gives states and municipalities more incentive to take responsibility for their own programs and finances. This is not a matter of just changing rules, but also of creating a culture of devolution. It will take time. The agenda here sets out some possible steps, which will build on those taken in the past decade.

Two features dominate the current assignment of expenditure responsibilities. First, there are many concurrent obligations at all three levels, especially between the federal and state governments for important services such as education, health, or social assistance. Second, few responsibilities are assigned to the municipal level, especially in areas with important benefits, such as education or health (see box O.3).

There appear to be five main problems with the current allocation of decentralized spending responsibilities: (a) inadequate *fiscal autonomy for*

Box O.3. Education and Health

Education

The 1992 *Acuerdo Nacional para la Modernización de la Educación Básica* was a pioneer step that established a limited decentralization precedent. According to the *Acuerdo*, the federal government remains responsible for general policies and standards (normative and policymaking functions), teacher training and territorial distribution, production of textbooks, evaluation and monitoring, and the provision of financial resources needed to ensure proper coverage and quality of the educational system.

In 1998, Ramo 33 complemented the *Acuerdo Nacional* by guaranteeing transfers and introducing greater transparency in resource allocation for education. However, inasmuch as Ramo 33 enshrined inertia in territorial allocation of resources for education, it may be considered more a tool for deconcentration than a decentralization measure that enhances efficiency. Indeed, Ramo 33 brings no incentives for improving subnational performance or mobilizing additional local resources for education, which are two goals of the decentralization processes.

Health

Decentralization in the health sector started earlier and proceeded more gradually, allowing states and municipalities more time to learn. Six features of the system today make it work relatively well:

1. Resource allocation from the federal level to states according to well-recognized criteria;
2. Fundability for states and sanitary jurisdictions in the use of health sector funds;
3. Careful and effective transfer of human resources from the federal level to the states, negotiated with the national union;
4. Complete transfer of infrastructure, goods, and equipment to states;
5. Municipal cofinancing of new infrastructure and participation in planning;
6. *Consejo Nacional de Salud* has resolved many conflicts and monitored the process of decentralization.

states, given their political and economic power and the scope of service delivery responsibilities delegated to them; (b) inefficient and nontransparent basis for *allocating sectoral transfers;* (c) remaining ambiguities in the *assignment of expenditure responsibilities* and failure to take account of *disparities between municipalities* in their capacity; (d) unclear responsibility and therefore generally inadequate funding for *pensions* (elaborated in the debt and borrowing section); and (e) lack of effective *procedures for dispute resolution* (discussed above).

State Autonomy to Increase Efficiency

Although more resources pass through their books than ever before, states in some ways have less fiscal autonomy now than they had a decade ago. With the exception of the Fund for Strengthening State Finances and the Program of Support for Strengthening the Federal Entities, most of the resources they receive from the federal level (including from shared revenues) are effectively earmarked either for transfers to municipalities or social sector salaries, especially schoolteachers and university professors with federally mandated pay scales, or they are claimed by the terms of matching grant programs (pari passu). This situation is inconsistent with the growing economic and political power of the states.

The Fund for Strengthening State Finances was set up within Ramo 23 in the wake of the 1995 crisis and disbursed money on the condition of a state's fulfilling a fiscal adjustment program agreed with SHCP. Although the agreements for these funds were not transparent or by uniform formula, they represented an advance of the earlier pattern of the President personally allocating major resources to states, also via Ramo 23. In 1998–99, as the fiscal reform agreements ended, the fund was phased out, with a residual going to a national disaster relief fund with transparent rules of access. In 1999, a few incidents, especially with Chihuahua and Nuevo Leon, demonstrated power of states to demand ad hoc resource transfers—debt relief or federal spending on state-priority projects. In the budget for 2000, the Program of Support for Strengthening the Federal Entities was created in Ramo 23, but with Congress allocating the funds to states, not at executive discretion. It remains to be seen how much the nominal earmarking of the fund will be binding, or whether the funds will be fungible and relatively free for the states to spend. But freedom to allocate funds will not be enough. A more fundamental way to increase autonomy of the states would be to give them greater control over spending, especially for personnel, and over taxes, as discussed below.

Efficient and Equitable Basis for Sectoral Transfers

Transfers for education and health are allocated mainly on the basis of the number of staff and physical sites (schools, clinics, hospitals). In the education sector, staffing in 1992 is the base from which allocations are adjusted at the margin for inflation and population growth, and sometimes increased further by special request. Although this system does not explicitly penalize states that have controlled costs since 1992, neither does it penalize those that fail to improve efficiency, and it actually hurts states that improve student attendance rates, in the sense that they have fewer resources per attending student. In health, the allocation is still based mainly on the current number of establishments and staffing, but the system has improved since 1996. Now, requests by the states for incremental health resources are evaluated by SHCP and the Ministry of Health on the basis of demographic and health data. It is understandable that the initial values of the transfers matched previous cost levels, because the states had neither the authority nor the time and money to change staffing quickly. But now it makes sense to move to a system with better incentives. Evidence from a number of countries indicates that formulas for sectoral transfers are more equitable and encourage efficiency better if they are based on a capitation formula, with adjustments made for population density, age, and gender. Moving toward such a system, as the social security system is starting to do, would improve the efficiency and equity of transfers.

Assignment of Responsibilities

The broad assignment of responsibilities by sectors in Mexico is reasonable: education and health to the states, local streets and sanitation to municipalities, and other sectors to the federal government. The problems are in the details. Concurrent obligations at all three levels and especially between the federal and state governments in important services such as education, health, or social assistance often leave functions like maintenance, regulation, and inspection without any level taking adequate responsibility. Responsibility is ill-defined for roads, water, and higher education. The water issue is especially problematic, because it has so many dimensions in terms of users and geography. A separate study on water is needed to clarify the issues, only some of which relate to decentralization. Although some states have shown strong interest in local environmental issues where their involvement would make sense, the mandate and funding remain largely at the federal level. A pilot program in the 2000 budget offers some federal funding to encourage states to develop their environmental sector capacity and cost recovery. Federal involvement in personnel issues remains problematic. The municipal level has few assigned responsibilities, especially in social sectors. Individual schools and hospitals have little autonomy or community involvement, although international experiences in Colombia (the New School Program), Nicaragua (the Participatory Fund for Maintenance of Social Infrastructure), and El Salvador (the EDUCO Program) indicate that this part of decentralization does the most for performance on various indicators: attendance, test scores, and cost control.

The thorny problem of nationally negotiated teachers' salaries probably cannot be solved with direct confrontation and will not need to be. The fundamental problem is not that their pay is too high. As Mexico's private sector grows and its labor market gets more integrated domestically and more closely linked with the rest of the world, the most serious problem will be that a national salary does not attract qualified teachers in the areas with the fastest private sector growth and the most international linkages. These areas will have to pay more or witness a decline in quality, because only less-qualified personnel will stay or they will spend more of their time and energy in outside employment. If the federal government cannot afford to pay for wage increases nationwide, it may need to give local governments and voters the option to raise more resources locally to improve pay and working conditions above the national (minimum) standard. At the other end of the spectrum, isolated areas are already having trouble attracting enough teachers that meet the usual national standard, even though the national salary is high compared to local wages. The federal transfer system may need to provide extra support there. Faced with these economic realities, the teachers may see the necessity and benefit of having their union focus less on negotiating national raises and more on setting standard negotiating frameworks for local branches.

Separating the assignment of responsibilities for maintenance and operation of infrastructure facilities from responsibility for capital investment has been a persistent problem in Mexico. For example, municipalities are in charge of maintaining school buildings, while the federal and state governments carry out most capital investments. This dichotomy often leads to insufficient levels of both maintenance and infrastructure investment. Each level of government can blame the other for not doing its part, and each has an incentive to refrain from using its own resources, with the expectation that the other levels will give more. Rigid separation of construction, maintenance, and operation decisions has led to notorious inefficiencies in allocation and production, as evidenced by all Latin American countries that transferred building responsibilities to specialized funds while keeping operation under traditional sector ministries and leaving maintenance responsibilities unspecified.

Subnational Taxes and Revenue

Subnational governments in Mexico should raise more taxes for three reasons. First, the public sector needs more tax revenue for when revenues from oil decline, not only temporarily because of low oil prices but also permanently as a share of gross domestic product (GDP) because of economic growth and diversity. Second, to give citizens more control over the size of public spending within their jurisdictions, subnational governments need to have adequate taxing authority. If they want to spend more money in an area, they can raise taxes; if they decide to save money on a program, they can reduce taxes. This involves, primarily, having control over marginal (incremental) revenue—what a subnational government can affect by its own actions, especially by changing tax rates, but also by imposing new taxes or repealing old ones, by changing the tax base, and by varying administrative effort. Third, and related to the second, states that borrow need to have some source of funds to repay their debts. If they experience an unexpected adverse shock, relative to their fiscal plan at the time of borrowing, they need to be able to raise additional revenue (or cut costs) by enough to sustain their debt service.

States typically have their own payroll taxes, annual taxes on automobiles, and fees. Currently they are legally prohibited from taxing interstate trade and some excises. Taxes represent only about 4.5 percent of total revenues of states (other than the Federal District). Payroll taxes are the most important, levied in 23 of the 32 states. Rates range from 0.5 to 4 percent, with most rates in the range of 1 to 2 percent of payrolls (18 states). Only one state has a rate above 2 percent. The definitions of taxpayers are generally similar, but tax bases and exemptions differ substantially across states. The structure of these taxes is not consistent with the bases for the federal payroll taxes that finance social security and housing; making them more consistent would reduce the costs of enforcement and of compliance (and audit) for firms operating in more than one state. The federal personal income tax has a different, narrower, base than the payroll taxes. Moreover, each state administers its own payroll tax, following its own procedures, which are independent of those used for federal payroll taxes. Inconsistent tax bases and duplicate administration are wasteful practices for both taxpayers and administrators. The administration and, for most states, the rate of the payroll tax, both offer substantial opportunities to increase states' own revenues. Most states seem to lack the incentive, however, because they have too little control over how they spend money and relatively too much opportunity to negotiate discretionary transfers, at least prior to 1999. Most of their resources, however, come from formula-based transfers, mostly unconditional. See figure O.1, which is illustrative and based on preliminary estimates for 1999, as described in Chapter 5.

Municipal governments are on average only slightly less dependent than the states on revenue sharing and transfers. In the aggregate, municipal governments receive about two-thirds of total net revenues from these sources. This pattern differs markedly across and within states. The incentive structure in revenue-sharing arrangements partly accounts for low rates of tax collection. At least the larger municipal governments would benefit from having access to additional sources of revenue and from improved incentives. The main sources of revenue for municipalities are taxes on

Figure O.1. Composition of Total Subnational Revenues, 1999

Pesos per capita

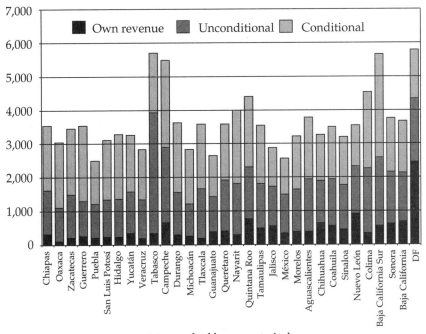

states ranked by poverty index

Source: Courchene and Diaz (Chapter 5).

property and water-user charges. Property taxes average only 13 percent of total municipal revenues, although some municipalities have significantly increased their property tax revenues in recent years. Property taxes constitute 22 percent of revenues in the Federal District, showing the potential in large cities.

The most challenging institutional issue in the case of property and payroll taxes is to find the right incentives for states and municipalities to raise their taxation to levels compatible with tax efficiency and equity, and to limit tax distortions of the market allocation of resources.[9] The problem seems to go back to the states' revenue initiative, which diminished as a result of the federal Fiscal Pact.

A good strategy for many countries, including Mexico, would consist of surcharges levied by subnational governments on a tax base (or bases) defined by the federal government and administered by them either alone or jointly with the states. In this scheme, subnational governments would exercise the politically important choice of tax rates, while avoiding most of the complexity, inequities, tax exporting, and locational distortions that result from independent subnational legislation and administration. That is, tax surcharges combine the simplicity of tax sharing with the advantage of allowing subnational governments to determine tax rates. Canada makes substantial use of this type of system. Such surcharges could be imposed on excise taxes, a residence-based income tax, or even the value added tax (levied at the destination of sales). This could be accomplished with a compensating value added tax. States might still impose payroll taxes, preferably with a unified base. For any such piggyback tax to work for states in Mexico, the federal level would need to improve the design and implementation of its corresponding tax, the value added tax, or the income tax.

Excise taxes, for example on alcoholic beverages and tobacco products, are good candidates for assignment to the states, as is done in many countries. State excise taxes should be levied by (or on behalf of) the states where consumption occurs, not the states where production or importation occurs. Because excise taxes are relatively visible, they would help to ensure the accountability of state officials. The federal government might wish to impose floors, below which state excise rates could not go, to prevent a "race to the bottom" caused by competition among states seeking to attract sales of products they know are intended for smuggling to other states, and to protect local merchants from competition with products smuggled from low-tax states.

States that support their municipalities in administering the property tax—compiling and updating the cadastre—could negotiate some revenue sharing with the municipalities, with formulas that reward states for their support. Similar arrangements exist in Colombia, where the Antioquia Department manages a multipurpose tax for its municipalities. In El Salvador, larger municipalities and municipal associations keep registration and current accounts for smaller municipalities. The federal government in Mexico might support such arrangements by sponsoring pilot programs and disseminating lessons from foreign and domestic experiences.

As a practical approach for simulation and policy analysis, it is useful to consider reform measures that would be revenue-neutral, substituting revenues from state and municipal taxes for transfers from the central government. Such measures would (a) lower federal taxes to provide "tax room" that state and municipal governments could fill or not, at their option; (b) reduce aggregate transfers to states by the amount of the reduction in federal revenues; (c) assign taxes to state and municipal governments that could, on average, replace lost transfers if levied at similar rates;[10] and (d) adjust transfers to maintain funding levels for individual state governments, if they use the tax room provided. However, Mexico may want to reduce the overall reliance of the public sector on oil revenues. In that context, it may be useful for part of the increased national tax effort to occur at the subnational levels.

Intergovernmental Transfers

Intergovernmental transfers perform a variety of roles in federal systems. First, they balance the interplay between expenditure needs and the revenue of subnational governments. Second, they integrate fiscal federalism and social and political dimensions of federations. For example, more conditionality for intergovernmental transfers signals an increase in the centralization of the federation and vice versa—less conditionality means more decentralization. The alternative approaches to transfers offer the flexibility to generate a desired degree of horizontal equity across subnational governments and can embody important incentives by enhancing accountability or encouraging tax effort. They are also the main channel for implementing society's intentions regarding the nature of the Fiscal Pact and the degree of equality of opportunities among citizens living in different states.

Mexico has undergone an amazing degree of decentralization in the past few years, enabled by a great increase in the number and variety of transfers. Although selected aspects of these new transfer arrangements may need rethinking, the bold expenditure-cum-transfer revolution in Mexican fiscal federalism is impressive.

The two main categories of transfers are *participaciones* and *aportaciones*. *Participaciones* were originally revenues of states and municipalities whose collection was delegated to the federal level in the Fiscal Pact for tax efficiency reasons. Legally, the federation only collects those taxes and distributes the proceeds to their owners. In practice, the federal government writes the formula for distribution of these funds and augments them from federal sources, like oil revenues, so they are different from tax sharing (where revenue collected in a state stays there) and are more like a transfer program of the general revenue-sharing type. Most of these transfers go out under Ramo 28. *Aportaciones* were conceived as federal money earmarked to pay for (formerly) federal commitments and transferred to the states and municipalities together with those commitments (for example, education and health). These funds, formerly under Ramo 26, now go out under Ramo 33.

The transfers to states from revenue sharing within Ramo 28 (not counting ramos that pass directly to the municipalities or Ramo 33 funds earmarked for teachers and health sector workers) were almost six times as large as states' own revenues in 1996. Federal and state transfers to municipalities under Ramo 28 were almost twice municipalities' own revenues.

Including Ramo 33, total state revenues equaled about 6 percent of GDP and total municipal revenues equaled about 1.5 percent. The shares were even higher in 1999.

There are also Ramo 23 funds that relate neither to previous revenues of the states nor to previous responsibilities of the central government. Once they were partly at the discretion of the president, but then most of them went into the Fund for Strengthening State Finances that individual states negotiated with federal ministries, mostly SHCP. In 1998 and 1999, discretionary transfers under Ramo 23 declined to less than one-tenth of their pre-1995 value. In the 2000 budget, the transfers at the discretion of the executive ended completely.

There are important transfers within the budgets of sectoral ministries, too. Some go to the states as matching funds under state-by-state agreements (described in the institutional section). These are especially important in the education, road, and health sectors. Sector ministries also spend money directly for projects in particular states, which can be important implicit transfers. Both of these kinds of transfers were traditionally negotiated with the governors, with the terms not disclosed publicly. In 2000 SHCP is publishing the standard rules for access to the pari-passu programs and the matching-grant ratios for all major programs.

In Mexico, as in many countries, society's intentions with regard to transfers are in flux and unclear. There were at least 10 major transfer programs in the 1999 budget, up from three in 1997. In the 2000 budget, Congress added another major transfer in the Program of Support for Strengthening the Federal Entities, which is allocated by Congress in the budget law, rather than by executive discretion. Each program addresses multiple objectives, and each objective is addressed in several programs. This makes it harder than necessary for subnational governments to calculate how much money they will receive and for the federal government to determine how well the transfer system is addressing its objectives. The constitution and the revenue-sharing law do not give explicit goals for the transfers, but their actual pattern reveals something about the intentions. The principal objectives of transfers in Mexico seem to be to (a) let states share in the federal government's greater potential to raise revenue, (b) subsidize subnational governments' provision of services with national externalities (basic health and education), (c) strengthen the autonomy of municipalities, and (d) provide additional resources to states with a high incidence of poverty. A fifth possible objective would be to compensate states with low per capita tax bases, as Canada does. Mexican transfers do not address this objective explicitly, although they address it partially through poverty-targeted transfers, because poverty is positively correlated with low tax base per capita.

Reflecting the first objective, the federal government makes transfers to the states and municipalities under Ramo 28 in order to bolster their revenue capacity, which is weak compared with their expenditure mandates. The states seem to receive considerably more mandates than funding, and municipalities (especially small ones) seem to receive more funding than mandates. For the states, about half of transfers are earmarked funds under Ramo 33; unconditional funds are mostly from Ramo 28. Furthermore, part of the "unconditional" funds have to be used to match funds from other federal programs or to pay federally mandated salaries that are not covered by Ramo 33. State population is important in the formulas for some funds (*Fondo General de Participaciones* and *Fortamun*), and a few (mainly *Fondo de Fomento Municipal, Tenencia,* and Excise Shares Ramo 28) attempt to share revenue with states on the basis of origin. In the past, when states could make a case that revenues were inadequate, the federal government often increased the transfers, although this approach may be coming to an end. These ad hoc transfers were neither automatic nor free from politics. For municipalities, in contrast, a little over half of federal transfers (passing untouched through state accounts) are unconditional revenue shares, and more than half of the rest (Ramo 33 transfers) are also unconditional.

Reflecting the second objective, many federal transfers are targeted to specific sectors—some, like education and health, apparently because they have national externalities. The sectoral targeting of transfers to municipalities (parts 3–7 of Ramo 33) seems to be a transitional arrangement intended to start decentralized municipal services at the same level of funding as they had under the previous system. Reflecting the fourth objective, the formulas of the infrastructure funds in Ramo 33 have strong poverty-targeting elements.

When all the programs are added, state by state, the amount of per capita resources available to the states (total of their own revenues and all the various transfer programs) varies considerably (mostly in the range of $Mex2,500 to $Mex4,500, estimated for 1999, with three states receiving almost $Mex6,000). The resources per capita are about the same on average for states with middle and high levels of poverty, however, and the richer states (low levels of poverty) have only slightly higher-than-average resources. High per capita revenues in rich, low-poverty states are counterbalanced on average by poverty-targeted transfers to high-poverty states. This equality of per capita government resources across income levels may reflect a basic social value in Mexico. The nominal equality across income levels corresponds to some progressivity in real terms, because the cost of public services is generally lower in poorer states, meaning that the same pesos per capita buy more.

The current transfer system has four main problems: (a) it is too complex to achieve a coherent set of purposes. Consequently the federal government distributes more resources than necessary to achieve its objectives, and states are treated inequitably. The main beneficiaries of this complexity are states that get more than they would under a simple and transparent system; (b) basing many transfers on historical or current costs, rather than using per capita or per potential recipient costs, is inequitable and discourages efficiency; (c) at least up until 1999, the availability of ad hoc transfers for politically favored states undermined the incentives for managing spending well and for enhancing revenue; and (d) earmarking and matching grant requirements leave states with little autonomy for improving efficiency or adjusting allocation to meet local needs.

Other Latin American countries have similar problems. Colombia's distribution formulas for general revenue sharing are too complex to convey transparent signals and effective incentives to subnational governments. The formulas include four criteria (per capita, per territorial unit, fiscal effort, poverty incidence), plus combinations of these criteria. Some of the criteria apply to indicators that are not readily available to subnational governments. As a result, subnational governments do not perceive clearly the intentions of the national level, nor do they respond appropriately to signals and incentives.

The future of the Mexican tax-expenditure-transfer subsystem will depend on the way the Mexican federal system itself evolves. There is a range of possible models. With the Canadian-type model—full legislative federalism—transfers would be characterized by:

- An equalization program to ensure that all states have some minimum acceptable level of untied revenues (that is, own revenues plus equalization). This could be the level of the national average, for instance.
- Formula-based conditional transfers, but only where there are obvious national externalities. These would likely be equal per capita to a large degree, since the horizontal balance across states would be addressed under the equalization program.
- Conditions associated with this transfer in the form of a set of socioeconomic principles relating to spending areas such as education and health. The idea would be to provide considerable discretion to subnational governments in implementing these principles.
- A federal-state "accord" or fiscal pact on the socioeconomic union, replete with provisions for addressing disputes. One version of such an accord would extend the procedures for appeal and dispute resolution to Mexican citizens.

With the German-type decentralization model—administrative federalism—a significant proportion of own-source revenues would come from revenue sharing, but there would still be a substantial vertical imbalance in the federation. This would be addressed by a set of conditional transfers designed to ameliorate both vertical and horizontal imbalances. The conditions on these grants could be of two sorts. First, the legislation relating to the spending area could be federal with the implementation delegated to subnational governments, or, second, the grants themselves could be targeted to specific spending areas with associated conditions. Over time, these conditions could be relaxed to allow for more subnational autonomy on the spending front, but there would always be more revenues under federal control than the alternative model where subnational governments have access to unconditional own revenues. The administrative federalism model would represent an evolution of the existing Mexican model, but it could also be an appropriate transition toward legislative federalism, if that is what Mexico ultimately chooses.

Subnational Borrowing and Debt Management

Subnational debt in Mexico has not been a national macroeconomic problem, but it could become one. More important, the burden of debt has been a fiscal problem for some states (municipal debt is small, except for the Federal District, which is effectively a state), and the way in which the federal government has treated subnational debt in the past has created inappropriate incentives for the states' fiscal affairs. For states to have an incentive to control costs and increase their revenues—a stated goal of state and federal governments—it is important that neither states nor borrowers expect a federal bailout. Otherwise, borrowing becomes a means through which states can obtain extra federal resources, transferred to them or their creditors. This has often been the practice in Mexico. (All states received bailouts in the wake of the 1995 economic crisis, and a few states have received bailouts since then when guarantees came due on large infrastructure projects.) Moving to a new practice of no bailouts will require not only changing the rules, but also assuring that challenges to the new rules are not overwhelming, especially during the transition, and that there is adequate political support for the rules.

Most borrowing by states and municipalities has been guaranteed with state *participaciones* as collateral. The federal government (SHCP) handled the collateralization, so the banks and their regulators treated the debt as being virtually riskless. Furthermore, the federal government was not always strict in reducing the *participaciones* of some states when creditors exercised the guarantee, meaning that the rest of the federation had to pay. Thus neither the states nor their creditors worried much about the repayment capacity. This contributed to a state-debt crisis during the general crisis of 1995. The federal government has been the only stakeholder with a strong motive for concern about the state's true creditworthiness; sometimes it has refused to register and collateralize state debt, but at other times politics or other considerations allowed the excess borrowing.

Following the 1995 series of bailouts, to prevent a recurrence, SHCP tried to end its involvement with the collateralization of state and local debt, but the states and commercial banks, still traumatized by the crisis, did not agree on mutually acceptable private sector *fideicomiso* arrangements to handle the collateralization. So SHCP agreed on a temporary basis to accept mandates from the states to act as *fideicomiso* for borrowing transactions of which they, SHCP, approved. In 2000 SHCP will end this role and is now working with banks and states to assure that an adequate regulatory framework will be in place for private *fideicomisos* to collateralize state debt with *participaciones*, if that is what the parties want.

Of the many political problems with imposing a hard budget constraint on the states, the most difficult arises because the large share of spending for wages has created strong political pressure to use federal bailouts to avoid large cuts in spending rather than to service debt. Solving the problem will require not only firm resolve by the federal government to avoid bailouts but also more fiscal authority and political responsibility by the states to raise additional revenue (to service debt or pay wages) and to control costs. In other words, there will be an interdependence between hard budget constraints that motivate fiscal responsibility for the states and true fiscal autonomy of the states that makes such constraints politically realistic.

Subnational debt rose from $Mex27 billion in 1994 to $Mex71.6 billion in 1998. The 1994–95 financial crisis, and the rise in the interest rate, expanded the states' real debt outstanding, but this was considerably reduced by the bailout package put in place by the federal government in 1996–97. In 1997 subnational debt was only about 6 percent of the total public debt and 2 percent of national GDP. By comparison, subnational debt was around 5 percent of GDP in Argentina, almost 20 percent in Canada, and somewhat above that in Brazil. Much of the subnational borrowing in Mexico has been from Banobras, a federally owned development bank. States with high debt ratios and a repeated history of needing bailouts have still received loans from Banobras, but this will presumably be less of a problem with the introduction of tighter lending practices and the end of implicit federal guarantees, through the *mandatos*. Banobras's cost of funds is higher than that of commercial banks (because Banobras cannot accept deposits), which have been getting an increasing share of the subnational business. None of the debt is external because the constitution prohibits states from borrowing in foreign exchange or from foreign creditors.

Borrowing has been low or zero by most states since 1995; some states have paid off their debt. But a few have borrowed heavily, and the debt imposes a burden on them, because they have so little disposable income with which to service it. The ratio of debt stock to disposable revenue, defined as own taxes plus untied transfers, ranges from a maximum of 1.8 (in Sonora) to a minimum of 0.02 (in Hidalgo). The Federal District, although it has the highest absolute debt, is ranked among the least-indebted relative to disposable income, because it collects substantial revenue. The eight most indebted states are Baja California Sur, Jalisco, the State of México, Nuevo León, Querétaro, Quintana Roo, Sinaloa, and Sonora, all with a ratio of debt stock to disposable revenue greater than 1.[11] If one uses an alternative definition of disposable revenue—total revenue minus wage payments (personnel and educational and health decentralization) and minus transfers to municipalities—the same states are the most indebted, with the addition of Baja California (Norte). The main difference is that the ratio is higher for states like Nuevo León that use much of their own revenues to pay salaries. By this measure, 12 states had debt stock greater than disposable revenue in 1997.

The debt stock of Mexico's subnational governments is considerably less than their accumulated past fiscal deficits. A substantial part of their fiscal gap has been repeatedly relieved by the federal government through extraordinary, discretionary transfers (to cover unanticipated wage increases, investment expansion, and so forth) and other forms of bailouts like the 1995 ad hoc transfers for debt reduction and rescheduling. The primary balance of subnational governments in Mexico was positive in 1995–97, in contrast to deficits in 1992–94 (see figure O.2). But this resulted mainly from an increase in extraordinary transfers from the federal level. Netting out these extraordinary transfers, the states still had a primary deficit in 1995–97 and,

Figure O.2. Mexico: States' Primary Deficit, 1989–97

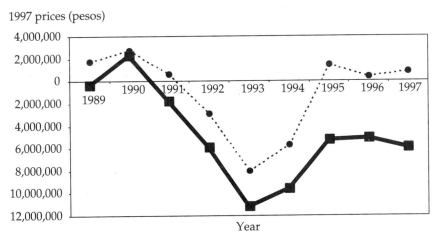

1997 prices (pesos)

··●·· BAL. PRIMARIO REAL

■■■ BAL. PRIM. REAL (Excluding extrodinary transfers)

Source: SHCP and World Bank estimates.

of course, a larger overall deficit. SHCP made annual fiscal adjustment agreements with each of the states (except the Federal District) as a result of the bailouts implemented after the 1995 crisis. The main federal program for these transfers (the Financial Strengthening of the States in Ramo 23) was dropped from the budget for 1999, and other parts of Ramo 23 were greatly reduced. It remains to be seen how states will cope and whether the federal government will remain committed to ending bailouts to the states.

They are also some important contingent liabilities of the subnational governments, such as pensions and health schemes for employees. Furthermore, the Federal District, states, and municipalities provide guarantees on loans to their respective decentralized agencies and public enterprises. There is a consolidated record of these only where they were registered in order to use the state's *participaciones* as collateral. In a few cases defaults of decentralized entities were large enough to trigger a federal bailout, as occurred with the Monterrey metro and the toll road in Coahuila. For most places, water companies are likely to be problem debtors.

Pensions of state employees are mostly unfunded, and few states have the fiscal capacity to operate them even on a pay-as-you-go basis. Nuevo León has reformed its pension system independently, but it was an incomplete reform and remains an exception. A partial estimate of the states' contingent debt for pensions reached $Mex167 billion in 1997 (about 6 percent of national GDP).[12] Among the 25 states with sufficient data to estimate the year in which the system would run out of reserves, given present contribution rates and so forth, five were already in deficit in 1998 and seven more were projected to be bankrupt in 1999–2002. Most state governments see the pension liability as a legacy left by the pre-1990 practices, when state governments were under the complete domination of the federal government. Consequently, some state governments view pensions as an implicit liability of the federal government. The lack of clear assignment has given both sides an incentive *not* to make adequate preparations, hoping that the lack of preparation will result in the other side bearing more of the cost in the end. When the problem is ignored, it grows quickly with the maturation of the labor force. Furthermore, when a large debt of this type becomes imminent, it reduces the incentives for a state to manage prudently the rest of its fiscal affairs.

The experiences of Argentina and Brazil show the absolute necessity of dealing with state pensions. Brazil has yet to reach a solution, although one is under active discussion; Argentina has federalized most of the responsibility. It may be best to separate the design of a future system, where options are wide, from the development of procedures to deal with pension liabilities built up in the past. The latter could be a federal responsibility, at least the part for workers originally hired by the federal government. In any case federal responsibility needs clear limits. The future system could be dealt with at the state level; experience indicates that a defined-contribution scheme is more likely to be sustainable.

The policies on subnational borrowing in the past evolved when Mexico's intergovernmental fiscal relations could be kept on track by ad hoc transfers and negotiations between players in the same party hierarchy. Now that states and municipalities are more independent politically and are often governed by parties in the opposition at the national level, the challenge has been to make a transition to a more strict and transparent system for managing subnational borrowing. Otherwise, debt problems could cripple the decentralization process and, in a worst-case scenario, eventually pose a macroeconomic hazard. Good fiscal behavior by states seems to be politically popular, which is fortunate, because much of the reform process will require actions by state governments and heightened vigilance by citizen-voters. The federal government is encouraging this by enforcing financial disclosure rules (as a condition for debt registration), demonstrating that governments are public entities using taxpayer money, not private operations with some right to privacy.

Although the past system at least prevented a major macroeconomic crisis from subnational debt, several things have already changed, the most important being the greater political independence of the states and the virtual elimination of extraordinary transfers. Thus a transition is already under way and requires further changes in order to be sustainable.

The federal government, as of 31 March 2000, ceased accepting *mandatos* from states to collateralize their loans with *participaciones*. States and their creditors will thus have to make alternative private *fideicomiso* or equivalent arrangements that do not carry an implicit guarantee by the federal treasury. SHCP will no longer be directly involved in the subnational borrowing process. Instead, it will only issue guidelines to explain what *fideicomiso* or other collateralization arrangements would be legally and financially sound, although a state and its creditors will have the option of agreeing on whatever guarantee arrangement suits them best. To make the transition to the new no-*mandatos* system as smooth as possible, during the first quarter of 2000 the federal government accepted *mandatos* only for states in the process of obtaining credit ratings from reputable international agencies (see below).

In parallel, bank regulation (and its impact on loan pricing) recently created incentives for more efficient and more transparent borrowing programs and financial management by states and municipalities, and for sounder, moral-hazard-free subnational risk assessments by their bank lenders. First, the so-called *régimen de excepción*, whereby all subnational lending was exempted from normal provisioning requirements and exposure concentration limits, was abolished in December 1999 formally and in practice. Second, bank loans to states and municipalities were subjected to a punitive capital risk weighting ratio (150 percent) if they were not registered with SHCP, a process that was in turn made conditional on the borrower being current in its publication of debt and fiscal data and in its debt service obligations to the government's development banks. Third, new regulations introduced differential capital-risk weighting that links the capital-backing requirements for (and, thus, the pricing of) subnational debt instruments to the borrower's credit rating, as measured by two, current, published, global-scale local-currency credit ratings performed by well-known international credit rating agencies.[13] There is always some danger of states shopping for ratings, but requiring two ratings from reputable international agencies will mitigate this risk. Using a global scale will increase the objectivity and reliability of the ratings, since the international firms will know that their rating of any Mexican state or city will be compared to the firm's other ratings around the world. Since the states cannot borrow abroad or in foreign currency, there is no exchange risk and thus local-currency ratings are appropriate.

To be complete, the hardening of budget constraints and the reduction in moral hazard requires a new lending framework for the public development banks, because they have not had the same corporate governance and market pressures as commercial banks. Thus, for their lending to state and municipal governments, the development banks (namely Banobras) will also be required to observe the same lending concentration limits and differential capital risk weighting as the commercial banks. In addition, and as a matter of corporate policy, the federal government (who owns the development banks) will allow development banks to grant loans only to subnational governments that require capital-risk weightings less than 100 percent.[14]

To avoid punitive capital risk weights of 150 percent, the state governments will also have to register their debt with SHCP, for which they will have to be current on their publication of debt and fiscal data and on debt service to development banks. The latter requirement will effectively prohibit Banobras from capitalizing interest arrears via new lending.

The new policies put in place in late-1999 and 2000 are moving Mexico toward a market-driven approach to state borrowing, excluding the possibility of federal guarantees and bailouts and including global credit ratings that determine capital-risk weighting and thus the cost and availability of bank credit to states. The federal government has an important role to play in motivating and facilitating improved accounting standards and public disclosure for states and municipalities, and financially prudent behavior by banks. Experience in Argentina, Colombia, and the United States shows how fiscally responsible behavior by states and their creditor banks requires good regulation and supervision of the banking system.

Options and Agenda for Action

It is useful to think of the policy agenda for decentralization not only as a list of actions for the short, medium, and long term, but also as steps that could initiate various paths of reform. Some important changes have already been made, such as ending discretionary transfers and the practice by the federal government of withholding debt service payments from states on behalf of the banks. Carrying on with these measures is an important part of the short-term agenda.

International experience points to a few principles that could guide the development of policies for the medium and long term:

- Authority and responsibility for delivering services should be devolved to the most local level that is compatible with efficiency.
- Within each sector, the responsibility for carrying out the essential functions should be clearly specified, and the responsible level of government should have access to adequate resources, including tax bases, to finance the service.
- As much as is feasible in terms of efficiency and equity, state and local governments should raise their own resources, and should do so in a way that makes the users of public services pay the costs.
- Governments should be able to borrow when, and only when, they are able and required to fully service the debt.
- The governments and agencies that do the spending should provide clear and transparent accounts, not only to the next level up but also, more important, to the public.
- The democratic process, not a technical process, must determine the degree of equalization in financing for states (and municipalities).
- New scenarios based on these principles will sometimes require legislation and other fundamental changes to the roles and responsibilities of governments.

Mexico faces some fundamental choices about the type of federal system it will have. Continued public debate would be fruitful, even if it does not lead to a clear choice of system. In many countries the choice has emerged gradually from many smaller choices. It is important, however, to understand that decisions to move in one dimension—for example, toward more reliance on subnational taxation—affect how decentralization will move in other dimensions, such as total tax resources, equality of per capita public resources across states, local autonomy in spending decisions, and control of borrowing.

At present subnational governments have weak taxation and depend on federal transfers, making them subject to federal controls on spending and borrowing. Mexico is following a model closer to the German end of the spectrum. Although there are many inequalities in funding across states, they are due mostly to historical and political factors, not to differences in the economic strength of the state economies. A variety of reforms would strengthen the institutions and clarify and simplify the rules.

In the longer term, the system may move part way toward legislative federalism—the Canadian model. This would occur if transfers do not grow as fast as the demand for spending on services that have been delegated to subnational governments, especially education, health, and roads. Then states, led by the ones with the best tax bases, might well choose to raise more of their own revenue. States can do that now in principle, but they will only do it in practice if they gain additional control over their spending and if the federal transfers do not penalize the state's tax effort. This requires not only the end of negotiable transfers, but also more autonomy for states. Moving on this path does not necessarily imply any reduction in resources for the poorer states with less tax base; indeed, such states will probably gain. But the rich states may increase their resources faster, thereby increasing inequality of per capita resources of local governments, unless there are stronger redistribution transfers than at present. In addition, the political market and the financial market would gain more influence on spending, taxing, and borrowing decisions than the central government.

Recent Steps: 1999–2000

The government's most recent step to improve the decentralization process focused on three main targets: (a) imposing hard budget constraints on federal resources provided to states and municipalities; (b) reducing moral hazard in subnational borrowing; and (c) increasing the transparency, efficiency, and public accountability of subnational fiscal and financial management and of the overall decentralization process. These will be valuable no matter where the system goes in the long term and will help create the incentives and capacity for taking the next steps, in the medium term, such as revamping the tax and transfers system and revising the assignments of spending authority.

Hard budget constraints will come about as rules rather than discretion govern subnational expenditure, transfers, and borrowing.[15] The federal government is ending all cash discretionary transfers to states and municipalities. All large pari-pasu programs will operate with transparent rules and will be available to all states that qualify according to published criteria. The state-by-state distribution of federal spending on local projects in education and transport will be published in 2000, to increase further the transparency in the use of federal resources.

Rules on discretionary financing from the federal government are being complemented with the efficiency-enhancing, market-based incentives in subnational borrowing, as described earlier, which will both harden budget constraints and reduce moral hazard.

Although there is little chance of solving the problem of state pension systems before 2001, it is important to get this issue on the table and initiate discussions. For this purpose, publishing a study of the state pension liabilities, including state-by-state estimates of them, seems a sensible step forward. This will be a key step in the process of clarifying the limits of federal responsibility, reducing the current impression that the states have a blank check from the federal government to cover pension liabilities, and eventually developing some common standards for allocating the burden.

Increasing the transparency of decentralized fiscal management, as a means of increasing the public accountability of both federal and subnational governments, is the third objective of the initial steps in the decentralization agenda. The federal government in the year 2000 budget increased the accountability of subnational governments for expenditures financed with federal resources. On a pilot basis, federal ministries and states will enter into performance agreements based on matching grant programs, which will be a signal that in the future subnational governments will be held more accountable for the sector-specific funds they receive through decentralization. To start, pilot performance agreements are being written and implemented for the environment and health sectors. These sectors appear particularly suitable for the performance agreement pilot because they enjoy a solid reform record with strong country ownership and ongoing decentralization agendas. The new Decentralization Committee, described above, will also improve transparency, especially when its Technical Secretariat makes more data and analysis publicly available.

To build a more consistent process of institutional development for decentralization, beyond the above-mentioned Decentralization Committee and Secretariat, a program of institutional training and strengthening at the state and municipal levels, covering accounting, budgeting, monitoring, reporting, auditing, and procurement, will be made available on demand. This program will be directly supported by an Inter-American Development Bank US$400 million line of credit approved in late 1999, and will capitalize on ongoing federal efforts, such as homogenization of accounting practices; and state efforts, as in Puebla and at the University of Monterrey.

The federal government can also support improvement of local accounting and reporting practices in several additional ways by (a) setting minimum standards for different categories of municipalities according to the absolute volume of transfers received. States would not be required to differentiate between municipalities, but the federal minimum standards would effectively invite states to differentiate in a way appropriate to their situations; (b) supporting the efforts of the *Contaduría Mayor de Hacienda de Honorable Camara de Diputados* to establish common guidelines for Ramo 33 and other subnational expenditures financed by federal transfers; (c) actively pursuing synergies between PROMAP, other similar programs at the federal level, and the *contaduría mayores* of the states. SHCP could document practices for covering the costs that states incur to administer Ramo 33 (project preparation, budgeting, accounting, and reporting); (d) evaluating the impact of laws and practices of states that have taken initiatives toward closer monitoring of Ramo 33; (e) evaluating the impact of external auditing by specialized firms wherever they exist; (f) providing information and recognition to encourage credible civil society organizations to keep and disseminate their own indicators of performance by subnational governments; and (g) beginning pilot-testing nonmonetary incentives to states that fully and promptly comply with the intergovernmental agreements reached under the *Homologación* Program. Initial incentives may consist of public recognition and dissemination of good practices.

Strengthen the Capacity of Subnational Governments. Documentation, recognition, and dissemination of good practices have a powerful training and demonstration effect, especially in the early years of decentralization. To encourage training activities, SHCP could collect and disseminate good practices with local spending of the Ramo 33 contributions since 1998 (the year they began), promote municipal-to-municipal training on the basis of good intrastate practices with effective allocation of Ramo 33 funds, and compare the benefits of horizontal training and technical assistance among municipalities with those of federal or state training programs. Training could include identifying priorities, preparing budgets and projects, conducting monitoring and evaluation, and writing procurement contracts. To encourage capacity building in municipalities, the federal government could increase the amount of funds from Ramo 33 that can be used for capacity building and encourage states and municipalities to follow the example of Puebla in concentrating and augmenting their training funds at the state level, in order to realize economies of scale.

Improve the Budget Preparation Process. Budget preparation and presentation offer a significant opportunity for the federal government to communicate its commitment to ensuring the fiscal transparency of sector units and subnational governments. The federal government may—as an experiment and while complying with the legally established timetable for budget preparation and approval—provide preliminary (and contingent) estimates of proposed transfers to states and municipalities, so that subnational governments may formulate tentative budget plans before the beginning of the fiscal year.

Clarify and Rationalize Intergovernmental Relations with the Federal District. To reduce current and future conflicts, the federal government could clarify the rules of intergovernmental fiscal relations for the Federal District. These would include the technical criteria for reorganizing both vertical (federal to Federal District) and horizontal (Federal District to neighboring states and municipalities) transfers related to the Federal District and effective institutional arrangements for negotiations and dispute resolution. The proposed arrangements will need to be consistent with the Federal District's autonomy concerning revenues, borrowing, and spending responsibilities. A study may be necessary to support this proposal, drawing on international experience in intergovernmental transfers and institutional arrangements from other metropolitan areas (Buenos Aires, Santiago, and São Paulo from within Latin America, and other cities in Eastern Asia, Europe, and North America).

Medium- to Long-Term Agenda: 2001–2006

The decentralization reform agenda for the medium to long term includes revising the fiscal pact between state and federal levels—the joint design of tax allocation and transfers—and revisiting the assignment of authority to make spending decisions. Institutional development will need to continue in several ways. The national government will also need to sustain its reforms of 1999–2000 to the financial regulatory regime for subnational borrowing, so that the states will change their laws and practices appropriately.

Several states, including seven whose governors in December 1999 signed the Declaración de San Lazaro, have actively objected to the current system of transfers and taxes, demanding that they get more of the resources collected in their territories. Since there are no longer federal budget resources for cash transfers at the discretion of the executive, the immediate solution has been increased federal spending for local needs—effectively ad hoc, in-kind transfers—and the revival of the Fund for Strengthening State Finances, with allocations set by Congress. Almost all parties would benefit from a more regular and transparent solution, but agreeing on which particular solution will be difficult. Addressing several problems at once—especially both taxes and transfers—will allow more possible dimensions to the solution and thus could make it more likely.

Subnational Taxes

Both to have appropriate incentives for efficient spending and to allow state finances to withstand economic shock, states and municipalities need to have substantial control over their revenues at the margin.

INTRODUCE NEW TAXES, PIGGYBACKING ON FEDERAL TAXES, CHOOSING ONE OR TWO OF SEVERAL POSSIBILITIES. The federal individual income tax rate could be reduced to allow states to levy their own surcharge. There could then be a corresponding reduction in federal transfers or revenue sharing. Some share of revenues obtained from excise taxes on motor fuels could be shifted from the federal government to the governments of states where consumption occurs. A similar shift of revenues from excise taxes on alcoholic beverages and tobacco products to be implemented via state surcharges could also be considered. With respect to excise taxes, the state excise taxes that fit within the current constitutional and legal frameworks could be identified. Then, experimentation could proceed with one or a few of the most promising excise taxes through federal and state agreements. Finally, SHCP could evaluate, adjust, and promote replication. The federal government could also shift to state governments the revenues generated from a given percentage point of the value added tax, employing the dual federal/state value added tax and the compensating value added tax for interstate sales. Stronger federal tax administration would be a prerequisite for any of these.

Rationalize the Payroll Tax. The federal government could give incentives to states to harmonize the base for the payroll tax. One way would be to share in the collection costs if the states adopt the same base as the federal social security tax. The most challenging issue concerning payroll (and property) taxes is to find the right incentives to stimulate states and municipalities to increase revenues to higher levels that are still compatible with tax efficiency, equitable incidence, and limited tax distortions of market allocation of resources.

Tax Administration. The formation of cadastres, updating, and valuation, should be strengthened for the property tax. Exemptions (even intergovernmental exemptions) should be limited or eliminated to expand the tax base and make the taxes more neutral. Accounts of tax expenditures (via exemptions) could be kept and publicized, with models prepared by the federal government. Audit and collection should be strengthened for state payroll taxes and municipal (or state-administered) property taxes. To improve tax collection, Mexico could create a national tax agency, which would collect both federal and state taxes that have the same or similar bases. This would obviously become more relevant as states harmonize payroll taxes and (are allowed to) have their taxes piggybacked on federal taxes.

Support Local Property Tax Efforts. It would be useful for a study to identify and evaluate the incentives that account for which states are effective in their support for the municipal property tax. State and municipal agreements could be encouraged to allow states to recapture part of the costs of administering the property tax or to share part of the additional revenues produced by improved administration. New state-municipal incentives and agreements are needed to stimulate cooperation for higher local fiscal effort. The federal government could consider a program to recognize and reward municipalities with the highest gains in property tax revenues and states with the most effective support for the property tax. It would be helpful to explain the impact of the *ejido* (communal land holding) on property registration and fiscal cadastre. The Technical Secretariat for the Decentralization Committee could collect and evaluate information on revenues from and administration of the property tax.

On the basis of ongoing experience, the federal government could encourage states to establish rules for which municipalities can fully and efficiently administer the property tax by themselves and which municipalities would benefit from various degrees of state support for forming and updating the cadastre, keeping current accounts, billing, and collecting. Evaluating the impact and efficiency of the 100 Cities Program—insofar as it involves support for the formation and administration of the cadastre—would help to establish the capacity of cities vis-à-vis predominantly rural municipalities. Comparisons could include cost-effectiveness ratios and center-periphery distribution of revenues.

It would be useful to have technical and empirical studies (a) to identify and evaluate the reasons behind the relative decline over the past 20 years of property tax administration in some places (for example, Monterrey) and the relative strengthening in other places (for example, the Federal District)—studies should lead to proposals for policy reform and replication of good practices; and (b) to measure the impact of changes in rates of the payroll tax on fiscal revenue and on the state economies—employment, labor productivity, and competitiveness—compared with those of other states.

Intergovernmental Transfers

In coordination with the tax reform agenda, some of the matching grant transfers and perhaps even the *participaciones* could be reduced, along with the reduction of federal tax rates (for example, the individual income tax or the value added tax) and the devolution to the states of the right to collect surcharges on the taxes.

In the medium term, a simpler and more transparent system is needed to assure equal per capita resources (or whatever objective is agreed to by the national and subnational governments) and more equal treatment of states with similar levels of poverty. The measure of equity should be total per capita transfers plus the revenue that *could* be obtained from the state's tax bases. Conditions will need to respect state priorities and allow states to achieve equivalent standards in different ways. The formulas for transfers should not penalize states that increase their own revenue.

To simplify the transfer system, all special earmarked programs, such as the Plan for Public Security or the 100 Cities Program, could be included within Ramo 33. Lumping together these special programs under one rubric would facilitate policymaking and move toward a simpler, more transparent system of transfers and greater subnational autonomy.

Spending and Service Delivery

The federal government could clarify sectoral responsibilities between levels of government, coordinating responsibilities for investment and maintenance and for hiring and salaries. States could be encouraged to adapt salaries and staffing to local conditions of demand for teachers and health personnel. This is already being done in Oaxaca for low-income areas and could be expanded to other states. States with an adequate tax base and extra demand for education could be allowed to raise teachers' pay above the national level, covering the extra cost with their own taxes. They could also take initiatives in the areas of performance indicators, pay, promotion, and incentives for improving public sector management.

IMPROVE INCENTIVES FOR EFFICIENCY. Some sector-specific reforms would improve the efficiency of incentives. In education, a new system of transfers could take existing allocations as a nominal floor and move the increases (or freezes) toward a formula based on the number of school-age children, according to the census and transparent projections from it. The federal formula eventually might try to reflect actual pupil attendance, but that sort of incentive should probably be left to the states. In the health sector, with existing allocations as a nominal floor, the increments should continue to move the allocations toward a formula based on some indicator of potential demand, like age- and gender-adjusted population. International experience shows that states should be encouraged to devolve authority and public accountability down to the units that directly provide services, such as hospitals and schools.

SHCP might evaluate the various state laws, de facto practice, and manuals that regulate state incentives and disincentives for municipal autonomy and for efficient allocation of Ramo 33. SHCP and SECODAM could compare state laws and practices on Ramo 33 with the tools of the *Programa de Mejoramiento de la Administración Pública* (PROMAP) and the new, results-oriented *Nueva Estrategia de Programación* (NEP), and propose recommendations for training *Comités de Planeación para el Desarrollo del Estado* (COPLADEs) and *Comités de Planeación para el Desarrollo Municipal* (COPLADEMUNs) (planning committees for state development and municipal development, respectively) in the new programming techniques. The study could compare those states where the COPLADE is responsible for executing a program with those states where it is not.

CLARIFY PENSION RESPONSIBILITIES ON A SUSTAINABLE BASIS. An agreement between federal and state governments is needed to clarify which level of government is responsible for the pensions of state employees. Perhaps it would be necessary for the federal government to recognize explicitly some base-line part of a state's pensions not under its control (such as former federal employees and those over age 50) in return for the state undertaking fiscal reforms, such as servicing the remaining obligations, including social security. Alternatively, as was done in Argentina, the federal government might offer to take over the states' pension schemes (to reform them), along with the collection of contributions. Specific steps would come from the initial study to make explicit the size and nature of the pension liabilities.

Core Institutions for Decentralization

IMPROVE DISPUTE RESOLUTION. To deal with problems that arise even in the best-designed system and to give participants an incentive to find cooperative solutions, better institutions are needed for resolving disputes. Creating these institutions will take time, but starting soon is desirable. For major sectors such as health and education, sectoral boards could be developed. In the medium term, with lessons learned from the experience in the sectors, an overall intergovernmental board could be established to handle systemwide issues and appeals from the sectoral boards. Once the federal-state models are working, states could establish their own municipal-state boards to handle issues among municipalities and between them and the state.

IMPROVE ACCOUNTING STANDARDS AND INFORMATION. It is important to maintain clear accountability of each level of government—municipal reporting to the states and state monitoring of allocations. Some states currently impose sanctions on municipalities for slow reporting by suspending transfers, and this practice could be linked with the process of documentation and evaluation. Evaluation of ongoing practices could also distinguish executive controls from the controls exercised by the states' Congressional accounting offices. SHCP could evaluate whether the model being prepared by the *Contaduría Mayor de la Unión* adequately stimulates efficient allocation, and then formulate and publish corresponding recommendations. It is also important to implement uniform accounting and exchanges of sectoral and intersectoral information, both top-down and bottom-up.

IMPROVE COORDINATION BETWEEN AND WITHIN LEVELS OF GOVERNMENT. The Federal government may want to stimulate municipal associations to (a) achieve economies of scale (in procurement, specialized services, sharing of equipment, administrative costs); (b) identify fiscal or other technical solutions through coordinated, subregional efforts undertaken jointly by two or more municipalities (garbage disposal, interjurisdictional distribution of pollution charges); (c) identify and evaluate ongoing experiences; and (d) undertake short-term pilot projects that can be launched and evaluated quickly. Intersectoral, interstate, and intermunicipal forums could be created to allow integral budgeting for a given region or subregion. Although initially informal or ad hoc, these forums could establish the basis for more flexible budgets and integral regional budgeting in the future.

ACCORD MUNICIPALITIES DIFFERENT TREATMENT ACCORDING TO CAPACITY. It is important to establish a set of criteria for certifying municipalities as having the capacity to execute certain programs or to borrow. Financial reporting requirements should be set according to the fiscal size of the municipality, whether it is a state capital, and whether it wants to take on additional responsibility and authority.

In conclusion, the agenda envisioned here has six main objectives:

1. Sectoral and intersectoral decentralization policies need to be formed within a more coherent strategic framework. This would help to address the need for clearer allocation of responsibility, more subnational autonomy, and more effective implementation strategies.
2. The administrative capacity of subnational governments needs to be strengthened, particularly at the municipal level.
3. The capacity of the states to tax and borrow needs to be expanded in a sound and sustainable way to match their new responsibilities.
4. To have adequate incentives for responsible fiscal autonomy, states need to face hard budget constraints from the federal government regarding transfers, debt, and responsibilities for service delivery.
5. Accounting practices need to be improved at all subnational levels because intergovernmental coordination and monitoring of the decentralization process require the exchange of uniform and relevant information. Such information has to be shared between governments and with citizen-voters, who are the ultimate champions of reform in a democracy.
6. Consensus-building processes and preemptive conflict and dispute resolution mechanisms are needed to help the widening circles of economic and political actors participate in the dynamic process of decentralization.

Although the steps outlined here may be politically and economically difficult, all stakeholders in Mexico are aware of the costs and risks of taking no coherent action. These costs would include underutilization of subnational tax capacity, inefficient spending due to lack of clear accountability and controls on service delivery, and potentially explosive subnational indebtedness, particularly arising from contingent debt or pension liabilities.

Perspectiva General *N A*

Marcelo Giugale, Vinh Nguyen, Fernando Rojas y Steven B. Webb

AUNQUE LA "DESCENTRALIZACIÓN" es un fenómeno que se vive en todo el mundo y su significado, aplicación y efectos varían de un país a otro, la experiencia indica que hay tres lecciones que son pertinentes en cualquier parte.

En primer lugar, la descentralización tiene efectos muy importantes en diversas areas: desde la estabilidad macroeconómica hasta la disminución de la pobreza, la prestación de servicios sociales y la calidad de la gestión gubernamental (Burki, Dillinger y Perry, 1999). Por esta razón, un país que descentraliza su sector público necesita idear una *estrategia de descentralización* que sea coherente. Cuando ésta se lleva a cabo de manera correcta, puede generar muchos beneficios económicos, tales como la mayor eficiencia, receptividad y transparencia en la prestación de servicios que solicita la población local. Si la descentralización se hace de manera inadecuada, puede tener consecuencias poco deseadas, provocando el desequilibrio macroeconómico, intensificando las diferencias y conflictos regionales, o disminuyendo la calidad y cantidad de los servicios públicos. Prestar la debida atención a cómo interactúan diversas políticas económicas puede evitar muchos problemas con la descentralización. Aunque no exista una única senda "correcta" para la descentralización, y sea una decisión política para el país determinar el alcance y naturaleza adecuados de ésta, pueden evitarse muchos errores comunes. Por ejemplo, siempre es erróneo descentralizar los ingresos sin hacer lo propio con el correspondiente conjunto de responsabilidades; y, por lo general, es incorrecto asignar exactamente el mismo ingreso y responsabilidad a gobiernos municipales grandes y pequeños.

Segundo, dado que en todos lados la descentralización es una actividad progresiva y en evolución, una buena estrategia requiere una *adecuada infraestructura institucional* para formular una política de descentralización, seguirla muy de cerca y aplicarla. La infraestructura necesaria incluye contar con marcos normativos y legales, organizaciones que se encarguen de coordinar, así como programas de capacitación. Incluso las estrategias mejor planeadas no se sustentan por sí solas sin un apoyo institucional de ese tipo. En particular, la experiencia en todo el mundo ha puesto de manifiesto la necesidad que existe de preparar y divulgar información exacta, completa y confiable sobre todos los aspectos que implica descentralizar. Esto disminuye la confusión así como los conflictos políticos y burocráticos que invariablemente acompañan a cualquier cambio importante.

Tercero, la experiencia latinoamericana en el proceso de descentralización muestra que las campañas abruptas y uniformizantes generalmente han fracasado. Los países han tenido que regresar a una descentralización incremental, con reglas diferenciadas conforme a la diversa capacidad administrativa de las unidades territoriales. Esta fue la experiencia con la legislación colombiana de 1986, la constitución brasileña de 1988, la Ley Orgánica de Descentralización de Venezuela en 1988, y las leyes bolivianas de Participación Popular y Descentralización de 1994 y 1996.

Estas lecciones se aplican a México. El país está progresando en conceder más autonomía, asignar más responsabilidad fiscal y pedir más informes de resultados a los niveles inferiores de gobierno (o subnacionales). En la actualidad, los estados gastan cerca de la mitad de lo que gasta el gobierno federal (Ver el Cuadro sinóptico 1). También ha crecido el porcentaje del gasto público municipal, aunque esta tendencia no está totalmente documentada. Este proceso está encauzándose gracias a la mayor competencia política en todos los niveles de la administración pública y al deseo del gobierno federal de incluir la descentralización en su programa para una mayor participación política.

Cuadro 0.1. Magnitudes Fiscales: Gobiernos federal y estatales, 1997

Concepto	Porcentaje del Producto Interno Bruto	
	Federal	Estatal*
Gasto propio	11,5	4,9
1991	8,4	3,0
1996	7,7	4,9
Ingresos propios	15,8	1,0
Ingresos disponibles	13,2	5,4
Saldo original	−1,3	0,0
Saldo general	−4,9	−0,1
Intereses de la deuda	18,4	0,3
Obligaciones	31,0	1,5

* No incluye Tabasco ni Tamaulipas; sin información.
Fuentes: SHCP y cifras estimadas de los autores.

Sin embargo, cada país debe diseñar su propia estrategia de descentralización y su propia infraestructura institucional particular de acuerdo con su historia, sus objetivos y las restricciones que enfrente. En el mundo se observa un variado espectro de modelos de descentralización. Uno de sus extremos, el caso de Canadá, puede calificarse como un federalismo legislativo total en el sentido de que la principal fuente de recursos de los gobiernos provinciales y territoriales es su propia recaudación fiscal; y su autonomía es casi total en cuanto a cómo gastar esos ingresos. La autonomía provincial de Canadá es tal que no hay restricciones federales de ningún tipo al endeudamiento de las provincias, dejando la tarea normativa completamente en manos del mercado de capitales, aunque las provincias imponen estrictos controles al endeudamiento municipal. Las desigualdades regionales en Canadá a causa de las diferencias en la base impositiva se nivelan en forma parcial mediante las transferencias federales. Suiza y Estados Unidos se apegan a variantes de este modelo, aunque con menos igualación (ninguna en Estados Unidos), políticas tributarias menos uniformes a nivel estatal y tentativas federales más detalladas para influir en el gasto estatal. En América Latina, la descentralización brasileña está más cerca de este extremo del espectro; los estados más grandes recaudan gran parte de sus propios ingresos y diseñan sus programas sociales. Sin embargo, el gobierno federal de Brasil ha participado frecuentemente en las políticas de personal y administración de la deuda de los estados, en muchos casos de manera negativa.

En Alemania y Austria se observa un federalismo administrativo, el modelo al otro extremo del espectro. Las transferencias son la principal fuente de ingresos de los estados y las políticas federales (o conjuntas) orientan la mayoría de los gastos en los niveles inferiores de gobierno. Las políticas de compensación regional, ejecutadas en buena parte mediante las transferencias, son muy firmes. Además, el gobierno central impone estrictos controles al endeudamiento subnacional. Colombia y Venezuela siguen este modelo en América Latina, aunque el factor de igualación está ausente en gran medida.

En otros países pueden encontrarse variadas combinaciones de las características mencionadas: independencia en ingresos, autonomía para ejercer el gasto, autonomía para adquirir obligaciones e igualación. En Argentina, por ejemplo, las transferencias son más importantes que en Brasil; pero los estados tienen más autonomía para controlar los costos de personal y el mercado desempeña un papel más importante en la administración de la deuda.

En principio, Mexico podría combinar y acoplar estas características de acuerdo con sus deseos. En vista de que este país ya ha tomado las principales decisiones respecto a descentralizar la responsabilidad del gasto y el endeudamiento en los niveles inferiores de gobierno, la siguiente decisión crítica se refiere a la importancia de las transferencias y hasta qué punto debe descentralizarse el sistema fiscal. Esto irá de la mano con la decisión que se tome respecto al grado en que las transferencias federales compensarán las desigualdades regionales, que de otra manera surgirían a raíz de la descentralización tributaria. Una tercera decisión importante, que puede requerir modificaciones a medida que evolucione el sistema de transferencias, es en qué medida el gobierno central orientará, supervisará o controlará los gastos en detalle (por ejemplo, mediante la regulación de los mercados financieros o mediante condiciones impuestas a las transferencias). Las estructuras institucionales antes mencionadas serán necesarias para lograr el consenso sobre estos objetivos de política, y para ponerlos en práctica y mantenerlos.

México ya ha empezado el camino hacia la descentralización con un modelo propio diseñado por el país, como debe de ser. Parece que algunas de las medidas que ya se han tomado son convenientes y deben preservarse y fortalecerse; por ejemplo, el fin de las transferencias discrecionales y el apoyo a la confección de informes estatales públicos y contables más comprensibles y uniformes. Otras medidas parecen ser menos deseables. Este libro reúne una serie de ensayos que aprovechan las experiencias que ha dejado la descentralización en el ámbito mundial, con el propósito de concentrarse en lo que es necesario para desarrollar una estrategia de descentralización sustentable y coherente en México, y en las medidas institucionales necesarias para apuntalar este proceso.

En esta Perspectiva General, extraemos los principales mensajes de los autores de dichos ensayos. Este análisis se organiza en torno a cinco temas: (1) instituciones; (2) gasto y prestación de servicios; (3) impuestos e ingresos subnacionales; (4) transferencias intergubernamentales; y (5) endeudamiento y administración de la deuda subnacional. Surge así un panorama de la trayectoria y alternativas de México en cuanto a la descentralización, panorama que luego se expresa para el corto, mediano y largo plazos.

Las Instituciones de la Descentralización

En México, las cuestiones institucionales fundamentales que se presentan al descentralizar son el fortalecimiento de la confianza en este proceso entre los principales interesados, el mejoramiento de la coordinación intergubernamental y la solución de conflictos, el afianzamiento y de la democratización del proceso de control y presentación de informes de resultados, la coordinación del proceso presupuestario en múltiples niveles, las diferencias entre municipios con distinta capacidad administrativa, la cooperacion en el fortalecimiento conjunto de capacidades, y las características singulares de la relación del Distrito Federal con sus vecinos y el gobierno federal.

Coordinación intergubernamental

La experiencia internacional muestra la importancia y dificultades de las instituciones colectivas que dirigen el proceso de descentralización y que funcionan como foros para evitar negociar y solucionar conflictos (consulte el recuadro 1). Desarrollar instituciones de ese tipo constituye un desafío sobre todo para México, por su enfoque de tanteos hacia la descentralización y la consecuente fragmentación política, regional, intersectorial e, incluso, intra-sectorial. Hasta ahora, México ha mejorado su coordinación intersectorial e intergubernamental en buena parte mediante mecanismos verticalistas, como las transferencias condicionadas y la supervisión federal. En la actualidad, parecería necesario establecer un mecanismo para crear consenso, en el que confíen todas las partes y que se encargue de las tareas que a continuación se mencionan y que son de importancia fundamental:

- Proponer una perspectiva a largo plazo de la descentralización, metas intermedias y ajustes continuos;
- Promover foros para analizar y negociar medidas fiscales intergu-bernamentales, y evitar conflictos entre jurisdicciones.
- Elaborar un informe anual del avance y los asuntos en curso respec-to a la descentralización, manteniendo al tanto a las dependencias fe-derales y a los gobiernos estatales sobre sus responsabilidades en el proceso de descentralización;
- Proporcionar información confiable para el análisis público de la política financiera y fiscal local, federal y estatal; y evaluar el diseño e intercambio de información;
- Diseñar, recabar y divulgar indicadores importantes para llevar a cabo la descentralización, supervisar los cambios de responsabilidades en lo que se refiere a ingresos y gasto; y evaluar la capacidad de los go-biernos estatales para asumir nuevas responsabilidades.

A principios del año 2000, y con el propósito de ayudar a satisfacer estas necesidades, el gobierno federal mexicano estableció un Comité de Descentralización en el seno de la Secretaría de Hacienda y Crédito Público (SHCP), con una secretaría técnica presidida—en forma rotativa—por los tres subsecretarios: de Ingresos, Egresos y Crédito Público. Este comité intersecretarial desempeñará un papel decisivo coordinando las relaciones fiscales intergubernamentales y preparando una modificación del pacto fis-cal y una nueva *Ley de Coordinación Hacendaria* (que aborda los ingresos, las transferencias y las responsabilidades en todos los niveles de gobierno.) La secretaría técnica será responsable del análisis de la evolución del proceso de descentralización, a fin de orientar la política federal en la materia. La unidad diseñará y evaluará los indicadores para supervisar las relaciones fiscales intergubernamentales y la descentralización en conjunto; recabará información y publicará estadísticas fiscales sobre los niveles inferiores de

---

Recuadro 0.1. Coordinación de la descentralización: Lecciones de América Latina

La experiencia latinoamericana en cuanto a coordinar el proceso de descentralización deja las siguientes lecciones:

1. Los acuerdos horizontales entre los diferentes ministerios (nivel nacional) o las reuniones de gobernadores, alcaldes o ministros de finanzas (nivel subnacional) han tenido sólo modestos efectos, generalmente limitados a unas cuantas políticas específicas. Parece que los acuerdos con una esfera de acción más amplia requieren el apoyo presidencial y el compromiso explícito del Ministerio de Finanzas federal.

2. Las comisiones presidenciales pueden ser más eficaces; sin embargo, el continuo apoyo presidencial es lo que determina su sustentabilidad, según señaló la experiencia en Venezuela de la Comisión Presidencial para la Reforma del Estado (COPRE, por su sigla en español).

3. El apoyo presidencial a dependencias de menor nivel generalmente es efímero, como el caso boliviano de la Subsecretaría de Participación Popular; esta sólo duró mientras contó con el apoyo ilimitado del presidente.

4. Una sola entidad a nivel ministerial, como la secretaría de gobernación o el ministerio del interior o de la presidencia, generalmente ha fracasado; mientras el ministerio de finanzas o el encargado de la programación se volvía fundamental para el avance de la descentralización.

5. Un órgano específico a nivel presidencial, como la Secretaría de la Presidencia, generalmente carece de una capacidad de coordinación eficaz comparada con los ministerios y sobre todo con el de finanzas.

6. Las experiencias en los lugares donde ningun ministerio es el responsable de manera fundamental, como en Chile y Colombia, pone de manifiesto que el ministerio de finanzas o la oficina nacional de programación por lo general se hace cargo si el proceso de descentralización no es encabezado de manera rotunda por otro ministerio.

---

gobierno; divulgará análisis periódicos; promoverá el debate público y mantendrá comunicación con los congresos, sus oficinas contables— denominadas *Contaduría Mayor de Hacienda de la Honorable Cámara de Diputados*—y la Secretaría de Contraloría y Desarrollo Administrativo (SECODAM). El Comité integrará y coordinará las tareas de descentralización que actualmente promueven las tres subsecretarías; y coordinará los diversos programas de apoyo técnico y fortalecimiento subnacional que ofrecen la Secretaría de Hacienda y Crédito Público, Banobras y otras instituciones federales. El comité no se institucionalizará oficialmente durante la administración del presidente Zedillo, dejando que el próximo gobierno decida si lo hace y en qué forma.

Prevenir y solucionar conflictos

La coordinación intergubernamental acertada necesitará instituciones específicas que lleven a cabo las negociaciones y solucionen los desacuerdos, porque una descentralización eficaz requiere algo más que el diseño de ingresos, transferencias, endeudamiento y responsabilidades. Ningún sistema puede prever y especificar todo por adelantado. Surgen controversias y cuestiones que necesitan resolverse, y el método para hacerlo produce importantes efectos de estímulo respecto a cómo funciona en realidad el sistema.

Al igual que otros países en proceso de descentralización, México tiene un número cada vez mayor de conflictos interjurisdiccionales. Los tribunales necesitan reforzar su capacidad para atender las controversias administrativas y constitucionales que surjan a causa de la descentralización. El país también podría fomentar otros medios para la resolución de controversias, porque los trámites en los tribunales tienden a ser caros, requieren mucho tiempo y a menudo son innecesarios. Algunos desacuerdos están conjurándose o son resueltos mediante negociaciones informales y la buena disposición para llegar a un arreglo. La falta de canales institucionales alternos para resolver controversias a menudo hace que el resultado sea cuestión de qué parte tiene mayor poder político y esto debilita la credibilidad de las reglas. Sería útil si se institucionalizaran los medios no judiciales para resolver desacuerdos entre jurisdicciones, y se preparara a jueces y expertos en conciliación en los principios y reglas de operación de la descentralización. En el área de salubridad, el *Consejo Nacional de Salud* resuelve muchas controversias; y esta institución podría ser un ejemplo para otros sectores con temas importantes relacionados con la descentralización, como el sector educativo, los recursos hidráulicos, el transporte vial y el medio ambiente.

Responsabilidad y control democráticos

Los controles eficaces son un requisito previo y un elemento indispensable para consolidar la capacidad de gestión, la autonomía y la presentación de informes de resultados en los niveles inferiores de gobierno. Como en México el ímpetu para la descentralización ha provenido no sólo del gobierno federal sino también de la competencia democrática en el Congreso y de los gobiernos estatales, es importante que todas las cuentas del gobierno se divulguen pública y sistemáticamente abriendo las posibilidades para un control democrático descentralizado.

En un México descentralizado, el desarrollo institucional para disponer de controles eficaces debe aprovechar las capacidades de los mecanismos actuales. Mexico ha adquirido considerable experiencia y conocimientos técnicos en la SECODAM y en algunas de las contralorías estatales (en la rama ejecutiva). Las contadurías de los congresos, órganos independientes de congresos cada vez más pluralistas, están surgiendo como algunas de las instituciones que gozan de más confianza en el país. El Programa de Homologación de la SHCP también trata de estandarizar los informes financieros de los estados. Además de estos organismos oficiales, algunos estados y dependencias federales ya llevan a cabo auditorías externas efectuadas por empresas especializadas.

En el modelo mexicano, los controles son cuestión de coordinación intergubernamental. La Contaduría del Congreso establece los principios generales a los que deben apegarse las contadurías de las legislaturas estatales. A fin de consolidar la autonomía política y la credibilidad de estas instituciones, México podría considerar los modelos de la Contaduría General de Estados Unidos de América, a la que el Congreso concede autoridad autónoma considerable en materia de investigación; o el de los comités de finanzas parlamentarios de algunos países de la Comunidad Británica de Naciones, que la Constitución establece bajo la presidencia del partido opositor. En el aspecto ejecutivo en México, la SECODAM coordina el trabajo con las contralorías estatales y les ayuda con programas de capacitación y diseminación. Desde el punto de vista legal, los estados son responsables del control fiscal de los municipios. Aunque en principio cada nivel de gobierno debe contar con sus propios controles independientes, el nivel federal ha dispuesto medidas que sirven de base para reforzar los controles en todos los niveles durante la transición a un sistema más descentralizado.

Cooordinación presupuestal

En la actualidad, coordinar el presupuesto en México implica ante todo equilibrar las prioridades del gasto en diferentes niveles de gobierno. Los mecanismos para coordinarlo son distintos en cada nivel: federal–estatal, estatal–municipal y federal–municipal.

El presupuesto federal–estatal se coordina mediante el proceso diseñado para el presupuesto federal, y otros mecanismos. Los estados solían presentar planes operativos anuales por sector que a la sazón se ajustaban e incorporaban al plan sectorial federal que se sometía a consideración de la Secretaría de Hacienda y Crédito Público (POA por su sigla en español). La Ley de Coordinación Fiscal sustituye en parte este proceso mediante mecanismos de fórmula automática, pero las secretarías federales de educación y salud siguen exigiendo que los estados elaboren un cierto tipo de planes operativos anuales para el presupuesto por sectores. Una vez que el plan se presenta, la SHCP filtra aún más los planes por sector y presenta el proyecto de ley para el presupuesto ante el Congreso. Aunque los mecanismos actuales para elaborar el presupuesto garantizan cierto intercambio de información y oportunidades para conciliar las prioridades federales y estatales, aún se carece de normas transparentes y explícitas para la asignación de recursos federales en todos los estados.

Además de la preparación del presupuesto federal, las juntas ordinarias de coordinación federal–estatal (se trata de reuniones trimestrales entre la Secretaría de Hacienda y Crédito Público, las áreas de Ingresos y Egresos, y los secretarios de hacienda de los estados) y el Pacto Fiscal federal también son contextos en que se coordina el presupuesto. La coordinación de ingresos y el equilibrio tributario entre el gobierno federal y los estados se logra principalmente por medio del Pacto Fiscal y la respectiva transferencia de ingresos generales de casi el 22 por ciento de las llamadas participaciones (recaudación federal participable).[1] Sin embargo, como el ejercicio fiscal coincide con el año calendario en todos los niveles del gobierno, la información sobre el presupuesto federal va a los estados y municipios apenas en el momento del cierre mismo del ejercicio fiscal anterior o a principios del nuevo año; lo que hace que la elaboración del presupuesto en los niveles inferiores de gobierno sea cada vez más difícil, ya que los presupuestos y transferencias federales son menos previsibles y se autorizan en los últimos días de diciembre.

La coordinación adicional del presupuesto se verifica mediante el creciente número de programas pari-passu, acuerdos para donaciones de contrapartida por sector, y transferencias para fines específicos para la descentralización por sector; como el Programa de Federalización Educativa, el primer y más cuantioso fondo del llamado Ramo 33.[2] Las transferencias extraordinarias con fines específicos de inversión también pueden considerarse como mecanismos de coordinación.[3] De hecho, las transferencias extraordinarias han fomentado los acuerdos para que la presentación de informes y la contabilidad sean homogéneas entre el gobierno federal y los estados (Programa de Homologación).

La coordinación del presupuesto estatal–municipal se ejerce cuando el estado en cuestión autoriza los presupuestos y el endeudamiento de sus municipios.[4] En teoría, los presupuestos municipales tienen que someterse al plan de desarrollo del estado, primordialmente para inversiones, aunque esto rara vez se practica. Los acuerdos especiales entre estados y municipios pueden ser otra oportunidad para conciliar las prioridades de egresos de ambos niveles, y coordinar las metas y métodos para la recaudación de ingresos.[5]

La coordinación del presupuesto federal–municipal, incluso la federal–estatal–municipal, también se ejerce mediante la transformación del Ramo 26 en el Ramo 33 (categoría presupuestaria 26). Las fórmulas ya especifican que la mayor parte de la asignación de recursos especiales del Ramo 33 es fundamental, pero no exclusivamente, para fondos sectoriales.

Por consiguiente, el Ramo 33—en la práctica—es un mecanismo por medio del cual el nivel federal (el Congreso y la rama ejecutiva) garantiza la asignación territorial de recursos conforme a las prioridades federales. Sin embargo, los informes y la contabilidad para los recursos del Ramo 33 aún son deficientes, y ninguno fomenta la confianza intergubernamental ni deja un margen para supervisar o evaluar sus efectos.[6]

Los mecanismos actuales para coordinar el presupuesto—egresos en su mayor parte—obstaculizan la iniciativa y autonomía en los niveles inferiores de gobierno. En vez de fomentar la asignación más eficiente de recursos en los territorios, tienden a aumentar el control federal de la asignación de recursos, incluso aunque se otorgue más responsabilidad política a los estados en este sentido. Por consiguiente, estos mecanismos complican la distribución de responsabilidades entre los niveles de gobierno y reducen la responsabilidad de cada nivel. Además, estos mecanismos no contribuyen a una verdadera coordinación bilateral del gasto porque, ante todo, son métodos formales de programación y presupuesto.[7]

Clasificar los municipios

La diversidad de los gobiernos locales y estatales no está reflejada en las distintas normas federales para gobiernos locales (consulte el recuadro 2 sobre experiencia internacional). En México existe una amplia variedad en la escala, capacidad administrativa, bases gravables y niveles de pobreza en estados y municipios, pero el marco jurídico para la descentralización no reconoce estas diferencias. En la actualidad, las normas federales no clasifican a los municipios por tamaño y capacidad para diferenciar la autoridad responsable del gasto, la autoridad fiscal, la autoridad para solicitar créditos, los requisitos para la presentación de informes, o la elegibilidad ' para contar con apoyo técnico. Los detalles del problema y la solución adecuada pueden ser diferentes para municipios y estados.

México tiene más de 2.400 municipios, abarcando una amplia gama, desde ciudades con varios millones de habitantes, funcionarios responsables de formular las políticas con grados superiores de educación formal e información sobre cuentas fiscales procesada en computadoras, hasta poblaciones pequeñas con menos de 5.000 habitantes, y líderes con poca educación formal y prácticas contables informales en el mejor de los casos. Sólo del 25 por ciento al 40 por ciento de los municipios están a la altura de los indicadores de capacidad comunmente aceptados: tener una unidad de programación del presupuesto, una agencia de evaluación e información de cuentas procesada en computadora; contar con un código administrativo interno y utilizarlo, asi como reglamentos para el catastro;[8] y recaudar más de la mitad de sus propios recursos. Parece poco realista aplicar las mismas reglas a todos los municipios. En la práctica, los estados a menudo no exigen todos los requisitos legales a los municipios pobres y pequeños. Sin embargo, los municipios pequeños que cumplen

---

Recuadro 0.2. Experiencia internacional en el tratamiento diferencial de municipios

La experiencia en América Latina demuestra que si no se establece una diferencia categórica en las responsabilidades de los órganos inferiores de gobierno conforme a su capacidad de gestión y fiscal, o de ambos tipos, la diferenciación tiene lugar de hecho, a menudo en forma caótica. Por lo tanto, es aconsejable establecer una diferencia rotunda entre los órganos inferiores de gobierno, mientras al mismo tiempo se fijan los estándares para ascender de una categoría a otra. El proceso colombiano de certificación es un ejemplo de clasificación flexible que estimula a los gobiernos locales y regionales para habilitarlos a fin de que asuman responsabilidades en los sectores de la educación y la salud. Para obtener la certificación, los departamentos tienen que demostrar al gobierno nacional que pueden asumir las nuevas responsabilidades en salud y educación; y que han adquirido la capacidad requerida en programación, finanzas, supervisión y presentación de informes. Después de certificar a un departamento, sus municipios pueden solicitar a éste que haga lo mismo con ellos. En otro ejemplo de clasificación y ascenso de categoría, España ha aumentado paulatinamente las responsabilidades de las autonomías—áreas como Cataluña con estatuto especial—y ampliado sus responsabilidades.

---

con una cantidad adecuada de informes para su tamaño no deberían estar en un estado de incumplimiento. Los municipios grandes frecuentemente cumplen con un nivel superior al mínimo para satisfacer los requisitos de su propia administración o de sus acreedores del sector privado. Sin embargo, algunas ciudades más importantes tienen una administración inadecuada, aun cuando cumplen con la letra de la ley.

La capacidad administrativa y fiscal de los 32 estados de México también varía mucho. Por ejemplo, en 1997 sólo tres estados tenían una ley de coordinación fiscal, una ley de gasto público, contabilidad y presupuesto, y una ley de deuda pública; siete estados no tenían ninguna de estas leyes. En la actualidad, todos los estados cuentan con estas leyes aunque su eficacia varía en parte a causa de su novedad. Las transferencias identificadas para programas de fortalecimiento de las capacidades, como las que aparecen en el presupuesto del año 2000, podrían ayudar a los estados a llegar hasta norma uniforme. A medida que los gobiernos municipales y estatales sean más democráticos y más responsables, los ciudadanos exigirán que sus gobiernos rindan mejores informes.

Fortalecer la capacidad

Todas las partes interesadas coinciden en la necesidad de aumentar la capacidad técnica y administrativa de los gobiernos estatales. Por ejemplo, las deficiencias técnicas impiden que la contabilidad y presentación de informes de las transferencias del Ramo 33 sean adecuadas, sobre todo en municipios cuya capacidad de gestión y fiscal es mínima. Sin embargo, existe menos acuerdo respecto a la mejor manera de fortalecer la capacidad en los niveles inferiores de gobierno. A nivel federal, la ejecución de programas para fortalecer la capacidad administrativa subnacional—como el *Programa de Homologación*—ha tenido un efecto positivo pero limitado. Algunos recursos federales para el desarrollo de instituciones a nivel municipal provienen de la opción con que cuenta cada municipio de usar el 2 por ciento del fondo único del Ramo 33 para este propósito (infraestructura municipal). Sin embargo, para los municipios pequeños, losque más necesitan fortalecer su capacidad, la suma asciende apenas a unos cuantos cientos de pesos; demasiado poco y muy disperso para los 2.400 municipios de México. El estado de Puebla ha establecido una serie de acuerdos con sus municipios para concentrar e incrementar estos recursos a nivel estatal y proporcionar un programa de fortalecimiento de capacidades; con base en un sondeo de las necesidades locales. El gobierno federal también está planeando nuevos programas para apoyar el fortalecimiento de capacidades en los niveles local y estatal. Se estima que habrá presión sobre estos gobiernos para que mejoren su acceso a los mercados de crédito cuando éstos se reformen según se describe más adelante.

La reforma del servicio civil en los niveles subnaciones es necesaria y tal vez inevitable, pero tendrá éxito o efecto limitado mientras los antiguos incentivos sigan vigentes. Los funcionarios del gobierno local y estatal, al igual que los del gobierno federal, responden a los estímulos con los que se enfrentan. Si esos incentivos entorpecen la iniciativa y premian la ineficiencia, encontrar administraciones subnacionales ineficientes e irresponsables no resulta ser una sorpresa. Solucionar el problema de capacidad administrativa limitada en algunas jurisdicciones requerirá modificar el sistema de bonos al personal controlado federalmente para permitir que gente honesta y bien preparada encuentre una carrera atractiva en el gobierno subnacional.

Relaciones con el Distrito Federal

El Distrito Federal enfrenta desafíos singulares en sus relaciones con el gobierno federal y los estados aledaños. Por ejemplo, el Congreso federal debe aprobar cada año el presupuesto y límites de endeudamiento del Distrito Federal; éste no obtiene parte de los recursos del Ramo 33; tampoco es responsable de la educación básica. El Distrito Federal cree que subsidia a sus vecinos al apoyar el sistema del tren metropolitano; mientras que éstos sienten que subsidian al Distrito Federal con inversiones en el sector hidráulico. La rápida transformación de la categoría fiscal y política del Distrito Federal y la posible creación de municipios dentro de éste, han hecho necesarios un análisis y una reforma de sus relaciones intergubernamentales verticales y horizontales. La experiencia internacional, como la del área metropolitana de São Paulo, en Brasil, puede ayudar a dilucidar una gama de posibilidades.

Gasto y Prestación de Servicios

Se espera que la descentralización proporcione muchos beneficios económicos en las áreas de gasto y prestación de servicios. Estos beneficios incluyen elegir la combinación de actividades del sector público que satisfaga de la mejor manera el gusto y las necesidades de los ciudadanos en un área local, ofreciendo los servicios en una forma más rentable adaptando el método de prestación a las circunstancias locales; y permitiendo que la ciudadanía exprese en forma más directa sus inquietudes respecto a la prestación de servicios. Los beneficios también dependerán de que se fortalezca el vínculo entre las decisiones para fijarse impuestos y las opciones de gasto en los niveles inferiores de gobierno. Capitalizar estos beneficios en México dependerá de las medidas de las autoridades locales y de la intervención de los ciudadanos; pero el gobierno federal puede ayudar creando un ambiente que proporcione más estímulos a los estados y municipios para que acepten la responsabilidad de sus propios programas y finanzas. Esto no es sólo cuestión de cambiar las normas, sino también de crear una cultura de devolución de responsabilidad y autonomía. Tomará tiempo. La agenda que aquí se presenta plantea algunas posibles medidas, que se sustentarán y avanzan las que se tomaron la década pasada.

Dos peculiaridades predominan en la asignación actual de reponsabilidades del gasto en México. Primera, hay muchas obligaciones coincidentes en los tres niveles; especialmente entre los gobiernos federal y estatales para servicios importantes como la educación, la salud o la protección social. Segunda, se asignan pocas responsabilidades a nivel municipal, sobre todo en áreas con beneficios importantes, como la educación o la salud (consulte el recuadro 3).

Parecería que hay cinco problemas fundamentales con la asignación actual de responsabilidades descentralizadas en cuanto al gasto: (a) *autonomía fiscal* inadecuada para los estados, dado su poder económico y político y el alcance de las responsabilidades en la prestación de servicios que se les han delegado; (b) bases poco eficientes y no transparentes para la *distribución de transferencias sectoriales*; (c) ambigüedades remanentes en la *asignación de responsabilidades del gasto* y fallas para tomar en cuenta las *desigualdades entre los municipios* en cuanto a su capacidad de obrar; (d) responsabilidad poco clara y por lo tanto financiamiento generalmente inadecuado para las *pensiones* (explicado en detalle en el capítulo sobre la deuda y endeudamiento); y (e) la falta de *procedimientos eficaces para la resolución de controversias* (analizado líneas arriba).

Recuadro 0.3. Educación y Salud

Educación

El *Acuerdo Nacional para la Modernización de la Educación Básica* de 1992 fue una medida precursora que estableció un precedente de descentralización limitada. Según el *Acuerdo*, el gobierno federal sigue siendo responsable de las políticas y normas generales (funciones normativas y de formulación de políticas), la capacitación docente y la distribución territorial, la producción de libros de texto, la evaluación y supervisión, así como la asignación de los recursos financieros necesarios para garantizar la cobertura adecuada y la calidad del sistema educativo.

En 1998, el Ramo 33 completó el *Acuerdo Nacional* avalando transferencias e incorporando una mayor transparencia en la distribución de recursos para la educación. Sin embargo, en vista de que el Ramo 33 conservaba la inercia ya existente en la distribución territorial de recursos para la educación, puede ser considerado más un medio de desconcentración que una medida de descentralización que aumente la eficiencia. En realidad, el Ramo 33 no incluye ningún incentivo para mejorar el rendimiento de los niveles inferiores de gobierno o transferir otros recursos locales para la educación, que son dos metas de los procesos de descentralización.

Salud

La descentralización del sector salud empezó antes y tuvo precedencia de manera más paulatina, concediendo más tiempo a los estados y municipios para que se adapten y aprendan. Hoy, seis características del sistema hacen que éste funcione relativamente bien:

1. Distribución de recursos del nivel federal a los estados conforme a normas muy reconocidas.
2. Capacidad de financiamiento para estados y jurisdicciones sanitarias en el uso de fondos del sector salud;
3. Transferencia cuidadosa y eficaz de recursos humanos del nivel federal a los estados, negociada con el sindicato nacional;
4. Transferencia completa de infraestructura, bienes y equipo a los estados;
5. Cofinanciamiento municipal de nueva infraestructura y participación en la programación;
6. El Consejo Nacional de Salud ha resuelto muchos desacuerdos y supervisado el proceso de descentralización.

Autonomía estatal para aumentar la eficiencia

A pesar de que por sus registros contables pasan más recursos que nunca antes, los estados en cierta medida tienen menos autonomía fiscal ahora que hace una década. Con la excepción del Fondo para Fortalecer las Finanzas del Estado y el Programa para el Fortalecimiento de las Entidades Federativas, la mayoría de los recursos que reciben del nivel federal (incluyendo los que proceden de ingresos compartidos) de hecho se destinan a transferencias para los municipios o para salarios del sector social; sobre todo para maestros de escuela y catedráticos universitarios con escalafón de sueldos autorizado federalmente, o son reclamados conforme a los términos de los programas (pari-passu) de donación de contrapartida. Esta situación es incongruente con el cada vez mayor poder político y económico de los estados.

El Fondo para Fortalecer las Finanzas del Estado se instituyó dentro del Ramo 23 a raíz de la crisis de 1995 y aportó dinero con la condición de que el estado en cuestión cumpliera un programa de ajuste fiscal acordado con la Secretaría de Hacienda y Crédito Público. Aunque los acuerdos para estos fondos no fueron totalmente transparentes ni se realizaron mediante una fórmula uniforme, significaron un avance respecto al anterior modelo en que el Presidente distribuía personalmente recursos fundamentales a los estados, también mediante el Ramo 23. Durante el bienio 1998–99, a medida que los acuerdos de la reforma fiscal llegaban a su fin, el fondo se eliminó en fases escalonadas; un remanente se destinó a un fondo nacional de ayuda humanitaria para casos de desastre con reglas transparentes de acceso. En 1999, unos cuantos incidentes, especialmente con Chihuahua y Nuevo León, mostraron el poder de los estados para exigir transferencias de recursos para un propósito determinado, sea este apoyo para la deuda o gastos federales relacionados con proyectos prioritarios para el estado en cuestión. En el presupuesto del año 2000, se creó el Programa para el Fortalecimiento de las Entidades Federativas—dentro del Ramo 23—pero con asignación de fondos a los estados por parte del Congreso, no a discreción del ejecutivo. Queda por verse cuánto de la asignación nominal del fondo será obligatoria, o si los recursos serán fondos intercambiables y relativamente libres para que los estados los gasten. Sin embargo, la libertad para asignar recursos no será suficiente. Una manera más sencilla de aumentar la autonomía de los estados sería darles mayor control sobre el gasto, especialmente para el personal, y respecto a impuestos, como se analiza más adelante.

Bases eficientes y equitativas para las transferencias sectoriales

Las transferencias para educación y salud se asignan principalmente tomando en cuenta el número de personal total y de sitios físicos (escuelas, clínicas, hospitales). En el sector de la educación, el número de empleados en 1992 es la base para ajustar las partidas a las tasas de inflación y crecimiento demográfico, y en ocasiones éstas aumentaron más a solicitud especial. Aunque este sistema no castiga de manera explícita a los estados que han controlado costos desde 1992, tampoco sanciona a los que no logran mejorar su eficiencia y en realidad, sí perjudica a los estados que aumentan los niveles de asistencia a sus estudiantes ya que tienen menos recursos por cada estudiante que asiste a clases. En cuanto a la salud, la asignación aún se sustenta principalmente en el número actual de instalaciones y empleados; aunque el sistema ha mejorado desde 1996. Hoy en día, la Secretaría de Hacienda y Crédito Público y la Secretaría de Salubridad y Asistencia evalúan las solicitudes de los estados que piden recursos adicionales para el sector salud, tomando en cuenta información de sanidad y demográfica. Es comprensible que el monto inicial de las transferencias igualara los niveles de costos anteriores, porque los estados no tenían la autoridad, el tiempo ni el dinero para cambiar enseguida el número de empleados. Pero ahora es razonable cambiar a un sistema con mejores incentivos. El testimonio de muchos países indica que las fórmulas para transferencias sectoriales son más equitativas y fomentan mejor la eficiencia si se sustentan en una fórmula de capitación, con ajustes que tomen en cuenta la densidad de población, la edad y el sexo. Tomar medidas encaminadas a un esquema de ese tipo, como se está empezándolo a hacer en el sistema en de seguridad social, aumentaría la eficiencia y la equidad de las transferencias.

Asignación de responsabilidades

La asignación de responsabilidades por sectores en México es, en general, razonable: la educación y la salud van a los estados, las calles e higiene pública a los municipios, y otros sectores al gobierno federal. El problema estriba en los pormenores. Las obligaciones coincidentes en los tres niveles, y sobre todo entre los gobiernos estatales y federal en servicios vitales como la educación, la salud o la protección social, a menudo provocan que ningún nivel asuma una responsabilidad adecuada respecto a tareas de mantenimiento, regulación o inspección, por ejemplo. La responsabilidad en cuanto a carreteras, recursos hidráulicos y educación superior es poco clara. La cuestión del agua es especialmente problemática ya que implica muchos aspectos en cuanto a usuarios y geografía. Es necesario hacer un estudio independiente del agua para dejar en claro cuáles son las cuestiones relacionadas con este recurso, ya que sólo algunas de ellas tienen que ver con la descentralización. Aunque determinados estados han mostrado un gran interés en los problemas del medio ambiente en sus localidades, en las que su participación sería sensata, el mandato y financiamiento continúan en buena parte en manos del nivel federal. El presupuesto para el año 2000 incluye un programa piloto que ofrece algunos recursos federales para fomentar que los estados desarrollen capacidad por sector para fines ambientales y la recuperación de costos. La participación federal en cuanto a empleados del servicio civil de niveles inferiores de gobierno sigue siendo problemática. Al nivel municipal se le han asignado pocas responsabilidades, sobre todo en los sectores sociales. Las escuelas y hospitales específicos tienen poca autonomía o participación de la comunidad, aunque las experiencias internacionales en Colombia (el Nuevo Programa Escolar), Nicaragua (el Fondo Participativo para el Mantenimiento de la Infraestructura Social) y El Salvador (el programa EDUCO, Educación con la Participación de la Comunidad) señalan que este aspecto de la descentralización es tal vez el más importante para el mejoramiento de diversos indicadores, entre ellos, asistencia, calificaciones en exámenes y control de costos.

Es probable que el espinoso problema de salarios para maestros negociados a nivel nacional no pueda, ni necesitará, resolverse mediante la confrontación directa. El problema fundamental no es que sus sueldos sean muy altos. A medida que el sector privado de México prospere y que su mercado de trabajo se integre más a nivel nacional y establezca vínculos más estrechos con el resto del mundo, el problema más grave será que un salario nacional no atraiga a maestros competentes en las áreas con localidades crecimiento más rápido del sector privado y la máxima vinculación internacional. Estas áreas tendrán que pagar más o ser testigos de una disminución en la calidad educativa, porque sólo se quedará el personal menos calificado o dedicarán más tiempo y energía a otros trabajos. Si el gobierno federal no tiene capacidad económica para pagar aumentos de salarios en todo el país, quizá necesite dar a los gobiernos locales y al electorado la opción de recaudar más recursos—a nivel local—para mejorar el pago y las condiciones de trabajo por encima del nivel (mínimo) nacional. En el otro extremo del espectro, las áreas aisladas ya están teniendo problmas para atraer a suficientes maestros que cumplan con la norma nacional acostumbrada, aunque el sueldo nacional es elevado comparado con los salarios locales. El sistema federal de transferencias tal vez necesite proporcionar apoyo adicional en cuanto a eso. Enfrentados a estas realidades económicas, los maestros podrían considerar la necesidad y beneficio de hacer que su sindicato se concentre menos en negociar aumentos nacionales y más en establecer sistemas oficiales de negociación para las dependencias locales.

Separar la asignación de responsabilidades por el mantenimiento y operación de obras de infraestructura de la responsabilidad por inversión de capital ha sido un problema constante en México. Por ejemplo, los municipios son responsables de mantener los edificios escolares, mientras los gobiernos federal y estatales realizan la mayoría de las inversiones de capital. Esta dicotomía a menudo da por resultado niveles insuficientes tanto de mantenimiento como de inversión en obras de infraestructura. Cada nivel de gobierno puede culpar al otro de no cumplir con su parte, y cada uno tiene un incentivo para abstenerse de usar sus propios recursos, con la expectativa de que los otros niveles aportarán más. La estricta separación de decisiones en cuanto a construcción, mantenimiento y operaciones ha provocado notorias ineficiencias en el reparto y la producción, como es evidente en todos los países latinoamericanos que transfirieron las responsabilidades de construcción a fondos especializados mientran mantenían la operación bajo los tradicionales ministerios por sector y dejaban sin especificar las responsabilidades de mantenimiento.

Impuestos e Ingresos Subnacionales

Los gobiernos subnacionales en México deben recaudar más impuestos por tres razones. Primera, el sector público necesita más ingresos tributarios para compensar la futura baja en los ingresos petroleros, no sólo temporalmente a causa de los bajos precios de los energéticos sino también en forma permanente como un procentaje del porducto interno bruto (PIB) a causa de la diversificación y el crecimiento económicos. Segunda, para conceder a los ciudadanos más control sobre el monto del gasto público dentro de sus jurisdicciones, los gobiernos subnacionales necesitan contar con una adecuada autoridad fiscal. Si desean gastar más dinero en un sector, pueden aumentar los impuestos; si deciden ahorrar en un programa, pueden disminuirlos. Esto implica, principalmente, tener control sobre rentas públicas marginales en las que pueden influir las propias medidas del gobierno subnacional, sobre todo al cambiar las tasas impositivas, pero también imponiendo nuevos impuestos o abrogando los antiguos al modificar el régimen impositivo y reformar la labor administrativa. Tercera, y con relación a la segunda, los estados que solicitan créditos necesitan contar con alguna fuente de fondos para cancelar sus deudas. Si sufren una desfavorable e inesperada sacudida con respecto a su plan fiscal al momento de solicitar el préstamo, necesitan poder recaudar ingresos adicionales (o reducir costos) en cantidad suficiente para mantener el servicio de sus deudas.

En general, los estados de México tienen sus propios impuestos sobre nómina, gravámenes anuales sobre automóviles (tenencia) y tasas para el uso de servicios. En la actualidad, la ley prohibe a los estados gravar el comercio interestatal y aplicar algunos impuestos al consumo. Los impuestos equivalen apenas a cerca del 4.5 por ciento del total de los ingresos de los estados (excluido el Distrito Federal). Los impuestos sobre nóminas son los más importantes; este tipo de gravamen se ha fijado en 23 de los 32 estados. Las tasas van del 0.5 al 4 por ciento, la mayor parte de ellas en la escala del 1 por ciento al 2 por ciento de las nóminas (18 estados). Sólo un estado tiene una tasa superior al 2 por ciento. En general, las definiciones del término contribuyente son similares, pero la base impositiva y las exenciones difieren en forma considerable a través de los estados. La estructura de estos impuestos no es compatible con las bases para los impuestos federales sobre nómina que financian la seguridad social y la vivienda; hacerlas más compatibles reduciría los costos de ejecución, cumplimiento (y auditoría) para las firmas que operan en más de un estado. El impuesto federal sobre el ingreso de las personas físicas tiene una base diferente, más limitada, que los impuestos sobre nómina. Es más, cada estado administra su propio impuesto sobre nómina, de acuerdo a sus propios procedimientos, que son independientes de los que se utilizan para los impuestos federales sobre nómina. Las bases gravables contradictorias y la doble administración son prácticas antieconómicas tanto para contribuyentes como para administradores. La administración y, para la mayoría de los estados, la tasa del impuesto sobre nóminas, a menudo proporcionan oportunidades considerables de aumentar los ingresos propios de los gobiernos estatales.

Sin embargo, parece que la mayoría de los estados carecen del incentivo a inponer tributos, porque tienen muy poco control sobre la forma en que gastan el dinero y relativamente mucha oportunidad para negociar transferencias discrecionales (al menos antes de 1999). La mayor parte de sus recursos proviene entonces de transferencias federales que se sustentan en una fórmula, casi siempre sin condiciones. Consulte la gráfica número 1 que es ilustrativa de esa situación y se elaboró a partir de cifras estimadas preliminares para 1999, según se describe en el capítulo 5.

En promedio, los gobiernos municipales son moderadamente menos dependientes que los estados de la participación de ingresos y las transferencias. En forma agregada, los gobiernos municipales reciben cerca de dos terceras partes de sus ingresos netos totales de estas fuentes. Este modelo difiere notablemente en todos los estados y al interior de éstos. La estructura de incentivos en planes de participación de ingresos justifica de manera parcial los bajos porcentajes de recaudación de impuestos. Al menos, los gobiernos municipales más grandes se beneficiarían al tener acceso a otras fuentes de ingresos y mejores incentivos. Las principales fuentes de ingresos para los municipios son el impuesto predial y las cuotas por consumo de agua a los usuarios. El impuesto predial promedia apenas el 13 por ciento del total de las rentas municipales, aunque en los últimos años algunos municipios han aumentado de manera significativa sus ingresos por este concepto. En el Distrito Federal, los impuestos prediales constituyen el 22 por ciento de los ingresos, mostrando el potencial de este rubro en las ciudades grandes.

El problema institucional más difícil en el caso de los impuestos predial y sobre nómina es encontrar los incentivos adecuados para que los estados y municipios aumenten sus impuestos a niveles compatibles con la eficiencia y equidad fiscal y limiten las distorsiones que la tributación pueda tener en la asignación de recursos que el mercado lleva a cabo.[9] El problema parece remontarse a la iniciativa de ingresos de los estados, que disminuyó a causa del Pacto Fiscal federal.

Una buena estrategia para muchos países, entre ellos México, consistiría en recargos tributarios fijados por los gobiernos subnacionales sobre una

Gráfica 0.1. Estructura del total de ingresos subnacionales, 1999

Pesos por cabeza

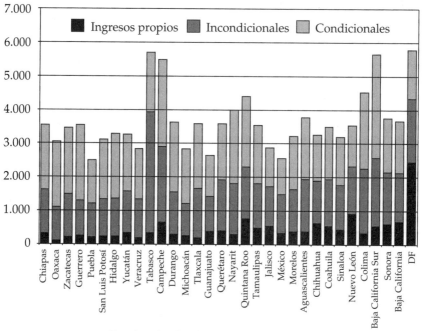

Estados clasificados índice de pobreza

Fuente: Courchene y Díaz (capítulo 5).

base (o bases) gravable definida por el gobierno federal y administrada por ellos, solos o en forma mancomunada con los estados. En este esquema, los gobiernos subnacionales ejercerían el importante derecho prioritario—desde el punto de vista político—de elegir tasas impositivas, al mismo tiempo que evitan la mayor parte de la complejidad, las desigualdades, la exportación de impuestos y las distorsiones por ubicación que generan una legislación y administración subnacionales independientes. Es decir, los recargos tributarios combinan la sencillez de la participación en los impuestos con la ventaja de permitir que los gobiernos subnacionales decidan sus tasas impositivas. Canadá utiliza este sistema en forma considerable. Los recargos de ese tipo podrían aplicarse a impuestos al consumo, al impuesto sobre la renta de acuerdo a la residencia, o incluso al impuesto al valor agregado (gravado en los destinos de venta). Esto último podría lograrse con un impuesto al valor agregado compensatorio. Los estados aún podrían imponer impuestos sobre la nómina, preferentemente con una base unificada. Para que cualquier impuesto concatenado de ese tipo funcione para los estados en México, el nivel federal necesitaría mejorar el diseño y aplicación de su impuesto correspondiente, el impuesto al valor agregado, o el impuesto sobre la renta.

Los impuestos al consumo, por ejemplo sobre bebidas alcohólicas o productos del tabaco, son buenos candidatos para asignación a los estados, como se hace en muchos países. Los gravámenes estatales al consumo deben ser impuestos por (o a favor de) los estados donde se hace el consumo, no por los estados donde se producen o se importan los productos en cuestión. Como los impuestos al consumo son relativamente visibles, ayudarían a garantizar la responsabilidad de los funcionarios estatales. El gobierno federal podría imponer mínimos, que las tasas estatales al consumo no podrían rebasar, a fin de evitar una "carrera para llegar al punto más bajo" provocada por la competencia entre los estados al buscar atraer la venta de productos que saben son pensados para pasar de contrabando a otros estados, y proteger a los comerciantes locales contra la competencia de productos introducidos fraudulentamente de estados con bajos impuestos.

Los estados que apoyan a sus municipios administrando el impuesto predial—recopilando información para el catastro, y actualizándolo—podrían negociar alguna participación en los ingresos con los municipios, con fórmulas que remuneren a los estados por su apoyo. En Colombia existen acuerdos similares, donde el Departamento de Antioquia maneja un impuesto para usos múltiples destinado a sus municipios. En El Salvador, los municipios más grandes y asociaciones municipales mantienen la registración y las cuentas corrientes para los municipios más pequeños. En México, el gobierno federal podría apoyar acuerdos de este tipo patrocinando programas experimentales y divulgando las lecciones que han dejado las experiencias nacionales y extranjeras.

Como un enfoque práctico para simulación y análisis de política, es útil tomar en cuenta las medidas de reforma que serían neutrales en cuanto a ingresos, sustituyendo las transferencias del gobierno central por ingresos de los estados e impuestos municipales. Este tipo de medidas (a) reducirían los impuestos federales para proporcionar un "espacio fiscal" que los gobiernos estatales y municipales podrían o no ocupar, a su elección; (b) reducirían las transferencias totales a los estados en la cantidad en que disminuyan los ingresos federales; (c) asignarían impuestos a gobiernos estatales y municipales que, en promedio, podrían sustituir las transferencias perdidas si se gravara a tasas similares;[10] y (d) se ajustarían las transferencias para mantener niveles de financiamiento para gobiernos estatales específicos, si utilizan el espacio fiscal proporcionado. Sin embargo, sería conveniente que México disminuya la dependencia del sector público agregado de los ingresos petroleros. En ese contexto, sería útil que parte del esfuerzo fiscal nacional ocurra en los niveles subnacionales.

Transferencias intergubernamentales

Las transferencias intergubernamentales cumplen diversas funciones en los sistemas federales. Primero, equilibran la interacción entre las necesidades de gasto y el ingreso de los gobiernos subnacionales. Segundo, integran el federalismo fiscal y las dimensiones social y política de las federaciones. Por ejemplo, establecer más condiciones a las transferencias gubernamentales es señal de un aumento en la centralización de la federación y viceversa; menos condiciones significa más descentralización. Los enfoques alternativos a la cuestión de las transferencias ofrecen la flexibilidad de generar un grado deseado de equidad horizontal en todos los gobiernos subnacionales y pueden incorporar incentivos importantes aumentando la responsabilidad o estimulando el esfuerzo fiscal. También son el principal método para llevar a cabo los propósitos de la sociedad en lo que concierne a la naturaleza del Pacto Fiscal y al grado de igualdad de oportunidades entre los ciudadanos que viven en diferentes estados.

México ha experimentado un sorprendente grado de descentralización en los últimos años, facilitado por un gran aumento en el número y diversidad de transferencias. Aunque podrían reconsiderarse aspectos seleccionados de estos nuevos planes de transferencias, la revolución en gasto y transferencias en el federalismo fiscal mexicano es impresionante.

Las dos principales categorías de transferencias son las llamadas *participaciones* y *aportaciones*. Las participaciones eran originalmente ingresos de estados y municipios cuya recaudación se delegó al nivel federal mediante el Pacto Fiscal por cuestiones de eficiencia tributaria. De acuerdo con la ley, la federación sólo recauda esos impuestos y los distribuye a sus dueños. En la práctica, el gobierno federal redacta la fórmula para la distribución de estos fondos y los aumenta con ingresos de fuentes federales, como los del petróleo, así que son diferentes a las participaciones de impuestos (donde las rentas recabadas en un estado permanecen ahí) y más bien son como un programa de transferencias de tipo general de participación de ingresos. La mayoría de estas transferencias se expiden bajo el Ramo 28. Las *aportaciones* se concibieron como dinero federal destinado a pagar obligaciones que eran previamente federales, y que es transferido a los estados y municipios junto con esos compromisos (por ejemplo, educación y salud). Estos fondos, que anteriormente pertenecían al Ramo 26, ahora proceden a través del Ramo 33.

Las transferencias—a los estados—de participaciones de ingresos dentro del Ramo 28 (sin contar los ramos que pasan directamente a los municipios o fondos del Ramo 33 destinados a maestros y trabajadores del sector salud) casi sextuplicaron los ingresos propios de los estados en 1996. Las transferencias estatales y federales a los municipios conforme al Ramo 28 casi duplicaron los ingresos propios de los municipios. Incluyendo el Ramo 33, los ingresos totales de los estados representaban cerca del 6 por ciento del producto interno bruto y las rentas totales de los municipios alrededor del 1.5 por ciento. Esos porcentajes se incrementaron de forma casi continua hasta el presente.

También hay fondos del Ramo 33 que no se relacionan con ingresos anteriores de los estados ni con obligaciones previas del gobierno central. En otro tiempo, hasta cierto punto eran a discreción del presidente, pero después todos se dedicaron al Fondo para Fortalecer las Finanzas del Estado que estados específicos negociaban con secretarías federales, la mayoría de las veces la Secretaría de Hacienda y Crédito Público. En 1998 y 1999, las transferencias discrecionales conforme al Ramo 23 cayeron a menos de una décima parte de su valor anterior a 1995. En el presupuesto del año 2000, las transferencias a discreción del ejecutivo terminaron completamente.

Los presupuestos de las diferentes secretarías de estado también incluyen transferencias importantes. Algunas van a los estados como fondos de contrapartida conforme a acuerdos estado por estado (descritos en la sección institucional). Estos son muy importantes en los sectores de la salud, el vial y el educativo. Las diferentes secretarías también invierten recursos directamente para proyectos en determinados estados, que pueden ser importantes transferencias implícitas. Estos dos tipos de transferencias tradicionalmente se negociaban con los gobernadores, sin hacer del conocimiento público los términos de la operación. En el año 2000 la Secretaría de Hacienda y Crédito Público publicará las reglas oficiales para acceso a los programas paralelos (pari-passu) y el porcentaje de donaciones de contrapartida necesarias para todos los principales programas.

En México, al igual que en muchos países, los propósitos de la sociedad en cuanto a las transferencias cambian continuamente y son poco claros. En el presupuesto en 1999, había por lo menos 10 programas de transferencias muy importantes, contra 3 en 1997. En el presupuesto del año 2000, el Congreso agregó otra transferencia importante en el Programa de Apoyo para Fortalecer las Entidades Federativas, que es asignada por el Congreso en la ley del presupuesto en vez que a discreción del ejecutivo. Cada programa aborda múltiples objetivos, y cada objetivo se consigna en diversos programas. Esto hace innecesariamente difícil para los gobiernos subnacionales calcular cuánto dinero recibirán; y para el gobierno federal determinar cuán bien está atacando sus objetivos el sistema de transferencias. La constitución y la ley de participación de ingresos no dan fines específicos a las transferencias, pero su modelo actual revela algo sobre sus intenciones. Los principales objetivos de las transferencias en México parecen ser: (a) dejar a los estados participar en el mayor potencial del gobierno federal para recaudar ingresos; (b) subvencionar la prestación de servicios de los gobiernos subnacionales que conllevan externalidades nacionales (salud básica y educación); (c) consolidar la autonomía de los municipios, y (d) proporcionar más recursos a estados con un elevado índice de pobreza. Un quinto posible objetivo sería compensar a los estados con una base impositiva baja per cápita, como hace Canadá. Las transferencias mexicanas no atacan este objetivo de manera explícita, aunque lo hacen en forma parcial mediante transferencias seleccionadas para combatir la pobreza, ya que existe una correlación negativa entre ésta y el tamaño de la base impositiva per cápita.

En cuanto al primer objetivo, el gobierno federal hace transferencias a los estados y municipios bajo el Ramo 28 a fin de reforzar su capacidad de recaudación, que es débil comparada con sus mandatos de gasto. Parece que los estados reciben considerablemente más órdenes que fondos, y parece que los municipios reciben más fondos que órdenes (sobre todo los pequeños). Cerca de la mitad de las transferencias para los estados son fondos para fines específicos bajo el Ramo 33; la mayoría de las veces los fondos no condicionados proceden del Ramo 28. Además, parte de los fondos "no condicionados" tienen que usarse para emparejar fondos de otros programas federales o para pagar sueldos decretados federalmente que no cubre el Ramo 33. La población del estado es un factor importante en las fórmulas para algunos fondos (Fondo General de Participaciones y Fortamun), y unos cuantos (sobre todo el Fondo de Fomento Municipal, Tenencia y Ramo 28 Participación de Impuestos sobre el Consumo) procuran compartir los ingresos con los estados en base a su origen. En el pasado, cuando los estados podían argumentar que las rentas eran inadecuadas, el gobierno federal a menudo aumentaba las transferencias, aunque este planteamiento puede estar llegando a su fin. Estas transferencias para un propósito determinado no eran automáticas ni ajenas a la política. En cambio, para los municipios un poco más de la mitad de las transferencias federales (al pasar intactas por las cuentas estatales) son participaciones de ingresos no condicionadas y más de la mitad del resto (transferencias del Ramo 33) tampoco son condicionadas.

En cuanto al segundo objetivo, muchas transferencias federales se designan a sectores específicos, algunos, como la educación y la salud, aparentemente porque tienen externalidades a nivel nacional. La selección de transferencias por sector a los municipios (secciones 3–7 del Ramo 33) parece ser un plan de transición que busca lanzar servicios municipales descentralizados con el mismo nivel de financiamiento que tenían conforme al sistema anterior. En cuanto al cuarto objetivo, las fórmulas de los fondos para obras de infraestructura en el Ramo 33 incluyen importantes factores destinados a combatir la pobreza.

Cuando se suman todos los programas, estado por estado, la cantidad de recursos disponibles per cápita para los estados (el total de sus propios ingresos y todos los diferentes programas de transferencias) varía en forma considerable (la mayoría de $2.500 a $4.500 pesos mexicanos, estimados para 1999, con tres estados recibiendo casi $6.000 pesos). Sin embargo, los recursos per cápita aproximadamente son los mismos en promedio para los estados con niveles de pobreza medios y elevados; y los estados más ricos (con bajos niveles de pobreza) sólo tienen un poco más de los recursos promedio. Los elevados ingresos per cápita en estados ricos con poca pobreza se contrarrestan en promedio por las transferencias destinadas a combatir la pobreza que se hacen a los estados más pobres. Esta uniformidad de recursos gubernamentales per cápita en todos los niveles de ingresos puede reflejar un valor social básico en México. La igualdad nominal en todos los niveles de ingreso corresponde a cierta progresión en términos reales, porque el costo de los servicios públicos generalmente es menos costoso en los estados más pobres, entendiéndose que los mismos pesos per cápita compran más.

El actual sistema de transferencias tiene cuatro importantes problemas: (a) es demasiado complejo para lograr un conjunto de propósitos coherente. Por lo tanto, el gobierno federal distribuye más recursos de los necesarios para alcanzar sus objetivos, y el trato que se da a los estados no es equitativo. Los principales beneficiarios de tal complejidad son los estados que obtienen más recursos de los que recibirían de acuerdo a un sistema sencillo y transparente; (b) al fundamentar muchas transferencias en valores iniciales o de reposición, en vez de hacerlo en base a costos per cápita o por posibles beneficiarios, es injusto y no estimula la eficiencia; (c) por lo menos hasta 1999, la disponibilidad de transferencias para propósitos determinados destinadas a estados políticamente favorecidos debilitaba los incentivos para administrar bien el gasto y aumentar los ingresos; y (d) los requisitos de asignación y las donaciones obligatorias de contrapartida dejan a los estados con poca autonomía para aumentar su eficiencia o ajustar las partidas de acuerdo a sus necesidades.

Otros países latinoamericanos tienen problemas similares. Las fórmulas de distribución de Colombia para la participación de ingresos general son muy complejas para transmitir señales transparentes e incentivos eficaces a los gobiernos subnacionales. Las fórmulas incluyen cuatro criterios (per cápita, por unidad territorial, esfuerzo fiscal, índice de pobreza) además de combinarlos. Algunos de éstos aplican a indicadores que no son fácilmente asequibles a los gobiernos subnacionales. En consecuencia, los gobiernos subnacionales no comprenden del todo las intenciones del nivel nacional, ni reaccionan oportunamente a las señales e incentivos.

La forma en que el sistema federal mexicano evolucione en sí mismo determinará el futuro del subsistema de transferencias-gastos-impuestos. Existe una gama de posibles modelos. Con el modelo de tipo canadiense— federalismo legislativo total—las transferencias se caracterizarían por:

- Un programa de igualamiento para garantizar que todos los estados tengan cierto nivel mínimo aceptable de ingresos no condicionados (es decir, ingresos propios más igualación). Éste podría ser el nivel del promedio nacional, por ejemplo.

- Transferencias condicionadas basadas en fórmulas, pero sólo donde hay evidentes externalidades nacionales. Probablemente éstos serían iguales per cápita en una medida considerable, ya que el equilibrio horizontal en todos los estados se corregiría conforme al programa de igualamiento.
- Condiciones vinculadas con esta transferencia como un conjunto de principios socioeconómicos y relacionadas a áreas de gasto como la educación y la salud. La idea sería proporcionar considerable arbitrio a los gobiernos subnacionales en la aplicación de estos principios.
- Un "acuerdo" federal–estatal o un pacto fiscal sobre la unión socieconómica, con abundantes estipulaciones para solucionar controversias. Una versión de ese tipo de acuerdo extendería los mecanismos para la apelación y resolución de controversias a los ciudadanos mexicanos.

Con el modelo de descentralización alemán—federalismo administrativo—un porcentaje considerable de los recursos estatales de fuentes propias vendría a través de la participación de ingresos, pero aún perduraría un importante desequilibrio vertical en la federación. Éste podría atacarse mediante un conjunto de transferencias condicionadas diseñadas para corregir los desequilibrios horizontal y vertical a la vez. Las condiciones para estos subsidios serían de dos tipos. Primero, la legislación concerniente al área del gasto podría ser federal delegando su aplicación a los gobiernos subnacionales o; segundo, las donaciones mismas podrían oritarse para áreas específicas de gasto con condiciones asociadas. Con el tiempo, estas condiciones podrían ser menos estrictas a fin de permitir más autonomía subnacional en el frente de gastos, pero siempre habría más ingresos bajo control federal que en el otro modelo en que los gobiernos subnacionales tienen acceso a rentas propias no condicionadas. El modelo de federalismo administrativo representaría una evolución del modelo mexicano actual, pero también podría ser una transición oportuna hacia un federalismo legislativo, si es por lo que México se decide a la larga.

Endeudamiento y Administración de la Deuda Subnacional

La deuda subnacional en México no ha sido un problema macroeconómico nacional, pero podría llegar a serlo. Más significativo, la carga de la deuda ha sido un problema fiscal para algunos estados (la deuda municipal es pequeña, excepto para el Distrito Federal, que de hecho es un estado), y la forma en que el gobierno federal trató la deuda subnacional en el pasado ha creado incentivos inadecuados para los asuntos fiscales de los estados. A fin de que los estados tengan un incentivo para controlar costos y aumentar rentas—una meta que se han fijado los gobiernos federal y estatales— es importante que ni los estados ni los prestatarios esperen que el nivel federal los saque de apuros. De lo contrario, los empréstitos se convertirían en un instrumento mediante el cual los estados puedan obtener recursos federales extras, transferidos a ellos directamente o a sus acreedores. En muchos casos, ésta ha sido la práctica en México. (Todos los estados recibieron rescates financieros a raíz de la crisis económica de 1995, y desde entonces se ha sacado de apuros a unos cuantos estados al vencer las garantías sobre proyectos de grandes obras de infraestructura.) Cambiar a una nueva práctica sin rescates financieros federales requerirá no sólo cambiar las reglas, sino también garantizar que los desafíos planteados a las nuevas reglas no sean abrumadores, sobre todo durante la transición, y que éstas cuenten con suficiente respaldo político.

La mayor parte de los empréstitos de los estados y municipios se ha respaldado con las *participaciones* estatales como garantías. El gobierno federal (Secretaría de Hacienda y Crédito Público) manejó el proceso de garantías, así que los bancos y sus instituciones reguladoras trataron la deuda prácticamente como si fuera sin riesgos. Además, el gobierno federal no siempre fue riguroso disminuyendo las participaciones de algunos estados cuando los acreedores ejercían sus derechos sobre la garantía, lo que significa que el resto de la federación tenía que pagar. Por lo tanto, ni los estados ni sus acreedores se preocupaban mucho sobre la capacidad para cancelar obligaciones. Esto contribuyó a la crisis de deuda estatal durante la crisis general de 1995. El gobierno federal ha sido la única parte interesada que tiene motivos sólidos para preocuparse sobre la verdadera solvencia de los Estados; en ocasiones se ha negado a registrar y garantizar sus deudas; pero en otras, los factores políticos o de otro tipo permitieron el endeudamiento excesivo.

Después de la serie de rescates financieros de 1995, para evitar que volvieran a suceder, la Secretaría de Hacienda y Crédito Público trató de terminar su parte en cuanto a garantizar deuda local y estatal; pero los estados y los bancos comerciales—aún traumatizados por la crisis—no se pusieron de acuerdo en planes de fideicomiso aceptables para ambas partes para manejar el proceso de garantías. Así que la Secretaría de Hacienda y Crédito Público convino, de manera provisional, aceptar la comisión de los estados de servir de fideicomiso para operaciones de endeudamiento que ellos—la SHCP—habían autorizado. En el año 2000, terminará esta función de la SHCP, y en la actualidad está trabajando con los bancos y los estados para garantizar que se aplique un marco normativo para fideicomisos estrictamente privados a fin de garantizar la deuda de los Estados con las participaciones, si eso es lo que quieren las partes.

De los muchos problemas políticos de imponer una enérgica restricción presupuestaria a los estados, el más difícil surge a causa de la cuantiosa proporción del gasto estatal dedicada a pagar por salarios. Esto crea una fuerte presión política para usar rescates financieros federales y evitar recortes considerables en el gasto en vez de pagar intereses de la deuda. Resolver el problema no sólo requerirá la firme determinación del gobierno federal para evitar rescates fiancieros, sino también más autoridad fiscal y responsabilidad política por parte de los estados para recaudar más rentas (para pago de intereses de la deuda o de salarios), así como control de costos. En otras palabras, habrá una interdependencia entre restricciones presupuestarias que motiven la responsabilidad fiscal por parte de los estados y su verdadera autonomía fiscal, algo que hará políticamente realistas dichas restricciones.

La deuda subnacional se elevó de $27 mil millones de pesos mexicanos en 1994 a $71,6 mil millones en 1998. La crisis financiera del bienio 1994–1995 y el aumento en las tasas de interés incrementaron la deuda real pendiente de los estados, pero ésta se redujo de manera considerable por el paquete de rescate financiero puesto en marcha por el gobierno federal en el periodo 1996–1997. En 1997, la deuda subnacional apenas llegaba a cerca del 6 por ciento del total de la deuda pública y al 2 por ciento del producto interno bruto (PIB). A diferencia de otros países, en Argentina la deuda subnacional era de alrededor del 5 por ciento del producto interno bruto; casi 20 por ciento en Canadá, y un poco más por encima de eso en Brasil. Gran parte del endeudamiento subnacional en México ha sido con Banobras, un banco de fomento de propiedad federal. Los estados con altos coeficientes de endeudamiento y una reiterada historia de necesitar rescates fiancieros han seguido recibiendo préstamos de Banobras, pero presuntamente esto será un problema mínimo con la introducción de prácticas de crédito más rigurosas y el final de las garantías federales implícitas. El costo de los fondos de Banobras es superior al de los bancos comerciales (porque Banobras no puede recibir depósitos), que han estado captando una porción cada vez mayor de los negocios subnacionales. Ninguna de las deudas es de tipo externo porque la constitución prohibe a los estados tomar préstamos en moneda extranjera o de acreedores extranjeros.

Desde 1995, los empréstitos de la mayoría de los estados han sido mínimos o cero; algunos han liquidado su deuda. Sin embargo, unos cuantos han adquirido muchos compromisos y la deuda es una carga para ellos porque tienen muy poco ingreso disponible para pago de intereses. La proporción del stock de deuda con respecto a los ingresos disponibles, definidos como impuestos propios más transferencias no condicionadas, comprende desde un máximo de 1.8 (en Sonora) a un mínimo de 0.02 (en Hidalgo). Aunque el Distrito Federal tiene la deuda total más alta, cuenta entre los menos endeudados en relación con el ingreso disponible porque recauda impuestos considerables. Los ocho estados más endeudados son Baja California Sur, Jalisco, el Estado de México, Nuevo León, Querétaro, Quintana Roo, Sinaloa y Sonora, todos con una proporción de obligaciones con respecto a sus ingresos disponibles superior a 1.[11] Los mismos estados son los más endeudados además de Baja California Norte, si se usa otra definición de ingresos disponibles: ingresos totales menos pagos de salarios (descentralización de personal, del sector educativo y de salud) y deduciendo las transferencias a los municipios. La principal diferencia es que el coeficiente de endeudamiento es mayor para estados como Nuevo León que utiliza gran parte de sus propias rentas para pagar salarios. Según esta medida, 12 estados tenían stocks de deuda superiores a sus ingresos disponibles en 1997.

La deuda de los gobiernos subnacionales de México son considerablemente menores que sus déficits fiscales acumulados anteriores. El gobierno federal ha cubierto repetidas veces una parte considerable del déficit fiscal de los estados, mediante transferencias extraordinarias discrecionales (para cubrir aumentos salariales no previstos con anticipación, desarrollo de inversiones, y otros conceptos) y otras formas de rescates financieros como el de 1995 y transferencias para propósitos específicos para disminuir y reprogramar la deuda. El saldo primario de los gobiernos subnacionales en México fue positivo durante el bienio 1995–1997, a diferencia de los déficits en el periodo 1992–1994 (consulte la gráfica 2). Sin embargo, esto se debió principalmente a un aumento de transferencias extraordinarias del nivel federal. Si se descuentan estas transferencias extraordinarias, los estados aún tenían un déficit primario en 1995–1997 y, por supuesto, un déficit general más cuantioso. La Secretaría de Hacienda y Crédito Público realizaba acuerdos anuales de ajuste fiscal con cada uno de los estados (excepto el Distrito Federal) a causa de los rescates financieros llevados a cabo después de la crisis de 1995. El programa federal más importante para estas transferencias (el de Fortalecimiento Financiero de los Estados en el Ramo 23) fue excluido del presupuesto para el año 1999, y otras partidas del Ramo 23 se redujeron mucho. En el futuro, será importante observar cómo se las arreglarán los estados y si el gobierno federal mantendrá su compromiso de terminar con los rescates a los estados.

Existen tambien importantes pasivos contingentes de los gobiernos subnacionales, como las pensiones y los planes de servicios médicos para sus empleados. Además, el Distrito Federal, los estados y los municipios proporcionan garantías sobre préstamos a sus respectivas dependencias descentralizadas y empresas públicas. Existe registro consolidado de estos pasivos sólo cuando se contabilizaron para utilizar las participaciones del

Gráfica 0.2. México: Déficit Primario De Los Estados 1989–1997

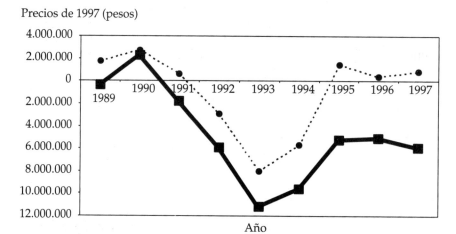

Precios de 1997 (pesos)

··•·· BAL. PRIMARIO REAL

━■━ BAL. PRIM. REAL (Excepto extraordinarias transferencias)

Fuentes: SHCP y cifras estimadas por el Banco Mundial.

estado en cuestión como garantía. En unos cuantos casos los incumplimientos de las entidades descentralizadas fueron lo suficientemente cuantiosos para inducir un rescate federal, como ocurrió con el metro de Monterrey y la carretera de cuota en Coahuila. Para la mayoría de los lugares, es probable que las companías de agua sean deudores morosos.

Los sistemas de pensión de los empleados públicos de los estados no están, en su mayoría capitalizados y pocos estados tienen capacidad fiscal para operarlos aún como sistemas de reparto ("pay-as-you-go"). Nuevo León reformó su sistema de pensiones de manera independiente, pero fue una reforma incompleta y sigue siendo una excepción. Un estimado parcial de la deuda contingente de los estados por concepto de pensiones llegaba a $167 mil millones de pesos mexicanos en 1997 (cerca del 6 por ciento del producto interno bruto del país).[12] Entre los 25 estados con suficiente información para calcular en qué año se agotarían las reservas de sus sistemas, y tomando en cuenta los porcentajes actuales de aportaciones y otros conceptos, en 1998 cinco estados ya tenían un déficit, y se proyectaba que siete más podrían quebrar durante el periodo 1999–2002. La mayoría de los gobiernos estatales considera los pasivos por concepto de pensiones como un legado de las prácticas anteriores a 1990, cuando los gobiernos estatales estaban, en la prática, bajo el dominio absoluto del gobierno federal. Por consiguiente, los gobiernos estatales consideran las pensiones como una obligación implícita del gobierno federal. Al no haber funciones definidas, se proporciona un incentivo a ambas partes para que *no* hagan los trámites pertinentes, con la esperanza de que la falta de trámites hará que, al final, el otro cargue con más parte del costo. El problema se pasa por alto, pero éste crece rápido con la maduración de la fuerza de trabajo. Además, cuando una deuda considerable de este tipo se vuelve inmanente, se disminuyen los incentivos para que un estado maneje prudentemente los demás asuntos fiscales.

Las experiencias de Argentina y Brasil muestran la necesidad absoluta de atender a las pensiones estatales. Brasil aún tiene que llegar a una resolución, aunque ya está analizándose una de manera diligente; Argentina ha puesto bajo la autoridad del gobierno federal la mayor parte de la responsabilidad. Quizá sea mejor separar el diseño de un sistema futuro, donde existe una gama de opciones, de la elaboración de procedimientos para atender los pasivos por pensiones que se formaron en el pasado. Esa elaboración podría ser responsabilidad federal, por lo menos la parte para los trabajadores contratados originalmente por el gobierno federal. En todo caso, la responsabilidad federal necesita límites claros. En el futuro, son los estados quienes deberían encargarse del sistema; de acuerdo a la experiencia, un plan de capitalización con aportaciones definidas ("defined contribution") tiene más posibilidades de ser sustentable.

En el pasado, las políticas de endeudamiento subnacional de México evolucionaron en un contexto en el que las relaciones fiscales intergubernamentales podían mantenerse encarriladas mediante transferencias para propósitos específicos y negociaciones entre integrantes en la misma jerarquía del partido en el poder. Ahora que los estados y los municipios son más independientes desde el punto de vista político, y en muchos casos son gobernados por partidos de la oposición a nivel nacional, el desafío ha consistido en dirigir la transición hacia un sistema más estricto y transparente para administrar el endeudamiento subnacional. De lo contrario, los problemas por la deuda podrían debilitar el proceso de descentralización y, en el peor de los panoramas, llegar a representar un riesgo macroeconómico para el país en general. El buen funcionamiento fiscal de los estados parece ser políticamente popular, lo que es una suerte, porque gran parte del proceso de reforma exigirá que los gobiernos estatales tomen medidas al respecto asi como una mayor vigilancia por parte del electorado. El gobierno federal está fomentando esto al poner en vigor reglas de divulgación financiera (como una condición para el registro de la deuda), demostrando que los gobiernos son entidades públicas que usan el dinero de los contribuyentes, no operaciones privadas con algún derecho a la privacidad.

Aunque el anterior sistema por lo menos impedía una crisis macroeconómica grave a causa de la deuda subnacional, ya han cambiado algunas cosas, la más importante de las cuales es la mayor independencia política de los estados y la eliminación de hecho de las transferencias extraordinarias. Por consiguiente, hay una transición en marcha que requiere más cambios para que sea sustentable.

A partir del 31 de marzo del año 2000, el gobierno federal dejó de aceptar *mandatos* de los estados para garantizar sus préstamos con *participaciones*. Por lo tanto, los estados y sus acreedores tendrán que instituir un fideicomiso privado o tomar medidas equivalentes que no incluyan una garantía implícita del erario federal. La Secretaría de Hacienda y Crédito Público ya no participará de manera directa en el proceso de endeudamiento subnacional. En vez de eso, únicamente hará pública una serie de principios generales para explicar cuáles serían los planes de fideicomiso o de otro tipo de garantías adecuados desde un punto de vista legal y financiero; aunque los estados y sus acreedores tendrán la opción de acordar el plan de garantías de cualquier tipo que más les convenga. A fin de que la transición al nuevo sistema sin mandatos sea lo menos complicada posible, durante el primer trimestre del año 2000 el gobierno federal aceptó mandatos sólo para estados que estaban ya tramitando una calificación crediticia con reconocidas firmas calificadoras de valores (consulte más adelante)

De manera simultanea, nuevas regulaciones bancarias (y sus repercusiones para determinar el costo del crédito) crearon recientemente incentivos hacia un mejor control financiero y programas de empréstitos más eficientes y más transparentes por parte de los estados y municipios, y hacia evaluaciones de riesgo subnacional más acertadas y sin riesgo moral por parte de sus acreedores bancarios. En primer lugar, en 1999 se derogó—oficialmente y en la práctica—el llamado régimen de excepción por medio del cual todo el crédito subnacional estaba exento de los requisitos normales para la constitución de reservas y los límites de concentración de riesgos. En segundo, los créditos bancarios para estados y municipios estan ahora sujetos a un coeficiente de ponderación punitivo de riesgo del capital (150 por ciento) si no se registran ante la Secretaría de Hacienda y Crédito Público, proceso que a su vez está condicionado a que el prestatario esté al corriente en la publicación de sus informes fiscales y de deudas y en sus obligaciones de pago con los bancos de fomento del gobierno. En tercero, las nuevas regulaciones introdujeron una ponderación diferencial del riesgo de capital que vincula los requisitos de capitalización para instrumentos de deuda subnacional (y, por consiguiente, la determinación de su costo) con la calificación crediticia del prestatario, conforme al avalúo de dos calificaciones crediticias actuales en moneda nacional, hechas en escala internacional, publicadas y efectuadas por firmas calificadoras de crédito conocidas en el ámbito internacional.[13] Siempre existe cierto peligro de que los estados solo contraten a las agencias calificadoras que les dan las calificaciones favorables, pero al exigirse dos avalúos de reconocidas calificadoras internacionales se atenuará este riesgo. Al usar una escala internacional se aumentará la objetividad y fiabilidad de las calificaciones, ya que las agencias calificadores sabrán que el avalúo que hagan de cualquier estado o ciudad mexicana será comparado con los que hagan en otras partes del mundo. Como los estados no pueden solicitar préstamos al exterior ni en moneda extranjera, no existe riesgo cambiario y por lo tanto es adecuado que las calificaciones sean en moneda nacional.

Para ser completo, el endurecimiento de los límites presupuestarios y la reducción de riesgo moral requieren un nuevo marco de crédito para los bancos públicos de fomento porque no tiene el mismo control empresarial ni las presiones del mercado que los bancos comerciales. Por lo tanto, cuando los bancos de fomento (específicamente Banobras) otorguen préstamos a gobiernos estatales y municipales también se les exigirá que cumplan con los mismos límites de concentración de crédito y la ponderación diferencial del riesgo de capital que los bancos comerciales. Además de eso, como asunto de política empresarial, el gobierno federal (propietario de los bancos de fomento) permitirá que los bancos de fomento otorguen préstamos sólo a los gobiernos subnacionales que requieran ponderaciones del riesgo de capital inferiores al 100 por ciento.[14]

Para evitar el coeficiente de ponderación punitivo de riesgo de capital del 150 por ciento, los gobiernos estatales también tendrán que registrar su deuda ante la Secretaría de Hacienda y Crédito Público, para lo cual deberán estar al corriente en la publicación de sus informes fiscales y de deuda y en sus obligaciones de pago con los bancos de fomento. De hecho, el segundo de estos requisitos impedirá que Banobras capitalice intereses atrasados vía nuevos préstamos.

Las nuevas políticas aplicadas a finales de 1999 y en el año 2000 están encaminando a México hacia un enfoque del endeudamiento estatal regido por el mercado, que excluye la posibilidad de garantías y rescates federales e incluye calificaciones crediticias internacionales que determinen la ponderación de riesgo de capital y, por consiguiente, el costo y disponibilidad del crédito bancario para los estados. El gobierno federal tiene una función importante que desempeñar, impulsando y facilitando mejores normas contables y la divulgación de informacion por parte de los estados y municipios, así como el funcionamiento prudente de los bancos desde el punto de vista financiero. La experiencia en Argentina, Colombia y Estados Unidos muestra cómo la conducta fiscalmente responsable de los estados y sus acreedores exige la regulación y supervisión adecuada del sistema bancario.

Opciones y Agenda de Trabajo

Es útil pensar en la agenda de políticas para la descentralización no sólo como una lista de medidas para el corto, el mediano y el largo plazo, sino también como una serie de etapas que podrían poner en marcha varias líneas de reforma. Ya se han realizado algunos cambios importantes, como dar fin a las transferencias discrecionales y a la práctica del gobierno federal de retener pagos de intereses de deuda de los estados en favor de los bancos. Proseguir con estas medidas es una parte importante de la agenda de corto plazo.

La experiencia internacional señala unos cuantos principios que podrían guiar el desarrollo de políticas para el mediano y el largo plazo:

- La autoridad y responsabilidad para la prestación de servicios debe recaer en el mayor nivel local que sea compatible con la eficiencia.
- En cada sector debe especificarse con claridad la responsabilidad para desempeñar funciones esenciales, y el nivel de gobierno responsable debe tener acceso a recursos adecuados, incluyendo bases gravables, para financiar el servicio
- Los gobiernos estatales y locales deben recaudar sus propios recursos tanto como sea viable en términos de eficiencia y equidad, y deben hacerlo de manera que los usuarios paguen los costos de los servicios públicos que consumen.
- Los gobiernos deben poder solicitar préstamos si, y sólo si, son capaces de, y se les exige, pagar los intereses y reembolsar el capital de la deuda completamente.
- Los gobiernos y las dependencias que ejerzan el gasto deben entregar cuentas claras y transparentes, no sólo al nivel inmediato superior sino también, lo más importante, al público.
- El proceso democrático, no uno de tipo técnico, debe determinar el grado de igualamiento en la distribución de recursos a los estados (y municipios).
- Las nuevas perspectivas que se sustenten en estos principios en algunos casos requerirán importantes cambios legislativos y de otros tipos en las funciones y responsabilidades de los gobiernos.

México enfrenta algunas disyuntivas importantes sobre el tipo de sistema federal que tendrá. El debate público continuo sería provechoso, incluso si no se llega a una elección definida del sistema. En muchos países, la opción ha surgido de manera paulatina a partir de muchas elecciones de menor trascendencia. Sin embargo, es importante comprender que la decision de avanzar en una cierta dimensión—por ejemplo, hacia un mayor uso de los sitemas tributarios subnacionales—afecta la forma en que la descentralización progresará en otras dimensiones, por ejemplo: el total de recursos fiscales, la igualdad de recursos públicos per cápita a través de los estados, la autonomía local en ejercer el gasto, y el control del endeudamiento.

Hoy en día, los gobiernos subnacionales tienen sistemas tributarios débiles y dependen de las transferencias del gobierno central, supeditándolos al control federal en cuanto a gasto y endeudamiento. México está siguiendo un modelo cercano al extremo alemán del espectro. Aunque hay muchas desigualdades en el financiamiento para los estados, en su mayoría se deben a factores históricos y políticos, no a diferencias en la fuerza económica de las economías estatales. Una diversidad de reformas consolidaría las instituciones y pondría en claro las reglas, además de simplificarlas.

A un plazo más largo, el sistema puede encaminarse—en parte—hacia el federalismo legislativo, el modelo canadiense. Esto ocurriría si las transferencias no crecen tan rápido como la demanda de gasto en servicios que se han delegado a gobiernos subnacionales; sobre todo en cuanto a educación, salud y carreteras. Los estados, entonces, encabezados por los que cuenten con las mejores bases gravables, bien podrían optar por recaudar más ingresos propios. En principio, los estados ya pueden hacer eso, pero sólo lo harán en la práctica cuando obtengan más control sobre sus egresos y si las transferencias federales no castigan el esfuerzo fiscal de los Estados. Esto requiere no sólo terminar con las transferencias negociables, sino también que los estados sean más autónomos. Tomar medidas en este sentido no necesariamente implica una reducción en los recursos para los estados más pobres con menos base impositiva; en realidad esos estados probablemente salgan ganando. Sin embargo, los estados ricos pueden incrementar sus fondos más rápido, aumentando así la desigualdad de los recursos per cápita de los gobiernos locales, a menos que haya una redistribución de transferencias más decisiva que en la actualidad. Además de eso, el mercado político y el mercado financiero cobrarían más influencia sobre el gasto, los impuestos y las decisiones de endeudamiento que el gobierno central.

Gestiones recientes: 1999–2000

Las recientes medidas tomadas por el gobierno federal para perfeccionar el proceso de descentralización se concentraron en tres objetivos fundamentales: (a) imponer estrictas limitaciones presupuestarias a los recursos federales que se proporcionan a estados y municipios; (b) reducir el riesgo moral en los empréstitos subnacionales; y (c) aumentar la transparencia, la eficiencia y la calidad de la rendición de cuentas en la administración financiera y fiscal de los niveles inferiores de gobierno y del proceso de descentralización en general. Estas medidas serán valiosas independientemente del curso que siga el sistema en el largo plazo; y ayudarán a crear los incentivos y la capacidad para tomar las medidas subsecuentes en el mediano plazo, como reformar el sistema fiscal y de transferencias y reconsiderar las asignaciones de responsabilidades por el gasto.

Las limitaciones presupuestarias estrictas tendrán verdaderamente lugar a medida que reglas claras remplacen a la discreción en materia de gasto, transferencias y endeudamiento subnacional.[15] El gobierno federal está terminando con todas las transferencias discrecionales en efectivo a estados y municipios. Todos los programas paralelos (pari-passu) importantes funcionarán con reglas transparentes y estarán a disposición de todos los estados que cumplan con los requisitos conforme a los criterios publicados. La distribución estado por estado del gasto federal para proyectos locales en educación y transporte se publicará en el año 2000, a fin de aumentar más la transparencia en el uso de los recursos federales.

Las reglas que gobernarán el financiamiento del gobierno federal a los estados complementan los incentivos dirigidos a aumentar la eficiencia y el rigor de mercado en el endeudamiento subnacional, según se describen líneas arriba. Esto hará más estrictas las limitaciones presupuestarias y, a la vez, reducirá el riesgo moral.

Aunque hay pocas posibilidades de que el problema de los sistemas de pensiones de los estados se resuelva antes del año 2001, es importante llevar este asunto a la mesa de discusiones y empezar a estudiarlo. Para este propósito, la publicación de un estudio de las obligaciones estatales por concepto de jubilación, incluyendo cifras estimadas para cada estado, parece ser una medida sensata. Este será un paso fundamental en el proceso de esclarecer los límites de la responsabilidad federal, disminuyendo la impresión existente de que el gobierno central le ha expedido un cheque en blanco a los estados para cubrir las obligaciones de jubilación, y en un momento dado idear normas comunes para distribuir dicha carga.

El tercer objetivo de las medidas iniciales en la agenda de descentralización consiste en aumentar la transparencia en la administración fiscal descentralizada, como un medio para aumentar la responsabilidad pública (y la rendición de cuentas) tanto del gobierno federal como de los estatales. En el presupuesto del año 2000, el gobierno federal aumentó la responsabilidad de los gobiernos estatales en cuanto a los gastos financiados con recursos federales. En forma experimental, las secretarías federales y los estados celebrarán acuerdos a partir de programas de donaciones de contrapartida, lo que será indicativo de que en el futuro se imputará responsabilidad a los gobiernos subnacionales por los fondos que reciban para sectores específicos gracias a la descentralización. Como primer paso, se están redactando y ejecutando los convenios de desempeño—de tipo experimental—para dos sectores: salud y medio ambiente. Éstos parecen particularmente adecuados para el programa piloto de convenios de desempeño, porque disfrutan de una trayectoria uniforme de reformas, con fuerte consenso en el país y agendas de descentralización ya avanzadas. El nuevo Comité de Descentralización, antes descrito, también aumentará la transparencia; sobre todo si su Secretaría Técnica hace asequibles al público los análisis e informes respectivos.

A fin de crear un proceso de desarrollo institucional más congruente para la descentralización, además de los mencionados Comité de Descentralización y su Secretaría Técnica, se contará con un programa de capacitación y fortalecimiento institucional para municipios y estados que estará a disposición de quien lo solicite, que incluye cursos en los siguientes temas: contabilidad, presupuesto, supervisión, presentación de informes, auditoría y contratación de bienes o servicios. Dicho programa será respaldado directamente por una línea de crédito del Banco Interamericano de Desarrollo por $400 millones de dólares, autorizada a finales de 1999, que aprovechará el trabajo federal ya existente (por ejemplo, la homologación de las prácticas contables) y los esfuerzos estatales (como en Puebla y la Universidad de Monterrey).

El gobierno federal también puede respaldar el perfeccionamiento de las prácticas contables y de presentación de informes a nivel local de diversas maneras: (a) estableciendo normas mínimas para categorías diferentes de municipios de acuerdo al volumen total de transferencias recibidas. A los estados no se les exigiría diferenciar entre municipios, pero las normas federales mínimas instarían de hecho a los estados a diferenciar en una forma que sea adecuada a sus situaciones; (b) apoyando las labores de la Contaduría Mayor de Hacienda de la Honorable Cámara de Diputados para establecer principios generales comunes para el Ramo 33 y otros gastos subnacionales financiados por transferencias federales; (c) buscando de manera diligente sinergias entre PROMAP (Programa de Mejoramiento de la Administración Pública), otros programas similares a nivel federal y las contadurías mayores de los estados. La Secretaría de Hacienda y Crédito Público podría documentar las prácticas para cubrir los costos en que incurran los estados para administrar el Ramo 33 (preparación de proyectos, presupuesto, contabilidad y presentación de informes); (d) evaluando el efecto de las leyes y prácticas de los estados que hayan tomado iniciativas para supervisar de manera más estrecha el Ramo 33; (d) evaluando las repercusiones de auditorías externas realizadas por firmas especializadas dondequiera que existan; (f) proporcionando información y reconocimiento a organizaciones creíbles de la sociedad civil para que mantengan y divulguen sus propios indicadores del desempeño de los gobiernos subnacionales; y (g) dando, de manera experimental, incentivos no monetarios a los estados que cumplan pronta y plenamente con los acuerdos intergubernamentales pactados conforme al Programa de Homologación. Los primeros incentivos pueden constar de reconocimiento público y divulgación de las prácticas adecuadas.

FORTALECER LA CAPACIDAD DE LOS GOBIERNOS SUBNACIONALES. La documentación, el reconocimiento y la divulgación de prácticas eficaces tienen un poderoso efecto en términos de demostración y aprendizaje; sobre todo en los primeros años de la descentralización. A fin de estimular la capacitación, la Secretaría de Hacienda y Crédito Público podría reunir y divulgar las mejores prácticas en el manejo del gasto local realizado con recursos del Ramo 33 desde 1998 (año en que este empezó), promover la capacitación de municipio a municipio en base a prácticas intraestatales eficaces en la distribución de los fondos del Ramo 33, y comparar los beneficios de la capacitación horizontal y la asistencia técnica entre municipios con los programas de capacitación federales o estatales. Los cursos de capacitación podrían incluir identificar prioridades, preparar prespuestos y proyectos, llevar a cabo la supervisión y la evaluación, y redactar contratos para la adquisición de bienes o servicios. A fin de fomentar el desarrollo de capacidad de los municipios, el gobierno federal podría aumentar el total de fondos del Ramo 33 que pueden usarse para este concepto e invitar a estados y municipios a seguir el ejemplo de Puebla, en cuanto a concentrar y aumentar sus fondos para capacitación a nivel estatal, con objeto de desarrollar economías de escala.

MEJORAR EL PROCESO DE PREPARACIÓN DEL PRESUPUESTO. Preparar y presentar el presupuesto es una oportunidad significativa para que el gobierno federal dé a conocer y demuestre su compromiso de asegurar la transparencia fiscal de los gobiernos subnacionales y unidades sectoriales. Como experimento y mientras cumple con el programa establecido legalmente para la preparación y aprobación del presupuesto, el gobierno federal podría proporcionar estimados preliminares (y contingentes) de transferencias propuestas para los estados y municipios, de suerte que los gobiernos subnacionales puedan formular planes de presupuesto provisionales antes del principio del año fiscal.

ESCLARECER LAS RELACIONES INTERGUBERNAMENTALES CON EL DISTRITO FEDERAL. A fin de reducir los conflictos existentes y futuros, el gobierno federal podría poner en claro las reglas de las relaciones fiscales intergubernamentales para el Distrito Federal. Éstas incluirían los criterios técnicos para reorganizar las transferencias verticales y horizontales relacionadas con el Distrito Federal y las medidas institucionales en vigor para la negociación y resolución de controversias (las transferencias verticales son del nivel federal al Distrito Federal, y las horizontales del Distrito Federal a los estados y municipios aledaños). Las medidas propuestas necesitarán ser consecuentes con la autonomía del Distrito Federal respecto a ingresos, endeudamiento y responsabilidades para ejercer el gasto. Quizá sea necesario elaborar un estudio para respaldar esta propuesta, aprovechando la experiencia internacional en transferencias intergubernamentales y los arreglos institucionales de otras áreas metropolitanas (Buenos Aires, Santiago y São Paulo en cuanto a América Latina; y otras ciudades en Asia Oriental, Europa y América del Norte).

Agenda de mediano a largo plazo: 2001–2006

La agenda de reformas para la descentralización del mediano al largo plazo incluye reconsiderar el pacto fiscal entre los niveles federales y estatales—el diseño conjunto de asignaciones tributarias y transferencias—

y pasar revista a la asignación de autoridad para tomar decisiones relacionadas con los egresos. Será necesario continuar el desarrollo institucional de diferentes maneras. El gobierno nacional también necesitará preservar las reformas que realizó en el bienio 1999–2000 al régimen regulatorio para el endeudamiento subnacional, de suerte que los estados reformen uniformemente sus correspondientes leyes y prácticas.

Algunos estados, incluyendo siete cuyos gobernadores suscribieron la Declaración de San Lázaro en 1999, se opusieron enérgicamente al actual sistema de transferencias e impuestos exigiendo una participación mayor en los ingresos que se recaban en sus territorios. Como ya no hay recursos presupuestarios de tipo federal para transferencias de caja a discreción del ejecutivo, la solución inmediata ha sido aumentar el gasto federal para las necesidades locales —transferencias en especie, de hecho y para propósitos determinados— y la reactivación del Fondo para Fortalecer las Finanzas del Estado, con partidas establecidas por el Congreso. Casi todas las partes involucradas se beneficiarían de una solución más transparente y uniforme, pero sería difícil acordar qué solución en particular. Atacar varios problemas al mismo tiempo, sobre todo las transferencias y los impuestos, permitirá que haya más dimensiones para solucionarlos y, por consiguiente, haría más probable la solución.

Impuestos subnacionales

Los estados y municipios necesitan tener considerable control sobre sus ingresos al margen, a fin de que tengan incentivos adecuados para un gasto eficiente y que sus finanzas resistan las sacudidas económicas.

INTRODUCIR NUEVOS IMPUESTOS, APOYARSE EN LOS IMPUESTOS FEDERALES, ESCOGER UNA O DOS ENTRE VARIAS POSIBILIDADES. El porcentaje del impuesto federal sobre el ingreso de las personas físicas podría reducirse para permitir que los estados fijen sus propios impuestos suplementarios. Luego podría haber una reducción correspondiente en las transferencias federales o en la participación de ingresos fiscales. Algunas participaciones procedentes de impuestos al consumo sobre combustible para automóviles podrían transferirse del gobierno federal a los gobiernos de los estados donde se realiza el consumo. También podría considerarse un desplazamiento de ingresos por impuestos al consumo de bebidas alcohólicas y tabaco para ser aplicado vía impuestos suplementarios estatales. En cuanto a los impuestos generales al consumo, podrían identificarse los que encajen mejor para convertirse en impuestos estatales, dentro de los marcos constitucional y normativo existentes. Luego, la experimentación podría continuar con uno o algunos de los impuestos al consumo más prometedores mediante acuerdos federales y estatales. Por último, la Secretaría de Hacienda y Crédito Público podría también evaluar, adaptar y promover su duplicación. El gobierno federal podría también trasladar a los gobiernos estatales las rentas generadas por un punto porcentual dado del impuesto al valor agregado, empleando el impuesto al valor agregado dual—federal/estatal— y el impuesto al valor agregado compensatorio para ventas interestatales. Un control fiscal federal más firme sería un requisito previo para cualquiera de éstos.

RACIONALIZAR EL IMPUESTO SOBRE NÓMINAS. El gobierno federal podría dar incentivos a los estados para homologar la base para el impuesto sobre nóminas. Una forma podría ser participar en los costos de recaudación si los estados empiezan a usar la misma base que el impuesto federal del seguro social. El asunto más difícil respecto a los impuestos sobre nóminas (y predial) es encontrar los incentivos adecuados para estimular a estados y municipios para que aumenten sus recaudaciones a niveles más elevados pero que sigan siendo compatibles con la eficiencia tributaria, la incidencia equitativa y la limitación de distorsiones fiscales en la asignación tributaria de recursos.

ADMINISTRACIÓN TRIBUTARIA. Debe fortalecerse la formación de catastros, la actualización y avalúos del impuesto predial. Las exenciones (incluso las intergubernamentales) deben limitarse o eliminarse para ampliar la base impositiva y hacer que los impuestos sean más neutrales. Las cuentas de gastos fiscales (vía exenciones) podrían conservarse y divulgarse, con modelos preparados por el gobierno federal. Deben fortalecerse las auditorías y la recaudación de los impuestos estatales sobre nóminas y los municipales de tipo predial. Para aumentar la recaudación de impuestos, México podría crear una dirección nacional de impuestos, que recaudaría los impuestos federales y estatales con bases iguales o similares. Es obvio que esto se volvería más pertinente a medida que los estados homologuen el impuesto sobre nóminas y (se les permita que) tengan sus impuestos apoyados en los impuestos federales.

APOYO A LOS ESFUERZOS LOCALES PARA EL IMPUESTO PREDIAL. Sería útil realizar un estudio para identificar y evaluar los incentivos que llevan a los estados a prestar apoyo al impuesto municipal sobre bienes raíces. Podrían fomentarse acuerdos estatales y municipales para permitir que los estados recobren parte de los costos administrativos del impuesto predial o compartan parte de las rentas adicionales producidas por una mejor administración. Se necesitan nuevos incentivos y acuerdos estatales–municipales para estimular la cooperación para un mayor esfuerzo fiscal local. El gobierno federal podría considerar un programa para reconocer y premiar a los municipios con los aumentos más altos en rentas por ingreso predial y a los estados que ofrezcan el apoyo más eficaz para recaudar esos impuestos. Sería útil explicar el efecto del denominado ejido (propiedad comunal de la tierra) sobre el registro de la propiedad y el catastro fiscal.

La SecretaríaTécnica para el Comité de Descentalización podría recabar datos sobre la administración y las rentas generadas por el impuesto predial y evaluarlos.

Tomando en cuenta la experiencia que vaya surgiendo, el gobierno federal podría estimular a los estados para que instituyan reglas por las cuales los municipios mismos puedan administrar con eficiencia y del todo el impuesto predial, y que determinen qué municipios se beneficiarían de los distintos grados de apoyo estatal para formar y actualizar el catastro, mantener las cuentas al corriente, facturar y cobrar. Evaluar el efecto y eficiencia del Programa 100 Ciudades, hasta donde implique apoyo para la formación y administración del catastro, ayudaría a desarrollar la capacidad de las ciudades en comparación a municipios predominantemente rurales. Las comparaciones podrían incluir coeficientes de rentabilidad y la distribución de ingresos centro-periferia.

Sería también útil contar con estudios técnicos y empíricos para (a) identificar y evaluar las razones del descenso relativo durante los últimos 20 años en la administración del impuesto predial en algunos lugares (por ejemplo, Monterrey), y el relativo fortalecimiento en otros sitios (como el Distrito Federal); los estudios deberían arrojar propuestas para efectuar reformas de políticas y replicar las prácticas que hayan resultado eficaces; y (b) calcular el efecto de los cambios en las tasas del impuesto a nóminas sobre las rentas fiscales y las economías de los estados—empleo, productividad laboral y competitividad.

Transferencias intergubernamentales

En coordinación con la agenda de reformas tributarias, algunas de las transferencias con contrapartida (pari-passu) y tal vez hasta las participaciones podrían reducirse, junto con la disminución de tasas impositivas federales (por ejemplo, el impuesto sobre el ingreso de las personas físicas o el impuesto al valor agregado) y la delegación del derecho—a los estados— para cobrar recargos sobre los impuestos.

A mediano plazo, es necesario contar con un sistema más sencillo y más transparente que garantice recursos iguales per cápita (o cualquier otro objetivo acordado por los gobiernos nacional y subnacionales) y un tratamiento más equitativo a los estados con niveles de pobreza similares. La medida de equidad debe ser las transferencias totales per cápita más las rentas que *podrían* obtenerse de las bases gravables del estado en cuestión. Será necesario respetar las prioridades de los Estados y permitir que estos alcancen estándares equivalentes de diferentes maneras. Las fórmulas para transferencias no deben sancionar a los que aumenten sus propias rentas.

A fin de simplificar el sistema de transferencias, todos los programas especiales con fines específicos, como el Plan de Seguridad Pública o el Programa 100 Ciudades, podrían incluirse en el Ramo 33. Al agrupar todos los programas especiales bajo un solo rubro se facilitaría la formulación de políticas y se avanzaría hacia un sistema de transferencias más sencillo, más transparente y con mayor autonomía en los niveles inferiores de gobierno.

Egresos y prestación de servicios

El gobierno federal podría poner en claro cuáles son las responsabilidades por sector entre los niveles de gobierno, coordinando las responsabilidades en cuanto a inversión y mantenimiento, así como contratación de empleados y sueldos. Se podría aconsejar a los estados que ajusten los sueldos y el número de maestros y personal del sector salud de acuerdo a las condiciones de demanda locales. Esto ya está realizándose en áreas de bajos ingresos en Oaxaca y podría extenderse a otros estados. A los estados que tengan una base impositva adecuada y demanda adicional de educación, se les podría permitir que aumenten los sueldos de los maestros por encima del nivel nacional, pagando esa diferencia extra de sus propios impuestos. También podrían tomar iniciativas en las áreas de indicadores de desempeño, sueldos, promoción e incentivos para mejorar la administración del sector público estatal.

AUMENTAR LOS INCENTIVOS HACIA LA EFICIENCIA. Algunas reformas específicas por sector aumentarían la eficiencia de los incentivos. En educación, un nuevo sistema de transferencias podría tomar las partidas existentes como un mínimo nominal y hacer avanzar los aumentos (o congelamientos) hacia una fórmula con base en el número de niños en edad escolar, conforme al censo y a proyecciones transparentes a partir de éste. A la larga, la fórmula federal trataría de reflejar el actual nivel de asistencia a los educandos, pero ese tipo de incentivos probablemente debe dejarse a los estados. En el sector salud, con las partidas existentes como un mínimo nominal, los incrementos deben seguir desplazando las partidas hacia una fórmula que se sustente en algún indicador de demanda posible, como población ajustada por sexo y edad. La experiencia internacional demuestra que debe estimularse a los estados para que deleguen autoridad y responsabilidad pública a las unidades que proporcionan los servicios directamente, como es el caso de hospitales y escuelas.

La Secretaría de Hacienda y Crédito Público podría evaluar las diversas legislaciones estatales, las prácticas de facto, así como los manuales que regulan los incentivos hacia la autonomía municipal y la distribución eficiente del Ramo 33. La Secretaría de Hacienda y Crédito Público y la Secretaría de Contraloría y Desarrollo Administrativo podrían comparar las legislaciones estatales y las prácticas respecto al Ramo 33 con los métodos del Programa de Mejoramiento de la Administración Pública y el nuevo programa, enfocado a resultados, denominado Nueva Estrategia de Programación; y ofrecer recomendaciones a fin de que se impartan cursos para enseñar las nuevas técnicas de programación a los Comités de Planeación para el Desarrollo del Estado y los Comités de Planeación para el Desarrollo Municipal (comités de programación para el desarrollo estatal y municipal respectivamente). (Las siglas en español de los organismos y programas antes citados se mencionan a continuación, en el mismo orden en que aparecen: SHCP, SECODAM, PROMAP, NEP, COPLADEs y COPLADEMUNs) El estudio podría comparar aquellos estados en que el COPLADE es responsable de aplicar un programa con los estados en que no tiene esa responsabilidad.

Esclarecer las Responsabilidades por Pensiones Conforme a una Base Sustentable. Es necesario contar con un acuerdo entre los gobiernos fe-deral y estatales para poner en claro cuál es el nivel de gobierno responsable de las pensiones para los empleados públicos subnacionales. Quizá sería necesario que el gobierno federal reconozca explícitamente que cierta parte de una línea base de las pensiones de los estados no es responsabilidad de estos últimos (como por los ex empleados federales y los que han rebasa-do los 50 años de edad) en recompensa porque el estado en cuestión emprenda reformas fiscales, como pagar los intereses de obligaciones sobrantes, entre ellas el seguro social. O bien, como se hizo en Argentina, el gobierno federal podría ofrecer hacerse cargo de los planes de pensiones de los estados (para reformarlos), junto con la recaudación de contribu-ciones. El estudio inicial arrojaría medidas específicas para hacer explícito el monto y naturaleza de las obligaciones de jubilación.

Instituciones fundamentales para la descentralización

Mejorar la Resolución de Controversias. A fin de resolver los problemas que surgen incluso en los sistemas mejor diseñados y ofrecer a los partici-pantes un incentivo para que encuentren soluciones en las que colaboren todos los involucrados, es necesario contar con mejores instituciones para resolver las controversias. Crear estas instituciones llevará tiempo, pero es deseable empezar a hacerlo pronto. Podrían promoverse comisiones sec-toriales para áreas importantes como salud y educación. A mediano plazo—con las lecciones aprendidas gracias a la experiencia en cada sector—podría instituirse una comisión general gubernamental para que atienda los asun-tos y apelaciones de todo el sistema que le envíen las comisiones sectoria-les. Una vez que los modelos federal–estatal funcionen, los estados podrían crear sus propias comisiones municipales–estatales para atender los asun-tos entre los municipios, y entre ellos y el estado.

Mejorar la Información y las Normas Contables. Es importante que se sigan rindiendo cuentas claras en cada nivel de gobierno; la presentación de informes municipales a los estados y la supervisión de partidas por parte del estado. En la actualidad, algunos estados imponen sanciones a los municipios por atrasarse en los informes suspendiéndoles las transferencias, y esta práctica podría vincularse al proceso de documentación y evaluación.

La evaluación de prácticas ya existentes también podría diferenciar los controles ejecutivos de los que ejercen las contadurías mayores de cuentas de los congresos de los estados. La Secretaría de Hacienda y Crédito Público podría evaluar si el modelo que está preparando la Contaduría Mayor de la Unión estimula de manera adecuada una distribución eficiente y, más adelante, formular y publicar las recomendaciones que considere pertinentes. También es importante establecer un sistema contable uniforme e intercambios de información sectorial e intersectorial, tanto de los niveles superiores a los inferiores como en sentido inverso.

Mejorar la Coordinación Dentro y entre los Diferentes Niveles de Gobierno. Es posible que el gobierno federal quiera promover alianzas municipales para (a) obtener economías de escala (en la contratación de bienes o servicios, servicios especializados, equipo compartido, costos administrativos); (b) identificar soluciones fiscales o técnicas de otro tipo mediante esfuerzos subregionales coordinados que emprendan de manera conjunta dos o más municipios (recolección de basura, distribución interjurisdiccional de comisiones para control de la contaminación); (c) identificar y evaluar experiencias en curso; y (d) emprender proyectos experimentales de corto plazo que puedan acometerse y evaluarse pronto. Podrían también crearse foros intersectoriales, interestatales e intermunicipales para elaborar el presupuesto de manera integral para una región o subregión dada. Aunque al principio sean informales o para propósitos específicos, estos foros podrían sentar las bases para presupuestos más flexibles y para la elaboración integral en el futuro de presupuestos por región.

Dar trato diferente a los municipios acorde a su capacidad. Es importante establecer un conjunto de criterios para certificar que los municipios cuentan con la capacidad necesaria para aplicar ciertos programas o tomar préstamos. Los requisitos de informes financieros deben determinarse según el tamaño fiscal de los municipios, que se trate o no de la capital de un estado, y si quiere asumir responsabilidad y autoridad adicionales.

En conclusión, la agenda que aquí se contempla incluye seis objetivos principales:

1. Las políticas sectoriales e intersectoriales de descentralización necesitan desarrollarse dentro de un esquema estratégico más coherente. Esto ayudaría a obtener una asignación más clara de responsabilidades, más autonomía subnacional y estrategias de ejecución más eficaces.
2. La capacidad administrativa de los gobiernos estatales necesita consolidarse, sobre todo a nivel municipal.

3. La capacidad de los estados para fijar impuestos y endeudarse necesita ampliarse de manera consistente y sostenible para permitirles enfrentar sus nuevas responsabilidades.

4. A fin de tener incentivos adecuados para una autonomía fiscal responsable, los estados necesitan enfrentar estrictas limitaciones presupuestarias del gobierno federal en cuanto a transferencias, deuda y responsabilidades por la prestación de servicios.

5. Necesitan perfeccionarse las prácticas contables en todos los niveles subnacionales de gobierno, ya que la coordinación y supervisión intergubernamental del proceso de descentralización requiere el intercambio de información pertinente y análoga. Esa información tiene que compartirse entre los gobiernos y el electorado, quienes son los defensores fundamentales de la reforma en una democracia.

6. Es necesario contar con procesos para crear consenso y con mecanismos para resolver controversias y conflictos prioritarios, como una forma de ayudar a que los círculos cada vez mayores de actores políticos y económicos participen en el dinámico proceso de la descentralización.

Aunque las políticas aquí esbozadas pueden ser difíciles desde un punto de vista político y económico, todas las partes interesadas en México están conscientes de los costos y riesgos que implica no tomar medidas coherentes. Estos costos incluirían la subutilización de la capacidad tributaria subnacional, un gasto ineficiente debido a la falta de claridad para rendir cuentas y de controles sobre la prestación de servicios, y un endeudamiento subnacional potencialmente explosivo, sobre todo surgiendo de deuda contingente y obligaciones de jubilación.

1

(Mexico)

Principles of Decentralization

Thomas Courchene, Jorge Martinez-Vazquez,
Charles E. McLure, Jr., and Steven B. Webb

H77 023
H50 H70 017

STUDIES OF FISCAL DECENTRALIZATION in many countries, some of size similar to Mexico, have led economists, political scientists, and policy-makers to agree on some useful principles for policy design. First, political and cultural considerations take priority in determining the appropriate model, and many models can work. The next section outlines several possibilities. Within the political and cultural constraints, the economic characteristics of the model need to be optimized, and a section on market-preserving federalism provides four economic criteria for performance. While no model is perfect, and "working" means having ways to compensate for weaknesses, there are certain decentralization-design strategies that can improve performance, and other design flaws that need to be avoided. The bulk of this chapter addresses these design issues in four areas: spending, taxation, transfers, and debt management.

Different Federal Models

At least three models or theories of federalism are relevant to Mexico and, indeed, are partially realized. The first model—"classical" federalism—assigns expenditure and taxation among the levels of government, with financial shortfalls accommodated by a set of conditional and unconditional transfers.

The second model relates to the direct federal-municipal relationship that exists not only in practice in Mexico, but in the constitution as well. Brazil's national constitution also recognizes in detail the municipal level. In some federal systems (such as Canada), municipalities are creatures of the provinces or states and are not even mentioned in the constitution. The United States' Constitution also makes no mention of the municipal level, but this is taken to mean that, while the states define and govern the municipal level, the federal government can have all kinds of direct programs for cities and other substate entities.

The third model—administrative federalism—is the German model where most legislation is federal, but most implementation and administration (even in the areas of federal jurisdiction) are conducted at the *länder* (state) level. As they currently exist in Mexico, expenditures on education would resonate well with this model. The appendix to this chapter elaborates on the cases of Australia, Canada, Germany, and the United States.

These three models could coexist in long-term equilibrium, as they do now in Mexico. For example, expenditures on some set of national (pan-Mexican) public goods could be legislated federally but implemented by the states. In this context, federally imposed conditions would comprise a set of principles, rather than specific and binding conditions. This would provide some degree of state autonomy in determining how best to satisfy these principles. Likewise, in any long-term scenario, municipalities could retain their constitutional status and their financial links with the federal government (via pass-through transfers). Given the apparent ascendancy of the states as economic and political actors, however, a more likely scenario might be one in which conditions are placed on state transfers regarding how these transfers are redirected to the municipalities. Aspects of classical federalism will surely play a key role in any federal system in Mexico. There is considerable scope for creative options. For example, conditional transfers can be rationalized, formula-driven, and designed so that states can take into account their own preferences, cultures, and economic requirements in satisfying the conditions. Moreover, the Ramo 28 revenue-sharing unconditional transfers could give way to more subnational taxation, and the mix between conditional and unconditional transfers could shift toward the unconditional as a result of pressures for further decentralization.

The message is twofold. First, Mexico has many avenues along which to pursue decentralization. Second, the transitional status quo embodies a variety of structural components that could, with creative applications, generate a more decentralized federation. Building or rebuilding a federal model has many objectives, including cultural and political ones on which this book does not dwell (Riker 1964; Stepan 1997). The economic objectives are more than fiscal—the focus of this book—and have to do with providing a better context for economic development.

Market-Preserving Federalism

What Weingast (1995) and McKinnon (1998) refer to as "market-preserving federalism" provides a useful summary of the immediate economic objectives of decentralization. According to McKinnon, market-preserving federalism comprises four key components:

1. *Monetary separation.* State governments cannot own or control commercial banks.
2. *Fiscal separation.* State governments do not have access to discretionary or additional central government financing to cover state deficits.
3. *Freedom of interstate commerce.* Goods, services, people, firms, and capital are allowed to move freely across state lines.
4. *Unrestricted public choice.* States are allowed to design and deliver alternative bundles of public goods and services and to finance them by alternative means of taxation.

The first two principles ensure that there are no bailouts. States can, of course, still borrow on capital markets, but credit-rating agencies and financial markets generally are more vigilant if they realize that the states face hard budget constraints. Unrestricted public choice is possible only if the first three principles are in place. In this market-preserving context, the exercise of competitive federalism enhances efficiency and welfare.

The Federal-State Fiscal Accord

To create and sustain the conditions for market-reserving federalism, federal and state governments may sign a federal-state fiscal accord preserving and promoting the socioeconomic union as the federation decentralizes. The specific elements can vary considerably, but the provisions generally include the following:

- Principles to ensure the free flow of goods, services, people, firms, and capital across state borders.
- Provisions to ensure that people who move across state boundaries continue to have uninterrupted access to basic services such as health and education.
- A code of tax conduct to ensure that states do not discriminate against residents of other states.
- A principle similar to the "national treatment" provision under the North American Free Trade Agreement (NAFTA), referred to in the fiscal accord as "state treatment," meaning that each state agrees to apply its policies equally to all residents of the state, even if they have migrated from other states.
- Commitment of the federal government to these provisions, except where the federal constitution dictates otherwise.

These are the core elements in any fiscal accord. But the fiscal accord could be made more encompassing. For example, it could incorporate principles or conditions associated with the system of intergovernmental grants. As in NAFTA, there would have to be mechanisms for resolving disputes, replete with sanctions (such as withholding part of the grant). The dispute-resolution process should be timely and transparent.

"Opting in" Provisions

Mexico is a complex federation. The constituent states differ in their cultural heritage, level of economic development, and relationship with the outside world. It would be surprising if all states viewed the prospects of decentralization in the same way. In some policy or program areas, it may be appropriate to provide for "opting in" provisions. If a state does not support the details of tax decentralization, for example, it need not embrace the new system immediately. Instead, it could continue to follow the existing system and to receive revenues from grants rather than from taxes.

Opting in can provide considerable flexibility, and states would have the option of switching to the new system at any time. Although there will be some asymmetry of treatment, the transfer would be designed to ensure that, overall, all states are treated in a comparable manner.

Regardless of the model followed, Mexico will need to improve the allocation of spending, the system of taxation, the system of transfers, and the management of subnational borrowing and debt. The rest of this chapter addresses these four topics.

Spending and Service-Delivery Assignment

Decisions about which level of government has responsibility for a particular public service must be judged by how well the assignment achieves the basic criteria of fiscal performance, namely, efficiency, income redistribution, and macroeconomic stability. These objectives sometimes conflict, and the government has to determine the tradeoffs.

COST AND PRODUCER EFFICIENCY. Efficiency means satisfying the needs and preferences of taxpayers at the lowest possible cost. Services should be provided by the lowest level of government compatible with the size of benefit area associated with them. Local officials are more familiar with the needs and preferences of individuals residing in their jurisdiction. They are also likely to be more politically accountable, and therefore responsive to, these needs and preferences. Because these needs and preferences are not uniform throughout the country, it is unlikely that the central government will be able to deliver more meaningful services for a given budget. Lower-level governments, especially if they are democratically accountable, are better able than central government to match expenditures with preferences and needs, making decentralization a means of increasing consumer efficiency within government budgets. Moreover, efficiency is enhanced if consumption benefits are linked to the costs of provision via fees, service charges, or local taxes.

A second type of economic efficiency, producer efficiency, also needs to be considered. Because there may be significant economies of scale, it may be more cost-efficient to produce certain public services on a larger scale at a higher level of government. Producer efficiency also reflects the skills and qualifications of government officials, which may be better at the higier levels of government, although not always. Better accountability, competition, and scope for innovation may render the delivery of services by lower-level government more cost-effective than delivery by central government.

The optimal degree of decentralization depends on the nature of the service. For example, the benefit area is clearly the local community for sanitation services, but the national territory for air traffic control. On the other hand, leaving the supply of public services with wider benefit areas to smaller units of government is likely to result in the inefficient underprovision of services, as when, for example, a tertiary hospital providing regional services is financed by a single municipality. Where there is wide variation in the size and capacity of local government, as in Mexico, it may be optimal to have various options for the extent of local fiscal control, with objective criteria and appropriate financing arrangements corresponding to each.

INCOME REDISTRIBUTION AND MACROECONOMIC STABILITY. Public expenditures for equity or income equalization, such as social welfare or low-income housing, should be primarily the domain of central government. Local or regional governments cannot sustain independent programs of this nature because doing so would attract the needy from other areas, while taxing (potentially mobile) residents more heavily. In addition, the need for redistribution and social welfare assistance may be particularly high within subnational governments that are themselves relatively poor. Although policy formulation and funding should be the responsibility of central government, implementation can be left to local governments that may have better information on the identity and needs of the poor. However, it is not uncommon for subnational governments to legislate and fund their own social welfare policies. This is sustainable as long as these policies fit a national or regional norm or pattern.

Expenditures undertaken to stabilize the economy, such as massive investment or unemployment compensation, are ascribed to the central government. The economies of regional and local governments are too open and dependent on those of the rest of the country for these governments to be able to affect employment or aggregate demand in a meaningful way.

LEGISLATION, FINANCING, AND DELIVERY OF PUBLIC SERVICES. The provision of any public service involves three functions. The first is the legislation of principles and norms. Often, the public function is limited to this activity alone, as is the case with environmental laws and regulations, regulations for the use of airwaves, or traffic laws. The second element is financing. The characteristic of a public good legitimizes the funding of the service out of a general pool of funds raised through taxes. In some cases, funds can be earmarked from some particular service, and these funds may come from cost-recovery fees associated with the service. The last function is the production or delivery of the service. At times, this activity may be undertaken by the private sector.

The design of a clear and efficient system of expenditure assignment should address each of these functions. Different levels of government may handle different functions for any expenditure area. For example, the central government legislates and regulates the content and standards of general basic education (curriculum content, teacher qualifications and training, and so on), the state finances the education system, and the local school district runs the schools. Efficiency means making the best use of available resources, and accountability means ensuring that government officials are responsive to their constituents. Concentrating regulation, financing, and delivery of a public service in a single level of government usually enhances accountability, but this is not always possible or desirable. National interests and goals may dictate that national standards be stated and controlled by the central government. The lack of adequate resources or considerations of equity may dictate that funding be provided by the central government and that services be delivered or produced at the local level. This may be the case for many social welfare programs.

NO SINGLE-BEST ASSIGNMENT. These principles should guide the assignment of expenditure responsibilities, but they are not definitive for all times and all places. Some public services, such as primary education and primary health services, may be local in nature because of the size of their benefit area; but, because of their relevance to welfare and income redistribution, they may also be considered a concurrent responsibility of the regional or central governments. Economic efficiency calls for greater autonomy of subnational governments in expenditure and taxing decisions, but this may lead to fiscal disparities among subnational governments that are unacceptable in a given country. There are other important trade-offs in the implementation of intergovernmental fiscal relations. Achieving a more equal distribution of resources among subnational governments is a worthy objective. But to redistribute resources to poorer regions, central authorities need to tax better-off regions more heavily. Placing higher tax burdens on better-off regions limits their ability to grow. Different countries and governments make different choices in the tradeoff between redistribution and growth. Even in a single country, the "best" expenditure assignments will change over time, responding to changes in costs and technology or in citizens' preferences.

It is often argued that an explicit assignment of expenditure responsibilities is not possible because some responsibilities will always be concurrent among different levels of government. This argument is fallacious. Although many types of expenditure responsibilities should be shared among different levels of government, failure to have a concrete and explicit assignment leads to instability and friction, if not open conflict, in intergovernmental relations. Worse, it leads to the inefficient provision of public services.

Common Problems with Expenditure Assignments: Lessons from International Experience

LACK OF CLEAR DELINEATION BETWEEN THE PUBLIC AND PRIVATE SECTORS. Often subnational governments and, of course, central governments get involved in the financing and provision of private market activities. This hinders economic development because subnational governments tend to compete unfairly with private entities. Involvement in the private sector by local authorities creates conflicts of interest and opportunities for corruption and fraud, and this undermines the appropriate regulatory functions of both central and subnational governments. Ultimately, public funds in private activities decreases the amount of funds available for the provision of public services. The best that subnational governments can do to promote economic development in their jurisdictions is to provide the best possible level of public services, capital infrastructure and, where appropriate, other regulation.

LACK OF FORMAL ASSIGNMENT. The country's constitution often assigns expenditure responsibilities among different levels of government, but the assignment is usually not specific. Expenditure responsibilities should be specified mostly in the law, not the constitution, providing specificity as well as flexibility. The lack of clear, formal assignment of responsibilities tends to destabilize intergovernmental relations. This was the case early on during the transitions in Kazakhstan, Russia, and Ukraine. What confuses expenditure assignments in practice is that even though responsibility for implementation or delivery may be assigned explicitly, responsibility is not assigned for designing policy, imposing norms over expenditure functions, or financing those expenditure responsibilities.

LACK OF AN INSTITUTIONAL MECHANISM FOR COORDINATION AND CONFLICT RESOLUTION. No assignment of expenditure responsibilities can cover all the possibilities and contingencies in a legal document. It is important to introduce well-developed institutions of cooperation and coordination among different levels of government that can discuss and resolve disagreements.

Conflicts involving expenditure assignment and inefficiencies in service delivery are more likely where the different levels of government are involved in the same sector, but there is little communication and exchange between them. When multiple levels of government are involved in most sectors, governments need broad and formal coordination institutions, as with "cooperative federalism" in Germany. In the United States, the pattern of assigning responsibilities varies widely from sector to sector and from state to state, so the only sector coordination is done by technocrats in some areas where there is a clear need, such as highways and law enforcement. Somewhere in between, Australia, Canada, and New Zealand use formal gatherings of politicians and bureaucrats to discuss mutually important fiscal issues.

MISALIGNMENT OF CAPITAL AND RECURRENT EXPENDITURE ASSIGNMENTS. In general, capital expenditure responsibilities should be assigned among the different levels of government in the same manner as recurrent expenditures. Decentralization in both capital investment decisions and recurrent expenditures increases the efficiency associated with being closer to the needs and preferences of taxpayers and improves government accountability and responsiveness. Furthermore, maintaining infrastructure at efficient levels in general requires local ownership. Responsibility for capital infrastructure should be placed at the level of government in charge of delivering specific services, including the operation and maintenance of facilities. In this way, only capital infrastructure facilities that are desired by subnational governments will be built, encouraging their maintenance and repair. To assign capital expenditure responsibilities properly, it is necessary to address the issue of long-term financing. Subnational governments need to be allowed to borrow from banks or in capital markets, and that borrowing needs to be regulated either directly or through the market. Borrowing for justified, long-lived infrastructure is both efficient and equitable.[1] Most countries only allow borrowing for capital investment purposes.

MISMATCH OF FINANCING CAPACITY AND MINIMUM LEVELS OF SERVICE. Do subnational governments have enough resources to provide some minimum level of service in the functions assigned to them in areas of national interest (education, health, social welfare, and so forth)? The concept of a minimal level of service, in contrast to what people of a subnational area can or choose to afford, has operational meaning only when the wider society has an interest in assuring such a minimum. In substance, the issue is whether it is desirable to introduce mechanisms that force or encourage subnational governments to spend (some of) their funds in a particular way in order to provide some minimum standard of service (provided the funds or the sources of funds are present).

One approach, commonly followed, is for the central government to rely on conditional grants or matching grants to induce subnational governments to provide the minimum level of service. This is another example of how expenditure assignment directly relates to the design of other elements of fiscal decentralization, in this case, the transfer system. To protect the principle of subnational autonomy—the core operational concept of fiscal decentralization—minimum standards and similar restrictions on subnational governments should be used sparingly.

ONE SIZE OF MANDATE DOES NOT FIT ALL. Achieving the optimal scale in local service provision is an issue in many transition and developing countries, especially when the constitution or the law treats all municipalities the same. Municipalities with small populations cannot take advantage of minimum economies of scale. To improve efficiency, small municipalities could be consolidated into larger ones; associations of municipalities or special jurisdictions could be created; local governments could deliver services through private contractors; or the state or national government could provide the service in small municipalities, with appropriate finance. Asymmetric decentralization is often a practical solution, providing options and incentives by giving more responsibility and resources to entities that demonstrate satisfactory administrative and fiscal capacity. It is important to recognize, however, that regional and municipal governments may be underdeveloped precisely because they have never been given responsibilities or the resources with which to carry them out. Small and poor municipalities often need technical assistance to help achieve adequate capacity.

UNFUNDED EXPENDITURE MANDATES. Unfunded mandates—the imposition of expenditure requirements on subnational governments without adequate funding by central or federal authorities—are a common problem in countries with decentralized fiscal systems. Unfunded mandates take different forms, including the setting of wages at the central level, mandatory increases in pension payments, and the setting of standards of provision for services. As expected, subnational and central governments tend to have quite different views of what is and is not an unfunded mandate. Central governments often argue that subnational governments receive funds through general funding sources (for example, revenue sharing or general transfers). Of course, subnational governments argue that general revenues should remain at the discretion of subnational governments.

Prohibiting unfunded mandates by law is not always respected in practice, and some may be desirable and acceptable to subnational governments (such as equal opportunity for citizens or environmental standards with cross-regional effects). Universal or blanket reimbursement policies, international experience shows, can easily create an administrative nightmare. An important step is to clarify expenditure assignments as much as possible. Other solutions include requiring supermajority votes in Congress to impose central mandates without funding, introducing mechanisms of self-restraint in Congress, establishing closer working partnerships among the various levels of government, and introducing categorical grants to fund large mandates.

TIMING. The assignment of responsibility for expenditures needs to precede or at least coincide with the design of other pieces of a decentralized system. Failing to do this is a common mistake. Many countries of Latin America assigned revenues to subnational governments and put transfers in place before transferring functional competencies from the central government to subnational governments. This approach produced weak subnational governments and fiscally overburdened central governments, which in many cases continued to take on most expenditure responsibilities with fewer resources.

Tax Assignments

Definition and Purpose

Other things being equal, the jurisdiction responsible for spending should also be responsible for raising the requisite revenues. Although this is a favorite principle of federalism scholars, in reality it seldom occurs. Most federations have significant vertical imbalances where a level with more revenue sources than spending responsibility makes vertical transfers to a level with revenues less than responsive. The challenge is to design intergovernmental transfers with an eye toward ensuring that, at the margin, states view transfers as they do their own revenue. For example, transfers should not be open-ended.

Tax assignment considers which level of government should tax what (the tax base) and how. Possible techniques of tax assignment include independent legislation and administration by subnational governments, surcharges on the tax base of a higher level of government, and tax sharing. (Revenue sharing is also considered, even though it is not a form of tax assignment.) The purpose of tax assignment is to provide subnational governments with revenues that they control and thus to decentralize the control of public spending.

It is important to distinguish between two concepts. *Own revenues* belong to subnational governments by law. They may include revenue-sharing funds as well as shared taxes and taxes levied by or for the subnational government. (Whether borrowing is considered a source of revenue depends on the context. For the present discussion it is not.) For decentralization to be viable, subnational governments must have their own revenues that are adequate to cover their current expenditures, including debt service. *Marginal (incremental) own revenues* are revenues that subnational governments can affect by their own actions, especially by changing tax rates, but also by imposing new taxes or repealing old ones, by changing the tax base, and by varying administrative effort. Access to marginal revenues is key to fiscal decentralization because it gives subnational governments control over the size of public spending within their jurisdictions.

Objectives and Constraints

Although the overriding objective of tax assignment is to increase the access of subnational governments to marginal own revenues, not all ways of increasing access are equally satisfactory. Subsidiary objectives and constraints inevitably influence the means used to increase access.

DESIRABLE ATTRIBUTES OF SUBNATIONAL TAXATION. Decentralization works best when taxes and the benefits of public spending (or costs incurred by governments) are closely related. In the extreme case of user charges and fees, payments act almost like prices for private goods, in that citizens get what they pay for and pay for what they get. The implication for tax assignment is that revenues from taxes closely related to identifiable benefits or public expenditures should be levied by the level of government that provides the benefits or incurs the costs. For example, revenues from taxes on motor fuels are intended to reflect the benefits of using roads and highways, and therefore should go to the governments that finance their construction and maintenance; revenues from taxes on alcoholic beverages and tobacco products should go to the governments that incur the health-related public costs occasioned by consumption of those products.

This raises a subsidiary question: should revenues from benefit-related charges and taxes be assigned (earmarked) to finance the corresponding activity, or should they be part of the general revenue of the level of government that provides the services in question? Optimal resource allocation requires that prices (or taxes intended to serve as quasi-prices) equal the marginal cost of providing services. Marginal cost pricing may provide more or less revenue than is needed to finance activities (depending on whether average cost is rising or falling), and funds that are earmarked may be trapped in suboptimal places, as when gasoline taxes are used to fund freeways, instead of mass transit in the United States.

User charges, fees, and taxes related closely to benefits are most likely to be feasible for financing services that, although provided publicly, exhibit an important characteristic of private goods: the feasibility and likelihood of excluding those who do not pay. Toll roads cannot be used without paying for access. Those who do not pay motor fuel taxes cannot use roads and highways, even if access is not restricted. In theory it would be possible to deny access to education and health care, but this is rarely done for social reasons, especially in the case of primary education and basic health care. Inherent in the nature of public goods is the inability to charge those who benefit from them. Thus much of public spending provides *generalized benefits* that must be financed by taxes that are only loosely related to the benefits of public services: general sales taxes, income taxes, and property taxes.

When production and consumption do not occur in the same jurisdiction (because goods are traded between jurisdictions) or individuals do not earn income where they live (because they commute between jurisdictions or have investments in other jurisdictions), an important two-stage question arises in the attempt to identify beneficiaries of generalized public services. First, are the benefits of public services provided primarily to businesses or to individuals? And, second, when such benefits are provided to individuals, are they more closely related to (a) consumption or the residence of taxpayers, or to (b) production or the source of income? If generalized benefits are provided primarily to business (and are thus more closely related to production than to consumption), an origin-based sales tax or a commercial property tax might be appropriate.[2] If such benefits are provided to individuals and are more closely related to consumption or residence of the taxpayer, a destination-based sales tax, a residence-based individual income tax, or a residential property tax might closely reflect the benefits of public services. But if such benefits are related more closely to the earning of income, a source-based individual income tax would be more appropriate.

Tax assignment must recognize administrative reality. Some taxes that are attractive in theory may not be administratively feasible or may require inordinate amounts of administrative resources, something Mexico cannot afford.

Subnational governments ordinarily should employ debt financing only for capital projects; they should not borrow for current expenditures. If this rule is to be respected, subnational governments need stable sources of own revenue (expenditures of subnational governments are assumed to be relatively stable.) Therefore, relatively volatile sources of revenues, such as the corporate income tax and taxes on natural resources, should not be assigned to subnational governments.

Undesirable Attributes of Subnational Taxation. If the benefits of free markets are to be realized, subnational governments should not impose taxes that distort the location of economic activity. Taxes levied at the origin of production or the source of income are more likely to distort locational decisions than are taxes levied at the point of consumption or residence, unless they reflect benefits of services provided to businesses or to employees at their place of employment.

Governments often wish to levy taxes on business that exceed the value of benefits provided to (or costs incurred on behalf of) business. This may be done because taxing business is more popular than taxing people (or the products they buy) or because it is thought that taxes on business can be exported to nonresidents of the taxing jurisdiction. Taxes on business that exceed the value of benefits provided are likely to distort the location of economic activity, unless they are levied at uniform rates throughout the country. But taxes that must be levied at uniform rates do not provide a marginal source of revenue for any one subnational government, and thus do not further fiscal autonomy. Moreover, agreements between jurisdictions to fix tax rates (or the imposition of uniform rates by a higher level of government) represent a form of cartelization that encourages overexpansion of the public sector and inefficiency. Competition among subnational governments both prevents excess taxation of business and impedes inefficiency in government.

Some taxes can be exported to nonresidents if they are imposed by (or for) subnational governments. The best examples of exported taxes are taxes on business that cannot be shifted to consumers or to labor and thus are borne by owners of business, many of whom may be nonresidents. (The view that taxes on business will automatically be shifted to consumers, many of whom are nonresidents, is generally incorrect. Exporting to nonresident consumers is likely to occur only when the taxing jurisdiction dominates the national market for the product taxed.) In the absence of untaxed competition (for example, from imports), excises imposed on products by the producing jurisdiction could be exported to consumers throughout the nation.

Tax exporting is generally undesirable. Not only does it impose unfair burdens on nonresidents, but it also cheapens the provision of public services in the taxing jurisdiction, encouraging overconsumption. An important exception involves taxation that is closely related to the benefits of a public service (such as taxes on motor fuels that finance roads used by nonresidents); in this case, failure to export taxes to users is undesirable. Again, this points to the superiority of destination-based sales taxes and residence-based income taxes over production-based sales taxes and source-based income taxes. The former are much less likely to be exported than the latter.

Except in rare cases, subnational governments within a nation differ substantially in their inherent fiscal capacity. Fiscal capacity may be measured by applying a representative tax system—that is, by calculating how much revenue each state would receive, per capita, if it levied the taxes typical of all states. Although such measurement depends on the structure of the typical state tax system, it is unlikely to be misleading. Some states are simply richer or poorer than others, as measured, for example, by per capita income or per capita GDP. But there may be other explanations. For example, some activities (for example, tourism) are easier to tax than others. Particularly important is the presence of geographically concentrated, high-value natural resources that can be taxed by subnational governments. Where *horizontal fiscal disparities* are important, equalization grants may be appropriate to allow all states to provide comparable levels of services with comparable levels of tax effort. (Tax effort can be measured by comparing actual tax collections with collections under the representative tax system. Subnational governments that collect substantially more than under the representative tax system are exerting high tax effort; those that collect substantially less are exerting low tax effort.)

OTHER CONSIDERATIONS. Responsibility for income redistribution via taxes should be lodged primarily with the central government. Attempts by subnational governments to redistribute income are likely to be futile, for example, because taxes intended to be borne by capital are likely to be shifted to labor and to owners of land. Moreover, they are likely to distort the location of economic activity or to result in tax exporting.

Public spending should be lodged at the lowest possible level of government to avoid spillovers of benefits between jurisdictions, realize economies of scale, and maximize the fiscal autonomy of those affected by public spending. This principle has a counterpart in the field of tax assignment, because of the seemingly inevitable existence of vertical fiscal imbalance. Higher levels of government can effectively administer virtually any tax that lower levels can administer, but the converse is not true; some forms of taxation do not lend themselves to implementation by or for lower levels of government. Moreover, some taxes are not appropriate for local governments, even if they are administratively feasible; customs duties are perhaps the best example. To minimize vertical fiscal imbalance, it is desirable to assign to subnational governments all taxes that are administratively feasible and appropriate for them. In judging administrative feasibility and appropriateness, one should consider the use of subnational surcharges on the tax base of a higher level of government and independent legislation and administration by the subnational government.

It is often suggested that subnational governments should be rewarded for exerting high tax effort, for example, by providing matching grants that reflect tax effort. In general there is little analytical support for this proposition. Unless there are good reasons to believe that tax effort would otherwise be artificially low, it is generally better to assume a neutral stance toward subnational tax effort. To overcome inertia, however, it may be desirable to encourage tax effort during the transition to a decentralized system.

Assignment of Taxes to Cover Generalized Benefits

Subnational governments should, to the extent possible, rely on taxes, fees, and charges that are related to benefits received. Using taxes to cover the generalized benefits of public spending has the following implications for tax assignment. First, if, as suggested, most of the public services provided by subnational governments are provided to individuals, not businesses, taxation that is likely to be borne directly by individuals or shifted to them by businesses in a predictable manner is preferable to taxation of business, including taxes that may be shifted to individuals, but in an unpredictable manner. This implies that a state individual income tax or a state value added tax is preferable to a state corporate income tax. If benefits are provided where people live, not where they work, destination-based indirect taxes and residence-based income taxes are likely to be preferable to origin-based indirect taxes and source-based income taxes. Finally, if subnational taxes are seen as payment for services providing generalized benefits, coverage should be as broad as possible, given concerns for equity; subnational taxes should be "mass taxes," not taxes paid by a select few.

Because the progressive individual income tax is the tax mechanism of choice for both income redistribution and endogenous macroeconomic stabilization, it should be reserved primarily for use by the central government. This does not mean, however, that subnational governments should not also rely on the individual income tax. A flat-rate individual income tax may provide a satisfactory surrogate for benefit-related taxation. Under certain circumstances, a flat-rate subnational tax can be imposed on the same base as a graduated-rate national tax.[3]

The assignment of taxes on natural resources raises difficult philosophical and political questions as well as economic issues (see McLure 1994). For the most part, economic arguments favor assigning taxes on economically important natural resources to the national government, especially if the resources are geographically concentrated in only some taxing jurisdictions. (Taxes on common low-value and ubiquitous resources such as sand and gravel can be assigned to subnational governments.) Because revenues tend to be unstable, taxes on natural resources are ill-suited for use by subnational governments, which generally need stable sources of revenue. Moreover, subnational governments may not be in as good a position as national governments to impose taxes on economic rents, generally agreed to be the most satisfactory form of tax on natural resources. In theory, taxes on economic rent, being a tax on surplus, do not affect production decisions; the pattern of production that maximizes before-tax income also maximizes after-tax income. Taxes on production encourage inefficient exploitation (high-grading) by discouraging production that would cover marginal costs, but not the tax. Property taxes on deposits of natural resources are even worse, because they encourage uneconomically rapid exploitation in order to avoid future taxes.

If effective ownership of natural resources is in private hands, subnational taxes may be exported to nonresident owners. Effective ownership may be in private hands even if the state owns the natural resources. This may occur, for example, when resources are exploited under concessions, subject to terms that are not adjusted for changes in taxation. Finally, if important natural resources are distributed unequally across a nation, subnational taxation may produce or aggravate horizontal fiscal disparities. Besides raising questions of equity—probably the most important reason to assign taxation of natural resources to the federal government—such disparities may induce economically inefficient allocation of private resources to jurisdictions with low tax rates or high levels of public services. These inefficiencies are likely to be relatively small, except in extreme cases, as in Alaska, where the combination of vast natural resources and a small population allows the financing of generous public services (including annual per capita grants) with low tax rates (see Mieszkowski and Toder 1983). Table 1.1 summarizes the current wisdom on tax assignment.

Philosophical arguments are more ambiguous. Advocates of taxation by subnational governments commonly argue that natural resources and the right to tax them are part of the "heritage" of such jurisdictions. But it can equally be argued that the resources and tax revenues are the heritage of the entire nation. The resolution of this issue calls into question the concept of nationhood as it is understood in particular countries. All things considered, it seems appropriate to assign most taxes on important natural resources to the federal government. Since the Mexican constitution makes this assignment, taxes on natural resources are not discussed further here.

Methods of Revenue Assignment

This section evaluates four methods of revenue assignment, including tax assignment: independent legislation and administration, tax and revenue sharing, state surcharges, and dual administration of surcharges.

INDEPENDENT LEGISLATION AND ADMINISTRATION. A system of tax assignment based on independent legislation and administration provides maximum state sovereignty, but this sovereignty is bought at a high price—a price that Mexico can ill-afford and need not pay. State taxes in the United States illustrate these problems. Inconsistent state laws and administrative practices

Table 1.1. Attributes, Strengths, and Weaknesses of Various Techniques of Tax Assignment

	Techniques of revenue assignment				
	Subnational legislation and administration	*National legislation; subnational rate and administration*	*Subnational surcharge: base of higher level government: administered by higher level*	*Tax sharing*	*Revenue sharing*
Assignment of taxing powers—best practice:					
Defining Tax Base	Subnational	National	National	National	National
Setting Tax Rate(s)	Subnational	Subnational	Subnational	National	National
Administration	Subnational	Subnational	National	National	National
Criteria of choice:					
Autonomy	Best	High: choice of tax rate	High: choice of tax rate	None	None
Complexity	High	Low: tax on local activity	Low	Low	Low
Horizontal Disparities	Potentially high	Potentially high	Potentially high	Potentially high	Can offset horizontal disparities
Overall	Generally not appropriate for Mexico		Generally best approach	Poor	Current practice
Most appropriate method of assigning revenues from major taxes to subnational governments:					
Excises			Best	Transition	
VAT			Best	Transition	
Individual Income					Best
Payroll Tax			Best		
Corporate Income					Best
Property		Good (greater state control)	Good (most efficient solution)		
Natural Resources					Best

raise the costs of compliance and administration and create inequity. Use of source-based taxes such as the corporate income tax distorts the geographic allocation of resources and may result in tax exporting. Even the retail sales tax, which is imposed by 45 states and the District of Columbia, contains an origin-based component that distorts locational decisions, since a substantial amount of revenue (an estimated 40 percent) is derived from taxes levied on sales to businesses instead of sales to households.[4] Taxes on natural resources generally take the form of state severance (production) taxes, income taxes, and local property taxes, all of which are distortionary. (Distortion is mitigated by the fact that the corporate income tax and sales taxes on business inputs are deductible in calculating liabilities under the federal tax.) There is substantial tax exporting, especially by resource-rich states.[5] In short, this system is not appropriate for Mexico.

TAX AND REVENUE SHARING. In tax sharing the central government directs given fractions of revenues from selected taxes to the various states where the revenue originates. In this approach, widely used in the former Soviet Union, states have essentially no control over the choice of taxes, tax base, tax rates, or tax administration; they are thus fiscally weak.[6] Although different in appearance, tax sharing closely resembles revenue sharing and grants. Unlike tax sharing, revenue sharing returns funds to subnational governments on the basis of formulas, instead of to the jurisdictions of origin. Like tax sharing, it provides no subnational autonomy over the choice of taxes, the definition of the tax base, the setting of tax rates, and tax administration. The use of formulas does, however, offer the possibility of reducing horizontal disparities among jurisdictions.

STATE SURCHARGES. An ideal system for many countries (including Mexico) consists of subnational surcharges levied on a tax base (or tax bases) defined and administered by the central government, perhaps with input from the states. In this scheme, subnational governments would exercise the all-important choice of tax rates, but most of the complexity, inequities, tax exporting, and locational distortions inherent in subnational choice of tax bases and administration of taxes would be avoided. That is, state surcharges combine simplicity with subnational sovereignty over tax rates. Canada makes substantial use of this type of system.

Ideally, surcharges could be imposed on some combination of excise tax, residence-based income tax, and value added tax (levied at the destination of sales). States might impose payroll taxes, but on a uniform base. State surcharges on the corporate income tax may be required in order to raise adequate revenues.

Of the three methods of tax assignment, subnational surcharges provide the optimal combination of subnational autonomy and simplicity.

Subnational governments have autonomy over rates—the most important issue for determining the level of subnational spending—while the central government defines tax bases and administers taxes, minimizing the costs of administration and compliance. By comparison, independent legislation and administration are too complicated, and tax sharing eliminates all subnational autonomy. Since tax surcharges may produce horizontal fiscal disparities and vertical fiscal imbalance, they can be combined with revenue sharing from the federal taxes.

Despite the manifest advantages of tax surcharges as a system toward which Mexico should move, the movement could be a gradual one consisting of three stages. In the first stage, the present system of tax sharing/revenue sharing would be replaced with a system in which revenues from certain taxes are shared with the states on a derivation basis. For this purpose, the determination of derivation for each shared tax should approximate as closely as possible the technique that would be used to impose a state surcharge on the federal tax in question. In the second stage, tax sharing would be replaced with a system of subnational surcharges in which state tax rates are constrained to be equal. In the third stage, states would be given greater—perhaps complete—control over state surcharge rates.

DUAL ADMINISTRATION OF SURCHARGES. It is common for surcharges of subnational governments to be administered by national governments. This arrangement seems preferable to the alternatives of dual administration, in which the federal government administers federal taxes and state governments administer surcharges. In some countries, subnational governments administer national taxes, but this is less common. Administration of the value added tax by the German länder and the Canadian province of Quebec are notable examples. This option deserves little discussion in the Mexican context, where it has an unsuccessful history. On the one hand, federal administration of state surcharges raises several concerns: Will the federal government efficiently transfer the revenue collected on behalf of the state? And will the federal and state governments have different priorities in the assignment of scarce administrative resources? On the other hand, dual administration raises the specter of costly duplication of administrative efforts, overly burdensome compliance, and the possibility that administration will not be consistent between states or between states and the federal government.

The risk that the federal government will not pay to state governments the revenue collected on their behalf can easily be addressed by having taxpayers deposit taxes directly in the bank accounts of each government. A greater risk is that taxpayers might meet their obligations to the federal government, but not to state governments, and that the federal government would condone this behavior. It is desirable to find ways to prevent this.

Federal and state tax administrations may have quite different priorities. First, the federal government may prefer to concentrate its resources on administering the taxes that yield the greatest marginal revenue for the federal government; these may not be the taxes that yield the greatest marginal revenue for the state.[7] Second, in the administration of a particular tax, the federal government will presumably prefer to concentrate its activities on taxpayers whose expected marginal yield of revenue for the federal government is highest. Since economic activity is not homogeneous throughout the country, the federal tax administration might pay less attention than state tax administrations to taxpayers in some states. (What might be a "big fish" for the state might be a "small fry" for the federal government.) To the extent that the federal administration ignores taxpayers in poorer states, horizontal fiscal disparities are accentuated. Third, the assumption that the federal tax administration allocates its resources rationally may not be valid; the administration's coverage of taxpayers in various parts of the country may vary widely for reasons that have no basis in sound policy. (It may be difficult to hire trained auditors to work in the hinterland; alternatively, coverage in some rural areas may be "denser" than in the major cities.)

One risk of dual administration is obvious: instead of filing a single tax return with the federal government, the taxpayer would file a return with each state where there is an actual or potential tax liability. Similarly, the return would be potentially liable to audit by the tax authorities of all these governments. Under a system of dual administration, tax administrators in all states must apply the law consistently. Although a single law might, in principle, apply throughout the country, it might not be interpreted uniformly by state tax administrations.

The treatment of interstate transactions is especially important. In a system with federal tax administration, the flow of information on interstate sales would stay with the federal government.[8] By comparison, in a dual system, the information on interstate transactions would have to flow between state administrations.

The states could be given a role in the supervision of the federal tax administration, essentially making it a *national* agency that is accountable to both the federal and state governments, instead of a *federal* agency that is accountable only to the federal government. This would bring the benefits of uniformity, avoid duplicate effort, and respect state priorities.

Transfers and System Integration

Federal systems are characterized by a formal (constitutional) division of powers between central and subnational levels of government. These powers can be assigned to one or the other order of government (self-rule) or they can be concurrent (shared rule). Theoretically, there could be a serendipitous matching of revenue and expenditure responsibilities among the two orders of government such that there would be no need for intergovernmental transfers. However, in virtually all federations, the central government has de facto, if not de jure, capacity to raise revenue in excess of its expenditure responsibilities. This is certainly the case for the Mexican federation, even more so now that state taxation responsibilities have been transferred to the center and significant expenditure responsibilities devolved to the states.

As mentioned earlier, in general, two sorts of fiscal balance (or transfer) issues arise in federal systems—*vertical* fiscal imbalance and *horizontal* fiscal imbalance. Vertical fiscal imbalance relates to the allocation (or, rather, misallocation) of revenue-raising capacity relative to expenditure responsibilities. The Mexican federal government has revenue-raising capacities well in excess of its expenditure responsibilities. Although a high degree of vertical fiscal imbalance in favor of the federal government can be rationalized on a variety of grounds (such as economies of scale in tax collection) and does exist in some mature federations (such as Australia), a corresponding set of intergovernmental grants (federal-state and perhaps federal-municipal) is required to address the revenue shortfall of subnational governments.

Horizontal fiscal imbalance has to do with fiscal capacity across the states. Fiscal capacity has a precise meaning: it relates to standardized per capita revenues, where these are calculated as the product of the all-state average tax rates and commonly defined per capita state tax bases. The intergovernmental transfers associated with alleviating these horizontal fiscal imbalances are typically referred to as equalization transfers and programs.

Analytical Underpinnings of Intergovernmental Transfers

Expenditure responsibilities at the state (subnational government) level usually exceed the states' revenue-raising capacity, lending to both vertical and horizontal fiscal imbalances. These imbalances occur for various reasons. The most obvious is that they arise from the allocation of taxing and expenditure responsibilities under the constitution. Or they could result from "first-mover" advantage. That is, according to the constitution, the states may have adequate capacity to raise revenue but may have to share the major sources of revenue with the federal government, which has preemptively occupied these tax areas. Unless the federal government is willing to transfer tax room to the states, there is no way, short of excessively high tax rates, that the states can exercise their taxing authority. Third, it may be more efficient for the federal or central government to collect taxes on behalf of the states. This can also occur for a variety of reasons—inadequate state-level collection capacity, economies of scale, and the presence of spillovers. This last reason is becoming more important: with increasing economic integration the optimal jurisdiction for collecting taxes is expanding (that is, the tax bases are becoming more "mobile") relative to the optimal jurisdiction for spending. In order to "internalize" these potential spillovers or externalities, taxes are collected at the national level with an understanding that some or all of the revenues will be returned to the states under a set of transfer arrangements. Whatever the reason, both horizontal and vertical fiscal imbalances exist at the subnational level. What is the role of intergovernmental transfers in ameliorating horizontal fiscal imbalances across the states?

Accommodating Horizontal Imbalances. The literature focuses on two criteria for assessing horizontal imbalances: fiscal efficiency and fiscal equity. Drawing on Boadway and Hobson (1993), the underlying theoretical model postulates that an individual's "comprehensive income" is the sum of his or her market income, W, and net fiscal benefits (NFBs), defined as the difference between the value of government expenditures and taxes paid. This leads to the following basic equation of labor-market equilibrium:

$$W_i + \text{NFB}_i = W_j + \text{NFB}_j$$

where subscript i refers to state i and subscript j refers to state j. Thus an individual will be indifferent between living in state i and state j when comprehensive incomes are the same in both states. But now assume that $\text{NFB}_j > \text{NFB}_i$. Net fiscal benefits in state j can exceed those in state i for a variety of reasons. For example, states with high source-based tax revenues (from, say, resources or corporate income taxes) or with high residence-based revenues (because they are higher-income states) could finance a given level of public goods and services with lower tax rates, which, in turn (and in the absence of capitalization) implies higher net fiscal benefits. Moreover, NFBs could also arise on the expenditure side: it may be more costly to provide a representative bundle of goods and services in some states than in others. These differences in NFBs provide the backdrop for what the theoretical literature refers to as the fiscal efficiency and fiscal equity rationales for equalization, that is, for ameliorating horizontal differences in fiscal capacity.

Fiscal Efficiency. Consider fiscal efficiency first. Output maximization requires that $W_i = W_j$, namely that individuals distribute themselves across states so that their market-based marginal products are everywhere identical (that is, in state i and state j). However, if, as assumed, $\text{NFB}_j > \text{NFB}_i$, then individuals will be willing to move to state j even if this means that $W_j < W_i$, in order to ensure that their comprehensive income ($W + \text{NFB}$) is in equilibrium. The result is inefficient or fiscally induced migration. The solution proposed in the literature is to provide a set of intergovernmental transfers (they could be federal-state transfers as in Canada or interstate transfers as in the German federation) in order to ensure that $NFB_j = NFB_i$, which, in turn, implies that, in equilibrium, $W_i = W_j$. Hence, migration will be efficiency-driven, not NFB-driven.

Several caveats are in order. First, since the underlying model focuses on individuals, equalization payments to provinces are a second-best solution. The first-best solution is a set of payments to individuals. But this is typically ruled out on constitutional or practical grounds. Hence, the literature argues that the presence of equalizing grants allows states, in principle, to equalize NFBs. In practice, this is highly unlikely to occur since it implies that similarly situated individuals in both states are treated similarly by taxes and expenditures. Second, the model implicitly assumes zero migration costs. If there are costs to migration, then NFBs can differ up to this cost differential with no deleterious impact on migration efficiency. The third caveat is more important. Although the model is general in the sense that it can accommodate any degree of capitalization of NFBs in terms of rents and wages, its typical application tends to argue for full equalization of revenues up and down, as in Australia. This application effectively assumes zero capitalization. Phrased differently, it assumes that an increase in revenues in state i, for example, is equivalent to an increase in NFBs in state i. But this does not hold if the revenue increases become capitalized in wages, rents, and so forth. This is not a defect in the theory, only in the way the theory tends to be applied. Finally, in Canada at least, the emphasis is shifting away from the fiscal efficiency case for equalization to the fiscal equity case, because the efficiency gains may not be very significant in any event (Watson 1986).

FISCAL EQUITY. The traditional case for equalizing federal-state transfers in a federation is premised on fiscal equity, which in turn is based on the public finance concept of horizontal equity—equal treatment of equals. The argument is straightforward: individuals with similar employment incomes ($W_i = W_j$) should, on horizontal equity grounds, also have similar NFBs. Thus "fiscal equity requires that all differences in NFBs be equalized regardless of their source" (Boadway and Hobson 1993, p. 89). Under what has come to be viewed as "broad-based horizontal equity," the underlying assumption is that people who are equally well off in the absence of government should also be equally well off *in the presence of both levels of government*. Hence the role for the federal government, under broad-based horizontal equity, is to design discriminatory transfers (essentially via equalization) to provincial governments so as to "undo" any differential NFBs that arise because of government policies (both federal and state). This approach turns the federation into something comparable to a unitary state (Boadway 1998; Hobson 1998). One can mount a convincing case, however, that the goal of broad-based horizontal equity is the very antithesis of federalism.

Nonetheless, the theoretical conception of fiscal equity underpins the comprehensive equalization system in place in Australia, where state revenues are leveled upward and downward to an all-state per capita level and then further adjusted to take into account differential state needs and costs of providing the average all-state expenditure bundle. Not all federations accept this approach to fiscal equity. The Canadian equalization system focuses only on revenues and then brings only low-revenue-capacity provinces up to some acceptable standard (it does not bring above-average provinces down to this standard). And the United States does not even have an equalization program, presumably on the grounds that differential NFBs will be fully capitalized so that there is "nothing to equalize." The degree to which federations seek to ameliorate horizontal imbalances across their subnational governments appears to be derived from the deeper political values and logic of the federal contract rather than from a simple application of fiscal theory.

Vertical Balance and Conditionality

This section reviews the theory and practice of vertical fiscal transfers, beginning with a focus on conditionality.

Conditional grants come in a variety of forms and rationales. The traditional public finance literature has devoted substantial attention to the "interjurisdictional spillover" rationale for conditionality. An interjurisdictional spillover (or externality) is said to exist when the activities of the public sector in jurisdiction A provide benefits to the residents of another jurisdiction (Boadway and Hobson 1993, p. 96). In the presence of such externalities, jurisdiction A has an incentive to underspend on the provision of public goods in the presence of such externalities. The greater the proportion of external to "own" benefits, the greater the underprovision will likely be. The obvious way to correct for this is to provide a matching conditional (expenditure-specific) grant where the degree of matching (degree of cost sharing) relates to the degree of interjurisdictional spillover. Although this argument is well grounded in theory, it is rare in practice to find open-ended, shared-cost conditional grants where the degree of cost sharing is predicated on the differences in intergovernmental spillovers. But this externality can be addressed in other ways. For example, the per capita value of conditional grants could vary across subnational jurisdictions in accordance with the degree of spillover. And the various equalization programs in federal systems imply that these moneys are designed to ensure that all states can provide national, average public services to their citizens. This can only be an implicit condition, since equalization grants are generally unconditional.

The most typical forms of conditional grants link the transfers to spending in specific areas or for specific purposes. These specific-purpose grants are intended to ensure that all individuals, as a right of citizenship, receive minimum levels of certain public goods and services. Presumably, this explains the degree of conditionality embedded in Mexico's Ramo 33 transfers, especially for health and education.

Although some forms of conditionality may embody problematic incentives (such as open-ended, 50-50 shared-cost grants that distort state expenditure priorities because states are spending "50 percent pesos" in the grant areas and "100 percent pesos" elsewhere), or overly strict conditions that prevent states from achieving the goals of the conditions in more efficient ways, conditional grants can also be employed creatively. Several examples come to mind. First, cost sharing can be combined with subnational spending priorities at the margin. For example, the cost sharing can be close-ended (intramarginal) rather than open-ended. And the amount of this intramarginal sharing can be different for different states (it even could accommodate the spillover rationale alluded to earlier). At the margin, however, states would be spending 100 percent their own pesos on all spending areas.

The United States' experience with shared-cost grants a few decades ago suggests another degree of flexibility. The federal government provided cost-sharing grants for highway construction, where the degree of sharing incorporated considerations relating to the states' fiscal capacities and the costs per mile of highway construction (mountain states required more than plains states, for example). In effect, this brought both fiscal capacity and fiscal needs into the design of conditional grants.

Canada's experience with conditional grants presents another perspective. In the 1950s and 1960s, when the Canadian welfare state was in its embryonic stage, the federal government provided generous shared-cost programs in areas such as welfare, health, and education. As these programs became established, they developed receptive and demanding citizens in their respective provinces and came to be viewed as an integral part of the Canadian social contract. As this occurred, the Canadian federal government could and did gradually abandon the shared-cost and highly conditional nature of these grants and converted them into block-funded unconditional programs, with the important proviso that the provinces agreed to a set of pan-Canadian principles in these expenditure areas. In turn, this suggests that there may be an optimal evolution of conditional transfers. Previously centralized federations that embark on a process of decentralization will probably have to resort, initially, to highly conditional grants. However, as the federation evolves and as citizens come to view these conditional-grant programs as entitlements, the federation can gradually eliminate the conditional nature of these transfers and use instead a set of mutually agreed operating principles. In either case the result is greater subnational autonomy.

Since Mexico is only beginning the process of meaningful decentralization, some of the federal-state transfers will probably have to be conditional. But even at this early stage of decentralization, the design and implementation of conditional grants can be flexible enough to accommodate both conditionality and an important degree of subnational autonomy.

Horizontal and Vertical Transfers in Practice

Different federations combine transfers in quite different ways. Canada is one of the few countries that compartmentalizes these two types of transfers. The federal government first overlays an equalization system on the taxation capacities of the various provinces. This is "pure" horizontal equalization since the equalization payments only go to low-fiscal-capacity provinces. Then, with all provinces thus brought up to the equalization standard, the vertical transfers are designed to be equal in per capita terms, subject to a set of pan-Canadian principles on which Ottawa and the provinces have jointly agreed.

The Australian system is quite different. Because the degree of subnational fiscal imbalance is so large, the unconditional financial adjustment grants overseen by the Commonwealth Grants Commission (CGC) incorporate both horizontal and vertical fiscal-balance concerns. That is, *all* Australian states receive CGC grants. One could interpret the per capita level of grants going to the "richest" state, Victoria, as embodying the all-state level of vertical transfers and the additional grants going to the other states as embodying the horizontal component of the grants. Beyond this, Australia has a set of specific-purpose payments (conditional grants) that, in the aggregate, exceed the unconditional CGC grants. The continuing importance of conditional grants in Australia reflects the more centralized nature of their federation (or, analytically equivalent, citizen preferences do not differ across states and that the conditions effectively capture these preferences).

The German system is different again. The shared taxes are distributed to the länder according to criteria that embody derivation, equal-per-capita, and equalization principles. The resulting differences in fiscal capacity are then subject to an overarching interländer revenue-sharing pool; rich länder contribute to the pool, and poor länder draw revenues from the pool. This revenue-sharing pool is an exercise in pure horizontal equalization.

No magic formula applies to all federations. Moreover, there is ample evidence that the approaches to intergovernmental transfers chosen are far from arbitrary; they find their rationale and underlying logic in the deeper political values of their respective federations.

Debt and Borrowing

Two levels of policy influence borrowing and debt management by state and municipal governments—the policies of subnational governments themselves and the policies of the national government (or the state for municipal government) that set the constraints and incentives for the local governments.

The proper policies for the subnational governments are straightforward—they should only borrow to fund an activity (investment) that will yield a rate of return to society above the interest rate and sufficient to service the debt. A project that generates its own direct revenue is most likely to meet these criteria, but it can also be met in an investment like local roads or school construction that is associated with growth of economic activity and tax revenue adequate to cover the debt service.

Since the principal of a loan typically comes due before the full benefits of the investment arrive, the stock of debt should be kept small enough so that debt service (interest plus amortization that is not scheduled for refinancing) is less than the current balance before debt service. Alternatively, amortization not scheduled for refinancing should be less than the current account balance.

To these minimum criteria for borrowing one must add a safety factor, so that even in the face of adverse shocks the local government will maintain its fiscal independence and thus meet the conditions for market-preserving federalism. Then, even after paying scheduled amortization, there is enough current surplus left to fund part of the investment program, that is, without borrowing for all investment. These rules apply to any level of government.

In a perfect world, decisionmakers would want to do this to maximize social welfare, or voters could discipline them to act this way. In the real world, there are many problems of information, and decisionmakers have short time horizons, so governments at all levels often borrow in excess of these rules. For local governments, there is an extra complication in that if they overborrow, a higher level of government may bail them out, in effect rewarding their imprudence with extra resources. In other cases, the higher level of government may impose spending requirements on them or limit their revenue options, making unsustainable deficits almost unavoidable and giving the local government a reason to expect a bailout from above. To deal with such problems, the higher level of government may establish and enforce rules that prevent the local government from borrowing imprudently. These policies are our central concern here.

Research on Latin America and the rest of the world indicates several conditions that are needed to achieve sound management of debt and borrowing by states and municipalities (see table 1.2).

Table 1.2 Institutional Arrangements to Set and Keep Hard Budget Constraints on States

Constraint	Institutional arrangement
Hard budget constraint from the central government to subnational governments	• Rule-based transfers • Firm allocation of spending responsibilities
Constraints on borrowing	• Ex ante constraints • Ex post consequences and resulting incentives • Enforcement of payment by subnational governments • Enforcement of losses on banks with bad loans to uncreditworthy subnational governments, via bank regulation • Independence of Central Bank and regulators
Autonomy of subnational government to reduce costs and raise own revenue	• Ability to control spending and costs • Ability to increase tax rates and improve enforcement
Transparency: timely disclosure of information to improve accountability of policymakers	• Regular publication of data • External auditing • Legislative oversight

Source: Dillinger, Perry, and Webb 2000.

HARD BUDGET CONSTRAINTS. First and foremost, a firm allocation of expenditure responsibilities is critical for establishing a hard budget constraint for subnational governments. If the central government can effectively delegate functions to subnational governments to go along with the delegation of revenue sources, central spending and deficits are more likely to be contained. If this is not the case—because, for example, the constitution or the law mandates resource transfers without allocating equivalent responsibilities—the central government can find itself with a constitutional obligation and political expectation to continue providing some services, even after revenues or tax bases have been turned over to subnational governments with the understanding that they will do the task. Or it may have to resume spending on functions when subnational governments experience a fiscal failure.

Basing transfers exclusively on clear rules is the other necessary ingredient for a hard budget constraint. Wherever there is recourse to significant discretionary transfers, including matching grants, subnational governments will have an incentive to overspend in the expectation that they can get a larger transfer.

BORROWING CONSTRAINTS. Although tax and spending policies create fiscal pressures, whether they cause problems for macroeconomic management depends on whether the subnational governments face hard limits on their ability to borrow or to spend more (Ter-Minassian and Craig 1997). Unsustainable deficits are less likely if the central government controls subnational borrowing ex ante. But how to enforce this in practice is not always clear when the subnational governments have considerable political autonomy. Pseudo-strict controls could make matters worse if central government approval creates the impression, and perhaps the self-fulfilling expectation, that the central government has extended a guarantee. The best controls would mimic the requirements of prudent lenders.

To run deficits, subnational government must find a source of financing, which potentially includes contractual borrowing from private foreign or domestic banks (especially banks owned by subnational governments), issuance of domestic or foreign bonds, and the running up of arrears to suppliers and personnel. A creditor and the subnational government would only agree to finance unsustainable deficits if both sides expected to gain, most likely through some sort of federal bailout. The bailout can take many forms, including allowing the financial system (implicitly insured by the government) to count as an asset a subnational government debt that is not being serviced. Unsustainable deficits are also less likely if the central government credibly commits not to have bailouts, prohibiting explicit bailouts and forcing subnational governments to service their debts, and if regulators force creditors to accept the losses implied by any failure of subnational governments to service debt. It is still an open question whether ex ante regulation or ex post enforcement of debt service is more effective in preventing excessive subnational government borrowing. Although conflicts are also possible, both can work together and complement each other. Ex ante controls keep the problem from growing so big that it threatens the entire system, and ex post consequences increase appropriately the concerns of individual borrowers and lenders.

Financing from the central bank often is what loosens the budget constraint for subnational governments, either directly by discounting subnational debt or indirectly by easing the national government's budget constraint or allowing commercial banks to roll over bad subnational debts. Unsustainable deficits are less likely when the central bank (and the bank supervisory agency) is more autonomous and has a strong anti-inflation mandate.

Subnational governments may also accumulate excessive contingent liabilities. This is more likely to happen wherever subnational governments are allowed to run their own pension regimes, when they own banks, and when they make concessions to the private sector without adequate regulation from above.

AUTONOMY TO REDUCE COSTS AND RAISE REVENUE. The third group of institutions relates to the capacity and autonomy of subnational governments to stay within the budget constraint. The first element is *expenditure autonomy*. If subnational governments do not have autonomy over their expenditure, there is no fiscal decentralization and no macro fiscal problem likely to come of it. Giving subnational governments autonomy over spending is, of course, the way in which decentralization can improve efficiency in matching the needs and desires of a diverse population. But to live within a sound budget constraint, subnational governments must have authority to control their costs. Too often central governments keep for themselves decisions (such as determining the wages of teachers and doctors) that critically affect the costs of subnational governments, and a liberal decision may throw subnational governments into deficit. In particular, subnational governments must have the authority to spend less, particularly to cut personnel, salaries, and pension benefits, collectively the largest single item of subnational expenditure, in order to be able to adjust to shocks or contribute to needed fiscal retrenchment. If central rules constrain this authority, it is more difficult to reduce deficits, and expectations of a central government bailout are higher. Thus unsustainable deficits should be less likely if subnational governments have authority to cut their costs.

With fiscal decentralization, subnational governments usually obtain certain tax bases, but for reasons of politics, equity, and efficiency, these bases rarely cover all their expenses. Subnational governments always receive significant federal transfers. It is commonly believed that subnational governments will have smaller deficits if they rely more on their own tax bases (and have the power to change tax rates on the margin), because then they have the ability to adjust to shocks by increasing revenue. In addition, relying on one's own resources may strengthen the incentives to control spending. Unsustainable overall public sector deficits are less likely if subnational governments raise much of their own revenue and have enough flexibility to change rates or impose new taxes.

TRANSPARENCY. Although increases in competitive democracy accelerated the process of decentralization, sometimes to a pace that is problematic, democracy can contribute to responsible macroeconomic management, as well as to other worthy ends. When congress and opposition parties have access to accurate and up-to-date information about public sector finances, they become effective watchdogs and bring the law and public opinion on the side of good management. It is thus important that subnational governments publish information on fiscal balances, revenues sources, expenditure composition, borrowing, debt structure, and contingent liabilities. A federal government can impose such requirements on subnational governments. This works well administratively because the federal government is giving the states transfers, which can be made conditional on transparency and reporting requirements. Politically it works, as well, when there is some balance of parties at the federal level, and each side wants to be sure that the other side cannot profit from lack of transparency in the subnational governments. In this context, transparency not only creates pressures for good fiscal management but also acts in a virtuous circle with political competition.

Interlinkages

While this chapter has dealt separately with the areas of spending, taxes, transfers and borrowing, in practice they are all closely linked. For example, states can only control their debt if they can control spending and/or borrowing. Further, a federation can maintain a tough budget constraint in its transfers to states only if state fiscal problems do not threaten the nation's financial system or do not result in politically unacceptable shortfalls in payments to service providers, like teachers. Or the dissatisfaction of a state with the tax transfers plan can lead it to threaten to withdraw from the fiscal pact if the government does not agree to increase transfers or pay for some expenditures that are normally the state's responsibility. Reforms to any part of the system must thus take account of the rest of the system and often must be accompanied by other reforms.

Appendix

Intergovernmental Transfers in Developed Federations

All federations have a constitution that allocates powers on a self-rule, shared-rule basis. Beyond this, some federations are highly decentralized (Canada), while others are highly centralized (Germany, Australia). Some are *legislative federalisms*, where subnational governments have substantial legislative powers especially with respect to expenditures (Canada, Australia, the United States). Germany, however, is a model of an *administrative federalism* because virtually all legislative power rests with the center and almost all implementation and administration is the responsibility of the länder.

All federal systems have to address both vertical and horizontal fiscal balance, although the United States, alone among federal systems, has no program of equalization directed toward ameliorating horizontal balances across subnational governments. Accommodating these fiscal imbalances falls to the system of intergovernmental transfers. In this sense, intergovernmental grants are the residual component of the expenditure, tax, and transfer assignment nexus, and the nature of these transfers varies markedly from federation to federation. Nonetheless, the nature and magnitude of, and incentives within, the system of intergovernmental transfers in each of these federal systems resonate closely with the underlying nature of the federation itself. Far from being merely a residual component of fiscal federalism, the transfer system tends to embody the values and norms of the citizen-government and intergovernmental relationship consistent with the federation's social and political contract. To be sure, causation may run both ways. If grants are unconditional, the balance of power tilts toward subnational governments, and vice versa. Decentralized federations may dictate that most grants be unconditional.

Phrased differently, the design of intergovernmental grants is not incidental to the underlying social and economic nature of the federation itself. This appendix examines intergovernmental transfers in a comparative federalism context, beginning with the Commonwealth of Australia and then turning to Germany, Canada, and the United States.

Australia

Australia is not only a highly centralized federation but also a highly egalitarian nation. For example, welfare payments are designed and delivered from Canberra and, as a result, are identical across the country, in sharp contrast to, say, Canada, where responsibility for welfare is provincial. Wage grids are also essentially uniform across Australia—university professors are on the same wage grid whether they teach in Perth, Sydney, or Launceston.

More relevant for our purposes, the Australian states do not have effective access to broad-based taxes (income taxes, sales taxes), and the taxes that they do levy are being eroded by a combination of global forces and high-court decisions (Courchene 1999). The Australian states are highly dependent on transfers: "Australia has by far the highest degree of vertical fiscal imbalance among the major federations in the world" (Walsh 1996, p. 115). However, the system of intergovernmental grants complements Australia's centralization and uniformity nicely. First, more than half of the cash transfers to the states are in the form of conditional grants (specific-purpose transfers, in the Australian context), which, in turn, enhances both centralization and uniformity. Second, Australia's approach to removing horizontal fiscal balances—the financial adjustment grants monitored by the Commonwealth Grants Commission—is the most comprehensive among federal nations. The fiscal equalization principle that guides the Commonwealth Grants Commission is as follows: "Each State should be given the capacity to provide the average standard of State-type public services, assuming it does so at an average level of operational efficiency and makes an average effort to raise revenues from its own sources" (Commonwealth Grants Commission 1995, p. 1).

Operationally, the equalization system works as follows. First, the 19 state revenues (at assumed common tax rates) are equalized both upward and downward to the all-state average. With revenues fully equalized, the 40 or so expenditure categories are then subject to upward and downward equalization to ensure that each state can deliver the average expenditure bundle at an "average level of operational efficiency." The end result of these calculations is a series of per capita "relativities"—that is, revenue- or needs-adjusted ratios relative to the national average. Hence, during 1994–95, for example, Victoria's relativity was 0.85 and Tasmania's was 1.54—that is, Victoria would receive 85 percent of its population share of overall Commonwealth Grants Commission grants, and Tasmania would receive 154 percent. This is *full* revenue and expenditure (needs) equalization.

The Commonwealth Grants Commission is the key institution in Australian fiscal federalism. Its operations are open and increasingly transparent, which ensures that the resulting "relativities" are accepted by all Australians. Beyond this, Australia has an effective process of state-commonwealth coordination to ensure overall macroeconomic cooperation and to preserve and promote the internal socioeconomic union (Courchene 1999).

Thus Australia has latched onto a highly egalitarian equalization program and, more generally, a system of intergovernmental transfers that meshes well with the underlying homogeneity and egalitarian nature of its federation.

Germany

The German federation is also highly centralized, but in a way quite different from Australia. Designated as an administrative federalism, all major tax rates are set centrally, with no variations allowed at the länder level (although the länder administer or collect these revenues). Apart from a relatively minor range of länder and municipal taxes (taxes on property, cars, and beer as well as fees of various sorts), most länder revenue comes from revenue-sharing arrangements with the center. The major shared or joint taxes include corporate and personal income taxes, capital taxes, and the value added tax. Some of this revenue sharing follows the principle of derivation, some of it is equal per capita, and some (especially for the new länder) is based on equalizing principles.

Beyond revenue sharing, there is a second and overarching tier—an interländer revenue-sharing pool. The rich länder contribute a share of their per capita revenues in excess of 102 percent of the national average (70 percent of per capita revenues between 102 and 110 percent of the national average and 100 percent of any revenues beyond this). The poorer länder then draw from this pool to bring them up to at least 95 percent of the all-länder average. The guiding principle underlying intergovernmental transfers in Germany is the constitutional provision assuring "the uniformity of living conditions." Needs are also taken into account in operations of the interländer revenue-sharing pool, meaning that the "standardized" revenues for purposes of the pool incorporate expenditure needs to a degree. Other things being equal, länder with large cities or dense populations are deemed to require more revenue and vice versa. (This is in sharp contrast to the Australian approach in which population scarcity is deemed to require greater expenditures, which, in turn, suggests that the approach to needs equalization in federations is rather subjective).

The key institutional/constitutional feature of German fiscal federalism is the upper house or Bundesrat, which is a house of the länder in that it is made up of direct representatives of the länder governments. All legislation pertaining to the länder, including the tax rates on shared taxes, must receive the imprimatur of the Bundesrat.

Canada

In contrast to Germany, the Canadian provinces have no formal role in the operations of the central government: members of the Senate (upper chamber) are appointed for "life" (up to age 75) by the government of the day, and, as a result, the Senate is not a federal chamber in a meaningful sense. Provincial concerns and issues tend to be articulated through the provincial legislatures and their premiers. Canada also differs from the typical federation in that there is an explicit and extensive listing of provincial powers under the constitution. Beyond this, other features of the Canadian federation propel it toward decentralization. The province of Quebec, with one-quarter of Canada's population, is linguistically, culturally, and institutionally distinct. Quebec has long advocated states' rights, which in turn has moved Canada toward not only greater decentralization, but greater asymmetry as well. (Quebec has its own, separate, personal income tax, whereas the rest of the provinces piggyback their tax rates on Ottawa's personal income tax system.)

The Canadian federation is highly decentralized on both the expenditure and tax fronts. For example, the provinces levy their own personal and corporate taxes and their own sales taxes (except for Alberta), and, in general, control the natural resources within their borders. Hence, the Canadian system of intergovernmental transfers accommodates this decentralization.

Focusing first on Canada's equalization program, the constitutional principle is less comprehensive than that in Australia: Parliament and the government of Canada are committed to making equalization payments to ensure that provincial governments have sufficient revenues to provide reasonably comparable levels of public services at reasonably comparable tax rates. Canada does this by providing equalization payments to the poorer provinces in order to bring their per capita revenues up to the so-called five-province standard (close to the national-average standard). Unlike Australia, however, the revenues of rich provinces are not "leveled down" to this five-province average, nor does Canada equalize for needs on the expenditure side. These equalization payments are wholly unconditional.

More interesting, perhaps, is the Canadian approach to vertical imbalance. When introduced in the 1950s and 1960s, vertical balance grants were of the shared-cost, conditional variety. Over time, as the programs that they were associated with became established in the various provinces, the federal government relaxed the conditionality. Currently, all vertical transfers are rolled into a single block fund, and the moneys can be spent where the provinces wish. However, a national set of social policy principles continues to guide *all* provincial spending, especially in the area of health.

Because of the decentralized nature of the Canadian federation, Canada has had to engage in creative measures to preserve and promote its socioeconomic union. For example, all provinces adhere to a mechanism that allocates corporate revenues across provinces for those enterprises that operate nationally. And recently (February 1999), the provinces and Ottawa have signed a framework to improve Canada's social union. The key coordinating institution has been what federal scholars refer to as executive federalism: the frequent meetings (more than 1,000 annually at last count) of federal and provincial officials (or executives) in areas of mutual concern and interest. More recently, the provinces have mounted their own national institution, the annual premiers conference, which is moving the provinces toward addressing some pan-Canadian goals. Nonetheless, the internal Canadian socioeconomic union remains less fully developed than that of Australia, for example.

The United States

The federal system in the United States probably suffers least from vertical fiscal imbalance, in part because U.S. states engage in a narrower range of activities than do Canadian provinces, for example. What is most fascinating about the U.S. approach to intergovernmental transfers is the *absence* of a formal revenue equalization program, although, on the expenditure side (for example, with respect to defense), regional considerations enter into allocation decisions, as they do in other federations.

One view of the U.S. approach is that Americans simply ignore any horizontal fiscal imbalances. Another view is that there really are no horizontal imbalances since any meaningful differences in per capita revenue across states are capitalized in property values, wages, and rents. Wallace Oates, one of the foremost scholars of U.S. federalism, takes this latter view:

> [E]xisting fiscal differentials (e.g., varying levels of taxable capacity) across jurisdictions will tend, to some extent at least, to be capitalized into property values so that those who choose to live in fiscally disadvantaged areas are compensated by having to pay lower land rents; from this perspective, horizontal equity under a federal system is, to some degree, self-policing. The need for equalizing grants in a federation is thus questionable. Perhaps it is best to regard their role as a matter of "taste" (Oates 1983, pp. 95–96).

It may well be that assuming full (or 100 percent) capitalization of differences in fiscal capacity is going too far. But so does the existing equalization literature, which, in general, assumes *zero* capitalization.

However one comes out on this issue, it is clear that the U.S. intergovernmental fiscal relations (or, rather, the lack of such) accord well with the laissez-faire U.S. constitutional rhetoric of "life, liberty, and the pursuit of happiness."

Recapitulation

Intergovernmental transfer arrangements are anything but arbitrary. Indeed, they complement the existing tax and expenditure allocation in a manner that integrates overall fiscal federalism in directions consistent with the implicit or explicit values and norms of the respective federal system. They are, in effect, part and parcel of the constitutional-institutional machinery that reflects and embodies the deeper societal values of the federation.

To be sure, the intergovernmental arrangements in the various federations represent the status quo. And in most of these federations, challenges are emerging on the transfer-intergovernmental front. For example, the Australians are about to introduce a value added tax, the proceeds of which will be allocated to the states. Whether this will be on a derivation basis or equal-per-capita basis, for example, is not clear. The likelihood is that it will be run through the Commonwealth Grants Commission. In Germany, the richer länder, such as Bavaria and Baden-Wurtemberg, are upset that they retain too small a share of any revenue increase they generate and have taken the equalization program to the German constitutional court. In Canada, the richer provinces are complaining that the federal government is mounting too many poor-province preferences in programs other than equalization. And so on.

This is to be expected in the best of times. But with the pervasiveness of the forces of globalization and the revolution in knowledge and information, all federations are examining their fiscal federalism arrangements in general and the nature of intergovernmental transfers in particular. What this means is that the arrangements (expenditure assignment, tax assignment, and intergovernmental transfers) will, on a continual basis, have to find their appropriate role in the deeper political logic and interests of the federation as it evolves. But what the comparative experience reveals is that the nature, magnitude, and incentives within the system of intergovernmental transfers, independent of the tax and expenditure assignment, can play a critical role in ensuring that the federal-state interface can accommodate the direction and values that the federation itself is pursuing.

Implications for Mexico

What implications does the role of intergovernmental transfers in developed federal systems hold for Mexico in its ongoing decentralization? Perhaps the most important lesson is that transfer arrangements can be designed to accommodate and integrate a wide range of expenditure and tax assignments in ways that are consistent with the overall equity and efficiency goals of the federation. For example, at the margin the system of transfers can embody incentives that encourage further decentralization. Or they can be tailored to produce the desired degree of fiscal equality across the Mexican states. Or by creative use of conditionality, they can ensure that all citizens have access to those public goods and services that ought to attend Mexican citizenship.

Beyond this, the transfer system can be designed in ways that will accommodate a smooth transition between the current status quo in tax and expenditure assignment and the longer-term evolution of subnational expenditure and tax devolution. To be sure, there is a sense in which intergovernmental transfers are, at any point in time, the necessary residual element in the interplay of subnational tax and expenditure assignment. However, and more important, transfers can do much more than merely bridge any vertical and horizontal imbalances resulting from the mix of subnational expenditure and taxation: they can and should ensure that the entire federal-state fiscal interface is in line with the deeper political and social logic of the federation. In this important sense, they are much more than a residual element in fiscal federalism.

2

Historical Forces: Geographical and Political

Thomas Courchene, Alberto Díaz-Cayeros, and Steven B. Webb

FISCAL FEDERALISM IS EVOLVING in Mexico. Expenditures have been significantly devolved over the past few years, and the associated financing has been incorporated in myriad conditional grant programs. Although the pattern of decentralization in Mexico is similar to that observed in other Latin American countries, the speed and depth of the process have gone beyond most expectations (Garman, Haggard, and Willis 1999).

How did the system of fiscal coordination and revenue-sharing agreements between states and federation in Mexico emerge? Why was such a highly centralized fiscal arrangement reached, notwithstanding centripetal forces for state autonomy and a long tradition of resistance in the "provinces" to imposition from the center? Contrary to conventional accounts, fiscal centralization in Mexico was not a necessary outcome, but a contingent result of political processes. Moreover, the specific revenue-sharing agreements between states and the federal government can be understood as consequences of incremental reforms, rather than of an overarching grand design. Although political actors in the first half of the century well understood the advantages of a certain degree of fiscal decentralization, they were unwilling to give up extensive fiscal authority.

Federal Concentration of Revenue

The basic dilemma in the Mexican political economy at the beginning of the twentieth century was the prevalence of fragmented markets and a weak tax authority, both state and federal. Local taxation was chaotic. Given the financial disarray of both local and the federal governments, public expenditure was mostly financed by debt and monetary emission. The *alca-bala*—the colonial tax on the movement of goods across jurisdictions which

123

inhibited the extension of markets in the nineteenth century—haunted the regional economies of Mexico. National and regional politicians in Mexico attempted to improve the regional flow of market transactions within the federal system, seeking to rationalize and unify state tax systems into a coherent national tax system and a system of tax settlement between levels of government. They met in National Tax Conventions in 1925, 1933, and 1947 for this purpose.

Alberto J. Pani, the charismatic federal finance minister who convoked governors to the First National Tax Convention, expressed the situation in 1925 this way:

> Each state establishes its own revenue system, the Federal Government maintains its own, and since the objects taxed happen to be the same, since there is no concrete and defined plan for the limitation between the federal capacity and the local capacities to create taxes, since states often rival each other leading into true economic wars and creating, in the name of a sales tax; e.g., true local import duties in order to sustain internal production taxes that are incorrectly established; the tax becomes increasingly burdensome due to the multiplicity of rates, fines and penalties, increasing the complexity of the system and increasing in a disproportionate and unjustifiable manner the deadweight expenses for revenue collection, surveillance and administration.[1]

While the first two National Tax Conventions made little progress, the Third in 1947 envisioned a centralized fiscal system that (a) local governments would rely on as exclusive sources of revenue on the property tax and some other minor taxes, eliminating their taxes on trade and industry; (b) states would receive revenue shares from federal excises on natural resources, alcoholic beverages, matches, and so forth, and they would be guaranteed 25 percent of any additional revenue collected through those federal taxes; (c) a national sales tax would be introduced where the rate would be shared between states and the federal government, but it would be administered as a centralized federal tax; (d) the income tax would become exclusively federal, although states would retain some tax authority over taxes with very low yields on agriculture and livestock; (e) the *contribución federal* would be finally reduced to 5 percent in all states, in order to gradually phase it out during the next years. These proposals were fully accepted by the assembly.

During the second half of the twentieth century the federal government consolidated its fiscal centralization by becoming the only level of government allowed to levy taxes on foreign trade, natural resources (including all oil and mining rights), banks, insurance institutions, electricity, tobacco, gas, matches, alcohol, forestry, and beer (art. 73-XXIX). Although states theoretically still retained the capacity to levy an income tax, payroll taxes, sales taxes, and other taxes not explicitly stated in article 73, in practice the federal government came to monopolize almost all sources of revenue. The federal treasury provided tax revenue shares (*participaciones*) to the states, which increasingly came to constitute the most important source of local government finance.

The system of tax coordination which characterizes the Mexican federal system today was the consequence of a regional compromise struck between the federal and state governments. The compromise required that local politicians delegate financial power to the president, in exchange for sources of patronage through the federal bureaucracies, attractive careers in the federal government, and an active involvement of the federal government in state development. The arrangement took almost two decades to become stable. The solution was achieved through institutional rules and a very peculiar political organization. The configuration of veto players made it self-enforcing, in the sense that local and national players were better off with this arrangement, and therefore willing to abide by it. The loser in this arrangement was federalism.

> [The weakening of the local machines] was coupled with the ever-increasing financial dependence of the formal state governments upon the central authorities, because just as the growing complexities of social and economic life called for greater expenditures by governmental agencies, the national government was busily preempting most of the major sources of tax revenue for itself. This forced the local officers to go to Mexico City, hat in hand, seeking grants from the national government to satisfy the demands of their constituents (Scott 1959; p. 135).

Electoral success compensated the governors for the loss of local financial independence and fiscal initiative, although many Mexicans disapproved of this tradeoff, since it led to an overwhelming federal government (Casanova 1965).

Two parallel developments converged to create the tax system that characterizes intergovernmental relations in Mexico today. The first was the establishment of a complex system of revenue sharing between states and the federal government at the beginning of the 1940s, which gave states unconditional transfers (*participaciones*) out of the collection of revenue from exclusive federal excises. The revenue-sharing system was complicated because it established state shares case by case, on each specific tax. The incorporation of all states into the same national sales tax in 1974 was achieved through what federal financial authorities called a "prudent strategy which quietly but stubbornly achieved its goal" (Secretaría de Hacienda y Crédito Público 1973, p. 6). In contrast with the Tax Conventions, which had been open debates, the changes of the 1970s were decided through closed bilateral negotiations.

The second development was the final implementation of a federal sales tax in 1947 (the *Impuesto Sobre Ingresos Mercantiles*—ISIM), which states could join if they agreed to coordinate their rate with the federal rate. By the early 1970s all states had joined the system, obtaining most of their local tax collection from this tax, in addition to receiving unconditional tax transfers through the revenue-sharing systems.

Both developments—the revenue-sharing system and the unified federal sales tax—came together in 1979 when fiscal relations between states and the federal government were merged into a single system, with the replacement of the ISIM with the Value Added Tax (*Impuesto al Valor Agregado*—IVA) at the federal level: all states would receive unique revenue shares out of federal tax collection, according to previously agreed formulas. This unification meant that local budgets would be financed mostly through unconditional federal transfers (*participaciones*) contained in the revenue sharing agreements. After 1980, state governments depended almost completely on federal revenue transfers.

While every state had been encouraged to join in the federal sales tax, the introduction of the Value Added Tax in 1979 produced a major redistribution of resources among states. On the one hand, the IVA would be collected where value was added, not where sales occurred, since the latter would require that when the tax was paid by the final consumer in one state, there had to be a credit for the tax paid in other states, with a consequent redistribution of where revenue is accrued. On the other hand, the success of the IVA required the elimination of some remaining state-level excises, in order to bring about more horizontal equity among regionally dispersed producers. These issues were addressed through the negotiation of the *Sistema Nacional de Coordinación Fiscal* (SNCF or *Pacto Fiscal*) among states and the federal government, including the Federal District. The arrangement tied *participaciones* to explicit formulas that considered population, education expenditure, revenue collected in the past, and indicators of state performance in tax collection.

The revenue-sharing arrangement of the SNCF was a contract between states and the federal government. There was no constitutional provision that forced states to give up their authority over taxation: states belonged to the system by agreeing to withdraw their own taxes and receive *participaciones* in exchange. Thus, governors retained the legal power to withdraw from the system. When the system was created, governors also signed

administrative collaboration agreements, which involved working closely with federal authorities on issues of federal tax compliance.

The creation of the SNCF was accepted by the states with almost no resistance. This was attributable to the political conditions, the timing of the
reform, and the state of federal finances. The dominance of the party in
office (the PRI) during the late 1970s was overwhelming: President López
Portillo ran unopposed in the 1976 election. The reform was also skillful-
ly timed around the temporal horizons of governors: during 1980 when the
reform would come into effect, most of the incumbent governors would be
just finishing their terms, according to the staggered timing of local elections. Finally, the country was in the midst of an oil boom, bringing the federal government a substantial amount of revenue from the windfall gains
of the nationalized oil company, PEMEX. Since taxation of natural
resources, and oil in particular, was exclusively federal, states were not
directly profiting from the expansion in available resources. They did
receive more resources and projects through *Inversión Pública Federal*, but
those transfers were ultimately controlled by the president and his bureaucracies. The SNCF offered the opportunity for states to reap part of the benefits of the oil boom as unconditional tax transfers, although the arrangement made state governments more dependent on the federal government.

The formulas have been changed frequently ever since. At first the main
ingredient in the formulas was to assure states the same revenue they
were previously collecting from local taxes, to ensure participation of all
states. Later on, the formulas also reflected some measures of the effort at
tax collection, in local taxes, federal IVA collection in each state, or formerly
federal taxes transferred to the state administrations collecting them (namely, the tax on new cars, *Impuesto Sobre Automóbiles Nuevos*, ISAN). This suggests that the system then moved into greater concern for incentive com-
patibility and performance. Since the beginning, the formulas also included
a complementary fund, which attempted to compensate states that were
receiving the least resources. This introduced an equalizing tendency in the
shares, which has been further reinforced in recent years by giving a greater
weight to population factors. (For discussions of the formulas and their
changes, see Chapoy Bonifaz 1992; Arellano 1996; Aguilar 1996; Díaz
Cayeros 1995.)

Thus, the overall pattern through time has been, abstracting from the
subtleties of each individual formula, that at the beginning states received
revenue shares much in line with the revenue they were collecting before-
hand from their own taxes, their rate in the federal ISIM, and their *participaciones*. That meant, in fact, that poorer states had smaller per capita *participaciones* than richer states. It also meant that the oil-producing states
received a disproportionate share of resources, because they had previously

been receiving high *participaciones* on federal oil taxes. However, as formulas have been changed, there has been a slight tendency toward per capita convergence, since poorer states have witnessed larger increases in *participaciones* than richer states, consonant with the larger weight given to population in the calculation of revenue shares (Díaz Cayeros 1995, pp. 94–95).

Rise of Democracy and Opposition Parties

The end of Mexico's hegemonic party system has accompanied democratization from below. This process, although limited at first, has been extended throughout the country. Local political forces have come to question the concentration of resources and authority at the federal level. Political pluralism is driving the decentralization witnessed during the past few years.

The dominance or control of the political system by a single political party intrinsically contradicts fiscal decentralization. From the viewpoint of governance, state and municipal governments are democratically elected in Mexico. To a large extent, the tradition of central control within a single dominant political party led at first to deconcentration—regional administrative units reporting to the center—rather than to decentralization proper, where territorial governments are chosen by and are accountable to the local populace.

Both decentralization and deconcentration have accelerated since the Zedillo administration came to power in December 1994. The impetus for decentralization is the result of the need to address the increasing levels of public debt held by some states and the need to improve efficiency and rationalize service delivery in key sectors, such as social welfare, education, health, and transportation. The Mexican government rightly sees decentralization of these services as the key to more efficient public expenditures. This has come in contradiction, however, to Mexico's long tradition of centralization and the federal government's de facto control of the tax system. This has added to the confusion about what is an appropriate strategy for decentralization and has had a direct impact on decentralization policy. The lack of a clear vision for sectoral policies, such as the final direction of education and health reform, has added to the state of flux of fiscal decentralization in Mexico.

Undoubtedly, the two most important events in Mexico's recent political history are (a) the winning of governorships by opposition parties since 1989, and (b) the loss of the PRI's majority in the federal Chamber of Deputies in 1997. Both of these events have affected the political processes and debates over Mexican federalism. Baja California was the first state governorship to be won by an opposition party (Partido Acción Nacional, PAN). Other PAN victories followed in Chihuahua, Guanajuato, and Jalisco. As of the beginning of 1999, the PAN controlled five governorships

(Aguascalientes, Baja California, Guanajuato, Jalisco, and Querétaro), while the other major opposition party, the Partido de la Revolución Democrática (PRD) controlled two more (Baja California Sur and Zacatecas) plus the Federal District. At the municipal level, by the end of 1997, opposition parties controlled 28 percent of municipalities, which account for 45 percent of the population. The partisan plurality of local governments has increased the demand for devolving power over resources, to the point where even PRI governors and mayors are advocating decentralization, federalism, and greater local autonomy.

The absence of a single-party majority in the federal Congress' Chamber of Deputies since 1997 is particularly important for federalism. All the major reforms tending toward greater decentralization pursued since then, such as the creation of Ramo 33 and the federal transfers (*aportaciones*) in the Fiscal Coordination Law, have required the support of at least one opposition party, namely the PAN. Any changes that deepen federalism will require partisan coalitions. The lack of a majority party in the lower chamber could continue in the near future no matter which party wins the presidency in 2000. Moreover, since the Senate does not have authority over the federal budget, the most important debates concerning further devolution of expenditure authority and the size, composition, and allocation of transfers will take place in the Chamber of Deputies.

By now, all the major parties are committed to federalism and to deepening the decentralization process. This was not true some years back, when the PAN was alone in advocating for greater local autonomy, consonant with its regionalist strategy of electoral competition and its stress on the subsidiarity principle, that each government responsibility should be assigned to the lowest level practicable. At that time, both the PRI and the PRD were highly centralist in their approach to national problems. But this has changed very quickly, as the presidency has relinquished some of its dominance, governors have become heavier political players, and the PRD has won governorships and seen its electoral support spread beyond Mexico City. By 1999 the most important contenders for the presidency had all been governors: Cuauhtémoc Cárdenas (Michoacán and the Federal District), Vicente Fox (Guanajuato), Roberto Madrazo (Tabasco), Manuel Bartlett (Puebla), and Francisco Labastida (Sinaloa).

Transfer-Led Decentralization

In the last ten years Mexico has rapidly decentralized public expenditures, quickly reaching almost the extent of the other large federations of Latin America—Argentina and Brazil—which have a long tradition of decentralization. Figure 2.1 shows this decentralization as a movement out along the x-axis, but the closeness to the x-axis also shows the small extent to

Figure 2.1. Subnational Tax and Spending Shares in Argentina, Brazil, and Mexico (Shares of GDP)

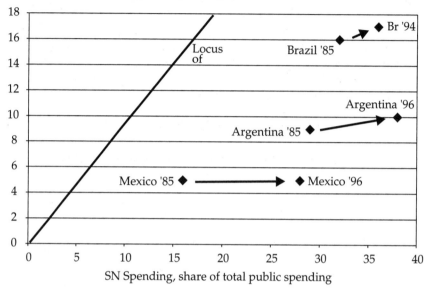

Source: IMF, *Government Financial Statistics;* World Bank estimates.

which the subnational expenditures are financed through their own revenues. The vertical distance from the diagonal line, the locus of fiscal balance along which taxes would equal spending, shows the dependence on transfers (and deficits). The great increase of subnational spending in Mexico over the past 12 years has all been accompanied by increases of transfers, with earmarking for broad sectoral purposes, as Chapters 3 and 5 describe in more detail. Tax authority of states and municipalities has not increased along with expanding responsibilities, and the rules for transfers have not provided incentives to intensify collection efforts. So states in Mexico depend much more heavily on transfers than in Argentina and Brazil.

History and politics explain this pattern. The first wave of decentralization in the late 1980s and early 1990s came right after the culmination of the centralization of taxes described above. Decentralization was at first really deconcentration, with the center delegating spending and responsibility, but keeping control over the priorities for spending. A prime channel for this control was the earmarking and conditions on transfers, control that would be lost if states were raising most of their own money. So the center did not delegate tax authority, and the states had little interest in trying to tax more, because it was easier to go to the federal executive for transfers.

In the second phase of decentralization, after 1997, the opposition parties were flexing their political muscle to get resources for their constituencies. The federal government offered some increased tax authority to the states, but in isolation it did not look politically attractive to the states, especially without any rollback of federal taxation. So the second phase of decentralization also came with transfers, but with much looser earmarking and linkage to expanded responsibilities.

Inequality and Globalization

Two initial conditions set the boundaries for the future evolution of fiscal arrangements in Mexico. The first has long been a feature of Mexican federalism, namely the degree of inequality across states. Understanding this inequality is critical to designing a more decentralized federation. The second is the impact of the North American Free Trade Agreement (NAFTA). As with selected provinces in Canada, some Mexican states are becoming fully integrated economically within the new environment created by NAFTA, and they are demanding more fiscal and economic autonomy than some other provinces can handle (see Courchene 1998 on Canada). Unless an appropriate system for transferring resources and responsibilities is devised, the uneven pattern of regional integration may exacerbate political and regional tensions.

Inequality and Federalism

In the nineteenth century, Alexander von Humboldt, the great political economist, labeled Mexico "the country of inequality." Income inequality in Mexico continues to be very high, even by Latin American standards. According to the 1996 income distribution surveys, the Gini coefficient for household inequality was 0.478, where the bottom 10 percent of the population had 1.8 percent of the income share, while the top 10 percent garnered 42 percent (INEGI 1996). Personal income inequality is also found at the state level, although to a lesser degree. According to the only available survey on income distribution at the state level, carried out by INEGI (the government's statistical office) in 1996, the Gini coefficients of Campeche, Coahuila, the Federal District, Guanajuato, Hidalgo, Jalisco, México, Oaxaca, and Tabasco, where the survey was conducted, ranged from a low of 0.41 for Guanajuato to a high of 0.47 for Campeche (INEGI 1999; an INEGI survey in 1989 indicated a coefficient for Tlaxcala of 0.38).

In 1996, in the wake of the economic crisis, 62 percent of the population was below the poverty line, with 30 percent in extreme poverty. Although growth since then has probably brought the rates down again, resuming the trend for the decade prior to 1994, the problem of poverty remains acute. Much of this poverty is concentrated in the southern states (Trejo and Jones 1998, p. 72). Inequality among households is also reflected in regional inequality.

Figure 2.2 highlights the differences in per capita gross domestic product (GDP) by state, according to the official statistics produced by INEGI for 1993. Some states have income levels similar to those in African countries, while others have income levels roughly at par with those of lower-income European countries. There is clearly a north-south difference in per capita GDP, with northern states generally much better off than southern states. Moreover, the regional distribution of GDP does not fully reflect levels of individual welfare since some southern states have high GDPs (for example, the oil-producing states, Campeche and Tabasco, on the one hand, and tourist havens, Cancún and Quintana Roo, on the other) that are not reflected in correspondingly high levels of welfare of the general population.

Figure 2.3 presents another overview of inequality—the index of illiteracy across Mexican states. Here, the north-south divide is even more strik-

Figure 2.2. Differences in Per Capita Gross Domestic Product (By State)

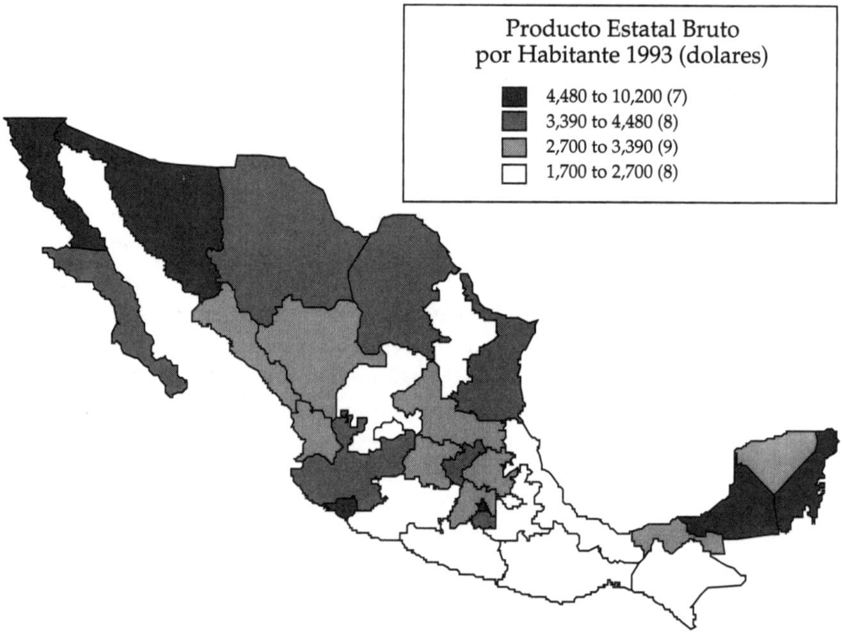

Producto Estatal Bruto
por Habitante 1993 (dolares)

4,480 to 10,200 (7)
3,390 to 4,480 (8)
2,700 to 3,390 (9)
1,700 to 2,700 (8)

Source: Authors' calculations from INEGI data.

Figure 2.3. Index of Illiteracy

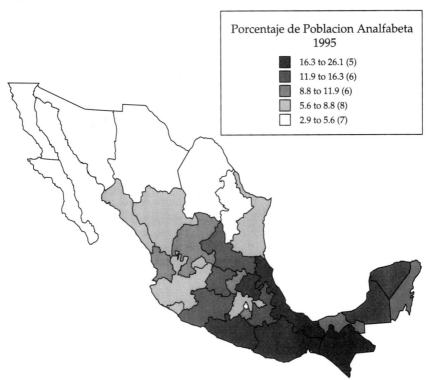

Porcentaje de Poblacion Analfabeta
1995

■	16.3 to 26.1 (5)
■	11.9 to 16.3 (6)
■	8.8 to 11.9 (6)
■	5.6 to 8.8 (8)
□	2.9 to 5.6 (7)

Source: Authors' calculations from INEGI data.

ing, with the differences reflecting, in part, the concentration of indigenous populations in southern states and the fact that the northern states have taken more advantage of the development opportunities from open international markets.

In an era when human capital holds the greatest promise of economic growth and betterment, this evidence of unequal outcomes challenges the claims of some advocates of decentralization that it will improve the responsiveness of the Mexican public sector to the needs of the population as a whole. In particular, these data speak directly to the citizenship rationale for intergovernmental transfers. Any evolution of Mexican decentralization will have to ensure that future expenditure and transfer arrangements provide an acceptable equality of opportunity across states in key public services such as education and health.

Will state per capita GDPs converge, as suggested by the growing literature on economic growth? According to the convergence hypothesis, since poorer states have less capital, any capital they get has a higher marginal return there and they tend to grow faster than richer states, and this will eventually lead to the convergence of income levels at the steady states. Within the neoclassical growth theory, once the steady state has been reached, differences in growth rates are attributable to variations in saving rates. There is also a technology argument for convergence, in that poor states have poorer technology and thus greater opportunity to catch-up by adopting state-of-the-art methods. Against this, some argue that the poor have less access to capital and are less able to access new technology. In its mild form, the convergence hypothesis does not require a reduction in the absolute gap between rich and poor, but it does require that poor states grow faster than rich states.

Table 2.1 and figure 2.4 provide indicators of convergence among Mexican states. (For definitions and the basic findings of this literature, see Barro and Sala-i-Martin 1991, 1995.) The coefficient of variation and the typical log deviation of per capita GDP suggest that regional inequality in Mexico peaked in absolute terms during the mid-1980s and decreased slightly but remained high in the early-1990s. The 1980–85 divergence (in terms of the coefficient of variation in table 2.1) presumably had its origins in the Mexican oil boom. Convergence is evident over the 1985–88 period, but this catch-up still results in a coefficient of variation higher than that for the earlier years. Arguably, the convergence process is running up against the highly unequal levels of education across states, as reflected in figure 2.1 (For a discussion of these issues, see Diaz-Cayeros 1999, Navarrete 1996, and Alzati 1998.)

Table 2.1. σ Convergence in Mexico

Year	Standard deviation (σ)	Coefficient of variation (σ/μ)	Typical log deviation
1970	17.21	.4169	.1762
1975	18.42	.3781	.1618
1980	27.24 (22.52)°	.4628 (.4181)°	.1731
1985	63.94 (23.39)°	.8889 (.3953)°	.2058
1988	34.07 (23.12)°	.5413 (.4108)°	.1804
1993	32.62	.5218	.1901

° estimates in parenthesis refer to measures excluding the outlier observations (Tabasco in 1980 and Campeche in 1985 and 1988).
Source: Authors' calculation with Banco de México and INEGI data.

Figure 2.4. Regional Convergence, 1960–88

Average annual growth (percent)

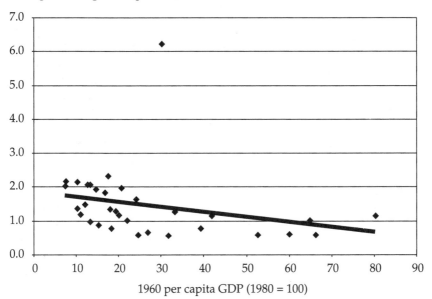

1960 per capita GDP (1980 = 100)

Source: Authors' calculations from INEGI data.

The convergence data can be placed in a longer-term framework. In figure 2.4 (which focuses on the 1960–88 period), the trend line is in the direction of convergence. However, from 1988 to 1996, this convergence effectively disappears (figure 2.5). Arguably, this reflects the move to trade liberalization, introduced on a gradual basis in 1985 and given a substantial boost in 1987. It will be important to extend figures 2.1 through 2.4 to incorporate more of the post-NAFTA (post-1995) data. One would expect the NAFTA environment to favor those states that are better-situated geographically and have better-developed infrastructure and human capital. All of these factors favor the northern states.

There is a high correlation between per capita GDP and a more accurate indicator of human welfare in each state, given by the Foster-Greer-Thorbecke poverty index (see Mogollón 1999). Figure 2.6 reports the Foster-Greer-Thorbecke index for all states calculated with official INEGI wage data for 1995, using a poverty line set at equal to twice the minimum wage and taking into account the depth of poverty. The correlation between the Foster-Greer-Thorbecke and per capita GDP is –0.4965. Except for the outliers of Campeche and Quintana Roo, which have high per capita GDP, but

Figure 2.5. Regional Divergence, 1988–96

Average annual growth (percent)

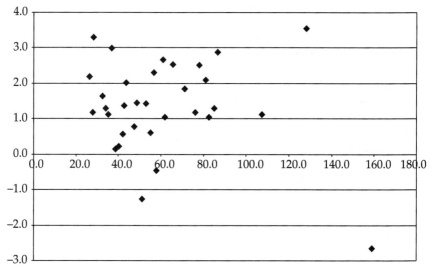

1996 per capita GDP (base 1980=100)

Source: Authors' calculations from INEGI data.

low levels of welfare as measured by poverty, there is a very close link between the two measures.

Thus regional inequality in Mexico is high and will likely remain high. Even if convergence were to take place at a rate of 2 percent, as has happened historically in other countries over the long run (Barro and Sala-i-Matin 1991), it would take more than 60 years for all states to arrive at the same level of welfare (estimates in Mexico find a slightly higher rate of convergence, but over a shorter period; see Navarrete 1996). Such convergence is doubtful without the achievement of similar levels of educational attainment; in the estimates for Mexico, education has sped up the convergence process. The rift between north and south, which is so obvious in the illiteracy indicators, is probably the greatest challenge facing Mexican federalism in the years to come.

North American Integration and Mexican Federalism

The opportunities presented by NAFTA might accrue, initially at least, primarily to the northern Mexican states, but the implications of NAFTA for Mexican federalism will likely go well beyond this economic dimension.

Courchene and Telmer's (1998) study of "region states," focusing on Ontario, Canada, reached some instructive conclusions:

- Ontario's economic future progressively lies in the North American market rather than in the Canadian market. Already, Ontario's exports to the United States are more than twice Ontario's exports to the rest of Canada. Indeed, roughly 45 percent of Ontario's GDP is now exported to the United States.
- Ontario's policies will be increasingly oriented toward making the province a more attractive location for penetrating the NAFTA market.
- When considering its competitive position, Ontario cares much less about tax rates in its sister provinces, (although they are typically higher), than it does about tax rates in competitive areas with which it competes directly, such as Michigan, Ohio, and New York.
- Moreover, Ontario wants to secure enough policy flexibility to ensure its economic future within the new NAFTA environment.

States like Nuevo León, the industrial powerhouse in northern Mexico, will surely fall into this category of North American region states. The only issue is the degree to which they will pursue this role. In fact, according to some preliminary estimates (Diaz Cayeros and Martínez 1999), the degree

Figure 2.6. Regional GDP Versus Poverty Index

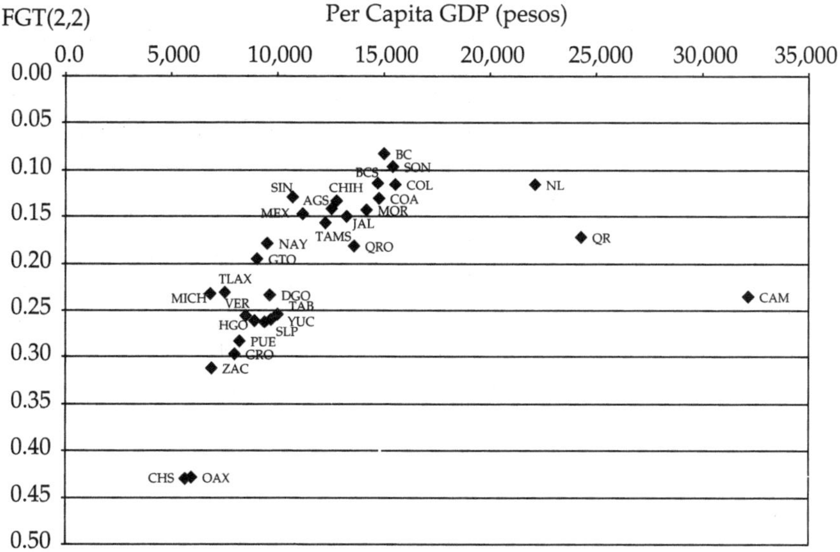

Source: Authors' calculations from INEGI data.

of regional integration of some border states is extremely high: foreign trade (imports plus exports) in Baja California, Chihuahua, and Tamaulipas already represents more than 100 percent of state GDP (171, 137, and 134 percent, respectively). Our view is that these border states, among others, will eventually press for more powers—taxation, expenditure flexibility, and the like. But border and rich states are not the only ones that will press for greater regional integration. Poor states like Oaxaca and Zacatecas already have highly developed networks of migration (both temporary and permanent), while worker remittances constitute a crucial component of the local economy. These pressures will complicate, if not exacerbate, the north-south divide and perhaps cut across unexpected lines. Unless the Fiscal Pact is substantially revised, some of these northern states may consider with increasing seriousness the option of withdrawing from the Pact and reintroducing state taxes.

The relevant point is that the transfer system (along with the rest of fiscal federalism) must be able to accommodate the preferences of these northern states while ensuring the social and political cohesion of all states within the federation. This is a tall order, but one that the transfer system can, in principle at least, deliver. Aspects of these inevitable north-south tensions will be an integral part of the simulations in Chapter 5, showing alternative scenarios of decentralization and future transfers.

3

(Mexico)

O77
O23
H70
H77
H50

Assignment of Spending Responsibilities and Service Delivery

Enrique Cabrero Mendoza and Jorge Martinez-Vazquez

THE MEXICAN CONSTITUTION REFERS to the division of some responsibilities—for example, it proclaims that education is the concurrent responsibility of the federal and state governments—but leaves explicit assignments to sectoral laws, such as those governing education and health. Many of the assignments in Mexico follow the generally accepted rules and principles of expenditure assignment (see table 3.1). The federal government provides public services with a benefit sphere that reaches the entire nation, such as national defense. State governments provide services with an intermediate benefit sphere, such as state roads and secondary hospitals, and municipal governments provide services with local benefit areas, such as sanitation and street lighting.

Two features dominate the present assignment of responsibilities. First, all three levels, especially the federal and state governments, have concurrent obligations for important services such as education, health, and social assistance. Second, few responsibilities are assigned at the municipal level, especially in education and health, where significant benefits could be obtained through decentralization to the lowest decisionmaking unit. The assignments often distinguish three elements of service delivery—regulation or normative design, financing, and implementation or actual delivery. The federal government tends to play a more significant role in normative design and financing, while states and, to a lesser extent, local governments, tend to take the lead for implementation and delivery but not financing.

In Mexico, expenditure responsibilities have been decentralized on a sector-by-sector basis and by unilateral decisions at the federal level. There is no all-encompassing scheme in which state governments engage in concerted agreements with the federal government to take over more responsibilities.

Table 3.1. Mexico's Expenditure Assignment

Expenditure function	Federal government	State governments	Municipal Governments
Defense	• 100 percent		
Foreign Affairs and Economic Relations	• 100 percent		
Labor Policies	• 100 percent		
Monetary and Financial Policy	• 100 percent		
Post and Telecommunications	• Government and private providers		
Education	• Setting policies and norms (SEP); financing through transfers (Ramo 33) • High schools and colleges (concurrent) • Federal technological institutes of higher education • Evaluation and audit of subnational performance • Labor relations and wage-setting • School construction supervision • All education in the Federal District • Approximately half of the technical schools • Most textbook production • Most teacher training	• Financing, implementation, maintenance, and equipment (concurrent) • High schools and state universities • Administration of programs and self-evaluation • Half of the technical schools • School construction (concurrent) • Adult education programs	• Minimal role, school maintenance, and some school construction (concurrent)
Health	• Setting policies and norms (Social Security Administration); financing through transfers (Ramo 33) • Evaluation and audit of subnational performance • Secondary and tertiary hospitals • Labor relations and wage determination • Most capital infrastructure decisions	• Primary care for the rural population and urban poor • Partly responsible for financing • Administration of programs and self-evaluation • Epidemiology and preventive care • Reproductive health	

(table continued on next page)

140

Table 3.1 continued

Expenditure function	Federal government	State governments	Municipal governments
Roads	• Federal highway construction and maintenance • Financing of rural road development	• State feeder roads (construction and maintenance) • Implementation of rural road development • Maintenance of secondary federal roads (with federal funds)	• Local streets
Police and Internal Security	• Federal transfer to the states to strengthen state police • Federal and border police • Special police (concurrent) • Coordination of state and municipal public safety	• Special police (concurrent) • State public order and safety	• Local public order and safety
Social Assistance and Social Security	• Funding through Ramo 33 and Ramo 26	• Implementation of school-lunch programs • Food assistance to the poor • Other programs in coordination with SEDESOL	• Implementing of social infrastructure programs
Culture and Libraries		• Public libraries	
Parks and Recreation	• Biosphere reserves • National monuments • National parks (concurrent)	• National parks (concurrent)	• Local parks
Public Transportation	• Most railways and airport operations have been privatized • Seaport operations being privatized	• Some airports	• Local transportation and transit

(table continued on next page)

Table 3.1 continued

Expenditure function	Federal government	State governments	Municipal governments
Environmental Protection	• National standards • Approval by INE, National Water Commission, the Ministry of Health, and the Ministry of Industry	• States can adopt their own standards	• Land use permits
Water, Sewerage, and Sanitation		• Water supply and sewage (concurrent)	• Garbage collection • Water supply and sewage; many water systems have been privatized (but municipalities retain debt liability) (concurrent)
Housing	• National programs for housing development	Some states have housing agencies	
Price Subsidies	• Market intervention programs (mostly phased out)		
Agriculture and Irrigation	• Funding for state programs in irrigation, water supply, and hydroelectric exploration • National irrigation programs and funding research • Rural development, rural roads, forestry • Funding for research	• Rural development • Extension services • Drilling • Some research	
Other Infrastructure	• Financing through Ramo 33 "social infrastructure" for the poor	• "State infrastructure"	• Cemeteries • Slaughterhouses • Public markets
Tourism	• National programs (concurrent)	• State programs (concurrent)	
Industrial Policy	• Concurrent	• Concurrent	

Source: Information provided by the Mexican authorities, the Constitution, General Education Law, General Health Law, and Amieva-Huerta (1997).

The sector-by-sector approach enables subnational governments to participate in planning and negotiating each step of decentralization, as has occurred in the decentralization of health services. Adequate planning has not always occurred, however, as the decentralization of education illustrates.

Current Assignments

To get an overview of the current assignment of expenditure responsibilities, this section examines the distribution of expenditures at different levels of government, using the data available. While refinements in the data might refine the picture, the information here illustrates well the trends, strengths, and weakness of the Mexican system, providing a departure point for how to improve the policies, and of the publicly available data.

Expenditure Shares and Composition of Expenditures

Table 3.2 presents the share of each level of government in total expenditures during 1989–96; more recent data are not available. These data show that Mexico has undergone decentralized spending over the past ten years.[1] Although the federal government still claims the lion's share of consolidated expenditures, its share decreased from around 84 percent in 1989 to around 75 percent in 1996. (The transfers, *aportaciones*, effectively earmarked for teachers' salaries, are still attributed here to the federal level, where the substantive decisions were made, even though the payments were made at the state level.) The trend was not monotonic. The share of federal expenditures

Table 3.2. Expenditure by Level of Government in Mexico, 1989–96
(Percent)

	Total			Programmables		
Year	Federal	State and federal district	Municipalities	Federal	States	Municipalities
1989	83.9	13.7	2.5	86.2	9.8	4.0
1990	83.2	13.7	3.0	85.5	10.0	4.5
1991	80.4	15.9	3.7	84.3	10.9	4.8
1992	76.8	19.4	3.8	82.9	12.3	4.8
1993	74.1	21.7	4.1	82.5	12.4	5.2
1994	72.5	23.5	4.0	81.7	13.5	4.8
1995	73.9	22.5	3.5	81.1	14.4	4.5
1996	74.8	21.8	3.4	81.2	14.5	4.3

Source: Authors' calculation based on INEGI 1998.

dropped to less than 73 percent in 1994. At the subnational level, the expenditure shares of both state and municipal governments increased over time, but in an unsteady fashion. State governments in particular increased their presence in total expenditures. The states' share was close to 22 percent in 1996, up from 14 percent in 1989. By comparison, municipalities' share was 3.4 percent in 1996, up from 2.5 percent in 1989. Municipalities represented 4 percent of total expenditures in 1993.

The distribution of programmable expenditures tells a similar story (table 3.2). Programmable expenditures exclude expenditures for debt service and financial restructuring as well as revenue sharing and transfers. For 1996 the shares of the federal and municipal governments were higher and the share of state governments was lower for programmable than for total expenditures. However, the share of municipal governments still was only 4.3 percent, while the share of state governments was 14.5 percent.

There is little information on the type of expenditure, in either functional or economic classifications, by level of government. Table 3.3 presents the share of each level of government in total education expenditures as a percentage of gross domestic product (GDP) during 1990–97. The table also shows expenditures in the private sector as a percentage of GDP. Given the central importance of education, decentralization of government expenditures still has a long way to go in Mexico. In 1997, states' share in public education expenditures was only 8.5 percent, or 0.4 percent of GDP. Municipalities' share was around 0.2 percent, or 0.01 percent of GDP.

Table 3.3. National Education Expenditure as a Percentage of GDP, by Source of Funds, 1990–97

Year	1990	1991	1992	1993	1994	1995	1996	1997[†]
Federal (SEP)	2.5	2.9	3.2	3.7	4.0	3.8	3.7	3.8
Federal (other)	0.5	0.5	0.6	0.7	0.6	0.5	0.5	0.5
Federal (subtotal of SEP and other)	3.0	3.4	3.8	4.3	4.6	4.2	4.2	4.3
State	0.7	0.6	0.6	0.6	0.6	0.5	0.4	0.4
Municipality	0.01	0.01	0.01	0.01	0.01	0.01	0.01	0.01
Public (federal, state, and municipal)	3.71	4.01	4.41	4.91	5.21	4.71	4.61	4.71
Private	0.3	0.2	0.3	0.3	0.3	0.2	0.2	0.2
Total	4.03	4.21	4.7	5.25	5.49	4.93	4.8	4.91
Federal education/ federal budget	19.1	21.7	23.9	26.4	26.1	26.7	26.4	24.6

†Estimates based on the document "General Criteria for Economic Policy."
Source: Statistical annex of the *Presidential Report 1997*, reproduced from World Bank (1998a).

During 1981–96, the share of resources at the state level going to current expenditures increased, and the share going to capital expenditures decreased (table 3.4). The same trend was true for municipalities. For both states and municipalities, with many ups and downs, the share of capital expenditures in programmable expenditures moved from one-third or more to around one-fourth or less. The increasing relative importance of current expenditures and decreasing relative importance of capital expenditures seems to have continued in 1997 and 1998.

State Expenditures and Financing

During 1989–96 states received more resources overall but became more dependent on federal sources of revenue (data are from *Instituto Nacional de Estadística Geografía e Informática*, INEGI). Federal revenue sharing (*participaciones*) was without doubt the most important component of state income, reaching approximately 47 percent on average for the period. States' own revenues represented an average of 14 percent for the period.

Table 3.4. Distribution of Programmable Expenditure by Level of Subnational Government in Mexico, 1980–96 (Percent)

	State		Municipal	
Year	Administrative expenses (current)	Public works and development (capital)	Administrative expenses (current)	Public works and development (capital)
1980	30.9	69.1	71.6	28.4
1981	76.2	23.8	66.6	33.4
1982	70.9	29.1	68.6	31.4
1983	65.5	34.5	65.5	34.5
1984	57.4	42.6	60.2	39.8
1985	55.8	44.2	62.4	37.6
1986	63.0	37.0	67.8	32.2
1987	60.9	39.1	69.7	30.3
1988	59.2	40.8	68.9	31.1
1989	61.9	38.1	69.3	30.7
1990	62.6	37.4	67.3	32.7
1991	61.8	38.2	68.7	31.3
1992	65.6	34.4	69.5	30.5
1993	70.4	29.6	69.9	30.1
1994	69.5	30.5	70.4	29.6
1995	72.3	27.7	73.9	26.1
1996	81.3	18.7	74.7	25.3

Note: Excludes the Federal District.
Source: Author's calculations based on INEGI (various years).

While states' own revenues increased in real terms through 1994, they dropped drastically in 1995 during Mexico's fiscal crisis. The significant increase in transfers (Ramo 26) in 1995 and 1996, and Ramo 33 during 1998–99, may have reduced tax effort by the states (figure 3.1).

Moreover, the growth of current expenditure crowded out capital investment. The increases in overall state income led directly to the enlargement of current expenditure. As shown in figure 3.2, the divergence of current and capital investment expenditures started in 1991 and accelerated in 1993. In 1993 and 1996, current expenditures clearly displaced capital investment expenditures.

Municipal Expenditures and Financing

During 1989–97 municipal income grew in real terms. However, the 1994 crisis caused a real decline in both own revenue and revenue sharing (figure 3.1). Nevertheless, in 1996 the trend was reestablished, both in own revenue and in revenue sharing. Since 1995 there has been a significant change,

Figure 3.1. State Revenue from Own Sources, Earmarked Transfers, and Participations (Constant Prices, 1993 = 100)

Miles de 1994 pesos (millions of 1994 pesos)

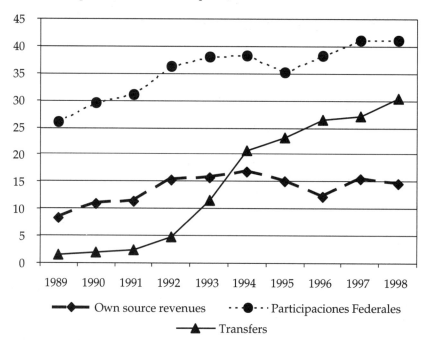

Sources: Based on INEGI's database and CPI from the Bank of Mexico.

Figure 3.2. Composition of State Expenditures, 1989–96 (Constant Prices, 1993 = 100)

Miles de 1994 pesos (millions of 1994 pesos)

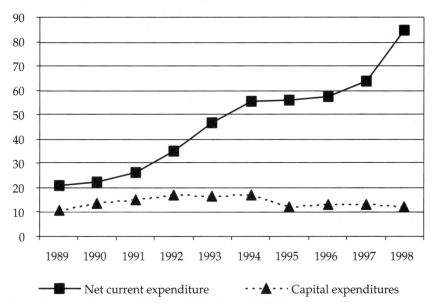

── ■── Net current expenditure   ·· ▲ ··· Capital expenditures

Sources: Based on data from INEGI and INPC, Banco de México.

with the appearance of the decentralized resources for municipalities in Ramo 26 and its successor in Ramo 33, the *Fondo de Aportaciones para la Infraestructura Social Municipal*. The question is how this new source of revenue will affect municipal fiscal effort. It is quite possible that fiscal effort fell in 1998, the year in which municipalities began to receive the direct flow coming from Ramo 33 resources. Unfortunately, there are no detailed nationwide data for 1997 and 1998.

The structure of revenues differs considerably by type of municipality. In 1993 the big urban municipalities (2 percent of all municipalities) counted on 40 percent or less from revenue sharing, the middle urban municipalities (13 percent of the total) counted on between 40 and 70 percent, while the middle and small rural municipalities (85 percent of the total) counted on between 70 and 95 percent. Because of the direct transfers coming from Ramo 26 for 1995–97 and Ramo 33 for 1998, municipalities across-the-board became more dependent on federal resources.

In municipal budgets, increases in real income have been accompanied by steady increases in the share of resources going into current expenditures. These increases may be explained by accumulated shortages in certain inputs, such as personnel, maintenance of infrastructure, or administrative expenditure. There is also the possibility that municipalities have become more wasteful simply because they have expanded the local bureaucracy unnecessarily. Capital investment expenditures declined vis-à-vis current expenditures from 1989 to 1996 (table 3.4). This trend could sharpen in the future due to the presence of direct transfers from Ramo 33 that are earmarked for capital investment. Because of Ramo 33 funds, municipalities will be able to spend more for current expenditures by freeing up funds formerly used for capital investment. However, the level of substitution will be limited by the size of Ramo 33 funds. Given that Ramo 33 is literally multiplying the funds available to municipalities and that much of the funds for municipalities in Ramo 33 are restricted to different forms of capital investment, the relative share of capital expenditures in municipal budgets may be on the rise.

In the case of education, the financial responsibilities decentralized to municipalities correspond strictly to the maintenance of school structures and the provision of basic equipment to schools. Municipal expenditures on public education have been very modest since the decentralization of education started in 1992. Municipal expenditures on education have been between 0.01 and 0.03 percent of GDP, while consolidated government expenditures on education have been between 4.41 and 5.21 percent of GDP. This is true despite the significant need to maintain school structures. A survey conducted in 1995 found that primary schools in 55 percent of the country's municipalities were in urgent need of repair and maintenance, as were junior high schools in 41 percent of municipalities (data obtained from Secretaría de Gobernación, CEDEMUN, and INEGI 1995). Despite the flow of resources from Ramo 26, municipal governments were not able to assume full financial responsibility for maintaining school facilities. It remains to be seen whether transfers under Ramo 33 will change this situation.

Since 1989, municipal governments have received more responsibilities and more funds for social programs and social infrastructure. First, these funds came from Ramo 26, where the federal government had considerable discretion, and in 1998 from the formula-driven Ramo 33. The total flow of resources from Ramo 26 was equivalent to 31 percent of gross municipal spending in 1989, 49 percent in 1992, and 45 percent in 1995 (table 3.5). In some small municipalities, resources coming from Ramo 33 tripled total municipal spending in 1998. In some medium and large municipalities, they covered only 6 to 10 percent of total municipal expenditures. In essence, they altered spending by small municipalities more than they did spending by medium and large ones.

There is little information on how the new Ramo 33 funds are being used. However, an informal survey conducted by the *Secretariat de Desarrollo Social* (SEDESOL) in 156 municipalities provides some data from 1997 that is help-

Table 3.5. Ramo 26 as a Percentage of Municipal Gross Expenditure, 1989–95

Year	Share
1989	30.61
1990	40.18
1991	44.47
1992	48.56
1993	46.07
1994	45.55
1995	44.57

Source: Zedillo (various years).

ful for understanding the subsequent changes in municipal expenditures induced by Ramo 33. In 1997, small rural municipalities spent only 38 percent of social infrastructure funds in the municipal seat of government, which indicates a better distribution of the benefits of the program. However, during 1998, they spent a higher percentage of the funds in the seat of government.

For 1997, FISM funds were spent on drinking water projects (15 percent), roads (13 percent), education (12 percent), and paving and urbanization (16 percent). For 1998, more investment was concentrated in paving and urbanization (37 percent), relegating to second and third place drinking water projects (9 percent) and roads (8 percent).

For 1997, 48 percent of the projects realized with FISM funds were executed by community committees, 35 percent directly by city councils, 12 percent in a combined way, and only 5 percent through contractors. For 1998, 35 percent were executed by community committees, 30 percent by city councils, and 30 percent by contractors.

Thus in the short life of the Ramo 33, it appears that decisions became more centralized, distribution of benefits worsened within municipalities, and potentially less productive use was made of the funds. The time period is too short, however, and the survey too informal, to permit firm conclusions.

Horizontal Disparities

Expenditures per capita across states for 1995–97 show significant horizontal disparities (table 3.6). These disparities seem to decrease over time, but they remain high by international standards.[2] Disparities in expenditures per capita are much more pronounced for capital investment than for total or current expenditures per capita. For 1995, Sonora spent 19 times more per capita than Guanajuato. For 1997, the state with the highest spending per capita, Baja California Sur, spent over five times more than

Table 3.6. Horizontal Disparities in Expenditures Per Capita, 1997

State	Net expenditure Total (millions)	Net expenditure Per capita (thousands)	Current expense Total (millions)	Current expense Per capita (thousands)	Investment Total (millions)	Investment Per capita (thousands)
Aguascalientes	2,501	2.71	2,221	2.41	279	0.30
Baja California	6,563	2.81	6,304	2.70	258	0.11
Baja California Sur	1,845	4.51	1,786	4.36	58	0.14
Campeche	2,956	4.29	2,326	3.38	628	0.91
Chiapas	10,577	2.70	9,716	2.48	861	0.22
Chihuahua	7,856	2.66	7,009	2.38	845	0.29
Coahuila	6,702	2.97	5,618	2.49	1,083	0.48
Colima	1,749	3.41	1,661	3.24	87	0.17
Distrito Federal	39,057	4.57	28,216	3.30	10,840	1.27
Durango	4,025	2.75	3,869	2.64	155	0.11
Guanajuato	5,880	1.26	5,299	1.14	581	0.12
Guerrero	8,570	2.77	7,636	2.47	934	0.30
Hidalgo	5,842	2.64	4,743	2.14	1,099	0.50
Jalisco	13,763	2.17	12,232	1.93	1,530	0.24
México	21,645	1.73	21,002	1.68	643	0.05
Michoacán	8,879	2.20	8,211	2.03	668	0.17
Morelos	3,808	2.45	3,416	2.20	392	0.25
Nayarit	2,940	3.17	2,413	2.60	527	0.57
Nuevo León	9,214	2.45	8,991	2.39	223	0.06
Oaxaca	8,267	2.39	8,044	2.33	223	0.06
Puebla	10,282	2.07	9,459	1.91	824	0.17
Querétaro	3,872	2.89	3,154	2.35	717	0.53
Quintana Roo	2,605	3.23	2,301	2.85	304	0.38
San Luis Potosí	4,987	2.16	4,744	2.06	243	0.11
Sinaloa	6,011	2.39	5,607	2.23	404	0.16
Sonora	6,251	2.84	5,775	2.62	476	0.22
Tabasco	7,396	3.97	6,328	3.40	1,069	0.57
Tamaulipas	8,422	3.18	5,797	2.19	2,625	0.99
Tlaxcala	2,598	2.77	2,518	2.69	80	0.09
Veracruz	18,685	2.60	16,213	2.26	2,472	0.34
Yucatán	4,088	2.49	3,823	2.33	265	0.16
Zacatecas	3,413	2.48	3,307	2.40	106	0.08
Minimum		1.26		1.14		0.05
Maximum		4.57		4.36		1.27
Mean		2.80		2.49		0.32
Standard deviation		0.73		0.59		0.29
Coefficient of variation		0.26		0.24		0.92

Source: INEGI 1998.

the state with the lowest, Guerrero. Moreover, the coefficient of variation in total expenditures per capita dropped from 0.45 for 1995 to 0.36 for 1997. The horizontal disparities in capital expenditures per capita for 1997 show a range of forty-sixfold between the lowest-spending state, Guanajuato, and the highest-spending state, Hidalgo. The coefficient of variation for capital expenditures per capita decreased only slightly from 0.61 in 1995 to 0.58 in 1997.

Not unexpectedly, total net expenditures per capita at the state level vary with the average economic resources available to state residents as measured by gross regional product per capita. In 1995, for each additional $Mex1,000 in per capita gross regional product, per capita expenditures increased around $Mex180 at the state level.[3]

There is little systematic information on expenditures per capita for functional areas. Significant disparities exist across states in expenditures per student in education and expenditures per capita in health. In the case of education, expenditure per student for 1995 was $Mex939 in Estado de Mexico, $Mex1,132 in Jalisco, $Mex1,198 in Guanajuato, $Mex2,569 in Nayarit, $Mex2,836 in Campeche, and $Mex3,535 in Baja California Sur. Poorer states such as Chiapas, Oaxaca, or San Luis Potosí had fewer funds to invest in primary schools or primary health clinics than other states.

These horizontal disparities may be much more significant across municipalities within states than across states. About 95 percent of the inequality in the "Carrera Magisterial" (grade school teacher) test scores is accounted for by within-state differences (World Bank 1998a). The state seats of government seem to receive more resources than other municipalities, especially the rural municipalities. In other words, the level of equalization achieved by federal programs designed for the states seems to be diluted within the states.

Problems with Expenditure Assignments

The current assignment of expenditure responsibilities still has three significant problems—unclear assignments, a dichotomy between investment construction and maintenance responsibility, and unfunded mandates.

Unclear Assignment

Without doubt, the most important problem is that the assignment of expenditure responsibilities in several important areas continues to be ill-defined. These areas include water resources, higher education, roads, and general infrastructure investment. Some responsibilities remain to be devolved pending the design of appropriate legal and regulatory frameworks. The devolution of responsibilities on the revenue side of the budget is tied to changes in revenue assignments and transfers. This is, for instance, the case for agriculture, tourism, and the environment.

Many services, including health, education, roads, and rural development and agriculture, are provided in a mode of shared responsibility rather than independent assignment to a particular level of government. In theory, there is nothing wrong with shared responsibilities. The problem arises when the responsibility of each level of government is poorly delineated. This is less of a problem in health services (but not insignificant) and much more of a problem in education, roads, and rural development and agriculture.

The lack of clarity in assignments is responsible for the inefficient provision and frequent underprovision of some services, because either the state or federal level of government attempts to free ride on the other level. Part of the confusion arises from ambiguity about Mexico's type of federalist system. Should the federal government work only through the states, or should it also work directly with municipalities, even though the constitution prohibits direct transfers? In a pure federalist system, the federal government works exclusively through the states, and the assignment of expenditures between the state and the municipalities is determined by each state.

Confusion about responsibilities also arises from the funding mechanisms used. The use of earmarked transfers reduces the ability of subnational governments to allocate resources as they choose and, in many cases, allows federal agencies to micromanage the activities of subnational governments. This works to the detriment of both subnational autonomy and production efficiency; it also limits the ability of subnational governments to respond to taxpayer preferences.

Dichotomy of Responsibilities for Construction and Maintenance

A persistent problem with the assignment of expenditure responsibilities in Mexico is the separation between the assignment of responsibility for maintenance and operation of infrastructure facilities and the assignment of responsibility for capital investment. For example, in the case of basic education, municipalities maintain school buildings, while federal and state governments carry out the vast majority of capital investments. This dichotomy reduces the expenditures for both maintenance and capital infrastructure, because each level of government can blame the other for not doing its part, and each level expects that the other will ultimately replace or renovate and maintain the property. As a result, neither maintenance nor new investment is adequate, and most of the physical infrastructure is decrepit and poorly maintained.

Unfunded Mandates

Unfunded mandates from the federal government impose expenditures on subnational governments without compensation and seem to be on the rise in Mexico. Without doubt, the most significant mandate on subnational governments is the setting of wages for education and health, which occurs at the federal level through negotiations between the national unions and the Ministries of Education and Health. The negative impact on state finances is especially pronounced in the case of education. There are 1.5 million employees in the state education sector compared with 130,000 employees in the state health sector. Other examples include decisions by the Federal Electoral Institute and the Ministry of the Interior that impose extra expense on state electoral institutes.

Decentralization in Specific Sectors

Decentralization has followed different patterns in the various sectors: education, health, water and sanitation, other infrastructure, agriculture, the environment, roads, social programs, and police and public safety. The first two are the largest and are examined in detail below; the others are briefly reviewed.

Education Sector

Decentralization in education is key to the government's overall decentralization policy (World Bank 1998a). Mexico's education system has an unusually complex structure and history (box 3.1). The division of responsibilities and the educational system in general are regulated in Article 3 of the Constitution and in the General Education Law. The process of decentralization in basic education started in 1992 with the National Agreement to Modernize Basic Education. This agreement was signed by the federal government, the state governments, and the National Union of Workers in Education. The critics of the National Agreement have argued that the process resembles administrative deconcentration rather than true decentralization. This criticism has significant merit.

Under the National Agreement, federal authorities (the Ministry of Public Education) remain in charge of all normative and policymaking functions for setting standards, developing curricula and teaching programs, training teachers, producing most textbooks, and evaluating and monitoring performance. They also provide the states with financial resources to ensure proper coverage and quality of the educational system, and all transfers for education are earmarked for specific purposes. The assignment of responsibilities to the states is general and somewhat vague. Specifically, the National Agreement charges the states with (a) delivering

---

Box 3.1. Mexico's Education System

The education system in Mexico consists of mandatory basic education (which includes primary education (from ages 6 to 12) and lower secondary education (from ages 12 to 16). The latter comprises a general and a vocational/technical track. Some of the secondary education is imparted through telesecundaria, a distance-learning approach for remote areas. Prior to basic education, there is a relatively small preschool program. Beyond basic education, there is upper-secondary or bachillerato, with a duration of about three years. With bachillerato, students again can choose between general education and technical schools. Finally, there is higher or tertiary education, imparted by teacher-training colleges, federal technological institutes, state universities, and autonomous universities.

The financing of basic education is the combined responsibility of the federal and state governments. Municipalities also contribute to school maintenance. For high school and college education, states have agreements with the federal government to share these expenditures. The federal government finances all basic education in the Federal District, adult education, and runs approximately half of all technical schools. These two activities are scheduled for decentralization but there is no concrete timetable.

The role of the private sector varies by level of education. The government or public sector is the predominant provider of basic education and bachillerato. Public school enrollment shares in 1994 were 94 percent in primary, 93 percent in lower secondary, and 78 percent in upper secondary. In higher education the private sector plays a much more significant role, accounting for 46 percent of all enrollments in 1994.

Source: World Bank 1998a.

---

basic education services in their territories, (b) guaranteeing the working rights and benefits of the transferred workers, (c) integrating the federal and state systems under one system, (d) allocating increasing financial resources in real terms to basic education, (e) designing a state evaluation system, (f) proposing regional contents for teaching programs, and (g) creating supervisory bodies.

The distribution between the federal and state levels of actual decisions on expenditures has changed little since decentralization began. The most apparent result of decentralization is that some of the deconcentrated organisms of the Ministry of Public Education have been replaced by state agencies. In particular, states now perform the payroll function.

The current difficulties with the education system go back many years but were exacerbated by drastic budget cuts during the 1980s. During 1982–90, federal spending on primary education decreased in real terms at an annual average rate of 1.2 percent, while enrollment increased 5 percent annually. Over this period, actual spending per pupil in real terms decreased 47.4 percent. As a result, few resources were available for maintenance of school buildings, new construction, and basic teaching materials, and real wages for teachers declined 40 percent.

Federal spending on education recovered sharply after 1991. As a share of GDP, real federal spending on education is now back to pre-1980s levels. Education expenditures continue to be concentrated at the federal level. Using average figures for 1990–97, 89 percent of education expenditures were funded at the federal level, 11 percent were funded at the state level, and less than 1 percent were funded at the municipal level. Of the federal government's share, 33 percent was spent directly by federal government agencies and 56 percent was transferred to the states. About 95 to 99 percent of federal spending that went to the states as transfers was earmarked for teachers' salaries, and the rest was earmarked for investment.

Funds are transferred to the states for the construction of schools (CAPFCE), compensatory programs (CONAFE), adult education (INEA), and special compensatory programs (PARE and PRODEI). Data by state on the relative importance of these funds are not available. All these funds are distributed to the states through annual agreements between the federal government and individual states, and they vary by state from one year to the next. At least part of this flow is being decentralized to the states, particularly CAPFCE. Other sources of education funding include SEDESOL (PROGRESA, "escuela digna") and *Desarrollo Integral de la Familia* (DIF, school breakfasts and scholarships).

The National Agreement gave states control of operations, but not of the entire education process. States can hire and fire teachers, but they cannot do so on a large scale, nor do they control wages and benefits. States coordinate school construction with funds from Ramo 33 for both states and municipalities and, very rarely, with state and local funds, but at least as of the time of writing, federal authorities have not completely transferred to the states the function of construction. In practice, the Ministry of Public Education continues to have a say in the planning and programming of teaching activities and a presence in the budgeting process. In reality, states have limited capacity to operate the system and limited scope to adjust curricula and programs for regional content.[4]

The lack of clarity between state and federal areas of responsibility has led to confusion and inefficiency in the delivery of services at the state level. The National Agreement has contributed to the confusion by failing to create an institutional mechanism for conducting a national dialogue between federal and state authorities about the process of decentralization and by failing to clarify the assignment of responsibilities and to adapt the decentralized system in a way that makes expenditure more efficient. In contrast, such an institutional mechanism has been effectively at work in the health sector and in police and internal security.

Municipalities and schools have had no significant responsibility or authority in the decentralization process. Municipalities have responsibility for maintenance and some school construction. The latter is nominal because municipalities have to count on state approval to staff any new schools. Although municipalities in many states have expressed their desire to assume more responsibilities for basic education, few states have expressed any intent or plan to decentralize further responsibilities to the municipalities. In some states, municipalities have gained flexibility for school schedules and school lunch programs. Previously, the school lunch program was administered entirely by the federal authorities. Parent associations in some states can also decide whether to charge students for textbooks. International experience shows that the delivery of educational services becomes more efficient when decentralization reaches the local level and, even more significantly, when it reaches the school level (Gershberg and Winkler, 2000).

The National Agreement of 1992 brought additional problems. Its impact on the states was uneven because some states had already developed their education systems and others had not. Its rapid deployment also caused logistical problems. Every state that did not have a special agency for basic education had to create one immediately. These new agencies came into direct competition with the ministries of education and culture in some states. The National Agreement did not abolish the duality between the federal and state systems of education prevailing in many states. Although the Agreement effectively unified salaries in both systems (state and federal), social benefits were not unified.[5] This forced states that had their own education system in 1992 to carry dual accounting systems. The National Agreement stated that wages would be set separately in state and federal subsystems, with states negotiating with state unions and federal authorities negotiating with the federal union. In practice, wages in the federal subsystem, which are negotiated in the Federal District by the Ministry of Public Education and the national union, set the wage level that all states have to follow in their negotiations with state unions.[6] State subsystems have little choice but to follow the decisions reached at the federal level.

The National Agreement also had a significant impact on the distribution of federal resources across states. The current distribution is quite uneven. Before 1992, some states had extensive (state) education systems financed from state budgets, others had less extensive (state) systems, and quite a few others had no (state) education system at all. All states also had the federal system of basic education managed by the Ministry of Public Education. In 1992, in effect, the federal government took a picture of the different ratios of federal to state teachers and, based on those figures, froze its obligations to support teacher salaries and benefits in the federal system. As a result, in some states the federal government pays the vast majority of teacher salaries, while in other states the majority of teacher salaries are paid by the state government. This approach not only was inherently punitive of states that had made an effort to develop education, but also ignored the fact that some states have much higher population growth than others and that Mexico's population is increasingly mobile. The system of basic education appears to show significant disparities in expenditures per student. These disparities, especially when they go against poorer states, are worrisome because access to basic education is likely to be the most effective means of equalizing income in the long term. Unfortunately, the quality of education is probably worse in poorer states.[7]

Under the National Agreement, states have inadequate incentives to fund education. Because of these perceived incentives, the states may not be fully reporting their education budgets. As frequently argued at the federal level, the states may be contributing more to education than is being reported, and the share of expenditures going to wages may be decreasing as a whole. However, these facts are not openly reported to the federal authorities because states fear that increases in their own funding will lead to decreases in federal funding. Although the federal authorities are not openly reducing their state spending at this time, historically this has been the pattern. States spending more of their own resources on education have received fewer resources for education from the federal authorities.

The National Agreement supposedly assigns states the responsibility for increasing their education expenditures. This does not seem to have occurred. In a recent study that uses data from the early part of the decentralization process (1993 and 1994) for a group of seven states, the ratio of state-funded education expenditures to federal expenditures dropped in all seven states following the start of decentralization (table 3.7; see Merino 1998). At the national level, the share of state-funded expenditure in consolidated

Table 3.7. State Expenses as a Percentage of Federal Education Expenses, 1989–94

State	1989–91	1993–94	Difference
Baja California	45.4	44.5	–1.0
Federal District	10.7	8.0	–2.7
Hidalgo	4.1	3.6	–0.05
Mexico State	44.7	39.3	–5.4
Nuevo León	47.6	40.2	–7.4
Sinaloa	32.8	32.4	–0.4
Tamaulipas	24.4	18.1	–6.3

expenditures fell from 13.2 percent in 1992 to 9.4 percent in 1995, and to 8.5 percent for 1996 and 1997. Clearly, the states are not matching federal expenditures on education.

The challenge is to undo the problems associated with the current distribution of federal resources for education. The historical pattern of funding provides flexibility in design for the future. Until recently, Mexico allocated resources after case-by-case negotiations, with pragmatic adjustments at different junctures and circumstances. This ad hoc process has been used as the distribution benchmark for the decentralization of federal resources since 1992. This distribution benchmark has also been incorporated in the Fiscal Coordination Law. These facts make it difficult to move toward more transparent, fair, and efficient formulas for allocating federal education funds. The most appealing option for reform is to transition over time to a "per student" funding formula, which might be adjusted for special costs of service delivery. Other formulas, such as those incorporating some measure of performance or existing inequalities, have been given some consideration. As shown in box 3.2, whatever formula is chosen, there will be significant changes in the distribution of resources vis-à-vis the current status quo.

In the short run, the most urgent need is to improve the transparency, equity, and efficiency of the allocation of federal education-related resources to the states. The current allocation has created incentives to accumulate teachers to the detriment of other key inputs. The absence of resources to allocate at the states' discretion prevents them from introducing their own potentially innovative projects for improving the education system.

The current earmarked programs have generated inefficient administrative structures and obstructed the comparison of efficiency and performance among states. For example, the relation between teaching staff (class teachers) and administrative personnel (teachers dedicated to administration or supervision) varies from a distribution of 65 percent teaching staff and 35 percent administrative staff in some states to 85 percent teaching staff and 15 percent administrative staff in others.

The efficiency of public expenditures is especially low in basic education, where 95 to 99 percent of all resources are used to pay teacher salaries. Little is spent on classroom materials, supplies, or maintenance. Efficiency and performance could be greatly improved if more funds were dedicated to inputs of production other than salaries. Getting these additional funds may be difficult because of the commitment and incentives to hire teachers. Nevertheless, the additional funds might be obtained by reducing the number of teachers at the margin through attrition (where enrollment is low or declining), by encouraging the private provision of post-secondary education, and by pushing for higher cost recovery in the public sector universities.[8]

Box 3.2. Impact of Alternative Distribution Formulas for Education Funds

The dominant criterion for the current allocation of resources to the states is the number of teachers employed in each state. This evidently generates perverse incentives, including a disproportional growth of personnel and the neglect of other inputs of production for the delivery of educational services. But even the use of this criterion does not produce a good balance across states in terms of students per teacher. For example in a group of six entities, for 1997 the proportions ranged from 17.7 to 32.8 students per teacher at the primary level, and from 13.9 to 33.8 students per teacher at the junior high level. Using other criteria would bring significant changes in the allocation of resources.

Distribution by school enrollments. It is clear that equality per student has not been the funding criterion used by the federal authorities to distribute funds to the states. Using this criterion, the corresponding distribution shows that some states would have been receiving a much larger percentage of funds than they have been getting. This is the case for states such as Baja California Sur (62 percent more funds), Durango (+44 percent), and Baja California (+39 percent). At the same time other states would have been receiving a lower percentage of funds. This is the case of Guanajuato (19 percent less funds), Puebla (-16 percent), Queretaro (-15 percent), and Michoacan (-10 percent).

Distribution by education efficiency. Allocation of federal funds by the level of the performance of the states' education system would promote a better use of resources. Of course, the use of this criterion would require adjustments for the fiscal capacity of the states and for inputs other than public expenditures, such as parents' level of education and income. The simplest benchmark for the distribution according to this criterion would be a national student performance evaluation system. Mexico has not yet developed such a system. Some states have experimented with standardized statewide tests (for example, Aguascalientes, Chihuahua, Nuevo Leon, and Sonora). In the absence of national test score data, resource allocation by entity can be simulated using data on the states' "terminal efficiency," that is, the proportion of students that finish their basic studies. This criterion is far from optimal, since states could relax standards to obtain more resources. With this criterion, the states of Estado de Mexico, Michoacan, Nuevo Leon, Puebla, and Guanajuato would receive more resources than they actually are now allocated. Baja California Sur, Campeche, Chiapas, Guerrero, Oaxaca, and Tamaulipas would receive significantly less.

Distribution as a compensatory criterion. Compensatory distribution, on the other hand, would allocate more resources to those states for which education lags and/or deficiencies are larger. The objective would be to provide these states with the necessary funds to allow them to perform at national average levels. With this criterion, the states of Chiapas, Oaxaca, Estado de Mexico, Yucatan, and Veracruz would receive more resources than at present

Source: World Bank 1998a, p. 49–55.

Health Sector

The recent process of decentralization in the health sector started with the adoption in 1995 of the Program to Reform the Health Sector, 1995–2000. The program sought to address inequalities in access to health care and the low quality and inefficiency of health services in the federal-state system administered by the Ministry of Health. This system covers the rural and poor urban population. In Mexico, health care services are also provided by the social security system (Mexican Institute for Social Security [IMSS] and other institutions) and by the private sector (see box 3.3). From 1983 to 1987, an attempt was made to decentralize health services, and 14 states were transferred some responsibilities for health services previously under the federal system. This system included people in rural areas who were attended to by IMSS-COPLAMAR, which has continued to work as IMSS-Solidaridad did earlier. During the 1980s decentralization was in fact mostly administrative deconcentration, not decentralization, since those 14 states continued to be subject to strict regulatory and budgetary controls by the Ministry of Health.[9] The current decentralization of the federal-state health care system is deeper and wider than that of the 1980s. The health care system provided by the IMSS is also being decentralized, and this process is in many ways more radical and more rational than that of the federal-state system.

The responsibilities assigned to the federal government and to the state governments are as follows.

Federal-level responsibilities:

- Ensure that national health policy responds to the national and subnational priorities and that it strengthens the national health system and the state systems
- Define and review the legal norms of the health care system and propose any needed changes in the legislation and implementation rules
- Evaluate the delivery of health services with the goal of amending deviations, reviewing objectives, reorienting activities, and improving the efficient use of resources
- Establish more effective mechanisms for coordinating with other health providers and among different levels of government
- Maintain through the Ministry of Health the legal framework, coordination, planning, and evaluation
- Deal exclusively through the Ministry of Health with labor relations pertaining to all workers in the non-IMSS part of the system.

State-level responsibilities:

- Organize and operate, among others, primary health services, child-mother services, family planning, and mental health

---

Box 3.3. Mexico's Health System

The health system in Mexico has several subsystems, each servicing different population groups. First, there are several social security schemes, the largest being the Mexican Institute of Social Security (IMSS), which covers the employees and the self-employed in the formal sector of the economy. Other social security schemes include those for government workers (ISSSTE), the employees of PEMEX, members of the army and air force (SEDENA), and the navy (MARINA). Social security schemes covered approximately 48 million people in 1997—half of the population. Second, the services provided by the Secretaría de Salud (SSA) and the state governments apply to the population not covered by social security (or "población abierta"). This is a heterogeneous group of people from rural areas and some poor urban areas. Health services for this population are provided directly through government health facilities or indirectly through the IMSS-Solidaridad, which is a program financed by the government and actually delivered by the social security institute (IMSS). In 1997, the federal-state health program provided health services to approximately 34 million people. Both the social security systems and the federal-state program for the "población abierta" have their own organizations of doctors, clinics, and secondary and tertiary hospitals. Third, the private sector provides services of different quality to all income groups. The three systems operate with little or no coordination. Although access to health care is a constitutional right for all Mexicans, in 1994 approximately 10 million people had very little or no access to health care (OECD 1998).

The main social security system (IMSS) is also undergoing a process of administrative decentralization. The regional deconcentration of the IMSS started in 1985 with the creation of seven regional offices, each one in charge of 70 to 80 hospitals, and by giving them more flexibility, although not autonomy, in decisionmaking. More recently, the IMSS has devolved more functions and responsibilities to the seven regional directorates and has decentralized decisions further to Medical Area Units. There are 139 Medical Area Units, an average of four per state, and each Unit typically consists of a secondary hospital and several clinics. These units have a good degree of authority over budget execution. Also significant for the federal-state system, the IMSS has designed and implemented a resource allocation system based on a risk-adjusted capitation formula. This is the resource allocation used to determine the amount of transfers in exchange for the provision of a standard package of care for a given population. The adjustment factor takes into account the greater costs implied by the specific demographic, socioeconomic, and epidemiological characteristics of the area.

- Overview and control nutrition issues
- Prevent and control environmental health threats
- Oversee occupational health and basic sanitation
- Prevent and control contagious diseases
- Implement social assistance programs

- Maintain the current level of financial participation and attempt to increase these contributions over time.

Spending by state governments on the health system was insignificant 15 years ago. More recently, state contributions to health expenditures appear to be increasing. In 1994 these contributions ranged from 5 to 15 percent of total state expenditures on health. There are few state-by-state data on the level and distribution of expenditures. For three states (San Luís Potosí, Aguascalientes, and Guanajuato), contributions on average almost doubled from 2 percent in 1993 to 4.4 percent in 1997. These three states show wide disparities in services. One state delivers health services to twice the population of another state with half the budget. Expenditure per patient in these three states ranged from $Mex37 to $Mex1,469 in the same year. Revenues from cost-recovery fees averaged around 10 percent, and on average 90 percent of total resources were used in recurrent expenditures and 10 percent in capital investment.

The ongoing decentralization in health services has many positive features. Even the limited experience gained from the decentralization experiment in the 1980s produced useful lessons for decentralization. In the case of health, state administrations appear to have been better prepared institutionally, administratively, and technically to assume their new responsibilities. To coordinate all aspects of the reform, the National Health Council (Consejo Nacional de Salud, CNS) was created in 1995 with representation from all states and federal authorities; it has been meeting on a monthly basis. The council not only has a role in coordination but also in negotiation, dialogue, and conflict resolution. It diagnoses issues, conducts surveys, and prepares recommendations. This institution is perhaps the most important element accounting for the relative success of decentralization in the health sector.

Unlike decentralization in education, more time and thought have been given to decentralization in the health sector. During 1996 each state evaluated the existing problems, set objectives for reorganization to increase coverage and efficiency, and issued specific proposals for reform. By 1997 all but one state and the Federal District had signed an agreement with the federal authorities for decentralization. In addition, the Ministry of Health created groups of experts to help the states strengthen their administrative capabilities. The reform created new agencies in the states, called public decentralization units (organismos públicos de descentralización, OPDs). During the decentralization, all federal health employees were transferred to the OPDs as state employees, and all state personnel were brought up to the pay levels of federal employees. The federal government paid the financial costs of this policy. These OPDs are part of the states' health budget and have considerable autonomy for allocating current resources in primary and secondary care.[10] The OPDs report to the states' health ministry on the allocation of resources and results; in turn, the health ministry reports to the state's congress and to the federal Ministry of Health. The Ministry of Health has introduced 21 indicators to measure performance at the state level and to supervise programs through federal delegations in the states.

The ongoing decentralization in health services also presents important problems. One is the lack of clarity on how much autonomy state authorities have in managing resources. The current legal framework gives states the freedom and flexibility to allocate resources, but only after they comply with minimum federal standards. There is still confusion on what these minimum standards are and how they should be interpreted. A similar source of ambiguity is the repeated reference to finding alternative or additional sources of financing for the health system while giving states no direct incentives to come up with additional resources.

At least until very recently, the distribution of health funds from Ramo 33 created perverse incentives to streamline cost and increase efficiency. The actual formula used to distribute health transfers under Ramo 33 is not known. The dominant criterion appears to be the existing physical infrastructure in the states (hospitals, clinics, storage, and other facilities).[11] Other types of information are also used. The resulting allocations achieved over time have no easy explanation. Using physical infrastructure in the formula for determining the distribution of health transfers creates perverse incentives to maintain obsolete infrastructure and keep excess capacity. A 1995 survey found that 23 percent of the hospitals in the federal-state system had average occupancy rates of 50 percent or less, which seems wasteful in the Mexican context of many unfilled medical needs.

Other problems at the current stage of decentralization include:

- Inequitable distribution of the incidence of disease, with children and adult males in rural areas being the worst affected
- Significant disparities across the states in the per capita allocation of federal health funds[12]
- The generally poor quality of the health services provided by the states and the Ministry of Health
- Inefficient allocation of resources, with too few health professionals other than doctors
- Difficult access to health facilities in rural areas[13]
- Funding formulas that are not based on a per capita, risk-adjusted basis[14]
- Insufficient operational autonomy of hospitals
- No clear regulations for contracting out hospital services such as laundry or cleaning

- Little cost recovery
- Inadequate budget transparency
- Failure to control hospital costs adequately because there is no separation of the double function as buyer and provider of health care
- Important investment decisions made at the federal level
- Transfers that consist of earmarked funds with very detailed mandates, leaving little room for discretion at the subnational level other than management of personnel[15]
- Perverse incentives for the states to contribute their own funds because higher matching rates from the states can result in reduced federal funding
- The determination of wages at the federal level, imposing a federal mandate on the states since they need to pay the salary raises determined at the federal level
- Complex regulations that are issued at the federal level, impeding autonomous decisions at the subnational level.

WATER AND SANITATION. There has been significant decentralization in water services. The National Water Program (1991–94) proposed to transfer responsibilities from the federal government to the jurisdictions that were operating the water and irrigation systems. These federal responsibilities were off-loaded taking into consideration the ability to pay and administrative capabilities of the jurisdictions.[16] The goal of the program, not fully achieved yet, is to have fully autonomous systems in administration and financing. Back in 1989 the National Water Commission (Comisión Nacional del Agua, CNA) provided water to 14 urban systems. By now the vast majority of these operations have been decentralized. Concurrent with this decentralization, a majority of the states have introduced legislation facilitating the decentralized operation of water and sewage services. The private sector has also invested in water and sewer projects in Aguascalientes, Cancun, Mexico City, and some of the northern states.

Legal reforms in the states have strengthened the role of local water authorities. Currently 118 out of 135 cities with 50,000 or more inhabitants have autonomous water authorities. Municipal governments set tariffs for about one-third of these local authorities. For the rest, tariff changes must be approved by the state congress. The Federal District does not have an autonomous water authority; some tariffs are set by the national Congress and others by the municipal government which provides the service. Even though local water authorities have been able to raise overall cost recovery, most systems are far from self-sufficient. Performance and willingness to collect fees differ considerably from state to state. There are still significant problems with cost recovery. In most cases, there is a lack of metering, and water fees are flat fees, so consumer waste is high. The administrative capabilities of water authorities are often weak, operational costs are high, and leakage and waste in the distribution system are significant. In the case of small companies that have not been able to survive, the responsibility for provision has returned to the state governments. The states also have assumed responsibility for water services for the poorest municipalities, although coverage in rural areas is still very low. However, deficits are no longer financed by the federal government, and accountability and transparency in budget operations have improved.

OTHER INFRASTRUCTURE. The first step in decentralization in other infrastructure was taken with the Solidarity Program managed by SEDESOL in the Salinas administration. But even in this period, all funds were federal, and states and municipalities mainly executed federal programs with funds earmarked for water, sewerage, school construction, and roads. With Ramo 33, there has been a step forward in the decentralization of these funds. Even though the funds are earmarked for a list of expenditures, subnational governments have more discretion in how they are used. The efficiency gains from decentralization will be reaped only after subnational governments have even more discretion over these funds. However, further discretion makes sense only if subnational governments have the administrative and institutional capacity, especially at the local level.

AGRICULTURE. Since the early 1990s many responsibilities previously performed by the Ministry of Agriculture have been decentralized, ranging from extension services to research. As in other areas, the response of the states has varied. In poorer states, some of the functions previously carried out by the ministry have not been taken over by state governments. There are now 32 state agricultural councils that include both government authorities and producers, and their agenda is to guide agricultural development in the states.

ENVIRONMENT. The 1993 Standards for Environmental Protection Law supposedly delegates a significant role to the states, which can adopt their own legislation and establish processes to enforce federal standards, but actual decentralization remains incomplete. For example, in some years, the federal authorities have not reached coordination agreements with some of the states. In order to operate, many industries must obtain a permit from the local authorities and also from the National Water Authority, the Ministry of Health, and the Ministry of Industry. The Institute of Environmental Protection in the Federal District is still the only agency that can issue permits for hazardous wastes, imposing an additional burden on businesses and discouraging compliance. A new pilot program in 2000 provides matching funds to states that sign performance agreements to improve their capacity for environmental protection.

ROADS. The Ministry of Communication and Transportation initiated a process of decentralization to the states in 1996 through a series of agreements involving the construction and maintenance of rural roads and the maintenance of secondary federal roads (World Bank 1998b). Despite its poor record on the maintenance of national roads, the federal government has been reluctant to devolve management of even part of the federal road network to the states. The budgetary difficulties of the federal government in providing adequate maintenance of the primary road network was the principal impetus for the private toll road scheme, which was introduced in 1989.[17]

SOCIAL PROGRAM. There has been some degree of decentralization, better called deconcentration, in the national programs for social assistance (DIF). These programs now operate through state offices in all the states and in local units in more than 3,000 municipalities. States and municipalities mostly implement federal programs, but also have their own smaller programs.

POLICE AND PUBLIC SAFETY. The decentralization process in this area has been laid out in the General Law of Coordination of the National System of Public Security. There is a national council with membership of the federal government and all the states including the Federal District. This council has been meeting regularly to coordinate joint financing of projects such as the construction of jails, purchase of modern equipment, and development of an information network.

Institutions of Coordination

Formal expenditure assignments can never be explicit enough to cover all contingencies. Similarly, conflicts can arise from diverse interpretations of the law. That is why, regardless of the vehicle and precision of formal assignments, a mechanism for dialogue and coordination between different levels of government is always needed. Mexico has no government-wide institution of this kind. The Ministry of Finance and Public Credit (Secretaría de Hacienda y Crédito Público, SHCP) has periodic meetings with the finance officers of the states to discuss the fiscal coordination agreements and revenue-related issues. SHCP is setting up a Decentralization Committee, chaired on a rotating basis by the three Subsecretaries, to coordinate decentralization within SHCP. A few sectors also have such coordination mechanisms, as in health with the National Health Council and in police and public safety with the National Council of Public Security. Other sectors, such as education, lack this type of mechanism but need it.

A general feature of Mexico's intergovernmental relationships is the use of individual agreements between the federal authorities and each of the states in areas of concurrent responsibility. Typically these agreements are not made public or even ratified by the state legislatures. This system dates back many years to the time when the president effectively appointed all the governors. Although explicit and more transparent agreements would help to coordinate concurrent activities between federal and state authorities, they are not substitutes for a national forum, such as the National Health Council, which brings all states and the federal government together in open discussion and dialogue.

At the state-municipal level, COPLADE traditionally established priorities for all investments of the state and municipal governments. State congresses have to approve the budgets for all the municipalities and for the state government. Formal responsibilities include formulating and updating the state's development plan, coordinating the federal, state, and local plans, and executing and evaluating state development plans. Practically all federal investment funds are channeled through this institution.[18] In states where COPLADE has functioned well, it has been organized by sectors, and each sector may have several subcommittees. Different departments of the state and its municipalities have representation in the COPLADE. In some states, the COPLADE has tried to respond to the proposals made by municipalities and by state government departments, but the governor clearly has controlled the ultimate decisions. One main objective of the COPLADE—to incorporate municipalities in the decisionmaking process of federal and state capital investment programs destined for the municipalities themselves—has been only partially fulfilled. In reality, COPLADE has worked more like a state planning institution, and the role of municipal authorities has been quite limited. Coordination and conflict resolution between state authorities and municipalities should follow the model of state councils for different areas of concurrent responsibilities and have membership of state authorities and all municipalities in the state. This may be more difficult to implement in states with highly fragmented municipalities, such as Oaxaca. In these cases, the state councils could function with representation of associations of municipalities.

More fundamentally, Mexico's institutional infrastructure for decentralization of expenditures is dominated by one key factor: the lack of autonomy at the subnational level. This seems to arise from four sources, some of which were mentioned earlier. First, a significant part of the federal transfers (*aportaciones*) are earmarked. This means that state governments have no discretion over spending outside the designated type of expenditure. This is the case with all transfers under Ramo 33 and with other decentralization funds and programs for education, health, agriculture, and so forth. Because of earmarking, decentralization has brought state officials not more autonomy, only much more work in accounting for funds. Second, discretion or expenditure autonomy for the states lies with revenue sharing and own revenues. To begin with, 20 percent of all revenue sharing goes directly to the municipalities. Many of the federal funds require matching arrangements by the subnational governments, leaving them few discretionary funds with which to pursue their own policies and expenditure priorities. Third, federal legislation imposes on subnational governments a detailed list of legal norms and conditions. These constrain the states' ability to deviate from federal policy, to develop and support their own policies, and to introduce innovations in their own programs. Fourth, the federal government has imposed unfunded mandates on the state governments. The most significant of these is the determination of wages for teachers and health care professionals at the national level.

A significant twist in municipal government autonomy has taken place with the recent introduction of Ramo 33 transfers to the municipalities. Many municipalities have seen their resources increase three- to fivefold. In an effort to prevent mismanagement, many state governments have tried to control how municipalities administer these resources. In a well-known case, Puebla established state-level criteria for the distribution and control of Ramo 33 transfers, a decision supported by the Supreme Court. Some other states have gradually introduced similar procedures.

Administrative Capacity and Democratic Governance

Decentralization will not increase efficiency if subnational governments do not have adequate administrative capacity or institutional development or if the institutions of democratic governance are absent or weak. In some cases, as with the Solidarity Program under the previous administration, municipal government institutions were weakened by the creation of parallel structures.

A significant feature of Mexico's fiscal federalism is the uneven distribution of institutional development and administrative capacity across states and municipalities. The disparities clearly are more pronounced among municipalities than among states, with urban and larger municipalities typically having more capacity than rural and smaller municipalities.

The management of state finances is influenced by the legislative framework of the state and by the type of laws regulating municipal finances. Three laws are important for regulating state financial management: (a) the Fiscal Coordination Law (which specifies the criteria for distributing resources among municipalities); (b) the Public Budget Process Law (which sets the process and policies for budget formulation, execution, and control); and (c) the Public Debt Law (which sets the criteria, procedures, and limits for the use of debt financing). In 1997, seven states had none of these three laws, six states had only one, 15 had two, and only three states had all three, but all states have them now.

The qualifications and skills of state officials directly affect the efficient use of budgetary resources. In the education sector, the professional training of state functionaries appears to explain the differences in performance across states. According to a study conducted in 1997, states that had the best management also had the best-trained officials (Cabrero, Flamand, and Vega 1998). States whose officials had been in the sector the longest, however, had the worst performance. This may suggest that time in service often reduces innovation and intensifies the use of traditional approaches.

At the municipal level, administrative and institutional capacity is more precarious. An official survey of municipalities in 1995 found the following deficiencies (Secretaría de Gobernación, CEDEMUN, and INEGI 1995):

- Even though the great majority of municipalities had a treasurer, only 39 percent had a specialized agency responsible for supervising and planning the budget process.
- About 60 percent of the country's municipalities did not have a computer system in 1995; accounting was done by hand in most municipalities.
- Regarding the existence of an internal legal framework, 63 percent of municipalities did not have basic regulations or manuals for administrative procedures.
- In roughly 80 percent of the municipalities there was no statutory framework for expenditure planning. In these municipalities, the budget document was improvised and very elemental.
- In more than 70 percent of the municipalities there were neither basic rules nor manuals for the collection and actualization of the property tax. In fact, the state administered the property tax for the vast majority of these municipalities.
- In 1994, 72 percent of the municipalities collected less than half of their budgeted revenues, 27 percent collected 50 to 85 percent, and less than 1 percent collected 86 to 100 percent of the expected revenues.
- Almost half of the municipalities spent more than half of their budget on wages and salaries. This reflects the narrow margins for expenditure decisions that are common in a large part of the country.
- Finally, citizens participated in government programs in just 51 percent of the municipalities, almost always in public works.

Although at least some states have made improvements, a comprehensive reassessment would be worthwhile. Without a major effort to develop institutional capacity of the poorer, smaller, and rural municipalities, it does not make sense to push decentralization at this level. The federal government has committed to make funds available for institutional development by states and municipalities.

Although many municipalities are ready to play a more significant role in the delivery of services, many more clearly are not. The general reforms promoted by local governments since 1983 and reforms to Article 115 of the Constitution have reached the limit of their efficiency because they do not recognize explicitly the diversity of Mexico's municipalities. Doing so will require both the federal and state governments to use asymmetric approaches to decentralization at the municipal level. The administrative and institutional limitations of the vast majority of municipalities are aggravated in cases where the entire staff of the municipality changes every three years with new elections. This is more damaging, of course, where the pool of skilled professionals is limited. The negative impact of this institutional feature of Mexican public governance cannot be exaggerated. There may be no point in training and increasing the qualifications of municipal officials if the training process has to start again in three years or less.

The majority of countries have dealt with the changes brought about by periodic democratic elections by separating elected officials or politicians (mayor, vice mayor, and local council) from technical staff (budget and tax officials, accountants, secretaries, and so forth). Often, technical staff are certified and made part of a professional career-oriented national or state body. In some countries, there is a local civil service. Allowing for the permanency and professionalization of technical staff at the municipal level is a fundamental reform that state governments need to consider. Interpreting and dealing with differences in institutional development and administrative capacity also require full acknowledgment that incentives are needed to make subnational governments develop. The lack of incentives can arise from the centralization of responsibilities and resources and from the lack of an appropriate institutional framework, including inadequate compensation for state and local officials or the perceptions that discourage honest and capable citizens from seeking public office.

Toward a More Efficient Expenditure Decentralization

The first priority is to assign expenditure responsibilities formally both at the federal-state level and the state-local level. This will help to clarify the existing confusion about who is responsible for what in education, health, the environment, water, and other infrastructure.

Although many countries formally assign expenditure responsibilities in their constitutions, this avenue is not recommended for Mexico. The constitution is difficult to change, and it cannot provide the level of detail needed. The proper vehicle for a formal and explicit statement of expenditure responsibilities is the law, such as the much-discussed (but not yet formally drafted) Treasury Law. If this law were not to progress for some time, a second-best vehicle would be federal sectoral laws, such as the General Education Law or the General Health Law. At the subnational level, the further division and clarification of responsibilities between states and their municipalities could be formalized in the Budget Process Law for municipal and state governments. Where concurrent sectoral responsibilities exist, responsibilities for regulation, financing, and delivery or implementation should be allocated explicitly among the three levels of government.

At the subnational level, state governments need to clarify the assignment of responsibilities between the state authorities (the Ministry of Education or the Ministry of Health) and municipalities and the units of implementation (schools or hospitals). The largest benefits from decentralization are typically achieved when decentralization reaches local agencies, empowering those directly involved in the delivery of services and ensuring accountability to local residents. The most appropriate vehicle for clarifying the division of responsibilities between state and municipal governments is the Budget Process Law of each state.

In terms of specific sector priorities, the assignment of expenditure responsibilities could be better clarified in the areas of water resources and drainage, higher education, school construction, road construction and maintenance, and other infrastructure.

The federal government could promote further decentralization from the states to municipalities, but only to municipalities with proven administrative capacity. The best approach is to adopt an opting-in system, under which municipalities that have adequate institutional and administrative capacity can receive further responsibilities and resources to carry them out.

It is inefficient to assign responsibility to different levels of government for capital expenditures and for maintenance, such as is currently the case with basic education and roads. In the longer run, it is more desirable to have a single level of government responsible for planning, financing, executing, and maintaining capital infrastructure. If subnational governments are deemed competent to take over the operation of services, they should also be made responsible for capital investments in this service area. This recommendation is cast in the long run because shifting capital expenditure responsibilities to state and local governments will require a corresponding adjustment in the assignment of tax instruments, revenue sharing, transfers, and long-term borrowing.

The clarification of expenditure responsibilities will also demand addressing the problem of unfunded mandates. The most important existing mandate for state government is the national determination between federal agencies and national unions of the salaries to be paid to education and health employees. This extremely complex issue will require time and tact to solve. However, true decentralization of education and health services will not happen as long as wages are mandated from the center. The challenge will be to gain the consent of the unions to decentralize the determination of wages and other labor issues to the state level. Perhaps this will happen if and when a number of state governments are able and willing to negotiate higher wages and benefits than those negotiated at the center.

One final issue will need to be clarified in the short run. Many state public employee pension funds are bankrupt or nearly bankrupt. The states believe that this situation developed because of mandates from federal legislation going back many years. Federal and state authorities need to discuss this issue and work toward a compromise for funding existing liabilities arising from past decisions. The agreement would eventually need to establish clear responsibility for any future liabilities within the states. This may require modifying the mandates contained in current federal legislation.

Institutions to Clarify Expenditure Assignments

Although the National Health Council has not worked as well as desired, it has clearly shown the benefits of a nationwide institution for encouraging dialogue and resolving conflicts among levels of government. Along similar lines, a National Education Council could be created with the mandate to mediate problems and differences in interpretation between the states and the federal government, make adjustments in the assignment of responsibilities, coordinate educational policies, and spread knowledge on the efficient management of expenditures. This could be accomplished in the short run by reforming the Fiscal Coordination Law to require the introduction of a National Education Council.

The current periodic meetings between SHCP and finance representatives from the states in the area of budget revenues could be expanded, or held separately, in the area of expenditures. Although all states should be represented in these institutions, it will be impossible to do the same for all municipal authorities. It is important, however, that municipal governments be represented in the dialogue. This can be addressed by allowing representatives of the national associations of municipalities or appointed representatives of municipalities to participate in these forums. At the state level, these institutions of dialogue and coordination could be replicated for expenditure responsibilities between state and municipal officials.

More Subnational Autonomy and Incentives for Increasing Efficiency

INCREASE SPENDING AUTONOMY AT THE STATE AND LOCAL LEVELS. To address the lack of expenditure autonomy at the subnational level, the federal government needs to reduce the degree of earmarking in federal transfers and increase unrestrained or lump-sum transfers of funds. In those sectors where national priorities need to influence the allocation of funds by state authorities, such as health and education, transfers could be earmarked only by sector—with the condition that some minimum level of service per student or inhabitant be achieved.

To increase the autonomy of subnational authorities, the federal authorities could increasingly use instruments of ex post performance and accountability, in place of ex ante control and regulations focused on input usage or "production function" decisions. Control should be transferred to the greatest extent possible to state legislatures, municipal councils, and ex post audit institutions, such as the Comptroller of the Treasury. The regulatory role of federal authorities should be limited to basic national programs that involve federal funds, and regulations could continue to move toward performance-based criteria.

GIVE INCENTIVES FOR INCREASED EXPENDITURE EFFICIENCY AT THE STATE AND MUNICIPAL LEVELS. Federal guidance, education, and the selective use of conditionality could help to spread the good practices and results across states. At the same time, the federal government needs to provide the proper incentives to state and local governments. In particular, the federal government needs to remove as soon as possible the perverse incentives provided in the Fiscal Coordination Law for the distribution of funds to education and health. These funds should not be distributed on the basis of physical capacity (registered number of school or health facilities) and number of employees (teachers and health workers). Instead, a simple formula could be used based on objective criteria, which cannot be manipulated by state authorities.

One way to improve efficiency would be to distribute funds on a per student basis (for education) and a per inhabitant basis (for health). These simple criteria should move state governments to seek economies in the delivery of services by consolidating facilities and in the use of staff. The per capita criterion may be adjusted, via a formula, to take into account different costs of provision due to differences in price levels or in the current stock of infrastructure. However, these adjustments should be kept to a minimum to exploit the advantages of a capitation system. The transition to the new system should be incremental, given the differences in funding that desirable new formulas will generate. In the short run, this calls for reform of the Fiscal Coordination Law to introduce over time a per student capitation formula, perhaps modified by educational outcomes and existing disparities.

Both the federal and state governments could promote the association of municipalities. For example, approved associations of municipalities could receive additional funding for investment and maintenance of facilities.

Moreover, government agencies could contract with the private sector for the full or partial delivery of public services. The experience with full privatization of services has been mixed in Mexico, but there are success stories that could be replicated throughout the country. The federal government could play a significant role in spreading and publicizing the positive experiences and in encouraging their replication. Similarly, state governments could encourage municipalities to make greater use of contracting with the private sector. The federal government could take the lead by supporting, through Banobras, the creation of joint ventures between the public and private sectors for building infrastructure and delivering services.

The most important check on the wastefulness of the public sector—or the most important incentive for an efficient use of public resources—should be the accountability of public officials to their taxpayers and electorate. To this end, the federal and state governments could promote electoral reforms that allow individuals to cast votes for members of the town council rather than for a party list, as is now the case.

State governments need to provide municipalities more discretion and resources and to increase accountability by implementing units, such as schools and hospitals. State governments also need to provide incentives for better performance and effective support mechanisms to develop technical and administrative capabilities.

Improvement of Administrative Capacity and Democratic Governance (Medium and Long Term) and Use of Asymmetric Assignments in the Interim (Short Term)

Weak administrative and institutional capacities constitute the most important impediment to increasing the efficiency of subnational public expenditures. Because of significant differences in administrative capacity and institutional development among states, it may be desirable to devolve more expenditure responsibilities only after each state government has achieved objective and transparent criteria that reflect a minimum level of administrative and institutional capacity. There is a need to promote the professional training of middle- and high-level officials in the finance departments of subnational governments. The federal government could make this a priority in its dealings with state governments and local legislatures. One possibility is for the federal government to offer funds supporting the modernization of finance departments under the condition that subnational governments establish professional service systems at least in the area of financial management.

The federal government could require states to update or develop a legislative framework for financial management. At the very least, this framework should include a fiscal coordination law for dealing with the municipalities, a budget, an accounting and public expenditure law, and a public debt law.

Federal policy could offer incentives for subnational governments to develop institutional and administrative capacity and to ensure that the asymmetric treatment of subnational governments does not create different classes of subnational governments, in particular an underclass of dependent governments under the paternalistic oversight of federal authorities. The federal government could help laggard states improve their administrative and institutional capacity. States that have not promoted or developed adequate democratic governance institutions in their municipalities—also stated in terms of objective and transparent criteria (such as municipal elections with separate executive and legislative powers, a local budget process law, and ex post audit)—should not be devolved functions or transferred funds destined for municipalities.

State governments could also be encouraged to use an asymmetric approach to municipal governments depending on their administrative capacity and record of democratic governance. Without a major effort to develop institutional capacity of the poorer, smaller, and rural municipalities, decentralization of responsibilities should not proceed. State governments could be encouraged to help municipalities improve their administrative and institutional capacities. Decentralization would proceed for those municipalities that opt to receive the training and demonstrate their administrative capacity.

Strengthening the administrative capacity of municipalities will require several tracks. First, the states should provide clear incentives to municipalities for upgrading their capacity. This may be done through a qualification system that devolves more responsibilities and resources to municipalities that improve their administrative capacity and institutions. Second, states need to find the technical means to do all the training, legal advice, and so forth. INDETEC is the type of institution that could be retooled for this type of training, but its operations and current status should be reconsidered. SEDESOL also gives technical assistance to municipalities in infrastructure, and Banobras has assisted municipal governments with evaluation studies for capital investment projects. Third, and most important, it is crucial to remove current institutional barriers to sustained improvement of these capabilities. In particular, municipal technical staff should not be removed every three years when elected officials are replaced. The states could be encouraged to professionalize municipal staff and to create a career ladder for municipal bureaucrats.

Part of the problem is that state governments have not had the right incentives to strengthen their municipalities. It may be desirable for the federal government to create a matching grant program through which state governments compete, winning earmarked resources for strengthening their own administrations, with the condition that a share of these funds go to a state program for strengthening municipal administrations.

4

(Mexico)

O17o23

H7O H77

H5O

Tax Assignment

Alberto Díaz-Cayeros and Charles E. McLure, Jr.

TAX REVENUES OF THE MEXICAN FEDERAL GOVERNMENT are unusually small as a percentage of GDP (11 percent in 1999, not including oil royalties) and of total federal revenues (76 percent). At the same time, federal transfers to states are an unusually large share of federal outlays (over half of outlays other than debt service) and of the revenue of states (over 80 percent for states other than the Federal District), which raise little revenue on their own. The Mexican public needs more resources for major economic infrastructure and human resources—areas in which the states carry a considerable part of the responsibility. The conjunction of these conditions today implies that a major source of increased revenue for the public sector should be more subnational taxation, which could be offset partially by decreases in aggregate transfers from the federal level.

The tax section of Chapter 1 provided some principles and a method for thinking about the major potential sources of revenues for state and municipal governments. This chapter applies these principles to the situation in Mexico, evaluates the possibility of assigning particular taxes to state or municipal levels of government, and provides rough estimates of the revenue effects of doing so.

Potential Sources of State Tax Revenues

This section looks at potential sources for increased state revenues, either by increasing use of existing taxes on payroll and automobile registration, introducing new taxes at the state level in the form of surcharges on federal taxes such as the income tax and VAT, or transferring excise taxes from the federal to the state level. It also reviews two potential taxes that the states should not use—corporate income tax and retail sales tax.

Payroll Tax

Twenty-one of the 32 states of Mexico rely on payroll taxes. These taxes are levied at rates that vary from 0.5 percent to 4 percent. Rates cluster in the range of 1 to 2 percent of payrolls (18 states); the modal rate is 2 percent (imposed by 11 states), and only one state levies a rate in excess of 2 percent (4 percent in Baja California Sur, which is due to a 2 percent surcharge to support higher education). Several states have multiple rates—lower rates for specific activities or incomes. Payroll taxes produce almost half of state tax revenues (45.6 percent, but this percentage jumps to 63.4 percent if one excludes the Federal District, the tax authority of which differs from that of the regular states because it includes the property tax). This constitutes 9.2 percent of own revenues of state governments—but, because of the preponderance of revenue sharing, only 2.7 percent of total net revenues. The percentage of states' own tax revenues among those states that do levy this tax varies from a low of 0.75 percent in Chiapas to a high of 10.74 percent in Nuevo León.

Conceptually, the payroll tax is not an attractive source of state revenues. The primary problem is that it is an origin-based tax on one of the key costs of production. As a result, it may distort the location of economic activity if levied at different rates in different states, unless rate differentials reflect differences in the level of public service provided to employers by the various states. State officials are naturally reluctant to impose payroll taxes that are far out of line with those levied by states with which they compete for business, fearing loss of jobs to other states.

A second objection is the presence of cities on or near state boundaries. Since payroll taxes are commonly collected at the place of employment, instead of the place of residence, revenues from taxes paid by commuters flow to the "wrong" state; that is, to the state where people work, instead of where they live. The problem is not merely that states where employees live have less revenue than they should and those where employees work have too much, relative to a residence-based system. That problem could be alleviated, and perhaps largely eliminated, by the structure of grants. A more pressing problem is that the exporting of payroll taxes to nonresident employees artificially lowers the political price of taxation in the state of employment. Similarly, to provide a given amount of revenue, the state where employees live must levy higher taxes than if it could levy a residence-based income tax.

Commuting across state boundaries seems to be a major problem primarily in the Mexico City metropolitan area, which spans two states (Estado de Mexico and the Federal District), but it could also be an issue in some northern cities in the future. There is no straightforward way to quantify commuting in the Mexico City metropolitan area. Since there are no personal income estimates at the state level it is hard to know how much of the tax base is being shifted from one jurisdiction to another. Moreover, the high prevalence of informal employment in Mexico City makes such estimation difficult. Some results from income distribution surveys carried out in 1996 for the Mexico City metropolitan area were released by 1999, but the aggregate results are not helpful because individual-level data analysis is necessary. Such analysis is a major task that should be undertaken by the local authorities, perhaps with federal support.

Despite these concerns, the payroll tax might play a greater role in the finance of the states. It appears to enjoy a reasonable level of acceptance, and it is one of the few potential sources of state revenues that is administratively feasible.

The way the payroll taxes are currently implemented is far from optimal. Each state is free to define not only the rate, but also the subject of taxation (which person) and the tax base (which part of their pay). While the definitions of taxpayers and tax bases seem to be generally similar, they are not identical to each other or to the payroll taxes levied by the federal government for social security and housing. (State definitions differ, for example, with regard to the treatment of fringe benefits such as commuting allowances and the value of housing and meals provided for employees.) Moreover, each state administers its own payroll tax, following its own procedures, which are independent of those used for the federal payroll tax. Duplication of administration is wasteful for both taxpayers and tax administrators. Differences in both administrative procedures and tax bases create unnecessary complexity and costs (compliance and audit) for multistate firms. There is some cross-checking of information between state and federal authorities, but this tends to be inefficient—and certainly less efficient than if the state and federal taxes were levied on the same base and collected by the same agency.

The most efficient way to implement state payroll taxes would be as a surcharge on the payroll tax levied by the federal government. The base for the federal and state taxes should be identical, except perhaps for different floors and ceilings on taxable payrolls.[1] Federal administration of state surcharges would appear, in theory, to be most efficient. States may, however, challenge this proposition for any number of reasons. If states insist on retaining their own administrations, calculation of liability for state payroll taxes should nonetheless begin with the base for the federal tax. This would require federal collection of data on tax base by state for each employer, something that is not now done. State administrative procedures could be made uniform to minimize compliance costs.

The modifications explored above, while important, are not fundamental—though they may be politically difficult to enact. They would improve the system by simplifying administration and compliance and would thus economize on the costs of administration and compliance.

These improvements might lead to some increase in revenues, but these are likely to be inconsequential.

Rate increases could provide increased revenues. Table 4.1 provides several estimates of the revenue potential of the payroll tax. The first column indicates present payroll tax revenues, by state. The second column provides an estimate of the revenues that could be gained by the 21 states that now levy payroll tax at rates below 3 percent by increasing rates to 3 percent. It involves simply scaling up existing revenues by the ratio of 3 percent to the present tax rate. (For example, for states now levying a tax rate of 2 percent, revenues are increased by 50 percent.) The estimate suggests that revenues would increase by 160 percent, an estimation that assumes a rate elasticity of 1, while separate econometric estimates by the authors suggest that the payroll tax revenue in Mexico is rather elastic at 1.5.

The third column presents the results based on econometric estimates of an equation that explains payroll tax revenues as a function of rates, employment in the formal sector, state GDP, and revenue sharing. Raising the rate to 3 percent would represent an increase in total net tax revenues[2] of around 8 percent in Campeche, Colima, Morelos, and San Luis Potosí; the increase in total net revenues would be less in other states, but it is important to note that in the 11 states that do have a payroll tax, an increase of their rates to 3 percent would mean at least doubling their revenue from this source. The bottom line is that substantial revenue could be derived from the payroll tax in the states that do not now have a payroll tax, and that even in those states that do have a payroll tax, if tax subjects and bases were more similar while compliance was taken to the national average, collection would improve. Since the payroll tax constitutes two-thirds of state tax revenues, this increase would be important.

Individual Income Tax

In theory, the individual income tax is an attractive source of revenue for the states of Mexico (or even for localities). Unlike the payroll tax, it could, in principle, be levied on the basis of residence, instead of the location of employment. Besides channeling revenues to the state (or locality) most likely to provide services to the employee's household, a residence-based tax is less likely to distort the location of economic activity. In addition, there is an intangible impetus toward use of the individual income tax by the Mexican states bordering the United States as they experience economic development induced by their northern neighbor: the desire to imitate the income tax systems of the U.S. states and the Canadian provinces.

Surcharges on the individual income tax are not without problems. First, residence-based taxation requires that most taxpayers file income tax declarations, an objective that is not likely to be realized—or even desirable—soon in Mexico.[3] Second, because the income tax threshold is quite

Table 4.1. Increase in Revenues from Increase in Payroll Tax (1996 Thousands of Pesos)

State	Current collection*	Proportional increase with 3 percent rate	Econometric estimate of increase for 3 percent rate
Aguascalientes	2,788	n.a.	51,402
Baja California	104,873	251,695	36,267
Baja California Sur	7,993	11,990	23,609
Campeche	29,071	43,607	86,962
Coahuila	60,854	182,562	138,500
Colima	102	n.a.	45,801
Chiapas	26,501	90,861	0
Chihuahua	104	208	201,469
Distrito Federal	1,929,602	2,894,403	34,118
Durango	21,540	n.a.	51,908
Guanajuato	0	n.a.	211,274
Guerrero	46,276	69,414	63,837
Hidalgo	22,773	68,319	73,892
Jalisco	305,182	457,773	131,679
México	488,127	732,191	149,611
Michoacán	0	n.a.	115,530
Morelos	279	n.a.	111,063
Nayarit	12,435	18,653	25,725
Nuevo León	374,368	561,552	137,476
Oaxaca	0	n.a.	61,647
Puebla	47,541	142,623	129,878
Querétaro	0	n.a.	91,057
Quintana Roo	45,985	68,978	62,062
San Luis Potosí	1,013	n.a.	112,628
Sinaloa	52,613	105,226	76,717
Sonora	118,880	178,320	29,069
Tabasco	38,175	114,525	0
Tamaulipas	182,137	273,206	0
Tlaxcala	11,322	33,966	12,697
Veracruz	10,033	n.a.	223,727
Yucatán	41,860	62,790	33,982
Zacatecas	0	n.a.	33,428
Total	3,982,427	6,362,858	2,557,018

n.a. = not applicable.
* Includes some minor personal income taxes levied in states without a payroll tax.
Zero in the third column indicates an econometric estimate below the 1996 actual. A blank in the second column indicates no true payroll tax in 1996.
Source: Author's calculations from INEGI data.

high and administration of the income tax is, by all accounts, quite weak, only a small percentage of the economically active population currently pays the individual income tax. The economically active population is calculated at 35.8 million, but only about 14 million people pay the payroll tax used to finance social security, and only 5.6 million pay the individual income tax, mostly withheld at source. The regional differences in compliance and individual filing are striking: 29 percent of the economically active population in the Federal District file returns, but in Oaxaca and Chiapas only 9 percent do. Thus, unlike the payroll tax, the individual income tax is not currently a "mass tax" that might provide significant additional revenues to pay for state services. If the individual income tax is to serve as a benefit-related state tax, it should be paid by a high percentage of the population.[4] Given the distribution of income in the states, which closely mirrors that of the country, for most states only the highest decile would be susceptible to pay income taxes, at least under the current federal provision that exempts incomes under three times the minimum wage.[5] Third, state individual income taxes would be characterized by substantial horizontal fiscal disparity. The disparity resulting from differences in per capita income across states would be aggravated by a tax threshold and graduated rates.

Under present conditions, allowing the states to levy surcharges on the individual income tax does not seem to achieve much that could not be achieved as well by the state payroll taxes.[6] Even so, the option could be considered, particularly if the subjects and base of the payroll tax are made more uniform, so that payroll and income taxes could be integrated.

There could also be a flat-rate state surcharge and a graduated-rate federal tax; both would be imposed on the base defined by the central government. It might be desirable to have a lower tax threshold for the state surcharges than for the federal tax, given the differences in objectives of the two taxes: benefit-related taxation in the case of the state surcharge and progressive taxation in the case of the federal tax.[7] This would complicate compliance and administration somewhat, because the two thresholds would need to be reflected in withholding tables, as well as rate tables used in completing tax returns.[8] Even more than in the case of payroll taxes, federal administration of the possible state or local income tax surcharges seems appropriate.

Excises

Excise taxes, for example, those on alcoholic beverages and tobacco products, would be ideal candidates for assignment to the states.[9] They would probably be politically acceptable as a means of financing state expenditures, and they could be linked to health care services provided by the states. They are reasonably assigned to the states under the principle of subsidiarity in taxation, and because they are relatively visible, they would help ensure accountability of state officials.

State excises should be levied by (or on behalf of) the states where consumption occurs, not the states where production or importation occurs. States where consumption occurs are more likely than producing states to incur public costs incidental to the consumption of excisable products. Moreover, taxation by producing states is likely to result in inappropriate exporting of tax burden to residents of other states. Even so, for administrative reasons, many excises should be collected at the point of production or importation. The ordinary way to implement state excises on alcoholic beverages and tobacco products is to attach distinct tax stamps to excisable products destined for various states. Taxes on motor fuels are commonly collected at the retail level by using sealed pumps.

The primary administrative problem might be smuggling from states with low excises to states with high excises. Smuggling is likely to be problematic for products with high ratios of value to weight and volume, such as alcoholic beverages and tobacco products.[10] This would tend to limit the differentials between state excise rates that could be sustained. It might be appropriate for the federal government to impose floors, below which state excise rates cannot go, in order to prevent a "race to the bottom" caused by competition among states seeking to attract sales of products they know are intended for smuggling to other states—and to protect local sellers from the onslaught of products smuggled from other states, where they are subject to lower taxes.[11]

Such floors on excise rates may also be needed for a political reason. The industries producing alcoholic beverages and tobacco products are sufficiently powerful that it is politically difficult to maintain the level of federal excises. This problem would be exacerbated by the assignment of excises on these products to the states, which would be even less able than the federal government to withstand the political influence of the industries. Moreover, the industries could play off states against each other, thus encouraging a race to the bottom. While a federal floor is inconsistent with the basic reason for assigning taxes to subnational governments—providing states with control over marginal sources of revenues through control of tax rates—it may be needed to avoid virtual elimination of excises on certain products, by concentrating political action in Mexico City. Of course, states should have freedom to go above the federally mandated minimum rates.

To maximize the latitude of the states to use excises, the central government should stop using them, effectively transferring them to the states. In 1996 federal excises on alcoholic beverages and tobacco products yielded total revenues equal to almost 11 percent of net state revenues (tobacco products 4.6 percent, beer 4.3 percent, and other alcoholic beverages 2.0 percent). This slightly overestimates what states could receive if they were to directly collect these taxes, since they would receive slightly less from revenue sharing.

Taxes on motor fuels are the most important excise. If they were fully transferred to states, they could represent 24 percent of net state revenues. It was not possible to get data on estimated consumption of these products by state, although there are regional breakdowns of the estimated potential revenues, by state in the case of beer, and by region for alcohol and tobacco. This information was obtained from the beer producer industry and a national health survey on addictions. With this data, a rough estimate is made of how much state excises in these products could yield (table 4.2). Better estimates should be generated when the government makes the actual proposals for change. The greatest problem is that the available fiscal statistics provide information about how much revenue is collected at the point of production, not at consumption. The state-by-state income distribution surveys conducted in 1996, discussed earlier, provide consumption information, but they cover only a third of the states. States and the federal government could work together to produce better consumption information.

Automobile Taxes

Although the registration tax on existing automobiles (*tenencia*) is formally a federal tax, revenues are actually assigned to the states, which is reasonable. The present tax could thus be assigned formally to the states. In theory, states could choose different rates for the tax, depending on the desire for public services. In fact, the possibility of illegally registering in low-tax states would probably constrain these tax rates to be similar, if not identical. It would be appropriate for the federal government (or the states acting in concert) to impose a national minimum, to prevent ruinous tax competition for the registration of vehicles. Automobile taxes cannot, however, provide a major source of revenue if they are not coupled with the excise on gas. The tax on new cars, ISAN, is also formally federal but its revenues are actually assigned to the states. It represents only around 1 percent of state net revenues, while tenencia reaches 8 percent. The tax base for these taxes is evenly distributed across states, since the per capita number of cars, except for Mexico City, is rather similar. One would not expect great increases in the yield of these taxes since compliance with them is already near the practical maximum, except for the problem of smuggled cars from the U.S. in several border states, most notably Chihuahua.

Corporate Income Tax

The corporate income tax is not a particularly good way to finance subnational governments, for reasons explained below. It should be used only as a last resort, if necessary, to reduce vertical fiscal imbalance.

Table 4.2. Increase in Own Revenues from Reassignment of Major Excises by State

State	All excises on beer and alcoholic beverages		All excises on tobacco products		50 percent of excises on motor fuels	
	Increase in own revenues	Percentage of net revenues	Increase in own revenues	Percentage of net revenues	Increase in own revenues	Percentage of net revenues
Aguascalientes	62,104	7.4	118,378	14.0	96,151	11.4
Baja California	268,524	11.2	294,617	12.3	237,467	9.9
Baja California Sur	48,875	10.6	52,703	11.4	42,480	9.2
Campeche	57,450	5.8	26,629	2.7	71,626	7.3
Coahuila	150,210	7.4	235,076	11.6	240,365	11.8
Colima	50,854	8.6	66,575	11.2	54,075	9.1
Chiapas	316,621	9.0	153,920	4.4	414,020	11.8
Chihuahua	288,058	9.6	303,749	10.1	310,583	10.3
DF	599,553	2.8	834,777	3.9	930,997	4.3
Durango	93,607	8.3	154,910	13.7	158,396	14.0
Guanajuato	337,785	11.0	325,461	10.6	495,935	16.1
Guerrero	246,074	13.0	233,044	12.3	329,147	17.4
Hidalgo	146,831	4.9	154,844	5.2	235,951	7.9
Jalisco	471,239	9.8	827,764	17.2	672,341	14.0
México	752,238	8.0	855,871	9.1	1,304,169	13.9
Michoacán	309,865	13.2	306,801	13.1	433,320	18.5
Morelos	111,005	8.2	105,695	7.8	161,057	11.9
Nayarit	83,802	11.8	122,216	17.2	99,269	14.0
Nuevo León	330,789	9.5	322,536	9.2	394,631	11.3
Oaxaca	265,144	7.6	262,375	7.5	370,574	10.6
Puebla	317,059	10.0	344,556	10.9	525,032	16.6
Querétaro	84,987	6.9	91,930	7.4	140,082	11.3
Quintana Roo	96,537	10.2	29,677	3.1	79,828	8.4
San Luis Potosí	136,183	9.6	201,092	14.2	246,042	17.4
Sinaloa	197,797	9.2	332,547	15.5	268,040	12.5
Sonora	214,692	8.6	287,233	11.6	231,516	9.3
Tabasco	142,222	3.9	72,704	2.0	195,562	5.3
Tamaulipas	239,164	10.6	228,986	10.2	280,171	12.5
Tlaxcala	56,588	6.7	64,487	7.7	98,264	11.7
Veracruz	504,373	8.3	542,923	8.9	766,815	12.6
Yucatán	116,693	8.3	64,212	4.6	172,719	12.3
Zacatecas	97,968	9.8	184,153	18.5	149,576	15.0

Source: Authors' estimates.

CONCEPTUAL ARGUMENTS. There is little reason to believe that corporate income taxes closely reflect the cost of services provided to business, especially if the taxes are levied only on corporations. There is no reason to believe that only profitable firms consume public services or that consumption of public services is closely related to profits.

ADMINISTRATIVE ARGUMENTS. It is inherently difficult to determine the geographic source of the income of corporations operating in more than one state (see McLure 1984).[12] Firms may manipulate transfer prices to shift income to the states where tax rates are lowest. Ordinarily it is even conceptually impossible to divide the income of multijurisdictional corporations accurately, because of the economic interdependence among activities in various jurisdictions. For this reason, it is common to use formulas to apportion the tax base among subnational jurisdictions. The "apportionment factors" that are commonly used in the United State are payroll, property, and sales; the Canadian provinces use payroll and sales.

ECONOMIC ARGUMENTS. Being origin-based taxes, corporate income taxes tend to distort the location of economic activity, be exported to residents of other states, and accentuate horizontal fiscal disparities.

LOCATIONAL EFFECTS. Using a formula to apportion income is equivalent to taxing whatever is in the apportionment formula, at a rate that depends on the nationwide profitability of the firm, relative to the apportionment factors (see McLure 1980). This being the case, it may be more appropriate simply to tax the apportionment factors (for example, payroll, property, and sales) directly. In either event, the tax will have economic effects, including distortion of the location of economic activity, that resemble those of taxes on the apportionment factors. Because payroll and property (and sales attributed to the state of origin) are origin-based factors, their inclusion in the apportionment formula tends to discourage location of production in the taxing state. By comparison, if the sales factor reflects sales at destination, its inclusion in the formula should have little effect on location.[13]

TAX EXPORTING. The incidence of a corporate income tax that is based on apportionment of profits among the states is likely to resemble that of a tax on the factors in the apportionment formula (for example, payroll, property, and sales; see McLure 1981). The portion of the tax that is related to property is likely to be exported in part to nonresident owners of corporations.

HORIZONTAL FISCAL DISPARITIES. As noted in Chapter 1, origin-based taxes tend to produce horizontal fiscal disparities. In the case of a tax based on formula apportionment, the forces creating horizontal disparities are probably strongest for the part of the tax that is related to property and weakest for the part related to sales (if at destination). Figures on GDP per capita by state provide some evidence on the potential for horizontal disparities that would be created by a state corporate income tax. While the Federal

District, Nuevo León, and the oil-producing states of Campeche and Tabasco have per capita GDP (in terms of purchasing power parity) comparable to those of the less wealthy European countries, the figures for Chiapas and Oaxaca are closer to those in Africa.

DESIGNING SURCHARGES. The only sensible way to implement a state tax on corporate income would be as a surcharge on the tax of the central government. Because of the need for uniformity in tax bases, apportionment formulas, and administrative practices, it would be a mistake to allow the states to define their own tax bases, choose their own apportionment formulas, or administer their own taxes. The central government would apply the relevant apportionment formula to the federal tax base to determine the income subject to the tax of the various states and then apply the state tax rates to determine liability for state taxes. It has been impossible to provide reliable estimates of how a state corporate income tax surcharge would be distributed across states. First, most of the federal corporate income tax is reported in Mexico City, where the company headquarters are often located. Second, the corporate income tax is fully integrated with the 2 percent asset tax, which although spread more evenly across the country, is offset by the possibility companies have of deducting the asset tax from the corporate income tax in their returns. Hence a high figure in a particular state in the asset tax could simply signal that firms in that state are in a downturn of economic activity, not reporting profits and hence income tax. The third issue is reliability of information. The numbers for corporate income tax provided by INEGI do not match those of the Cuenta de la Hacienda Pública Federal, which is supposedly the official source for this information.

Retail Sales Tax

The federal government of Mexico imposes a value added tax (VAT), and has recently proposed to allow the states to impose a retail sales tax (RST). If implemented, this proposal may create difficulties of compliance and administration—difficulties that have dissuaded most countries from attempting this particular combination of assignment of taxing powers. This subsection describes these difficulties and international experience in this area. Mexico could also consider adopting a system of dual national/subnational VATs. The next two subsections describe problems that have commonly been attributed to state VATs and consider briefly dual federal/state VATs. A particular dual VAT system that could work in Mexico is described in greater detail below and in McLure (1999).

The proposal to combine state RSTs with the federal VAT raises two concerns; they relate to the achievement of consumption-based taxation and the treatment of interstate sales to achieve destination-based taxation.

TAXING CONSUMPTION. A consumption-based tax applies only to sales to households; it does not burden sales to business.[14] In an ideal system, VAT is collected on virtually all sales by registered traders, except those for export, without regard to whether the sale is to a household or unregistered trader or to another registered trader. Taxation of business purchases is eliminated by allowing registered traders to deduct (take "input credit" for) taxes paid on purchases from tax due on sales. Thus the only tax that is not eliminated by input credits is that paid by households and unregistered traders.

An ideal RST would directly achieve the objective of exempting sales to businesses; it would apply only to sales to households (and unregistered traders) and exempts all sales to registered traders.[15] The administrative problem is how to achieve this objective without opening the door to evasion by households claiming to make business purchases. It would be sensible to condition exemption of sales to business on presentation of a business taxpayer identification number (TIN) to the seller, so that, in principle, only purchases that would be eligible for input credits under the VAT would be exempt under the RST.[16] The recent Mexican VAT proposal did not contain such a provision; it simply states that sales to businesses should be exempt.

The mechanics of the RST and the VAT operate in different ways. Under the RST the vendor collects tax only on sales to households and must keep track of exempt sales made to business purchasers and document the purchaser's eligibility for exemption. By comparison, under the VAT, since all sales are taxable, the vendor does not need to make the distinction between taxable and exempt sales, but is saddled with the task of accounting for the tax paid on purchases, in order to claim input credits. Both of these systems involve considerable administrative and compliance costs, especially for small businesses. Imposing both systems on businesses, as under the proposal to combine state RSTs with the federal VAT, would be quite onerous. Because the two systems operate differently, implementing both would be costly for tax administration, especially since the proposed legislation for the state RST indicates that the tax would be administered by state administrations.[17] Both the state and federal tax administrations would need to determine whether purchases by registered traders are for a legitimate business purpose, since only those are eligible for exemption (RST) or input credit (VAT).[18] In theory, state officials could use information obtained in administration of the federal VAT (or vice versa); in fact, the requisite sharing of information probably would not occur. Moreover, in the absence of substantial cooperation between federal and state administrations, vendors would be forced to provide essentially but not exactly the same information to both.[19]

Customarily sales taxes exempt a long list of products sold to households. This is true of the Mexican VAT, and it can be expected that states would also provide exemptions, because the proposal does not specify a uniform base for the RST. Exemptions substantially complicate compliance and administration, because taxpayers and tax administrators need to distinguish between sales of taxable and exempt products. The situation would be even worse if the exemptions provided by the state RSTs and the federal VAT were not substantially identical. Vendors would need to distinguish between four possible combinations of tax treatment, in addition to the distinction between sales to registered traders and other sales: taxable under both federal and state taxes, exempt under both, and taxable under one, but not the other. To minimize this type of complexity, the bases of the two bases should be identical (except for the difference in treatment of sales to registered traders and to others), so that a given sale to households is either taxed or exempt under both taxes. This implies, of course, identity of the bases of the state RSTs. As noted in Chapter 1, the lack of state sovereignty over the definition of tax bases is a small price to pay for autonomy over tax rates, and thus the level of public spending in the state.

DESTINATION-BASED TAXATION OF INTERSTATE TRADE. To the extent that sales to households and unregistered traders pass through locally registered merchants, it is relatively easy to achieve destination-based taxation of interstate trade under the RST, providing the state of origin does not tax interstate sales to registered traders.[20] Some sales to households and unregistered traders, called "remote sales" in the European Union, do not pass through locally registered merchants; mail-order sales of tangible products and electronic commerce in digital content fall into this category.[21] This "disintermediated" interstate commerce poses potential problems, because states of destination are likely to be unable to tax it, for reasons mentioned below.[22]

If states of origin tax interstate sales made directly to households and unregistered traders, revenues from the RST go to the "wrong" state, the state of origin, instead of the state of destination. While this may not be important in the aggregate, it could produce substantial amounts of tax exporting in some cases, for example, by the Federal District and certain other states where large cities are located and, most prominently, by the border state of Tamaulipas, where most of the RST on imports would be paid.

It seems more likely that states of origin would exempt all interstate sales, for competitive reasons. If states of destination could not tax sales to households and unregistered traders, there would be gaps in the tax base, and local merchants would be placed at a competitive disadvantage, relative to vendors in other states. Gaps in the tax base violate vertical as well as horizontal equity, because higher-income households are more likely to buy from out-of-state vendors.

It would be difficult to construct a workable system of destination-based taxation of remote sales under an RST. To implement such a system with precision, it would be necessary for each vendor to (a) calculate tax on each remote sale using the tax rate of the state of destination, (b) record taxable sales and tax due, by state, and (c) file a tax return and pay tax in each state to which it makes sales. Nothing comparable would be required under the federal VAT—or under the dual state/federal VAT described below. Similarly, each of the 32 states would, in principle, need to audit vendors engaged in remote commerce that are located in each of the other states.[23] This system seems too complicated for serious consideration, even if tax were due only from vendors making sales to a particular state in excess of a *de minimis* amount, since the alternative state/federal VAT described below is available.

An alternative would be to subject remote sales to households and unregistered traders to a uniform tax and divide the resulting revenue among the states in proportion to estimated consumption in the various states.[24] This is what would occur under the dual federal/state VAT. While this would address the problem of interstate trade, it would not address the first issue discussed above, the fundamental incompatibility in the way the VAT and the RST operate.

Value Added Tax: Traditional Concerns

The conventional wisdom has long been that subnational governments cannot use the value added tax effectively, especially as a stand-alone tax that they themselves administer.[25] As with the RST, the basic problems involve avoidance of multiple (cascading) taxation of business purchases and trade crossing borders between taxing jurisdictions within the nation,[26] especially the proper (destination basis) treatment of sales to households and unregistered traders.[27] Evidence and analysis in the late 1990s, however, have shown ways that state governments can effectively impose a surcharge on the VAT of the national government. The next subsection explains briefly the operation of two "dual" systems of destination-based federal/state VATs; one that is especially attractive for Mexico relies on imposition of a "compensating VAT" on trade between states; the state component of this system could be imposed either by the central government or by a consortium of the states.

The rest of this subsection indicates why a stand-alone state VAT is problematic, if not infeasible, whether imposed on the origin or destination basis. Poddar (1990, p. 105) sets out four criteria as a basis to judge state VAT systems: (a) lack of interference with the location of economic activity, which is inherent in the destination principle; (b) lack of internal border controls; (c) state autonomy over tax rates; and (d) simplicity.

ORIGIN-BASED TAXATION. Unless imposed at the same rate by all states, origin-based taxation distorts the location of economic activity and is difficult to administer, because all interstate transactions must be valued, to prevent artificial attribution of value added to low-tax jurisdictions.[28] But limiting all states to a single rate undercuts one of the primary reasons for assigning taxing powers to subnational governments, allowing subnational choice of tax rates. Moreover, there is a risk that triangular trade will produce undesirable patterns of fiscal flows, as has happened in Brazil.[29]

DESTINATION-BASED TAXATION. By comparison, destination-based taxation by states acting alone has several possible undesirable features, depending on how it is implemented: internal fiscal frontiers that interfere with trade between the states, the risk that revenues will be lost (if cross-border sales to registered businesses are zero-rated and diverted to households and unregistered traders without payment of tax), onerous burdens of compliance and administration, and complicated clearinghouse arrangements between states of origin and destination. These potential problems are described more fully.

Fiscal frontiers would impede the operation of a single market within a country. Destination-based taxation is achieved for international trade through the use of "border tax adjustments." That is, imports are subject to the VAT and exports are zero-rated (and tax collected on previous stages of the production-distribution process is refunded to exporting firms, if it exceeds their liability for the VAT on domestic sales). Implementation of this system requires fiscal frontiers, in order to collect the VAT on imports and verify that reported exportation actually occurs. This is ordinarily not a problem for international trade (except in the context of a customs union or common market), since goods commonly stop at the border for other reasons, including collection of customs duties and inspections for health and safety. But it is a problem within a country, where free internal trade is an important goal.

Zero-rating/deferred payment provides a conceptually attractive approach for dealing with interstate trade; the European Union employs it as a "transitional" scheme. Zero-rating of sales to registered vendors in other states would eliminate tax in the state of origin, and use of deferred payment by the state of destination would avoid the need for fiscal frontiers between states. (Since interstate sales would not be taxed, registered vendors who import from another state would have no VAT to claim as a credit against tax on sales. Tax is deferred from the time of importation to the time tax is paid on sales.) As in the case of the RST, sales to households and unregistered traders in other states could be taxed at the rate in the state of destination (with revenue submitted to that state) or, to simplify matters, at the rate in the state of origin (which would receive the revenue). The primary risk is that goods that have been zero-rated as sales to a registered trader in another state will be diverted to use by households or unregistered traders, perhaps even in the state of origin.

Taxation of all sales by the vendor at the tax rate of the state of destination (with submission of revenue to that state) also achieves the conceptually correct result, again without border controls.[30] Moreover, it avoids the need to treat cross-border sales to registered traders and to households and nonregistered traders differently. The primary drawback of this approach is complexity, which is similar to that of attempting destination-based taxation under the RST, but even greater, because it would apply to all interstate sales, not just those to households and unregistered traders. Vendors making interstate sales would potentially need to account for sales to 32 states and file returns in as many states. This alternative does not seem worthy of serious consideration.

Taxation by the vendor at the rate of the jurisdiction of origin, with a tax credit clearinghouse, seems also to be inordinately complicated. (Moreover, sales to households and unregistered traders would be taxed at the "wrong" rate and tax revenue would go to the "wrong" state, if such sales were accorded the same treatment.) Registered purchasers would be allowed credits for all tax on inputs, but credits would need to be identified by states collecting the input tax—and thus identified by vendors claiming the credits, so that destination states granting credits could be reimbursed by states of origin that had originally collected tax for which credit is granted. Since states of destination are to be reimbursed for the credits they grant for taxes paid to states of origin, they have little incentive to verify the validity of credits claimed for tax paid on interstate sales. This option also does not seem worthy of further consideration.

The Compensating VAT on Interstate Trade

It appears that the above analyses, which have usually implicitly assumed taxation by a single level of government, may overstate the difficulty of implementing a destination-based subnational VAT in the context of a national VAT. If a subnational VAT is possible, the state VAT could be a major source of own revenues for the states of Mexico and could increase their autonomy to raise own revenue *at the margin*, via state control of VAT surcharge rates. The remainder of this subsection discusses two alternative ways to implement a state VAT as part of a dual federal/state system.

ZERO-RATING/DEFERRED PAYMENT IN A DUAL SYSTEM. The dual system used in Canada by the federal government and the province of Quebec ("the Quebec system") relies on zero-rating and deferred payment for the taxation of trade between provinces. Bird and Gendron (1998) assert that the control provided by the presence of the federal tax is enough to prevent unacceptable abuse of the provincial tax.[31] (It would be difficult to evade tax on an interstate sale to a household or an unregistered trader by claiming that the transaction should be zero-rated upon export. Only interstate sales to registered traders would be eligible for zero-rating.) This argument may be less convincing in Mexico, where tax administration is weaker.[32] Some interstate purchases by households and unregistered traders masquerading as purchases by registered traders might escape tax. Primary reliance on state administration of the state VAT, combined with federal administration of the federal VAT, would accentuate the problem, due to the risk that communication and coordination among state administrations and between them and the federal administration would not be as good as within a centralized administration.

DUAL FEDERAL/STATE VAT, WITH COMPENSATING VAT ON INTERSTATE TRADE. A compensating VAT (CVAT) on interstate sales to registered traders would avoid most of the problems associated with stand-alone VATs and with Quebec's system of "unprotected" zero-rating/deferred payment.[33] Under the CVAT scheme, interstate sales to registered traders would be zero-rated by the state of origin and subject to deferred payment of VAT by registered businesses in the state of destination, as in the Quebec system. The risk that zero-rated sales would be diverted to households or to unregistered traders would be avoided (or reduced) by the collection of a federal "compensating VAT" on interstate sales to registered traders. (It is assumed here that the compensating VAT would be collected by the federal government in the context of the federal VAT.) Registered taxpayers would be allowed to claim credits for the compensating VAT, as well as the ordinary federal VAT, in computing federal tax liability; in principle, the two taxes need not be differentiated in calculating liability to the federal government.[34]

Assuming that the same compensating VAT rate would be applied to interstate sales to households and unregistered traders as to interstate sales to registered traders, vendors would need to deal with only three rates (plus zero, for international exports), only two of which would be relevant for any one domestic sale, as in any system involving taxation by two levels of government: the ordinary federal rate on all sales, the rate of the local state on sales within the state, and the compensating VAT rate on sales to other states. Vendors would not need to deal with the tax rates of any other states or to engage in interstate clearing of tax credits.

The dual federal/state VAT system has several administrative advantages over the combination of a federal VAT and state RSTs discussed earlier. Since both state and federal taxes are value added taxes, compliance and administration would be simpler. There would be no need to distinguish between taxable sales to households and unregistered traders, nor to exempt sales to registered traders, as under the RST. Under the VAT/CVAT system, vendors would need to distinguish between local and interstate sales (regardless of the nature of the buyer), but that seems to be easier than the multiple distinctions required under the RST.

Sharing of VAT Revenue as a Transitional Measure

As an interim measure, the federal government might share revenues from a joint federal/state VAT with the states on the basis of a formula reflecting the destination of taxable sales. Tax sharing would subsequently be replaced with uniform-rate state taxes on value added. Finally, states would be given latitude to choose their own tax rates. While it is very difficult to estimate what a state VAT would collect, very preliminary calculations suggest that the yield could be significant. Taking into account only domestic transactions susceptible to VAT, and keeping only the national oil company, PEMEX, susceptible to Federal VAT, if the federal government retained a value added tax rate of 12 percent, and during the transition state governments kept a 3 percent rate, state net revenue could increase by 10.9 percent. Such an increase would need to be offset by a decrease in revenue sharing, since federal VAT collection would be reduced, and hence sharable revenue. To this one would need to add an estimated 9.1 percent increase in state net revenues coming from the CVAT collected for imports.

Potential Sources of Municipal Revenues

Municipal governments are slightly less dependent than the states on revenue sharing and transfers. In the aggregate municipal governments receive 64.3 percent of total net revenues from the federal government and the states, 17.6 percent from taxes, and the rest from fees. Of course, this pattern differs markedly across and within states. While municipalities in Baja California, Chihuahua, the State of Mexico, Nuevo León, and Quintana Roo finance about a quarter of their expenditure with tax revenue, in Campeche, Chiapas, and Oaxaca this is close to 5 percent, and Morelos exhibits a dismal 1.3 percent. Thus, it would be advantageous to provide municipal governments with access to additional sources of revenue.

PROPERTY TAX. The property tax (*predial*) is the most important source of revenue for municipalities, besides the transfers received from the federal and state governments (*participaciones*). The property tax comprises 13 percent of municipalities' total net revenue, but 74.2 percent of their tax revenues. These numbers exclude the Federal District, which does not have municipalities and hence collects predial directly. The collection of property tax is best in Mexico City, where compliance has been improved and cadastres are updated more frequently. In fact, *predial* collection in the Federal District is almost as much as what is collected in all municipalities together. The two most important issues for property tax collection are the updating of the tax base and the problems of compliance. While initiatives are under way to help municipalities on both counts, successful experiences in specific municipalities could be better disseminated across the country.

EXCISES ON PUBLIC UTILITIES. Excises on public utilities have the advantage of being easily enforced. Moreover, demand for some public utilities is quite inelastic with respect to price, so that taxation does not create serious distortions. In some cases (for example, electricity) demand is also income elastic, but in others (water) it is income inelastic; taxation is progressive in the former case, but regressive in the latter.

The proper structure of a tax on electric power deserves attention. First, like other indirect taxes, such a tax should not be applied to business consumption of power. Taxing power used by business introduces an element of cascading into the system. Second, if power is subject to a special municipal excise, it should probably be exempt from the VAT, to prevent excessive disincentives to use power.[35] For electricity, there is a provision for revenue sharing to municipalities out of the federal excises, but the formulas are complex and not transparent. Part of the problem with municipalities charging excises on electricity is that utilities are public, and will remain so unless the constitution is changed. A number of municipalities have greatly improved their systems and practices for water charges over the last few years, but as with the property tax, successful experiences are scattered across the country and need systematic dissemination.

Constraints in the Constitution

According to Article 73, Section XXIX, of the Mexican Constitution, the national Congress has the power to levy taxes

1. On foreign commerce
2. On the utilization and exploitation of natural resources
3. On institutions of credit and insurance companies
4. On public services under concession or operated directly by the Federation
5. Special taxes on
   a. Electric power

    b. Production and consumption of processed tobacco[36]
    c. Gasoline and other products derived from petroleum
    d. Matches
    e. Maguey and its fermented products
    f. Forestry exploitation
    g. Production and consumption of beer.

It appears that this constitutional grant of powers to the Congress is interpreted to grant to the federal government the *exclusive* right to levy the taxes listed above. If so, it imposes severe limitations on the ability to achieve the tax assignments described above as appropriate. In particular, it would prohibit state excises on tobacco products, beer, and some other alcoholic beverages (but apparently not most other alcoholic beverages), and motor fuels and municipal taxes on electric power. Thus it appears that it would be necessary to change the constitution to enable the states and municipalities to levy excises on these products, as proposed above. The constitution would pose no barrier to the assignment of excises on other products (for example, soft drinks) to the states.

By comparison, there appears to be no constitutional prohibition on state entrance into the sales tax area.[37] A CVAT could be problematic if the system is run as a state tax arrangement, since the constitution explicitly forbids states from imposing sales tax at differential rates depending on where products come from. However, if the CVAT is a federal tax, there would be no perceived discrimination in the tax treatment of states to different products according to their origin. It would, however, be necessary to nullify or modify the revenue-sharing conventions and the provisions of the value added tax law that prevent the states from levying a VAT as long as they participate in the revenue-sharing program.

A final note on the politics of changing the constitution is in order. While ordinary laws are enacted by vote of the House of Deputies, amendments to the constitution must be approved first by the Senate and then by the House of Deputies.

Summary: Long- and Short-Run Reassignments of Taxes

Table 4.3 summarizes the actual assignment of taxes, proposed assignments, reasons for change, and caveats. The most important change proposed at the state level would be the introduction of a dual system of state and federal VAT. This change should not be undertaken, however, without careful planning and preparation. Canada is the only nation in the world that has a two-tier VAT that functions satisfactorily, and no nation employs the proposed system of a compensating VAT. (Brazil's two-tier system does not function satisfactorily now, but reforms of the VAT type are under serious consideration.)

The next most important change would be to make revenues from destination-based excises available to the states, which would require changing the constitution. These two fundamental changes could be highly beneficial but cannot be made quickly, for political and technical reasons.

Less significant changes involving state taxes are (a) rationalization of the payroll taxes by making definitions and administrative procedures uniform and identical to those for the federal social security taxes, and (b) formally transferring taxes on registration of motor vehicles to the state level. From a technical point of view, these changes could be made relatively quickly. Of course, except for the fears that the origin-based payroll tax will dampen economic activity, increases in the payroll tax could provide more revenues for most states.

At the municipal level greater reliance on the property tax may be possible, but not without a modern, up-to-date cadastral survey. This, of course, takes time to implement. Beyond that, taxation of electric power may provide revenues for some municipalities, and fairly quickly. Finally, it is important to increase charges for public services where they are priced below marginal cost, which is typical.

Short-term changes:

- An increase in the payroll tax rate to 3 percent in those states where the current rate is below 3 percent;
- A shift of all revenues from registration of automobiles to the states.

Long-term changes:

- A shift of revenues from 3 percentage points of the VAT from the federal government to state governments, employing the dual federal/state VAT;
- A shift of all revenues from excises on alcoholic beverages, tobacco products, and 50 percent of revenues from excises on motor fuels from the federal government to the governments of states where consumption occurs.

Table 4.4 provides preliminary estimates of the potential revenue available to the states from reassignment of taxes along the lines outlined above. It is based on the assumptions given in the table headings.

Table 4.3 Current and Proposed Assignments in Mexico

Tax	Current assignment	Proposed assignment	Rationale for proposal	Caveats/comments
Production Excises	Federal (constitutional)	Eliminate	Subsidiarity (reserve for states)	
Consumption Excises		State (federal administration, on destination basis)	Benefits of specific or generalized benefits; subsidiarity	New system; interstate smuggling
Vehicle taxes	Mixed federal/state	State	Subsidiarity	Convert purchase tax to annual tax
Value Added Tax	Federal/20 percent to revenue-sharing pool	Federal/state surcharges (Perhaps destination-based tax sharing in transition)	Specific or generalized benefits; subsidiarity; broad coverage; less horizontal disparities	Requires innovative technique
Individual Income	Federal/20 percent to revenue-sharing pool	Federal/revenue-sharing pool	Narrow coverage; horizontal disparities	State surcharge required for revenue
Corporation Income Tax	Federal/20 percent to revenue-sharing pool	Federal/revenue-sharing pool	Tax exporting; distortion of location; difficult to determine geographic source of income; horizontal disparities	
Payroll Tax	State	State, but perhaps with federal administration	Administration with federal payroll tax is more efficient	Lack of trust; less subnational autonomy
Natural Resources: Ordinary		Federal/ 20 percent to revenue-sharing pool	Federal/revenue-sharing pool	Avoid horizontal disparity; provide own state revenues
Extraordinary	Federal	Federal	Avoid instability of state revenue revenues	
Property Tax	Municipal	Municipal	Subsidiarity	Need to improve administration

Table 4.4. Increase in Own Revenues from Reassignment of Various Taxes, by State (Thousands of Pesos 1996)

State	Taxes potentially reassigned in the short run		Taxes potentially reassigned in the long run	
	Increase in payroll tax to 3 percent	State automobile taxes	State VAT of 3 percent	Destination-based excises
Aguascalientes	51,402	68,113	162,437	372,783
Baja California	36,267	120,373	401,177	1,038,075
Baja California Sur	23,609	21,302	71,765	186,537
Campeche	86,962	27,721	121,006	227,332
Coahuila	138,500	190,812	406,073	866,016
Colima	45,801	31,123	91,354	225,580
Chiapas	0	80,239	699,445	1,298,581
Chihuahua	201,469	183,401	524,700	1,212,974
DF	34,118	2,208,338	1,572,827	3,296,324
Durango	51,908	61,449	267,594	565,309
Guanajuato	211,274	231,126	837,833	1,655,116
Guerrero	63,837	73,307	556,061	1,137,411
Hidalgo	73,892	67,005	398,615	773,577
Jalisco	131,679	526,976	1,135,853	2,643,686
México	149,611	390,673	2,203,265	4,216,448
Michoacán	115,530	159,547	732,051	1,483,305
Morelos	111,063	82,041	272,089	538,813
Nayarit	25,725	32,695	167,704	404,556
Nuevo León	137,476	566,770	666,690	1,442,586
Oaxaca	61,647	49,248	626,048	1,268,668
Puebla	129,878	222,552	886,989	1,711,678
Querétaro	91,057	97,512	236,655	457,080
Quintana Roo	62,062	72,329	134,861	285,869
San Luis Potosí	112,628	111,721	415,664	829,360
Sinaloa	76,717	134,296	452,827	1,066,424
Sonora	29,069	148,445	391,123	964,958
Tabasco	0	83,573	330,383	606,051
Tamaulipas	0	180,702	473,321	1,028,492
Tlaxcala	12,697	23,757	166,008	317,604
Veracruz	223,727	236,421	1,295,457	2,580,926
Yucatán	33,982	87,666	291,791	526,342
Zacatecas	33,428	33,716	252,694	581,274

Source: Authors' calculations from INEGI data.

5

Transfers and the Nature of the
Mexican Federation

Thomas Courchene and Alberto Díaz-Cayeros

THIS CHAPTER ANALYZES THE CURRENT PRACTICE of transfers in Mexican fiscal federalism and then considers alternative approaches to transfer design and implementation. The first section focuses on those principles that ought to inform the system of intergovernmental transfers in any federation, Mexico included. The second section examines the constitution and the programs of the Zedillo administration for evidence on the nature of the social contract underlying Mexican federalism. Then the analysis directs attention to the description, quantification, and assessment of the current set of intergovernmental transfers, including unconditional *participaciones*, the mostly conditional *aportaciones,* and the infrastructure transfers. For each of these categories and their components, per capita data are presented both in absolute value by state and in relation to the state's ranking in terms of a poverty index. To these transfer data the following section adds data relating to own-source revenues which, then, allows an assessment of the degree of vertical and horizontal imbalance in the Mexican federation. What emerges is a relatively high degree of horizontal balance, provided one excludes a few of the obvious outliers. The final section turns attention to some alternative scenarios for the evolution of Mexican fiscal federalism.

Principles for Intergovernmental Transfers

The analysis of Mexico's theory and practice for fiscal federalism, described in the rest of the chapter, indicates that its system of intergovernmental transfers ought to satisfy eight principles.

First, intergovernmental grants should complement the associated expenditure and tax allocations in ways that make the overall system resonate well with the needs and underlying social values of the Mexican federation and society. For example, the importance of assuring relatively equal access to certain national public goods like education implies that the federation will have grants earmarked for those purposes.

Second, intergovernmental grants should deliver the conception and degree of equity embedded in the Mexican "political contract." This means that the equalizing or horizontal transfers to states should be tailored to deliver this degree of subnational equity. As an important aside, equity does not relate to the grants in isolation: it relates to the *sum* of the transfers and all other state revenues. That is, the states' *overall fiscal capacity* should be brought up to the equity standard.

Third, the transfer arrangements should be predictable over time. The set of transfers should be designed within a multiyear framework to allow the states a corresponding multiyear planning and budgeting horizon. Although absolute predictability cannot be guaranteed, a useful initial compromise might be a federal-state agreement over three or five years (preferably overlapping the presidential sexenio and the congressional three-year terms) with provisions requiring adequate notice for any changes.

The fourth principle is a variant of the last: formulas should determine transfers as much as possible. This implies that the procedures of calculation should be open and transparent, such that they can be reproduced by third parties. To facilitate this, Mexico could consider the establishment of a formal or informal agency representing both the federal government and the states. Australia's Commonwealth Grants Commission is the pre-eminent exemplar of a formal, quasi-independent agency, while Canada's technical working group of federal and provincial officials represents the informal variant. An important role for formula-based transfers is to de-politicize, at least to a degree, the overall transfer regime. These formulas will presumably be altered over time as conditions merit. But at any point in time the degree of objectivity and transparency of formula-based transfers tends to defuse what is, in effect, a zero-sum redistributional game.

The fifth principle relates to the nature of the conditions that are attached to grants associated with expenditure areas. Consistent with meeting the expenditure goals, the conditions should respect state priorities. For example, different states may be able to satisfy these conditions in different ways—ways that relate to the social, cultural, and economic needs of their respective constituencies. This argues not for a one-size-fits-all approach to conditionality, but rather for conditionality defined in terms of "equivalencies." In the fiscal federalism literature this has come to be associated with the term "competitive federalism" or "horizontal competition," which means allowing states sufficient flexibility to design their own bundles of goods and services consistent with the agreed upon conditions or, preferably, equivalencies. This should tilt the federation in the direction of dynamic efficiency, since demonstrably superior approaches to policy design in some states will be copied by other states. The focus here is on conditional grants: we take it as axiomatic that unconditional grants will be spent in ways that reflect state priorities.

The sixth principle relates to the objective of tax decentralization. Whatever the approach finally taken to equalization (or to the amelioration of horizontal imbalances), the incentives in this system should ensure that states that increase their tax effort or increase the effectiveness of their collection should be able to retain a meaningful share of the increased revenue. Even in developed federations one can still find equalization programs that embody 100 percent (that is, confiscatory) taxation with respect to subnational government revenue increases—transfers fall fully in line with revenue increases. The relevant formulas should prevent this and should retain some incentive for local tax effort.

The seventh principle also anticipates greater tax decentralization. The overall grant system should be designed in a way that anticipates and accommodates the desire of states to enhance tax revenue. For example, an expansion of states' access to tax revenues should automatically trigger the appropriate change in the flow of transfers; that is, the system should not have to be designed anew every time there is further tax decentralization. Any such institution of adjustment should respect principles three and six—assuring predictability and refraining from penalizing local tax effort.

Finally, but hardly exhaustively, any new grant design should take the initial conditions into account. Part of the rationale in this chapter is that the current set of transfers presumably embodies the implicit social contract. This must inform the evolution of transfers. Furthermore, to be politically feasible, any novel transfer arrangement must be accompanied by adequate and acceptable arrangements for transition from the old to the new system.

Mexican Constitution and Fiscal Federalism

The constitution is the framework document for all federations. Among other things, it specifies the division of powers among and between the various levels of government, including the assignment of responsibility for expenditure and taxation. In most federations, the constitution also speaks to the nature of the "federal social pact" and, therefore, provides some guidance on the nature and role of federal transfers. For example, in the Canadian federation, Section 36 addresses equality of opportunity for all citizens and also provides for equalization payments to provinces to "ensure that provincial governments have sufficient revenues to provide reasonable, comparable public goods at reasonably comparable tax rates." As an important aside, in 1999 the federal government and the Canadian provinces signed a social pact (Framework Agreement on the Social Union) designed to establish and promote the internal social and economic union. The German Basic Law embraces the concept of "uniformity of living conditions" for all Germans and actually enshrines the details of revenue sharing and the interländer revenue-sharing pool. Australia's federal social pact is reflected in the guiding principle of the Commonwealth Grants Commission—"each state should be given the capacity to provide the average standard of state-type public services, assuming it does so at an average level of operational efficiency and makes an average effort to raise revenues from its own sources." In other words, the constitution usually informs the design of intergovernmental transfers.

The Mexican Constitution, however, provides little guidance on the appropriate role, operational principles, and design of intergovernmental transfers. The Mexican Constitution proclaims, in Article 40, that Mexico is a representative, democratic, federal republic, composed of free and sovereign states in regard to their internal regimes. Article 124 assigns to the states the residual authority or power over all areas not explicitly assigned to the federal government. However, most of the other provisions then proceed to limit the authority of the states. In fact, the Mexican Federal Pact, as expressed in various provisions of the Constitution, reflects a certain distrust of the states. Moreover, except with respect to education, there is very little in the Constitution about the desired equality of conditions among constitutional units. Nor does the Constitution speak to the manner in which the federation should benefit citizens: that is, most of the references to federalism relate to the division of powers, not to the living condition of citizens within the federation.

Much of this distrust of states is rooted in an historical process of consolidation of national authority where, consonant with Riker's (1964) two principles of federalism, the federal arrangement was considered the only way to keep the country together in the face of the threat of the northern neighbor and the secessionist tendencies of some states (most notably Texas, but also Yucatán). At the same time, a highly centralized fiscal and political system was established once the country was pacified at the end the otherwise unstable nineteenth century. The Constitution limits state authority by granting exclusive tax rights to both the federal and the municipal governments. The granting of rights to the federal government is the result of a long process, culminating in the 1940s, when exclusive authority was granted to the federal government over several important taxes, although legislation to provide for explicit exclusive tax assignment was never approved by Congress (see Díaz-Cayeros 1997). The assignment of exclusive rights and responsibilities to municipalities is a more recent development, finding its expression in the 1983 reform of Article 115.

The federal Constitution explicitly mentions revenue sharing twice. The first mention is in Article 73, which assigns excises (IEPS) exclusively to the federal government and then specifies that a secondary law will determine the proportion that states will receive from those revenues. And in the case of electricity revenues, the Constitution states that the state congresses will establish a share for municipalities. The second mention of transfers is in Article 115, which gives states exclusive authority over the land tax. Here, it also provides that states should receive federal revenue shares according to conditions approved by the local congresses. These principles are important because they imply that revenue sharing is integral to the Constitution, but only for excises and for municipal governments. Revenue sharing arising from federal taxation in general is not considered explicitly, although it is the most important source of financing for subnational governments. Transfers to municipal governments are left for local congresses to decide, but a provision does imply that states must share revenues with their municipalities.

In terms of the overall fiscal authority, although Article 31, part 4, does not impose limits on tax assignment, it does provide that Mexicans must contribute to public expenditures of the federation, states, and municipalities on a proportional and equitable basis. Another article (Article 73, part 7), however, has been interpreted in practice to mean that the federal government has no limitation whatsoever on the taxes it can establish (the article states that the federal government can establish the taxes necessary to cover its budget). States, in contrast, have very specific limitations on several tax bases. The most important state limitation is related to the high-profile fiscal debate of the nineteenth century, which dealt with taxes on internal trade (the so-called *alcabala*). Such state taxes are now explicitly forbidden in Articles 116 and 117, although the provisions of those articles have often been violated de facto. The second major limitation is related to natural resources, which are now taxed exclusively under federal jurisdiction (Article 27 and Article 73). The third limitation is more recent: exclusive authority for municipalities over several areas, including property taxes, was established with the 1983 reform of Article 115.

Centralization of fiscal authority throughout the twentieth century was enhanced by increasing the authority of the federal Congress in areas as diverse as control over natural resources, regulation of financial institutions, and the exclusive right to impose taxes on foreign trade and the production of specific goods (tobacco, alcohol, beer, electricity, matches, fuel, forest products). All of these reforms were carried out by amending Article 73, concerning the attributes of Congress, which has been modified 36 times. Via Article 73, the federal government is allowed to impose taxes as needed to cover the budget; to prevent states from restricting interstate trade; to legislate with respect to oil, mining, cinemas, betting, financial services, electric and nuclear power, and labor; to coordinate states and municipalities on issues of public safety; to distribute and unify the education function "conveniently" among federation, states, and municipalities; to establish taxes on foreign trade, natural resources, credit and insurance institutions, public services granted to private providers, and sales of electricity, tobacco, gas, matches, alcohol, forestry products, and beer; and to enact laws on matters of concurrence between levels of government relating to population and environment.

Thus except for the provision granting the federal government responsibility for unifying education and distributing the education function among levels of government, there is little in the Constitution relating to the nature of transfers or what they ought to accomplish.

We must look elsewhere for an understanding of what federal transfers are meant to achieve. The Zedillo administration (1994–2000) has made the "new federalism" one of its major programs in government. The Program for a New Federalism (*Programa para un Nuevo Federalismo, 1995–2000*) explicitly states what the administration considers the most important changes needed to reinvigorate the federal arrangement. The program promises to decentralize resources in health, education, and the construction of physical infrastructure, much of which Ramo 33 has achieved. The program does not explicitly address the criteria to determine federal transfers for those functions. It does, however, seek to strengthen state autonomy and to redistribute "authority, functions, responsibility, and resources" from the federal government to the subnational governments (Programa 1997, p. 7). It also suggests that fiscal coordination should incorporate revenue, expenditure, and debt. But when it comes to stating the lines of action, there are only proposals to "carry out studies" and "propose new models of expenditure that should redistribute and balance both vertically and horizontally the assignment of resources for social spending and federal public investment" (p. 17). On the unconditional transfers granted through revenue sharing, the program does advocate revising the formulas for the distribution of revenue, but it fails to mention anything more specific than that. Indeed, the program is rather vague, calling for "including in the formulas, representative variables of the phenomena that are effectively sought to be measured" (p. 17).

The Program for a New Federalism gives some details on the devolution of expenditure and signals the future evolution of the federation, but not on the nature and characteristics of the accompanying transfer system. So, we look elsewhere for this vital information. In particular, we focus on the de facto overall distribution of the actual transfers and own revenues across states, which reveal the preferences in the social pact underlying the Mexican federation. The degree of overall horizontal imbalance across states is much less than one might expect from the interplay of more than 20 transfer programs and own-source revenues.

Current Intergovernmental Transfer Programs

Transfers in Mexico accounted for 39 percent of the total federal government budget in 1999. As figure 5.1 shows, this is a remarkable share, since it is larger than what is spent in all the ministries of the central sector (30 percent); the allocations to pay for the public debt (22 percent, including financial supports for banks and debtors as well as bills pending from previous periods); and support for the social security institutions and pension funds (9 percent). This 39 percent of the federal budget is made up by budgetary ramos or items—Ramo 23 for the president's discretionary fund, which is used for salary increases and natural disasters; Ramo 25 for support of education and salary increases in the Federal District; Ramo 26 for regional development; Ramo 28 for revenue sharing; and Ramo 33, started in 1998, for transfers (*aportaciones*) for education, health, social infrastructure, and other uses. Ramos 23 and 26 are being phased out, so 28 and 33 have become the main transfers.

This is not all the money that the federal government spends in states and municipalities. For example, there are matching grants for public investment projects with the states (which are substantially smaller than in previous years, but still remain important), and there are funds for social assistance such as PROGRESA, PROCAMPO, and other social welfare initiatives. Nevertheless, we focus here on the 39 percent share corresponding to funds that are transferred to states and municipalities, both

Figure 5.1. Composition of the Federal Government Budget

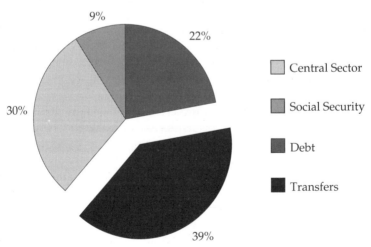

Source: Ley de Egreso 1999.

conditional and unconditional. We begin with the unconditional transfers arising from revenue sharing (Ramo 28).

Unconditional Revenue Sharing (Participaciones)

The most important element in the Mexican federal transfer system was, until December 1997, the revenue sharing (*participaciones*) determined by the National System of Fiscal Coordination (Sistema Nacional de Coordinación Fiscal) from 1980 onward. Laws relating to fiscal coordination existed before 1980, but the current system took shape once the value added tax was established at the federal level, substituting for a federal sales tax (Impuesto Sobre Ingresos Mercantiles, ISIM) that had existed for decades in most states. ISIM was not universally embraced by all states until the early 1970s, when the overall rate was increased from 3 to 4 percent, 2.2 percent of which was assigned to the states. (Accounts of the history of revenue sharing can be found in Bonifaz Chapoy 1992; Martínez Almazán 1980; Martínez Cabañas 1985; Retchkiman and Gil Valdivia 1981; and Diaz Cayeros 1995.) When the current system was established in 1980, the states surrendered not only their share of the federal sales tax, but also the multiple excise taxes on consumption and production that had been accumulating over the years. The 1980 agreement established two contracts between states and the federal government. The first was the *convenio de adhesión,* which established that states would voluntarily join the National System of Fiscal Coordination and hence restrain their own taxing authority. In return, the states would receive unconditional revenue-sharing transfers. The second was the *convenio de colaboración administrativa,* which provided guidelines for joint state surveillance and monitoring of federal tax compliance, providing incentives to states for detecting tax evasion.

Originally three funds comprised the revenue-sharing system: the *Fondo General de Participaciones* and the *Fondo Financiero Complementario,* which were distributed to states, and the *Fondo de Fomento Municipal,* which was transferred to municipalities via state governments, but according to a federal allocation formula. The states were also required to transfer 20 percent of these federal revenue shares to municipalities, in accordance with the states' own formulas or allocation criteria. The overall amount for the states and municipalities was determined as a percentage (now equal to 20 percent) of the *Recaudación Federal Participable* (RFP) or "assignable taxes." The main components of these assignable or shared taxes are revenues collected from the federal income tax, the value added tax, and the ordinary fees from oil. This meant that, except for the so-called "extraordinary" fees on oil and some other items, most of the domestic federal taxes were subject to sharing.

In addition to these funds, several specific federal taxes are shared on a case-by-case basis. The two most important for states are the property tax on automobiles (*tenencia*) and the tax on new cars (ISAN), which are both fully shared—that is, 100 percent of the revenues are transferred to the states. Both *tenencia* and ISAN are transferred on a derivation basis, so their collection in each state is a good indicator of the underlying tax base in the respective state. This is not true for value added and income taxes, which are typically reported regionally in terms of the companies' headquarters. To this we should add excises that are shared according to complex formulas depending on the product or service involved. Additionally, there are annexes to the *convenios de adhesión* that establish additional percentages when the states share other federal nontax sources of revenue.

The components of these unconditional revenue-sharing transfers appear as the first six rows of table 5.1. In addition to indicating their total values for 1999, the table also shows selected features of these transfers, including the method of allocation across provinces and whether it is formula based.

Far and away the largest transfer is the Fondo General de Participaciones, which appears in row 1. Although the allocation formula for *participaciones*, or that of its constituent components, has varied over the years, since 1993 (when these constituent funds were consolidated in the participation fund), the allocation has been as follows:

- 45.17 percent is distributed to the states on an equal per capita basis.
- 45.17 percent is allocated on a historical basis (referred to as an "inertial" basis), starting with the states' own revenues just before the system started in 1980 and modified gradually by relative state tax effort. In the figures that follow, the effect of the historical allocation is evident for the states of Tabasco and Campeche and reflects their high pre-1980 revenues as major oil-producing states.
- 9.66 percent is allocated in a way that "compensates" (or that is inverse relative to) the previous two allocations.

The original allocation principle gave primary weight to the derivation principle—the so-called *principio resarcitorio*—which in effect stipulated that no state should receive less from *participaciones* than they were collecting before joining the revenue-sharing system. This has been tempered over time by the shift toward an equal per capita basis for a significant portion of the overall allocation (although, as noted, the historical or inertial component still reflects some of this earlier allocation principle). Diaz Cayeros (1995) demonstrates a gradual convergence across states in per capita revenue shares; while Saucedo Sánchez (1997) shows a steady decrease in the population-weighted Gini coefficient for the distribution of state revenue shares over the years (the opposite result holds for a Gini coefficient weighted by state GDP, which has become more unequal).

The tendency toward capitation in the largest fund has led total revenue shares under Ramo 28 to be distributed fairly equally across states.

Table 5.1. Federal Funds Transferred to States and Municipalities (In Ascending Order of Federal Accountability)

Fund	Ramo	Amount	Percent RFP	Type of expenditure	Transfer	Nature of allocation	Formula
General de Participaciones (FGP)	28	117,801	20	States must transfer at least 20 percent to municipalities	Unconditional	Equal	Yes
de Fomento Municipal (FFM)	28	5,559	1	Mostly current	Unconditional	Derivation	Yes
Tenencia	28	7,984	n.a.	Works as own revenue in practice	Unconditional	Derivation	100 %
Automóviles nuevos (ISAN)	28	3,255	n.a.	Works as own revenue in practice	Unconditional	Derivation	100 %
Impuestos especiales	28	2,600	n.a.	Mostly current	Unconditional	Derivation	Yes
Other revenue sharing	28	1,437	n.a.	Mostly current	Unconditional	Derivation	No
de Aportaciones para la Educación Básica y Normal (FAEB)	33	86,481	n.a.	Current (teacher payrolls in basic education)	Conditional	Equal	No**
de Aportaciones para Servicios de Salud (FASS)	33	14,466	n.a.	Current (doctors and nurses payrolls)	Conditional	Equal	No***
de Aportaciones para la Infraestructura Social Municipal (FAISM)	33	12,245	2.037	Capital investment in the municipalities (public works)	Conditional	Compensatory	Yes
de Aportaciones para la Infraestructura Social Estatal (FAISE)	33	1,689	0.281	Capital investment, states can assign according to own criteria to municipalities	Conditional	Compensatory	Yes
de Aportaciones para el Fortalecimiento de los muncipios (FAFM)	33	13,098	2.5	Current, although recommendation to spend on specific items: public debt and safety	Unconditional	Equal	Yes
de Aportaciones Múltiples (FAM)	33	4,537	0.814	Current and capital (school breakfasts and school construction)	Conditional	Equal	No**
de Aportaciones para la Educación Tecnológica de Adultos (FAETA)	33/11*	1,251	n.a.	Current (technical institutes)	Conditional	Equal	No**
de Aportaciones para la Educación de Adultos (FAEA)	33/11*	1,062	n.a.	Current (adult literacy program)	Conditional	Equal	No**
de Aportaciones para la Seguridad Pública de los Estados y del Distrito Federal (FASP)	33	4,700	n.a.	Current, though some capital equipment	Conditional	Derivation	Yes

(table continued on next page)

Table 5.1 continued

Fund	Ramo	Amount	Percent RFP	Type of expenditure	Transfer	Nature of allocation	Formula
de Aportaciones para los servicios de educación básica en el Distrito Federal	25	10,767	n.a.	Current (teacher payroll)	Conditional	n.a.	No
Previsiones salariales por FAEB	25	10,935	n.a.	Current (teacher pay raises)	Conditional	Equal	No**
Previsiones salariales por FASSA	12	1,696	n.a.	Current (doctor and nurse raises)	Conditional	Equal	No**
Previsiones salariales	23	1,966	n.a.	Current	Conditional	n.a.	No
Desastres Naturales	23	4,000	n.a.	Current	Conditional	n.a.	No

* These funds come from Ramo 11 "Health" in the budget. Item 33 reports an appropriation of 0 in the fund, but article 17 establishes where the money is to come from.
** The Ley de Coordinación Fiscal does provide some vague guidelines, but they are so general that they do not become a binding formula.
*** A formula exists, but only for a compensating part of the fund, which constitutes 1 percent of it.
n.a. = not applicable.
Source: Based on CIDAC (1998), using data from the Presupuesto de Egresos de la Federación para 1999 and the Ley de Coordinación Fiscal and its reforms for 1999.

Figure 5.2 presents per capita data for the total revenue shares received by each state (including municipal funds). The graph ranks states according to their degree of poverty—the Foster-Greer-Thorbecke index with a poverty line set at two minimum wages—so that the leftmost state is the poorest and the rightmost is the richest.

Returning to figure 5.2, the per capita totals across states are the result of the interplay of various components of transfers, although, as noted, the participation fund plays a dominant role. Some of the other funds, such as the municipal promotion transfer, are extremely unequal across states. What tilts figure 5.2 in the general direction of richer states receiving more revenues is the influence of *tenencia* and ISAN, both of which are fully transferred to states on a derivation principle. Finally, the two prominent outliers, Tabasco and Campeche, benefit substantially from the "inertial" component of the allocation formula (which in turn reflects their historically high, oil-related revenues, which were grandfathered into the calculations).

Overall, then, figure 5.2 reveals a slight positive correlation—on average, richer states receive larger per capita revenue sharing than poorer states. This is what one would expect, given the emphasis on derivation in the various transfer components.

Conditional Transfers: Ramo 33 (Aportaciones)

Conditional transfers have existed in Mexico at least since the creation of Ramo 26 in the late 1970s, which was designed to provide matching grants

Figure 5.2. Total Per Capita Revenue Shares by State, 1999

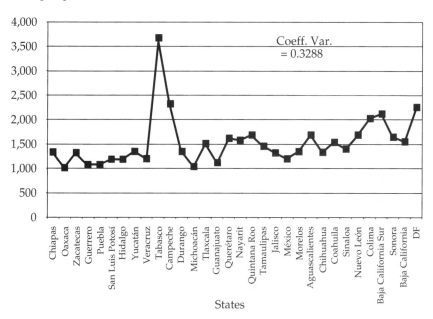

Per capita pesos

Coeff. Var.
= 0.3288

States

Source: Authors' calculations from INEGI data.

for states and municipalities to finance public works. The set-up of conditional transfers at that time reflected mainly the priorities in federal investment projects and not any set of rules for transfers to subnational governments. Funds in Ramo 26 became extremely important during the Salinas administration (1988–94), as the cornerstone of the poverty-alleviation strategy of the *Solidaridad* (Solidarity) Program. But even within this programmatic structure, solidarity funds remained highly discretionary and were often criticized for being managed electorally. (For the most prominent critiques of Solidarity, see Dresser 1991; Weldon and Molinar 1994; Bailey 1994; and Bruhn 1996; for some debates with these critics see Mogollón 1999; and Pineda and Gómez 1999.) These funds were transformed during the next administration into the so-called Municipal Social Infrastructure Fund, with their allocation determined by a complex poverty formula. This transfer was later incorporated into one of the funds in Ramo 33.

Most of the Ramo 33 transfers relate to expenditures originally undertaken by the federal government that were converted to conditional transfers. The most important of these new transfers does not relate directly to poverty alleviation and social infrastructure, but rather to the payroll of teachers, which was decentralized to the states through an agreement reached in 1993 (Latapí and Ulloa 1998; Merino 1998). Those funds were originally placed in Ramo 25 but were later grouped together with other transfers and placed in Ramo 33, which was created at the end of 1997 for the 1998 federal budget. The complex transfer of existing expenditures into Ramo 33 is captured in figure 5.3, based on a schema developed by Claudia Marcías Angeles and Jorge Rafael Manzano and reproduced from Guerrero (1998).

Figure 5.3. Where Ramo 33 Came From

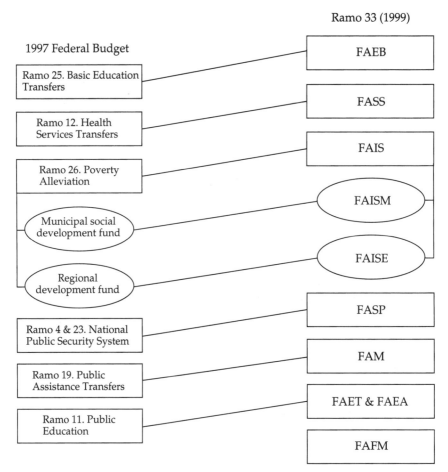

Source: Modified from CIDE (1998) and Macías and Manzano (undated), correcting for inaccurate attribution of FAFM as coming from item 28 (it does not, since item 28 was not reduced), and updating to 1999.

Table 5.1 presents the components of Ramo 33, including aggregate amounts for 1999, conditions, and methods of allocation. Figure 5.4 provides a graph, similar to the one for revenue sharing, depicting the allocation by state of per capita of the aggregate Ramo 33 transfers. The results reveal high variability across states. However, if one abstracts from the two major outliers at the "rich" end of the spectrum (Baja California Sur and Colima, which, as the smallest states, benefit from the manner in which the education fund is allocated), then poorer states tend to receive larger Ramo 33 allocations than do richer states, although there is a lot a variation around this tendency. This is the opposite of the pattern revealed in figure 5.2 for the Ramo 28 unconditional transfers.

The transfer related to education (FAEB) is by far the largest component of Ramo 33. The funds distributed under FAEB are highly unequal per capita (see Latapí an Ulloa 1998; Merino 1998). For 1999, according to budget data, and excluding the outlier Baja California Sur, these allocations range from $Mex1,611 per capita in Campeche to $Mex707 in Jalisco, with a coefficient of variation of 0.2394.

This inequality is attenuated considerably, however, if one also includes what the states spend from their own revenues on teacher salaries. The com-

Figure 5.4. Total Per Capita Ramo 33 (DF Includes Ramo 25)

Pesos per capita

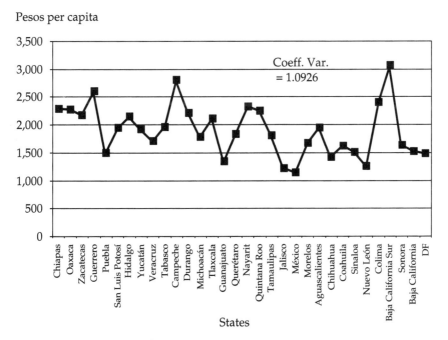

Source: Authors' calculations from INEGI data.

bined federal and state spending appears in figure 5.5. The lower (and light-shaded) area is the FAEB transfer, with the additional state expenditures displayed in the upper (dark-shaded) area. We made some key assumptions in generating these data on state teacher salaries or basic education spending. First, current expenditures on teacher salaries by state are only available for 1996 from the Ministry of Finance and Public Credit (SCHP), so those figures were extrapolated with inflation rates of 15.72 percent for 1997, 18.61 percent for 1998, and 13 percent for 1999. Second, data were unavailable for four states (Baja California Sur, Guanajuato, Tabasco, and Tamaulipas) and the Federal District, so this exercise might underestimate overall spending in these states, because it assumes that they spend nothing of their own revenue on teachers.

These state expenditures of their own funds on basic education are very unequal, since some states make substantial contributions to education, such as Baja California ($Mex669 per capita), Nuevo León ($Mex529 pesos), and Coahuila ($Mex403 pesos), while at least six states (Aguascalientes,

Figure 5.5. Education Transfers Complement State Expenditure

Pesos per capita

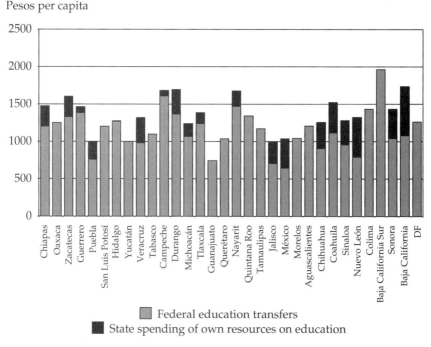

☐ Federal education transfers
■ State spending of own resources on education

States ordered by rank in poverty index

Source: Authors' calcualtions from INEGI data.

Colima, Moreles, Oaxaca, Quintana Roo, and Yucatán) spend nothing. The coefficient of variation of state expenditure for teacher salaries is 1.0827 for all states, including those not reporting any expenditures, and 0.6638 for states that do report some expenditure.

When one adds both federal and state expenditures (as is done in figure 5.5), the variation across states is reduced. Excluding the outliers (Baja California Sur on the top and Guanajuato on the bottom, both of which may be underestimated because we have no data for state teacher salaries), the minimum total expenditure on basic education is found in Yucatán with $Mex999 per capita, and the maximum is found in Baja California with $Mex1,739 per capita, producing a coefficient of variation of 0.1790, lower than the 0.2394 coefficient of variation for the federal FAEB transfers and well below the coefficient of variation for state spending on teacher salaries.

This is an intriguing result. While the overall impact is to generate more equality across states in basic education spending, the FAEB transfer is very problematical since the allocation formula effectively discriminates against those states that have opted to use their own revenues to finance aspects of basic education. Chapter 3 recommends basing the allocation for FAEB on criteria that are more equitable across states, for example, per student capitation. To do this, however, the overall transfer system itself must also become rationalized. Prior to an overview of all transfers and own-source revenues, one other transfer program merits discussion—federal public investment.

Federal Public Investment

During the late 1980s and the early 1990s, about one-third of the federal government's consolidated programmable budget (that is, the total budget of the federal government, excluding *participaciones* and interest payments on the federal debt) was allocated territorially to the states as federal public investment (*Inversión Pública Federal*, IPF). These funds were earmarked for specific projects considered important by the federal government, aiming to fulfill a developmentalist vision of the role of the state. Resources from IPF were two times higher than federal revenue sharing transferred to local governments (*participaciones*). Considering such relative magnitude, it is no wonder that IPF was a crucial financial flow to the states and has played a major role in debates on regional development in Mexico. The importance of IPF in Mexico has declined dramatically in recent years, however, to the point that in 1997 it was only 11 percent of the programmable budget, equal to only 32 percent of revenue sharing, precisely at a time when other transfers to states were steadily increasing.

Federal funds used to finance almost all local public goods in Mexico, although this is no longer the case. The money was allocated to subnational jurisdictions through a wide variety of federal agencies, programs, and bureaucracies, with the collaboration of local governments. Federal spending in Ramo 26—the poverty-alleviation program (PRONASOL)—commanded much attention in recent years not just because a lot of money was involved, but also because a whole bureaucratic apparatus was put together to make the program an instrument of the federal executive; it was just one of the parts of IPF. Funds were sometimes directly exercised by the local governments, but under very strict federal guidelines and oversight. That is, in Mexico federal funds are controlled by the federal bureaucracies, although they are spent, especially since the 1970s, jointly with the lower levels of government, according to development agreements.

Table 5.2 summarizes the main characteristics of the shares of IPF received by each state during 1960–93—the mean, standard deviation, coefficient of variation, and maximum and minimum. The most prominent feature of IPF is the high degree of discretion with which the federal government could increase or decrease the share of a specific state. In a way, these are really regional development grants by the federal government and so should be left out of the analysis of the transfer system.

This completes our description and brief assessment of the status quo with respect to the Mexican transfer system. The following section integrates state and municipal own revenues into the analysis, assessing the overall vertical and horizontal imbalances in the Mexican federation.

Vertical and Horizontal Balance

To provide a comprehensive overview of Mexican fiscal federalism, we need to bring state and municipal own-source revenues into the picture. This is the role of the first subsection. In the second, we present the aggregate revenue sources of state and municipal governments. This allows us to assess the degree of vertical fiscal balance in the federation. Moreover, by rearranging the transfers and revenues into their conditional and unconditional components, we obtain a measure of subnational fiscal autonomy. The final subsection focuses on aggregate state and municipal revenues and the degree of horizontal fiscal balance that exists in the Mexican federation.

State and Municipal Own-Source Revenues

Mexican states have little access to dedicated sources of revenue. No source is exclusively assigned to them constitutionally, and for those where they have concurrent jurisdiction, they have typically chosen to delegate authority to the federal government. The taxes and revenues that the states do collect fall into the following areas, as elaborated in Chapter 4: payroll tax, various fees, *tenencia,* and ISAN. The inclusion of *tenencia* and ISAN as own-source revenues of states merits further comment. Although, administratively, they fall into *participaciones* (and were included in the earlier dis-

Table 5.2. Summary Statistics of State Shares of IPF, 1960–93

State	Mean	Standard deviation	Coefficient of variation	Maximum	Minimum	Maximum/ minimum
Tlaxcala	0.42	0.06	0.01	0.49	0.34	1.44
San Luis Potosí	1.35	0.13	0.01	1.48	1.15	1.29
Morelos	0.73	0.12	0.02	0.90	0.57	1.58
Zacatecas	0.73	0.12	0.02	0.87	0.58	1.50
Oaxaca	2.41	0.20	0.02	2.62	2.07	1.27
Jalisco	2.69	0.29	0.03	3.11	2.32	1.34
Aguascalientes	0.57	0.15	0.04	0.79	0.39	2.03
Durango	1.19	0.22	0.04	1.57	0.99	1.59
Baja California Sur	0.84	0.21	0.05	0.98	0.43	2.28
Quintana Roo	0.73	0.21	0.06	0.98	0.42	2.33
Querétaro	0.88	0.22	0.06	1.29	0.66	1.95
Colima	0.89	0.22	0.06	1.21	0.61	1.98
México	3.95	0.49	0.06	4.60	3.33	1.38
Yucatán	1.10	0.28	0.07	1.56	0.80	1.95
Guerrero	2.36	0.48	0.10	3.11	1.84	1.69
Nuevo León	2.62	0.58	0.13	3.49	1.72	2.03
Baja California	2.28	0.58	0.15	3.26	1.50	2.17
Sonora	2.41	0.67	0.18	3.46	1.52	2.28
Coahuila	3.42	0.83	0.20	4.57	2.23	2.05
Nayarit	0.82	0.44	0.24	1.66	0.45	3.69
Puebla	1.90	0.74	0.29	3.36	1.32	2.55
Hidalgo	2.07	0.79	0.30	3.39	1.15	2.95
Guanajuato	2.25	0.82	0.30	3.60	1.46	2.47
Chihuahua	2.63	1.04	0.41	4.10	1.75	2.34
Veracruz	10.37	2.23	0.48	14.01	8.05	1.74
Chiapas	2.85	1.19	0.49	4.82	1.85	2.61
Sinaloa	3.11	1.27	0.52	5.20	2.03	2.56
Tabasco	4.78	1.72	0.62	7.77	2.94	2.64
Michoacán	3.77	1.69	0.76	6.87	1.95	3.52
Tamaulipas	5.11	2.25	0.99	8.16	2.20	3.71
Distrito Federal	26.34	6.35	1.53	37.27	21.18	1.76
Campeche	2.44	2.26	2.09	6.15	0.60	10.25

Source: Díaz-Cayeros 1997, table 6.2.

cussion of revenue sharing), they are fully transferred to the states on a derivation principle. Hence, they are, for all intents and purposes, state own-source revenues. Thus, for the analysis here, they are included in state own-source revenues and are deducted from revenue-sharing transfers.

Under the constitution, municipalities have exclusive authority (under Article 115) to provide drinking water and sewage, public lighting, markets, graveyards, slaughterhouses, streets, parks and gardens, and public safety. To fulfill these obligations, they are assigned control of the property tax. The municipalities also obtain revenues from various fees on the provision of goods and services (including water user fees in some municipalities).

Obtaining data for own-source state and municipal revenues in 1999 pesos (in order to make these comparable with the transfer data) requires several critical assumptions and extrapolations. First, the latest state and municipal revenue data (except for *tenencia* and ISAN) are for 1996. Lacking more recent data, we adjust these 1996 revenues for inflation to convert them to 1999 estimates. This is clearly unsatisfactory, but it is a further example of the data constraints facing researchers in this area.

With this caveat in mind, figures 5.6 and 5.7 present aggregate per capita own-source revenues for states and municipalities, respectively. The first observation is that we are talking about quite small amounts of money. Second, own-source state revenues tend to be higher in richer than in poorer states. This trend is even more apparent for municipal own-source revenues, although these revenues are even smaller. Third, the spikes in figure 5.5 for Quintana Roo and Baja California Sur reflect their importance

Figure 5.6. State Own Revenue

Pesos per capita

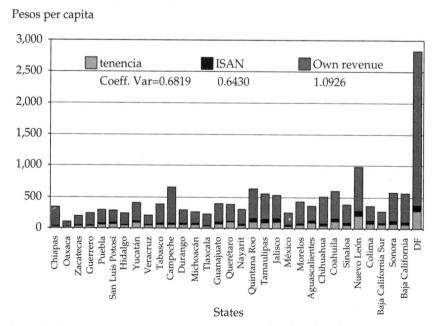

Source: Authors' calculations fron INEGI data.

Figure 5.7. Municipal Own Revenue

Pesos per capita

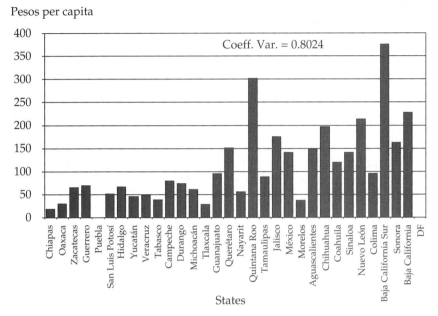

Source: Authors' calculations from INEGI data.

as centers for tourism. The Federal District is omitted in figure 5.6 because, while usually classified as a state, it has no municipalities.

Aggregate Subnational Revenues and Vertical Fiscal Imbalance

Total state own-revenues (the penultimate line in table 5.3) are estimated to be $Mex34.4 billion, with the comparable municipal own revenues totaling $Mex9.0 billion. Table 5.3 provides a capsule overview of state and municipal access to revenues. Focusing on the final three rows of the table, aggregate transfers account for 87.6 percent of combined state-municipal revenues, with own-source revenues accounting for 12.4 percent. This is one measure of the overall vertical balance in the Mexican federation.

This is a narrow conception of own-source revenues, however, in that it includes only those revenues that the states and municipalities themselves collect. One can make a case (as surely the states would) that the more appropriate definition of own revenues would include the unconditional *participaciones*. *Participaciones* account for 40.0 percent of aggregate state-municipal revenues from all sources. Under this conception, own-source revenues would account for 52.4 percent of total revenues (40.0 percent plus 12.4 percent).

Table 5.3. Total Transfers to Subnational Governments in Mexico, 1999 (Ranked in Ascending Order of Federal Conditionality)

	State	Municipal	Total	State (percent)	Municipal (percent)	Total (percent)
Total						
Aportaciones	124,952	25,342	150,295	43.0	41.3	42.7
FAEB[1]	97,248	n.a.	97,248	33.5	0.0	27.6
FASSA	14,466	n.a.	14,466	5.0	0.0	4.1
FIS	1,688	12,244	13,933	0.6	19.9	4.0
FORTAMUN	n.a.	13,097	13,097	0.0	21.3	3.7
FAIE[2]	2,467	n.a.	2,467	0.8	0.0	0.7
FAAS	2,069	n.a.	2,069	0.7	0.0	0.6
FASP	4,700	n.a.	4,700	1.6	0.0	1.3
FAETyEA[3]	2,313	n.a	2,313	0.8	0.0	0.7
Total salary						
Previsions	14,597	n.a.	14,597	5.0	0.0	4.2
Education[4]	10,935	n.a.	10,935	3.8	0.0	3.1
Health[5]	1,696	n.a.	1,696	0.6	0.0	0.5
General[6]	1,966	n.a.	1,966	0.7	0.0	0.6
Revenue sharing	113,756	27,055	140,811	39.2	44.1	40.0
Excises	2,600	n.a.	2,600	0.9	0.0	0.7
Incentives	1,437	n.a.	1,437	0.5	0.0	0.4
General revenue Sharing (FGP)	97,090	20,711	117,801	33.4	33.7	33.5
Municipal Promotion (FFM)	n.a.	5,558	5,558	0.0	9.1	1.6
New cars	3,254	n.a.	3,254	1.1	0.0	0.9
Car property	7,984	n.a.	7,984	2.8	0.0	2.3
Contingency Reserve	1,389	n.a.	1,389	0.5	0.0	0.4
Other[7]	n.a.	785	785	0.0	1.3	0.2
Total other	10,299	n.a.	10,299	3.5	0.0	2.9
Natural disasters[8]	3,640	n.a.	3,640	1.3	0.0	1.0
Sistema Nacional de Seguridad Pública	2,581	n.a.	2,581	0.9	0.0	0.7
Poverty regions	4,077	n.a.	4,077	1.4	0.0	1.2
Total transfers	255,887	52,397	308,285	88.1	85.3	87.6
Own revenue[9]	34,432	9,015	43,448	11.9	14.7	12.4
Total SNG resources	290,320	61,413	351,733	100.0	100.0	100.0

n.a. = not applicable.

This conception of the vertical fiscal balance corresponds closely to sub-national autonomy defined as the proportion of total revenues that are unconditional (that can be spent as and where the states wish). These unconditional grants would include own-source revenues and *participaciones* and a few other revenue sources (the FAFM component of Ramo 33 that is unconditional; see table 5.1). Figures 5.8 and 5.9 present the relevant data for states and municipalities, respectively. Taking into account the variability of these data across states, it is evident that for both states and municipalities the *absolute* amount of unconditional revenues is higher for richer states, and municipalities in richer states also have a higher proportion of total funds that are unconditional. The outliers in terms of the state data in figure 5.8 are Tabasco and Campeche (because of the allocation of *participaciones*) and the Federal District, for reasons noted earlier. The outliers in figure 5.9 result either from own-source municipal revenues or from states' pass-through to municipalities of roughly 20 percent of *participaciones* (which again makes municipalities in Tabasco and Campeche outliers).

Table 5.4 attempts to capture some of the dynamics relating to decentralization. The table is organized so that entries at the bottom are the most

Figure 5.8. State Funds

Pesos per capita

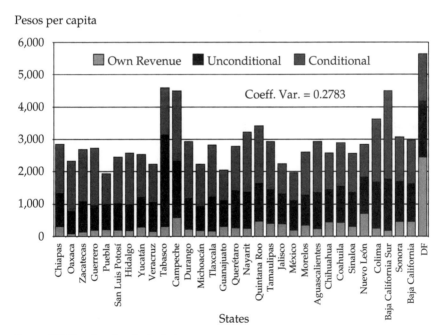

Source: SHCP and authors' calculations.

Figure 5.9. Municipal Funds

Pesos per capita

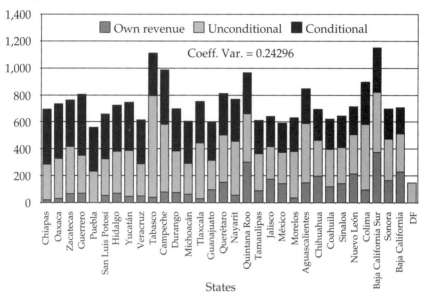

Source: SHCP and authors' calculations.

centralized (transfers), with the most decentralized (tax revenues) appearing at the top. The data indicate that there was some "decentralization" or increase in autonomy of state revenues during 1997–99. For example, highly discretionary federal transfers (row 1) fell from 10 percent of total state-municipal revenues in 1997 to 5 percent in 1999. Federal spending on behalf of the states (row 2) fell from 36.6 percent in 1997 to 1.9 percent in 1999. These were transferred to conditional *aportaciones* (embedded in Ramo 33), which rose from 3.2 percent in 1997 to 38.2 percent in 1999.

To be sure, this shows the ongoing process of decentralization and devolution in Mexican federalism. However, advocates of a more decentralist future would surely point out that none of this increase has been in the categories of unconditional transfer or own-source revenue, which would signal a more meaningful decentralization. As noted, these shares remained stable.

Aggregate Subnational Revenues and Horizontal Fiscal Balance

Our empirical overview of the Mexican transfer system concludes by looking at allocations across states of aggregate state or local revenues from *all*

Table 5.4. Transfers and Own Revenue as Percentage of Total Subnational Resources

	1997	1998	1999	1997 (percent)	1998 (percent)	1999 (percent)
Own revenue (taxes and fees)	32,390.0	38,450.1	43,448.7	12.7	13.5	12.1
Revenue sharing by origin (piggyback/ state rate)	6,140.6	6,712.6	7,984.0	2.4	2.4	2.2
Revenue sharing by origin (federal set rate)	4,071.7	5,333.2	8,078.2	1.6	1.9	2.2
Common pool revenue sharing	84,832.5	97,529.8	124,749.1	33.4	34.1	34.7
Unconditional Aportaciones	0	6,732.1	13,097.6	0.0	2.4	3.6
Earmarked Aportaciones	8,187.0	100,384.1	137,197.6	3.2	35.1	38.2
Matching funds	92,934.6	5,342.7	6,659.3	36.6	1.9	1.9
Negotiated and extraordinary transfers	25,528.9	25,135.6	18,237.0	10.0	8.8	5.1
Total	254,085.3	285,620.2	359,451.5	100.0	100.0	100.0

Source: Ley de Egresos, various years, and authors' calculations.

sources. Figure 5.10 shows a fairly equal allocation across states after taking into account the reasons for the outliers on the upside. The rationales for these outliers are similar to those noted earlier. Moving from left to right in figure 5.10, Tabasco and Campeche owe their position to the "inertial" feature of the *participaciones* formula. Quintana Roo is high because of a strong local tourist economy (Cancún); Colima and Baja California Sur benefit from being the smallest states (in population) and, therefore, favored by the educational allotment under Ramo 33. Finally, the Federal District tops the outliers on the basis of strong local finances (that is, an effective property tax system).

Dismissing these outliers, the overall picture presented in figure 5.10 is one of considerable horizontal balance. Yet this is the result of the interplay of more than 20 seemingly unrelated individual transfer programs plus own-source revenues. We view this as being more than coincidental and see the data as revealing a preference in the direction of a federal social pact. Although not explicit in the Mexican Constitution, the results in figure 5.10 signal an implicit social and political commitment to pursue a meaningful degree of horizontal balance in the Mexican federation.

Figure 5.10. Total Local Funds by State (Revenues and Transfers)

Pesos per capita

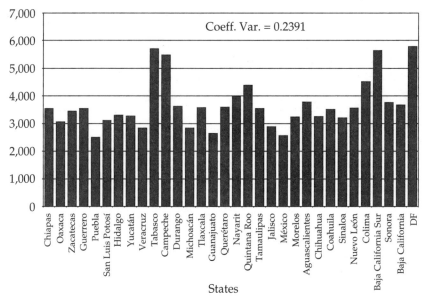

Source: SHCP and authors' calculations.

The Evolution of Mexican Federalism

This section speculates on some alternate futures for Mexican fiscal federalism and, within this, the alternative futures for the system of intergovernmental transfers.

The Mexican federation is evolving on many dimensions, led by a remarkable devolution of administrative spending authority. The transfer of financial resources for this spending devolution has taken the form of myriad conditional-grant programs falling largely under the Ramo 33 umbrella. It is possible that these recent expenditure and transfer initiatives could endure. More likely, however, they are creative transitional arrangements toward a more decentralized federal system. To understand what this more decentralized future might look like, we assess the contradictions and forces for change within the existing system.

The Inequality Challenge

Inequality across citizens and states alike presents an enormous challenge to the Mexican federation. The north-south illiteracy divide (as reflected in figure 2.3) is striking, and the North American integration pressures and opportunities under NAFTA may exacerbate the degree of inequality. For this reason the societal preference for approximate equality revealed in the pattern across states of the total per capita revenues deserves special emphasis. The data in figure 5.10 show considerable variability across states, but these deviations are not systematically related to how "rich" the states are. Approximate horizontal balance across states appears to be an underlying value of Mexican federalism.

Since the intergovernmental transfer system is, in effect, a zero-sum game, the challenge is to generate transfer programs that can withstand political pressure. Part of the solution is to ensure that these transfers are formula based, which, in turn, will tend to depoliticize them. The experience of the Municipal Social Development Fund in 1997, later transformed into a component of Ramo 33, should be helpful, since it demonstrates the possibility of establishing a formula that, although still too complex, can accommodate poverty criteria while being politically palatable. A viable scenario for the future will need an overall transfer system that addresses the enduring inequality issue in fair and acceptable ways.

The NAFTA Challenge

Mexican states, especially the northern tier, are being progressively drawn into NAFTA's orbit. Effectively, they are becoming North American region-states, along the lines of Ontario (as suggested in Courchene and Telmer 1998), and they will behave as such. They will use their available powers (and surely press for more powers) to make their states attractive locations for Mexican, North American, and foreign investment. Foreign policy will still be made in Mexico City, but the important wheeling and dealing on detailed trade issues will, to an increasing degree, rest with the states and governors. This is happening in Canada, and it seems inevitable that it will also intensify in Mexico.

This means the states will press for additional economic and fiscal powers in pursuing their regional-international interface within NAFTA. Many of these states are pressing for more freedom on the tax front. Legally any state can unilaterally withdraw from the voluntary tax concordat and reinstitute their own taxes and collection systems. This gives individual states a lot of negotiating leverage and contrasts to a situation like Argentina's, where any change in the fiscal transfer and tax system requires unanimous approval of all states and the federal government. Greater tax autonomy of these regions appears to be inevitable. Given the inequality in tax bases across states (and particularly the north-south dimension), this could create fiscal havoc within the fiscal-federalism framework if it is not done carefully.

The challenge is twofold: first, to accommodate the growing desires of selected states to acquire greater tax autonomy and, second, to design the overall transfer system to satisfy both the desire for more tax autonomy on the part of higher-revenue states and the equality imperative. As productivity and wages rise in these NAFTA states, they will make the case that their *cost* of public services is rising as well. (Canadian evidence suggests that roughly 60 percent of all provincial expenditures on public services relate to wages.) The southern states can and will make a convincing case that their *expenditure needs* are greater. Balancing these legitimate concerns will be priorities in the model outlined.

Alternatives for the Future

First, accountability and transparency at the state level are improving and will continue to improve. There will be tensions nonetheless, particularly regarding the "two-stage" procedure characterizing municipal transfers. Funds are first given to the state and then are allocated by the state to the municipalities, sometimes according to federal formulas, sometimes according to the state's own criteria. To be sure, accountability and transparency will vary across states, but over the longer term the states will have the analytical and managerial capacity to accommodate increased decentralization.

Second, the system of intergovernmental transfers should be formula based and should be set in a multiyear framework. Enhancing state-level analytical and managerial capacity will not mean much if they are stuck in the context of highly variable and unpredictable transfer regimes.

Third, as the system decentralizes, it will need some federal-state institutional machinery to secure the benefits of decentralization. This institutional evolution could take the form of a formal organization (along the lines of Australia's Commonwealth Grants Commission) or a more informal variant (along the lines of Canada's federal-provincial "executive federalism" arrangements). In any event, the following are among the likely roles for enhanced federal-state cooperation and coordination:

CONDITIONALITY ISSUES. Many of the transfers will probably have conditionality attached to them. This will be appropriate in the transition and to some lesser extent in any steady state. The issue is who sets these conditions. Initially, the answer probably has to be the federal government. Over time, however, it will become increasingly important to bring the states more formally into the determination of these conditions or principles.

INTERNAL TRADE ISSUES. As the federation decentralizes, state actions may fragment the internal Mexican economic union, either intentionally or inadvertently. Hence, a critical ingredient of any decentralization process is to preserve and, indeed, to promote the economic union. This harks back to McKinnon's principles of market-preserving federalism.

DISPUTE RESOLUTION. Initially, perhaps the federal government will serve as umpire. As decentralization proceeds, however, pressures will develop for a federal-state umpire—eventually a system of federal-state dispute-resolution mechanisms, complete with voting rules and sanctions.

CITIZENS AND DEMOCRACY. Too often fiscal federalism arrangements involve only governments. But federalism is presumably a system that also ought to benefit citizens. One way to accomplish this would be with a nonjusticiable citizens charter as an integral component of fiscal federalism. This might include, as a minimum, provisions granting citizens the rights for equality of access to some national public goods, such as education and health. Or it could be more proactive, allowing citizens to access dispute resolution procedures to redress perceived mistreatment under the new fiscal regime. To some extent, this may exist under the Mexican law of *amparo*, but the citizens charter would spell things out more specifically for federalism issues.

A Decentralist View of Mexican Fiscal Federalism

With the previous section as backdrop, we now attempt to spell out the defining features of a longer-term model that, in our view, is consistent with the existing values and norms and the emerging pressures being exerted on the Mexican federation. We give only the key features of the model, although we are specific about the forces driving the model. The basic approach is general and amenable to alteration.

The model has six general principles: tax decentralization, fiscal equity, conditional citizenship transfers, a federal-state fiscal covenant, a federal-state commission, and transitional guarantees. We deal with each in turn.

TAX DECENTRALIZATION. The first principle is to devolve more taxation authority to the states. Chapter 4 assesses the likely candidates for state taxation, including personal income taxation (perhaps an integration of payroll and personal income taxation), commodity sales taxation, and state surcharges on the value added tax. State access to some of these tax sources would require a constitutional amendment. In other areas, the federal government need not formally devolve authority. Rather, it might provide tax room for the states to apply surcharges on federal taxes, with collection still under federal (or national) supervision. Our goal here is not to recommend constitutional changes, but rather to note that selected states will progressively become more active players in the taxation area and that, somehow, the federation must accommodate this.

The problem arising from this recommendation, if implemented in isolation, is that the well-endowed states will have access to more per capita revenues than the poorer states. Thus accommodating one pressure in the federation would create another. How do we address this emerging challenge to horizontal balance?

EQUALIZATION AND FISCAL EQUITY. The second principle or component of the model is that the federation would mount an equalization program to offset the horizontal imbalances arising from increased state taxation autonomy.

The specific proposal follows Canadian lines. The federal government would provide unconditional transfers to ensure that all states are brought up to the agreed-upon equalization standard. For presentation purposes, this equalization standard is defined as what an average state's per capita revenues would be if the all-state tax rates were applied to the commonly defined state tax bases (see Courchene 1998 for more detail). This implies that all low-fiscal-capacity states will receive equalization payments to ensure that their own-source revenues are brought up to the national average of all states.

Three implications follow. First, these equalization payments must be unconditional, since the tax revenues of the richer provinces are likewise unconditional. Second, the existence of an equalization program will (or should) mean that *all* states are in favor of tax decentralization—richer states because they can pocket their per capita revenues in excess of the national average and poorer states because they receive unconditional equalization payments that bring their per capita revenues up to this national standard. Third, this can be a revenue-neutral exercise from the federal government's standpoint. The enhanced taxation autonomy of the states as well as the equalization transfers can come out of reductions in the existing *participaciones*.

Although this low-fiscal-capacity compensation is termed an equalization payment, in reality it is more like a social transfer, since it allows low-tax-capacity states to be put on some socially determined equal footing with high-tax-capacity states. Moreover, this equalization standard is, in principle, quite flexible—for instance, it could be defined in terms of the top 10 states rather than the all-state average. The key point is that much of the federal "cohesion" issue for inequality can be "solved" within the context of tax decentralization.

THE CONDITIONAL CITIZENSHIP TRANSFERS. With much of the social cohesion of the federation addressed in the context of the tax-autonomy-cum-equalization context, the stage is now set for a new approach to conditional transfers, namely that they should be equal per capita across all states. Their conditionality is predicated on the assumption that they are designed to deliver citizen-related public goods (health, education) equally to all Mexicans. It would be possible to have this aggregate transfer defined in terms of specific public goods, along the lines of the Ramo 33 funds. Although strict conditionality might apply at the outset, the spirit of this proposal is eventually to define conditions as a set of agreed-upon principles relating to minimum acceptable standards for these expenditures. This would allow states some flexibility in how they most efficiently achieve these standards and principles.

A FEDERAL-STATE FISCAL COVENANT. The fourth principle of the proposed model is the creation of a Mexican federal-state fiscal covenant. In turn, this covenant would include:

- A *code of fiscal conduct*, defined to ensure that states do not use their increased tax autonomy to fragment the Mexican economic union. More positively, the role of the covenant would be to preserve and promote the national fiscal union.
- A *social union agreement*, which would ensure that Mexican citizens moving from state A to state B do not suddenly find themselves deprived of social services. This may not be an issue today, but it could emerge as the federation decentralizes. There are many ways to accommodate this, but it must be accommodated.
- A *citizens rights charter*, which would be a political document, not a legal document. The charter would ensure that the evolution of Mexican federalism takes adequate account of related citizen concerns. Part of this would presumably be reflected in the principles that would attach to the conditional-citizenship grants. Part also would be reflected in a proposition that citizens have the right to move and work anywhere and everywhere in the federation (with the qualifications accepted on a mutual-recognition basis, as in the recent Canadian social union agreement). If the authorities wanted to go further still, they could allow citizens to invoke dispute-resolution procedures.

A FEDERAL-STATE COMMISSION ON MEXICAN FISCAL FEDERALISM. The fifth building block is a federal-state monitoring and coordinating agency. The development of such an agency is required on three grounds—technical, policy, and politics. The newly created Decentralization Committee in the Ministry of Finance is, with its Technical Secretariat, an important step in this direction.

On the technical front, and critically important if the Canadian federation is a guide, there is much to be done. For example, running an equalization program is technically demanding—handling increasing amounts of data, appropriately defining tax bases, determining the timing of the payment stream for equalization transfers, and the like. On the policy side, a federal-state monitoring and coordinating agency would be an ideal forum for working out, cooperatively, the set of conditions and principles that would inform the spending of the equal per capita conditional transfer. On the political front, the challenge would be to develop agreed upon dispute-resolution and dispute-avoidance procedures relating to the many issues that will surely arise. A variety of alternative institutional structures could fill this role.

TRANSITIONAL GUARANTEES. This final principle concerns a transitional solidarity program for the states, and perhaps for the federal government as well. There would be winners and losers in a direct transition to any model, although under reasonable assumptions the steady state could be a win-win solution for all. Appropriate transitional mechanisms are therefore needed to make the change generally desirable and politically acceptable.

This scenario is our conception of *one* potential future for Mexican fiscal federalism. We believe that it addresses in an appropriate fashion the various forces at play in Mexico today, but it is only one of many pathways along which the system might evolve.

Given the substantial effort involved in documenting the status quo with respect to the transfer system, we now present some empirical simulations relating to assumptions underlying this model.

Simulating Transfers with Tax Decentralization

We present two simulations relating to the evolution of the transfer system. Consistent with the recommendations elsewhere in this book, these simulations seek to assess the degree to which Mexican fiscal federalism can accommodate increased tax devolution to subnational governments. We focus on the *combined* state-municipal level, as in figure 5.10. By construction, these simulations are revenue neutral from the vantage point of the federal government. The methodology underpinning the simulations essentially marries the features of the status quo with characteristics of the scenario extrapolated in the previous section.

MEDIUM-TERM SIMULATION. The medium term simulation, with parameters drawn from tax decentralization recommendations in Chapter 4, is designed as follows.

First, we assume a relatively modest increase in devolution in tax assignment. Specifically, the payroll tax is adopted by all states at a 3 percent rate; a proportion of excises on beer, tobacco, and alcohol is transferred to state governments as own revenues; 30 percent of the (now federal) value added tax paid by individuals becomes a state value added tax; and 50 percent of the overall personal income tax rate is passed through to the states. These tax reassignments lead to an increase in state own-source revenues that is roughly double the status quo. The financing of this tax devolution is assumed to come out of the existing revenue-sharing grants (Ramo 28).

Second, we overlay an equalization program on these own-source revenues, which brings the per capita value of own-source revenues for low-fiscal-capacity states to the national average. Funds required for this equalization transfer also come from the Ramo 28 *participaciones*.

Third, since the sum of these two components does not exhaust the current aggregate level of *participaciones*, we allow the remainder of *participaciones* to be distributed in accordance with shares in the existing formula. This implies, for instance, that the revenue-sharing "spikes" for Tabasco and Campeche still exist, but at attenuated levels.

Fourth, and finally, we allocate the existing value of the conditional transfers (Ramo 33) to the states, but with a key difference: this transfer is now redesigned to be equal per capita across states.

Figure 5.11 presents the results of the modest tax decentralization scenario. The lowest part of the figure relates to existing own-source revenues; the next portion is related to the additional own-source revenues transferred to the states as a result of the simulation. The combined value of these own-source revenues is then equalized. As a result of equalization, all states now have access to the all-state average of own-source revenues, that is, the value

Figure 5.11. Medium-Term Simulation (Modest Tax Reassignment Proposal, Revenue-Sharing Formulas Unchanged)

Pesos per capita

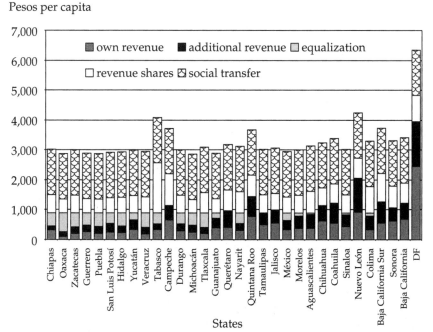

Source: Authors' calculations.

of equalization is equal to the difference between the equalization standard (just under $1,000 per capita) and the sum of the states' own revenues. As is to be expected, equalization payments flow to the poorer provinces (the left side of the figure). Next, the remainder of the *participaciones* are allocated to the states in terms of their current shares of these transfers (hence the spikes for Tabasco and Campeche). Finally, the equal per capita conditional transfer is then superimposed on all states.

In comparison with figure 5.10—the status quo—three features stand out. First, there would be much less variation across states. This is a result of the equalization transfer, on the one hand, and per capita equality of Ramo 33, on the other. Second, most poorer states would lose a little compared to the status quo, even though they would get a larger share of the (smaller) pie of transfers. Third, total revenues per capita would tend to be slightly higher for larger states, compared to the current system which penalizes them.

This is a revenue-neutral simulation, so there are losers as well as winners. These gains and losses appear in table 5.5. Compensating the states that lose would cost $Mex19 billion per year, or 15 percent of the Ramo 28 transfer. This estimate of the cost of compensating losers is the upper bound, because the costs would be less if both winners and losers were gradually brought up or down to their equilibrium levels. And assuming that the overall revenue pie is growing in real terms and even more in nominal terms, all states could be guaranteed their existing levels until the new system begins to generate equivalent overall revenues. If the new system gave states greater authority and incentive to increase their own revenues, then the revenue pie would grow faster and bring all the states more quickly to a situation with higher revenue than before.

LONGER-TERM SIMULATION. The longer-term simulation embraces much more tax decentralization. It is designed (a) to reflect the emerging reality if and when states do take on greater tax authority, and (b) to test the degree to which the general model outlined earlier can handle a tax-decentralized Mexican federation. The problem here is that we need a way of estimating what a substantial increase in derivation-based tax decentralization would look like across states. This model has only three components—a large own-source revenue component, an equalization component, and an equal per capita conditional transfer.

First, we assume that the entire Ramo 28 revenue-sharing fund will be transferred into tax room for the states. Although this could take the form of a variety of state taxes, we assume that the allocation across states will follow the average *tenencia* and ISAN allocations, which are based on derivation.

Second, as in the previous simulation, we now equalize these own-source revenues (that is, bring low-fiscal-capacity provinces up to the all-state average of per capita own-source revenues). Since the tax devolution (under the first point) "exhausts" Ramo 28, the funds for equalization must come from Ramo 33.

Third, the remaining funds in Ramo 33 will be allocated across states in equal per capita terms.

These two simulations assume a very passive reaction on the part of the states, which are not assumed to increase their tax rates on their existing taxes. Moreover, they are assumed to maintain the initial assigned tax rates on any new tax bases they acquire. Were they to increase these tax rates, their revenues could be higher than reported. Any such state tax-rate-enhanced increase in revenues should *not* be offset by a reduction in overall *participaciones*.

Figure 5.12 presents the simulation results for the scenario. The first important feature of this simulation is that own revenues (assumed to be according to current allocations for *tenencia* and ISAN) rise sharply for richer states, as one would expect.

Figure 5.12. Long-Term Simulation (Revenue Sharing Transformed into Derivation-Principle Own Revenue)

Percent

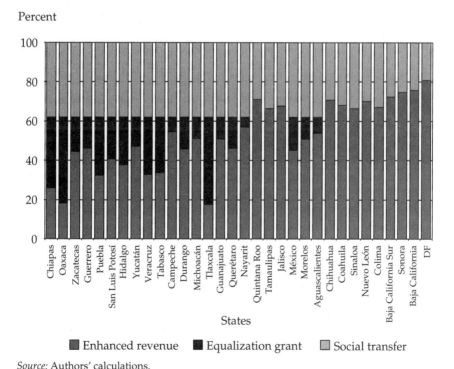

States

■ Enhanced revenue   ■ Equalization grant   □ Social transfer

Source: Authors' calculations.

Table 5.5. Fiscal Cost of Compensation

	Per capita gain/ loss	Gain/ loss as percent of status quo	Compensa- tion grant per capita	Compensa- tion grant ($)	Per capita gain/ loss	Gain/ loss as percent of status quo	Compensa- tion grant per capita	Compensa- tion grant ($)
Chiapas	−498	−14.0	498	1,954,587,633	−594	−16.8	594	2,332,560,241
Oaxaca	−158	−5.2	158	545,593,836	−105	−3.4	105	362,865,537
Zacatecas	−407	−11.8	407	561,655,896	−498	−14.4	498	685,916,935
Guerrero	−610	−17.3	610	1,886,370,780	−581	−16.4	581	1,797,544,942
Puebla	409	16.4	n.a.	n.a.	455	18.2	n.a.	n.a.
San Luis Potosí	−161	−5.2	161	370,695,816	−157	−5.1	157	361,934,273
Hidalgo	−331	−10.1	331	733,423,229	−343	−10.4	343	758,823,574
Yucatán	−253	−7.7	253	414,717,312	−322	−9.8	322	527,984,604
Veracruz	135	4.8	n.a.	n.a.	115	4.0	n.a.	n.a.
Tabasco	−1,546	−27.1	1,546	2,881,316,687	−2,753	−48.3	2,753	5,130,807,449
Campeche	−1,717	−31.3	1,717	1,183,654,212	−2,528	−46.1	2,528	1,742,040,044
Durango	−587	−16.2	587	858,788,283	−673	−18.6	673	984,689,013
Michoacán	56	2.0	n.a.	n.a.	120	4.2	n.a.	n.a.
Tlaxcala	−451	−12.6	451	422,760,670	−627	−17.5	627	586,992,779
Guanajuato	280	10.6	n.a.	n.a.	315	11.9	n.a.	n.a.
Querétaro	−368	−10.3	368	493,780,762	−637	−17.8	637	854,571,467
Nayarit	−828	−20.8	828	766,590,170	−1,032	−25.9	1,032	956,083,680
Quintana Roo	−670	−15.3	670	540,852,517	−495	−11.3	495	399,832,049
Tamaulipas	−486	−13.7	486	1,288,460,782	−219	−6.2	219	578,997,802
Jalisco	216	7.5	n.a.	n.a.	608	21.2	n.a.	n.a.
México	421	16.5	n.a.	n.a.	396	15.5	n.a.	n.a.
Morelos	−196	−6.1	196	304,948,531	−278	−8.6	278	432,081,645
Aguascalientes	−606	−16.0	606	560,052,569	−831	−22.0	831	768,158,068
Chihuahua	19	0.6	n.a.	n.a.	590	18.1	n.a.	n.a.
Coahuila	−89	−2.5	89	201,711,595	16	0.5	n.a.	n.a.
Sinaloa	−139	−4.3	139	349,170,404	137	4.3	n.a.	n.a.
Nuevo León	728	20.5	n.a.	n.a.	181	5.1	n.a.	n.a.
Colima	−1,174	−26.0	1,174	601,290,276	−1,113	−24.6	1,113	569,919,272
Baja California Sur	−1,865	−33.0	1,865	763,443,224	−1,573	−27.9	1,573	643,678,428
Sonora	−424	−11.3	424	933,104,902	702	18.6	n.a.	n.a.
Baja California	−220	−6.0	220	512,619,529	929	25.3	n.a.	n.a.
DF	598	10.3	n.a.	n.a.	14	0.3	n.a.	n.a.
Total fiscal cost of compensation				19,129,589,616				20,475,481,801
Fiscal cost as percentage of revenue sharing (Ramo 28)				15.0				16.1

n.a. = not applicable.
Note: States rank by descending rate of poverty.
Source: Authors' calculations.

The second feature is that, as a result of the pattern of own-source revenue, equalization now plays a much more critical role, that is, the equalization payments for Oaxaca and Tlaxcala appear, from figure 5.12, to be
as large as their equal per capita social transfer. As a result, the overall pattern of per capita revenue (not affected by the addition of the third tier, the
equal per capita conditional grants) is one of equal per capita revenues for

roughly half of the states, and then a rising level of overall per capita revenues for the richer states.

Our rationalization for this is that the equalization payment compensates for weak fiscal capacity and to a degree for expenditure needs, while levels across the rest of the states address the increasing "costs" of providing public services as their wages rise, and also provide an incentive for levying taxes. Moreover, it is relatively easy to defend these transfers politically. Some version of equalization exists in virtually all federal systems (except the United States) and, with equalization in place, the per capita equality of the conditional transfer would presumably be viewed as equitable.

But these distributional implications could be altered. Assuming that the own-source revenue pattern stays constant, the most obvious way to increase per capita revenues of the poorer states would be to raise the equalization standard. In figure 5.12, this standard is set at the all-state per capita average. Were it set higher, say at 110 percent of the average, the per capita value of the conditional grant would be reduced, and all of this would be transferred to the poorer states via equalization. Beyond this, one could introduce some additional "expenditure needs" components to modify the allocations of the conditional grant. And so on.

The obvious problem with the results presented in figure 5.12 is that some states lose a lot—especially Tabasco and Campeche—since the old *participaciones* revenue-sharing formula is gone and has been replaced by derivation-based tax decentralization. (But this result will arise under any scenario that contemplates enhanced subnational taxing authority but excludes the oil sector from the base). The costs of full compensation to the losers (table 5.5) under the simulation in figure 5.12 are estimated at 16 percent of the existing Ramo 28 transfers.

SUMMARY. These simulations illustrate the effects of introducing a combination of reforms—rationalizing the allocation of Ramo 33, introducing the notion of an equalizing transfer, and having greater subnational taxing autonomy. The debate about transfers needs to take the form of comparing alternate simulations of new systems, rather than complaints about individual programs or threats to disrupt the *pacto fiscal* or the political process if special grants of some sort are not forthcoming. Given Mexico's more than 20 separate transfer programs, simulation is an ideal way to experiment with alternative transfer mechanisms and, by implication, with alternative futures for Mexican fiscal federalism.

Our intention is not to defend these particular simulations. Rather, the goal is to drive home the point that in the not-too-distant future the Mexican federation will likely become more decentralized on the tax side and more challenged by cross-state inequality. These simulations attempt to design and test a transfer system that accommodates this reality. It is hoped that this will encourage others to simulate different and novel transfer mechanisms that accomplish similar objectives. If experience in federal systems elsewhere is a guide, it is not enough to develop a system of transfers that, at any point in time, delivers these objectives—the transfer systems themselves must resonate with citizens and states alike and be able to adjust to changing circumstances. We believe our approach to transfers will pass this political test.

As noted earlier the proposed model and the simulations represent only a fraction of the possibilities, but the more determining factor is that any significant increase in the states' tax autonomy will lead to a wide divergence in per capita own revenues. Were this to become reality, it might be politically very difficult to redesign the 20-odd existing transfers in ways that could accommodate this own-revenue increase and at the same time deliver an appropriate degree of horizontal balance. Therefore an equalization program may become a valuable instrument in the fiscal federalism arsenal.

In any event, the evolution of the Mexican federation and Mexican fiscal federalism will be determined not by the dictates of any given model but, rather, by the political, social, and economic values and norms of Mexican society. Viewed from this perspective, our study has aimed to give a framework for the variety of ways that creative designs for intergovernmental transfers can achieve the society's objectives.

6 Mexico

Subnational Borrowing and Debt Management

Marcelo Giugale, Fausto Hernandez Trillo, and João C. Oliveira

As a result of political opening and administrative decentralization, subnational governments in Mexico are demanding fiscal autonomy in order to improve their access to financial markets. But because the move toward fiscal decentralization is so recent, the allocation of fiscal responsibilities and borrowing autonomy among levels of government (federal, state, and municipal) is still being developed. State governments in Mexico have as yet limited flexibility in fiscal decisions, which limits their capacity to borrow for public investments. After several past attempts at reform, a new innovative regulatory system for subnational borrowing is being implemented which combines market discipline with rules.

Subnational Debt

The growth of subnational spending for public services and capital investments (in health, education, and basic infrastructure) does not yet pose a major threat to Mexico's macroeconomic stability. This distinguishes Mexico's experience from that of other large Latin American countries, notably Argentina and Brazil (Dillinger and Webb 1999; Burki, Perry, and Dillinger 1999).

Nevertheless, Mexico's subnational government debt grew from $Mex27 million in 1994 to $Mex71.6 million in 1998 (see table 6.1 which includes debt of both direct and indirect administrations, but not contingent debt). The 1994–95 financial crisis, and the ensuing increase in interest rates, expanded the states' debt stock in real as well as nominal terms, but the bailout package put in place by the federal government in 1996–97 reduced it considerably (figure 6.1). In 1997 subnational government debt represented 25 percent of the debt owed or guaranteed by the Ministry of Finance and

Public Credit (Secretaría de Hacienda y Crédito Público, SHCP), 10 percent of total public debt (including Banco de México debt), and only about 2 percent of national GDP. This compares favorably with Argentina, where subnational debt is 6 or 7 percent of GDP, and with Brazil, where it approaches 20 percent (Dillinger and Webb 1999).

Table 6.1. Mexico: Total Debt, 1994–98 (Millions of Pesos)

State	1994	1995	1996	1997	1998
Mexico	4,843	8,643	13,396	16,609	185,74
Nuevo Leon	2,348	6,427	5,463	6,706	7,470
Jalisco	2,811	3,371	3,876	4,006	4,418
Sonora	3,150	4,869	6,085	3,672	3,990
Sinaloa	873	1,337	1,677	1,931	2,212
Chihuahua	921	1,215	1,538	1,689	1,593
Baja Cal. Norte	999	960	1,214	1,380	1,528
Guerrero	515	858	983	1,168	1,255
Queretaro	1,282	1,090	1,016	1,061	1,163
Quintana Roo	450	643	740	842	1,009
Chiapas	1,024	992	1,088	961	931
Durango	552	462	606	713	806
San Luis Potosi	345	426	543	599	708
Coahuila	515	926	1,116	593	666
Tabasco	518	343	411	431	598
Guanajuato	405	411	464	517	569
Puebla	156	321	308	351	478
Baja Cal. Sur	304	296	350	450	452
Morelos	144	232	244	365	399
Yucatan	305	288	320	372	290
Tamaulipas	368	531	363	315	279
Oaxaca	260	147	192	202	261
Michoacan	249	256	251	216	251
Campeche	499	460	518	419	228
Aguascalientes	364	307	339	287	227
Colima	191	263	291	237	192
Zacatecas	123	380	468	235	136
Nayarit	222	187	178	115	104
Veracruz	348	379	262	78	52
Hidalgo	22	14	16	12	10
Tlaxcala	136	52	0	0	0
Subtotal	25,255	37,099	44,329	46,545	50,864
Fed. District	1,703	2,772	8,322	11,958	20,763
Total	26,958	39,872	52,652	58,503	71,627

Source: SHCP data.

Figure 6.1. Mexico: Subnational Governments' Total Outstanding Debt (1996 Prices)

Millions of pesos

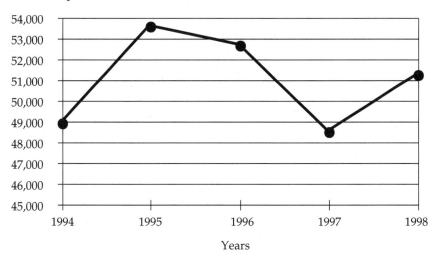

Years

Source: SHCP and authors' calculations.

Although subnational government debt continues to benefit from the effects of the 1995–96 bailout package, it recently began to increase considerably. Subnational debt increased 5.6 percent in real terms in 1998, mainly as a result of primary fiscal deficits of the Federal District (development and contractual debt with the commercial banks for the metro), the State of Mexico (development and contractual debt with commercial banks for the Atlacomulco Highway), the State of Guanajuato (bonds issued to pay for toll roads), and municipalities of Mérida (bonds) and Garza García (commercial and contractual debt with commercial banks for the construction of a tunnel linking this city to Monterrey).

Although it is expanding, subnational indebtedness does not yet threaten Mexico's macroeconomic management, because its share in the portfolio of the financial system is still relatively small. Two factors explain the relatively small size of aggregate subnational debt. First, subnational governments' access to capital markets is limited by their lack of borrowing capacity.[1] Second, the frequent implicit and explicit bailouts by the federal government softened subnational governments' budget constraints before their fiscal shortfall became a debt; that is, the federal government absorbed their potential debts. The first factor, a consequence of the architecture of Mexican fiscal federalism, indicates that reforms are needed to accord subnational governments adequate access to capital markets. The second factor was a consequence of ad hoc interventions by the federal government through ex post, extraordinary, and discretionary transfers. This second factor, in general politically motivated, indicated that the intergovernmental relationship in Mexico still embodied many channels that lead to moral hazard incentives. The federal government has acted in 1999-2000 to correct both factors by establishing a new market-based regulatory framework for subnational borrowing. This framework is explained in detail later on.

The subnational debt in Mexico is concentrated in a few states (see figure 6.2). During 1994–98, out of the nation's 32 states, six (Federal District, Jalisco, State of Mexico, Nuevo León, Sinaloa, and Sonora) were responsible for four-fifths of the subnational debt outstanding (table 6.2). Among

Figure 6.2. States' Real Debt, 1994–98

At 1996 prices (pesos)

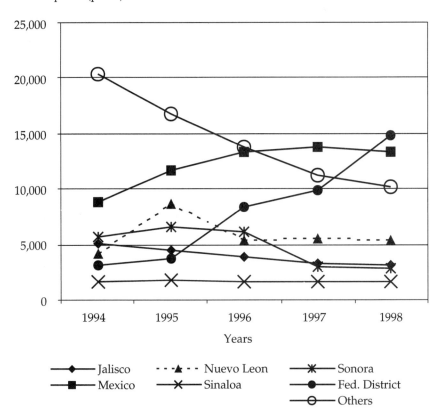

Source: Authors' calculations fron SHCP data.

these six entities, the Federal District, State of Mexico, and Nuevo León continued to expand their debt after the federal debt relief operation; the others, as a group, reduced their real stock of debt and their share of total debt.

The ratio of debt to revenue reflects an important aspect of financial vulnerability, but its relevance depends on the degree of fiscal autonomy of the states.[2] Therefore, the concept of revenue, for this particular purpose, should exclude all received transfers tied to nondebt expenditures. Table 6.2 shows the states according to three types of debt ratios: debt to total revenue, debt to disposable revenue, and debt to own revenue. Great dispersion is observed in the degree of indebtedness among states in any of these concepts, more so in the case of own revenue. Debt to disposable revenue, which includes only own revenue and unconditional transfers (Ramo 28), indicates that the degree of indebtedness varies from a maximum of 4.1 (Sonora) to a minimum of 0.02 (Hidalgo). The Federal District is ranked among the least indebted states, because of its relatively large capacity to collect own revenue. The eight most indebted states are Sonora, Nuevo León, State of Mexico, Querétaro, Quintana Roo, Baja California Sur, Jalisco, and Sinaloa, all with debt ratios greater than 1. The solvency and capacity to pay for debt in the medium term require analysis for the first three states, in particular.

Excessive indebtedness may have equity implications. In Mexico there is a clear, positive correlation between state indebtedness and state per capita GDP. Therefore, debt bailouts are likely to be regressive, since financial relief tends to go to richer-than-average states.

Fiscal Imbalances and Debt Accumulation

The stock of debt and the degree of indebtedness alone do not reveal the financial weakness of the Mexican states. In fact, the relatively "small" size of the outstanding debt of subnational governments in Mexico does not correspond to the capitalization of their past "large" fiscal deficits. The reason is that a substantial portion of their fiscal deficits has been repeatedly relieved by the federal government through extraordinary, discretionary transfers (to cover unanticipated wage increases, investment expansion, and so forth) and other forms of bailouts (the 1995 ad hoc transfers for debt reduction and rescheduling).

Since 1989 the aggregate fiscal deficit of states has always been larger than the sum of increases in indebtedness and changes in liquid assets of the states. The systematic federal government interventions to fill the financial gaps reveals the soft side of states' budget constraints. Figure 6.3 shows the evolution of the states' primary surplus or deficit and its financing. The states' fiscal stance deteriorated precipitously until 1993 (when the aggregate primary deficit reached 0.4 percent of national GDP). Since 1994 the situation has improved, and the statistics even show a primary surplus in 1995.

Table 6.2. Mexico: Total Debt, 1994–97 (Debt/Revenue Ratio in Descending Order of Total Debt)

	Total revenue		Disposable revenue		State-own revenue	
	1994	1997	1994	1997	1994	1997
México	1.0	0.9	1.0	1.4	5.9	9.6
Nuevo León	0.8	0.8	1.0	1.2	2.9	4.8
Sonora	1.1	0.6	1.6	1.1	4.4	6.6
Baja California Sur	0.5	0.4	1.2	0.8	16.7	12.4
Querétaro	0.9	0.3	1.6	0.7	6.9	4.9
Quintana Roo	0.6	0.4	1.1	0.7	5.2	2.9
Sinaloa	0.4	0.4	0.7	0.7	5.5	4.5
Aguascalientes	0.4	0.2	0.7	0.6	3.8	3.2
Jalisco	0.8	0.3	0.8	0.6	3.9	3.6
Baja California Norte	0.6	0.4	0.7	0.5	3.1	2.3
Chihuahua	0.3	0.3	0.6	0.5	2.0	1.6
Durango	0.8	0.2	0.9	0.5	8.7	5.0
Guerrero	0.2	0.5	0.4	0.5	2.9	3.4
Campeche	0.5	0.2	0.9	0.3	8.1	1.6
Colima	0.3	0.2	0.6	0.3	5.6	4.2
San Luis Potosi	0.3	0.3	0.4	0.3	5.2	6.5
Chiapas	0.2	0.1	0.6	0.2	3.6	0.9
Coahuila	0.2	0.1	0.4	0.2	2.1	1.4
Morelos	0.1	0.1	0.2	0.2	0.6	1.2
Yucatán	0.3	0.2	0.4	0.2	2.8	1.5
Zacatecas	0.2	0.1	0.2	0.2	2.0	2.7
Guanajuato	0.1	0.1	0.2	0.1	2.0	0.6
Michoacán	0.1	0.0	0.2	0.1	1.8	0.6
Nayarit	0.2	0.0	0.5	0.1	2.9	0.8
Oaxaca	0.1	0.0	0.3	0.1	5.7	1.1
Puebla	0.0	0.1	0.1	0.1	0.5	1.0
Tamaulipas	n.a.	0.1	n.a.	0.1	n.a.	0.7
Hidalgo	0.0	0.0	0.0	0.0	0.3	0.1
Tlaxcala	0.2	0.0	0.3	0.0	2.9	0.0
Veracruz	0.1	0.0	0.1	0.0	1.3	0.2
State average	0.4	0.3	0.7	0.6	3.7	3.4
District federal	0.1	0.4	0.1	0.4	0.2	0.6
Overall average	0.4	0.3	0.5	0.5	1.6	1.8

Source: SHCP and authors' calculations. Data for Tabasco are not available.

However, a closer look into the data reveal that during 1995–97 the states as a group were not generating a primary surplus before the extraordinary transfers, which should properly be counted as a financing item (below the line) not a revenue component; and that the primary *deficits* continued deteriorating even after 1995, because the debt restructuring did not lead, in most cases, to any effective fiscal adjustment in the states' budget *flows*. The financial deal involved basically a debt *stock* relief, and it did not resolve the structural fiscal imbalances. As a consequence, the fiscal stance of some Mexican states was not sustainable at least up to 1997, and they need serious fiscal adjustment.

The distance between real primary balance and real primary balance excluding extraordinary transfers basically shows the size of the bailout that benefited the states after 1995. Figures 6.4 through 6.9 depict the fiscal stance of the most indebted states and the Federal District. On the one hand, the states of Mexico and Sonora have been experiencing some fiscal improvements in the past two years, although they are still operating with insufficient primary surplus to sustain their high level of current indebtedness. On the other hand, the other states did not adjust up to 1997 and continued to increase their primary *deficits* up to that year. The states mostly improved their direct fiscal positions in 1998–99 as the extraordinary federal transfers phased out. These statistics do not reveal some important contingent liabilities for subnational governments; such as guarantees to public enterprises and pay-as-you-go pension and health schemes for state employees. Still incomplete estimates reveal that the size of outstanding contingent debt is daunting.

Figure 6.3. Mexico: Aggregate Subnational Governments' Fiscal Deficit, 1989–97

1997 prices (pesos)

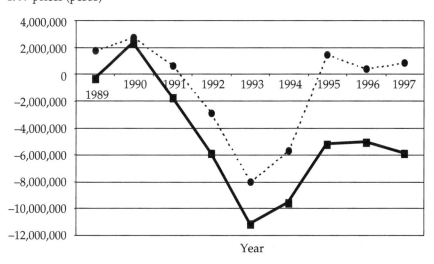

••●•• BAL. PRIMARIO REAL

━■━ BAL. PRIM. REAL (Excluding extraordinary transfers)

Source: Authors' calculations from SHCP data.

Figure 6.4. Jalisco: Fiscal Deficit, 1989–97

1997 prices (pesos)

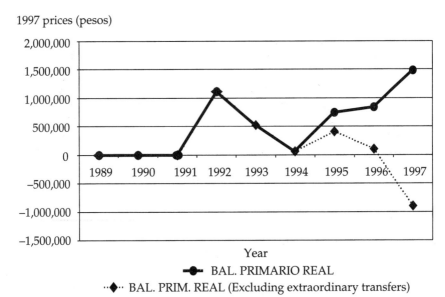

Year

⬤ BAL. PRIMARIO REAL

◆ BAL. PRIM. REAL (Excluding extraordinary transfers)

Source: Authors' calculations from SHCP data.

Figure 6.5. State of Mexico: Fiscal Deficit, 1989–97

1997 prices (pesos)

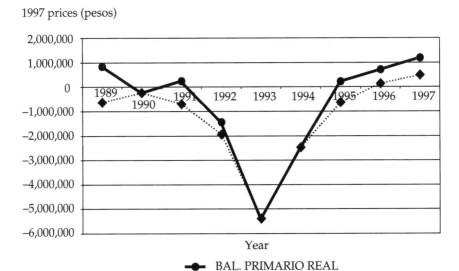

Year

⬤ BAL. PRIMARIO REAL

◆ BAL. PRIM. REAL (Excluding extraordinary transfers)

Source: Authors' calculations from SHCP data.

Figure 6.6. Nuevo Leon: Fiscal Deficit, 1989–97

1997 prices (pesos)

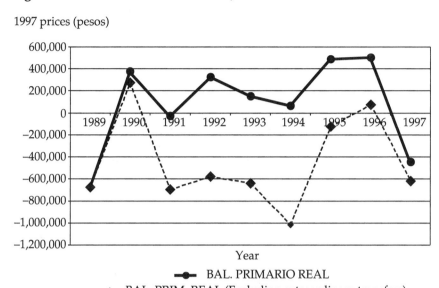

Year

— BAL. PRIMARIO REAL

- ◆ - BAL. PRIM. REAL (Excluding extraordinary transfers)

Source: Authors' calculations from SHCP data.

Figure 6.7. Sonora: Fiscal Deficit, 1989–97

1997 prices (pesos)

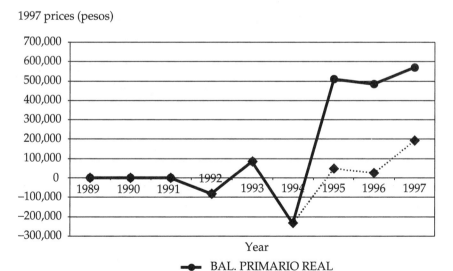

Year

— BAL. PRIMARIO REAL

···◆··· BAL. PRIM. REAL (Excluding extraordinary transfers)

Source: Authors' calculations from SHCP data.

Figure 6.8. Federal District: Fiscal Deficit, 1989–97

1997 prices (pesos)

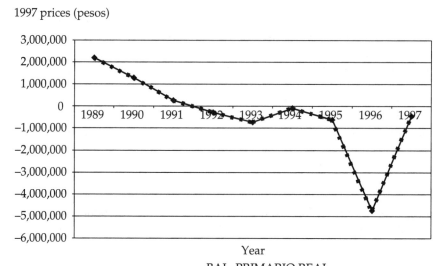

Source: Authors' calculations from SHCP data.

Figure 6.9. Sinaloa: Fiscal Deficit, 1989–97

1997 prices (pesos)

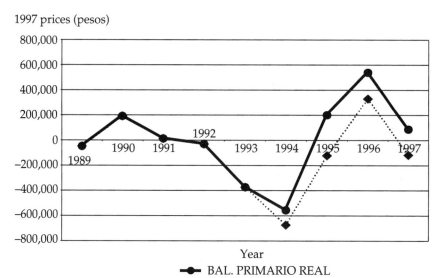

Source: Authors' calculations from SHCP data.

Subnational Borrowing: The Experience Up to 2000

Subnational governments can borrow mainly from development banks (38 percent in 1997) and commercial banks (62 percent). Other sources are available but rarely used by the states. The State of Guanajuato used bonds to finance construction of a road in 1997. The bond is guaranteed by the fees charged for use of the road. A fund (*fideicomiso*) was created to collect all the road revenues. The total amount of the issue was $Mex84 million. The capital of Yucatán (Mérida) has also issued a municipal bond. These are the only recent subnational experiences with bonds. The municipality of Garza García in Nuevo León, which is contiguous to Monterrey, needed a tunnel to connect two municipalities separated by a mountain. The government of Garza García, in coordination with the state government, put this construction to a referendum proposing that a property tax surcharge in Garza García be instituted for seven years to finance the construction. People in the municipality passed the referendum, and the municipality borrowed the resources from a commercial bank (Bancomer) using the property tax surcharge as a guarantee.

The Institutional and Legal Design

The institutional and legal design of the National Fiscal Coordination Law is important because it contains the incentives for both creditors and borrowers; some of those incentives are not desirable.

Subnational government borrowing is partly regulated by the national Constitution. The Federal Congress has the power to establish the bases on which the executive branch may arrange loans and take responsibility for public debt. All subnational governments must respect the criteria contained in Article 117, Section 8, for states; and Article 115, Section 6, for municipalities. The Constitution states that subnational governments can borrow only in Mexican pesos and only from Mexicans, and they can borrow only for productive investments. As a result, Banobras—a federal government development bank—and other financial institutions have found a way to lend in pesos with funds obtained in foreign currencies from international financial institutions, taking the exchange risk.

The details for guaranteeing credits are contained in Article 9 of the National Fiscal Coordination Law, created in 1980, which states that subnational governments can borrow from commercial and development banks to finance investment projects only after receiving authorization of the local congress. This law also states that around 20 percent of federal tax revenue must be transferred to state and local governments (that is, Mexico has a revenue-sharing system). In fact, the main source of revenue for subnational governments comes from federal transfers (*participaciones federales*), which, on average, account for about 85 percent of their total income.

Before a reform implemented in January 1997, after the tequila bailout, Article 9 allowed states and the Federal District to use their federal transfers as collateral. In case of arrears or a threat of default, the federal government would deduct debt service payments (on registered debt) from revenue sharing before the funds were transferred to states each month. This arrangement began in the 1980s when the banking system was nationalized.

Each year the state government would propose the debt level, and the state congress would approve the ceiling. This included the debt of municipalities. Municipalities, in principle, could incur debt, but the state had to guarantee it. That is why the state congress had to approve municipal debt.

The institutional arrangement before the 1995 crisis was simple. For *participaciones* to be used as collateral, states only needed to register the new debt contract with the SHCP, after receiving authorization from the local congress. This debt was backed by *participaciones*. SHCP could, in principle, deny the new debt and thus control the indebtedness of subnational governments, but this rarely happened.

This legislation had two implications for the behavior of suppliers and debtors. First, banks had incentives to make loans to subnational borrowers, because the credit risk was virtually nil, being guaranteed by the federal government. Second, states had incentives to borrow because the federal government would always bail them out. The latter is explained as follows.

Provided that federal transfers were the main source of revenues for the states and that current expenditures represented an average of nearly 80 percent of total expenditures, most of the disposable income of states and the Federal District was *tied*. This means that, if their revenue-sharing transfers were diverted to service debt, they would not be able to operate; this in turn brought high political costs at both the local and federal levels. Consequently, the federal government saw no alternative but to bail out the defaulting state by making the payments without deducting the amount from *participaciones*. This was typical when a commercial bank exercised a cross-default acceleration clause that would completely use up the state's *participaciones* or leave it without enough to pay for essential services.

These two points could explain in part the overborrowing in subnational credit markets and the lack of an explicit local regulation for borrowing or the lack of an obligation to present or publish financial statements. This, in principle, made it very difficult for lending institutions to evaluate a project. Until 1999 lending institutions rarely conducted an evaluation because the credit was risk-free.

When credit is not rationed and markets are competitive, economic theory suggests that spreads should be very small, reflecting only administrative costs. This is not the case in Mexico, where spreads are as high as 10 percentage points (see figures 6.4 through 6.9). In the absence of the possibility of a bailout, economic theory further predicts an equilibrium with credit rationing, where banks would be forced to evaluate the risk of a project, which in turn would force states to disclose information, both of which would promote market discipline.

To induce market discipline in subnational borrowing, Article 9 of the National Fiscal Coordination Law was reformed in 1997 to confer new obligations on state and local governments. Subnational governments could still use debt to finance their investment projects, and many still use their federal transfers as collateral. However, banks could not ask the Treasury Department to discount the corresponding amount from a defaulting state's federal transfers. They had to arrange the collateral according to state debt laws; that is, both parties had to create a repayment mechanism. In other words, subnational governments were responsible for repaying their contracted debts when federal transfers were used as collateral. In addition, they were obliged to publish their level of debt, and in turn, banks had to evaluate the risk of a project.

The modification had two purposes: to force states to exercise financial discipline and to force banks to analyze project risk when making a loan. These changes, in principle, were intended to induce discipline in subnational credit markets in three ways: (a) agents would respond to changes in interest rates; (b) states and local governments would define mechanisms under which borrowing is optimum and would be forced to present their financial statements when soliciting a credit; and (c) the possibility of a bailout would be reduced significantly because the federal government would be kept out of the market.

Did the Modification of the Law Induce Market Discipline?

Article 9 of the National Fiscal Coordination Law was modified to induce market discipline (a necessary but not sufficient condition for avoiding subnational bailouts). Its impact cannot be evaluated, however, because the changes it sought to impose were effectively circumvented.

After modifying Article 9 in January 1997, subnational governments had difficulty obtaining credit, especially from commercial banks. For this reason, in 1997 the federal government and the states designed a temporary scheme by which states would give the federal government a mandate to deduct debt service from *participaciones*. Under the mandate, banks were not forced to take losses, and they did not have incentives to evaluate the risk of the credit because they could obtain the *participaciones* independently of project evaluation. These actions, which were contrary to the spirit of the modified Article 9 (originally intended to instill discipline in the credit markets) also perpetuated the moral hazard problems. As long as the federal government stayed involved in the bank-subnational transaction, it was perceived as a guarantor in subnational credit markets.

Thus, in spite of the well-meaning reforms of January 1999, several weaknesses remained in the regulatory system for subnational borrowing. These weaknesses, which were addressed in a subsequent wave of reforms in early 2000 (see next section), included:

- Commercial banks still did not have an incentive to evaluate project risk because they were not effectively required to take any losses. This comes from the mandate given to SHCP. Most debt was issued by commercial banks. This debt was cheaper, but commercial banks did not evaluate the risk of the project and thus issued credit much faster than development banks, which did evaluate risk.
- `States and municipalities until at least 1998 still saw SHCP as the provider of last resort. This changed to some extent in 1999, when Ramo 23 virtually disappeared as a source of discretionary transfers. Ramo 23 was intended as a discretionary account of the president. Recently, a new fund was created for natural disasters, and another was created for wage increases. Ramo 23 could be used to help out states, and it was used from 1995 to 1998. In 1999 all resources were transferred to Ramo 33, and no resources are left to help out states although the case of Nuevo Leon in August 1999 shows how an emergency need for public works, combined with the threat of withdrawal from the *Pacto Fiscal*, could obtain special federal expenditures for what the state would ordinarily have financed.
- Matching transfers, such as for state universities, reduced the flexibility for managing debt. Such matching grants have the practical effect of earmarking some of the states' own revenue, cutting into what was counted as disposable revenue in our earlier calculations.
- Vertical imbalance persisted. As long as alternative sources of revenue were not developed, states would not be creditworthy. Most of their revenues were already tied.
- Domestic banks were virtually the only sources of debt financing for subnational governments. Alternative sources are needed to better access domestic as well as foreign savings.
- Before 2000, one rating agency gave debt ratings that considered past, not prospective, debt issues, and were on a Mexican scale (not a global scale). These ratings overlooked contingent liabilities and did not consider the perverse effects of fiscal imbalances, the matching transfer system, the moral hazard problem of past bailouts, and so forth. Debt had to be rated more seriously, as the new system will require.

A New Reform Initiative

The Overall Case for Subnational Borrowing Regulation

Fiscal decentralization in Mexico has been a political decision, and it seems irreversible. Mexican authorities are justifiably concerned with the risks involved in its scope, implementation, sequencing, and speed. Authorities are conscious about and well motivated by the political, efficiency, and equity benefits resulting from decentralization, but they are also aware of the possible tradeoffs between increased autonomy in expenditure and revenue decisionmaking and responsible macroeconomic management.

The potential of subnational governments to destabilize the country's macroeconomic situation is well known, especially in a federation like Mexico, where states are constitutionally sovereign in their territorial domain. Because states are free to increase outlays, even under a balanced budget they may affect macroeconomic equilibrium, since public expenditure multipliers tend to be larger than revenue multipliers.[3] Moreover, decentralized decisions tend to amplify the procyclical effect of fiscal policy and, in the absence of appropriate policies, to increase public debt. Subnational governments tend to increase expenditures during periods of economic expansion but are more reluctant to reduce expenditures during recessions. This reflects soft budget constraints in which subnational governments operate with a deficit and increase their indebtedness during recessions. Although the federal government has frequently used discretionary grant transfers (the so-called *transferencias extraordinarias*) to rescue states in financial trouble, the states of Coahuila, Guerrero, Mexico, Morelos, Nuevo León, Puebla, Quintana Roo, Sinaloa, Sonora, Tamaulipas, Zacatecas, and the Federal District increased their indebtedness substantially during the 1995 recession.

Soft budget constraints and increasing indebtedness of subnational governments may have deleterious macroeconomic effects in the short run, because of their direct impact on monetary expansion, inflation, interest rates, and balance of payments. In the medium and long term, excessive subnational indebtedness may crowd out private investments and reduce economic growth, and may have a perverse intergenerational equity effect, especially if the social rate of return on public spending is low and subnational governments cannot internalize all the benefits.

Therefore, a prior condition to guarantee successful and sustainable decentralization in Mexico is to ensure that decentralization, on the one hand, improves the social rate of return on public expenditures and, on the other, does not jeopardize short-term macroeconomic stability. Any policy strategy option should include incentives to assure that (a) a hard budget constraint is always in place, (b) public investments generate the highest possible social rate of return, and (c) public borrowers show enough capacity to pay back their loans (borrowers must be creditworthy). The incentives will be more effective if subnational governments are involved in the process of shaping the overall fiscal envelope and are accountable for their share of fiscal effects.

Management of Subnational Government Debt: The Initial Options

Who should evaluate the capacity of subnational governments to pay, in order to avoid excessive indebtedness, and how to do the evaluation? Many systems of subnational government debt management are possible for the Mexican government.[4] The most general and common systems are (a) financial market discipline; (b) strict case-by-case control by the federal government; and (c) the establishment of explicit, general rules by a national forum. Sometimes a combination of these systems is applied, depending on the particular market conditions.

RELIANCE ON MARKET DISCIPLINE. Market discipline is the most desirable code of behavior and set of benchmarks to follow. However, to work properly and effectively, market discipline has to be strict. This has rarely been achieved even in federations with well-developed financial markets. Many governments have decided not to rely solely on market discipline. Similarly, the following market failures prevail in Mexico, which means that market discipline alone may prove ineffective:

- *Restrictions on the financial market.* Market discipline is only effective if the financial market is free and open. The financial market is not entirely free or open in Mexico. Restricted access to foreign capital markets limits the available options, and compulsory allocation of resources (including those to official financial agencies and parastatals and the placement of government bonds) amplifies the borrowing capacity of the public sector and creates a suboptimal financial sector portfolio.
- *Lack of transparency.* Adequate dissemination and availability of information and full transparency on debt outstanding and capacity to pay are essential to market discipline. In Mexico, the effort to obtain reliable financial information, especially from subnational governments, is not a trivial endeavor. Not all states and municipalities follow a standardized plan of accounting, keep clear and uniform registers of their assets and liabilities, or publish and disseminate information on debt and capacity to pay on a satisfactory, systematic, and reliable basis. Moreover, extra-budget/contingent liabilities, hidden either under indirect indebtedness through parastatals or under soaring pension fund obligations, demand considerably more transparency in Mexico.

- *Moral hazard.* In the presence of moral hazard incentives, market discipline cannot serve as an effective check on subnational governments' excessive indebtedness. As mentioned earlier, in Mexico, the federal government has often intervened to rescue subnational governments in financial difficulties. These frequent bailouts (either by means of ad hoc extraordinary grant transfers or across-the-board debt rescheduling) have fed expectations of future rescue operations and encouraged moral hazard behavior on the part of both borrowers and lenders. As an example, the automatic federal guarantee and liquidation of debt (through the sequestration of federal transfers), still offered by Article 9 (via the so-called mandates from the states), encouraged lenders to disregard risk evaluation, and subnational governments to incur irresponsible indebtedness.
- *Insensitivity to market signals.* Market signals (interest rates and the possibility of market exclusion) can discipline borrowers to seek financial policies that are consistent with solvency. But for market discipline to be effective, the borrower must be sensitive to market signs. Increases in the interest rate should stop or at least make the borrower review its decision to borrow. However, governors and municipal presidents have rarely given adequate weight to market signals when determining their expenditure.

In Canada, market discipline alone is relied on to control subnational government indebtedness, and private rating companies evaluate public sector creditworthiness in a competitive environment. However, even in Canada, with its well-developed financial market, market discipline has been unable to check the excessive indebtedness of subnational governments. In the mid-1990s subnational debt reached 23 percent of GDP, prompting Canadian provinces to adopt fiscal adjustment programs to restrain themselves. But this only happened after the exclusion point had practically been reached, entailing high social costs.

Brazil, and to a certain extent Argentina, which do not have the necessary market conditions in place, have also taken some sort of market discipline approach since the late 1980s, with disastrous consequences. In Brazil, subnational debt jumped from 1 percent of GDP in the early 1970s to 20 percent in the mid-1990s, and in the past ten years the federal government intervened three times with large bailout operations to rescue the creditors of states, and twice to rescue the creditors of municipalities.

In Mexico, given present market conditions, relying solely on market discipline is not recommended, at least for the time being. Therefore, adequate regulation for checking excessive subnational government indebtedness is needed. In order to minimize distortions and encourage development of market practices, the necessary regulation should mimic desirable market discipline to the extent possible. But to what extent should the federal government or, alternatively, a national forum secretariat directly control subnational indebtedness in Mexico?

DIRECT ADMINISTRATIVE CONTROL. At the other extreme from the market is the enforcement of direct administrative control from the center to check excessive subnational government indebtedness. The direct control approach, however, has been used more frequently by unitary countries and less so by federations. States in Mexico also enjoy ample autonomy, and the direct control system may not be an adequate approach.

Direct controls (a) require the federal government's approval for each credit operation proposed by subnational government or (b) prohibit subnational governments from accessing capital markets directly. The approval of each credit operation inevitably requires an evaluation of the financial terms and conditions under which each operation is contracted. India is an outstanding example of central government approval on a case-by-case basis—the central government is a major creditor and guarantor of subnational governments, and the Constitution requires such intervention. During the 1980s, Australia prohibited subnational governments from accessing capital markets and centralized all loans through the Australian commonwealth government (the Loan Council), which then on-lent to the subnational governments. The direct control system in Australia was not effective, and now subnational governments are free to access capital markets directly. The Loan Council functions were restructured, and excessive indebtedness is now checked ex ante through a cooperative approach at the national level and is monitored closely ex post.

In Mexico the problems with a direct control system are clear: (a) centralizing all credit operations would involve the federal government directly in micromanaging each credit operation of every subnational government (the opposite of fiscal decentralization), entailing an unnecessary increase in federal bureaucracy and undesirable inefficiencies in the financial system; and (b) such prohibitions would be incompatible with the Mexican Constitution, which allows states free access to the domestic capital market, restricted only by approval of the state congress and by state indebtedness laws.

There are, nevertheless, strong arguments in favor of some prohibitions, or at least severe limitations, on some subnational government credit operations, in order to prevent systemic damage. These are operations concerned with (a) central bank financing, (b) noninvestment expenditure financing (the *golden rule*), (c) short-term loans for liquidity assistance, and (d) external financing. These kinds of subnational financing operations are banned in Mexico. Central Bank independence in Mexico rules out any kind of direct government financing. Similar rules could regulate other official financial institutions (for example, Banobras and Nacional Financiera). In addition, the Mexico Constitution prohibits expenditure financing for purposes other than investment (the *golden rule*). Yet, in the case of Mexico, the golden rule is not a sufficiently restrictive criterion, since (a) a clear definition of what constitutes investment is not yet in place, and (b) public savings need to be generated to help finance public investments.

Given the initial stage of decentralization in Mexico, the other two prohibitions (against short-term loans and external loans) will remain for the time being, and the government may want to revisit them in due time. Also because of the golden rule, subnational governments cannot yet use short-term loans for liquidity assistance purposes and are losing the opportunity to smooth out their cash flow through the year in order to optimize their financial inflows with outflows. The use of this kind of short-term loan by subnational governments is quite common and appropriate (for example, in the United States, Brazil, and other countries), as long as these governments can be forced to liquidate their debt during the same fiscal year.

The Mexican Constitution prohibits subnational governments from accessing foreign capital markets. Some compelling arguments support this prohibition. First, because changes in external debt have direct impacts on macroeconomic variables (exchange rate, foreign exchange reserves, and money supply), the federal government wants to keep full control over short-run stabilization policies to prevent federal policies from being either neutralized by or detrimental to subnational governments. Second, allowing the states and federal government to approach international capital markets in a fragmented fashion would be less efficient and would result in less favorable debt terms than a coordinated approach from the center. Third, there is always the possibility of a contagion effect in which the default of any one state would affect the creditworthiness and risk rating of other states and the federal government. Fourth, official international lenders usually require a federal government guarantee.

The arguments in favor of prohibiting external debt by subnational governments seem inescapable for the time being. Yet, as market conditions evolve and fiscal decentralization expands, the prohibition should be reexamined, since significant opportunities may be lost by not accessing the global capital market. A cooperative approach, with greater involvement, commitment, and accountability of subnational governments and improved coordination by the federal government, will make the arguments for prohibition less compelling and create conditions for a less radical approach based on more effective rules.

RULES-BASED APPROACH. There are strong reasons to support an adequate rules-based approach to curb subnational government access to capital markets. Rules can only be effective if they can be substantiated in a simple, transparent, and across-the-board set of legally binding instruments (the Constitution or ordinary laws). In general, these rules should comprise quantitative limits and procedural norms that respect or imitate, to the extent possible, the market practice of good financial discipline and creditworthiness indicators. Being constantly submitted for review, some of these rules should be established as preventative measures, others should only be implemented according to need. A rules-based approach has been adopted to different degrees in Brazil, Korea, Japan, Spain, and the United States, and other countries. Mexico can benefit from the extensive international experience in this area. The most common and essential lessons learned include

- *Limit the borrower's maximum debt service ratio.* Subnational governments should not be allowed to incur further debt if their debt service ratio (flow of interest due and amortization divided by flow of disposable revenue) exceeds a certain limit, say 12 percent. A debt service commitment above this limit will likely jeopardize the delivery of normal public services.
- *Limit the borrower's maximum level of total indebtedness.* Subnational governments should not be allowed to incur further debt if their total indebtedness indicator (ratio of outstanding debt, including indirect and contingent liabilities, to disposable annual revenue) exceeds a certain limit, say 0.8. This indicator of indebtedness will capture the debt burden of loans and credits that are still benefiting from a grace period.
- *Limit banks' portfolio exposure to the public sector.* Banks' portfolio exposure to the public sector should be constrained by a certain maximum limit. This limit should be enforced on total bank-by-bank assets to subnational governments as a group and to each public sector entity individually. Stricter norms and supervision should be applied on the official credit institutions (for example, Banobras, Nacional Financiera).
- *Enforce strict bank reserve requirements.* Besides the regular reserve requirements imposed on banks by the monetary authority, special provisions could be enforced on their operations with subnational governments. A special regulatory and supervisory framework could be in place to preempt problems with subnational governments that are experiencing financial difficulties.
- *Pass and regulate a public entity bankruptcy law.* In preparation for market discipline, the government could introduce a municipal and state bankruptcy law defining debt workout procedures in the case of default.

- *Pass and regulate a law of fiscal accountability.* This law would seek to stabilize public accounts over time (by limiting reiterated, excessive deficits and imprudent buildup of public debt), increase efficiency of public administration, achieve fiscal transparency (by clearly specifying an accounting code and full disclosure), and ensure the accountability of public officials, placing the risk on lenders rather than the federal government.
- *Encourage dissemination of risk rating of subnational governments.* To improve transparency and encourage the financial system to operate as close as possible to market discipline, the practice of creditworthiness analysis should be encouraged. In the United States and Canada, this practice is very common, and private risk-rating companies play a central role in helping subnational governments tap the capital markets, and in helping lenders gauge risks and limit subnational government's excessive indebtedness. Because of market failures, such practices are not well established in developing countries.

Rules-based systems of checking excessive subnational government indebtedness have the great advantage of being transparent and impartial—qualities that minimize political bargains and discretionality. Possible disadvantages are that excess inflexibility can damage the system and that some states will try to circumvent the rules. Although these disadvantages may operate in the short run, in the medium and long run, the rules can be changed and adjusted to new circumstances and necessities. As for short-run rigidities, the purpose of the rules is precisely to harden the budget constraints.

Mexico's New Regime for Subnational Borrowing: 2000 and Beyond

Faced with the challenge of both creating market-based mechanisms that ex ante would prevent excessive subnational borrowing and conveying a credible signal that the federal government would not, ex post, bail out parties involved in such borrowing, in late 1999 the Mexican federal government introduced (with full effect as of April 2000) a new regulatory framework for debt management by the states and municipalities. This framework has six components which innovatively combine market discipline with rules. The first two changes reinforce the government's commitment not to have bailouts. The next three (combined with the long-standing constitutional prohibition of foreign borrowing by states) limit ex ante the states' borrowing, in order to reduce the chance for states to create a debt crisis that would make the rules too costly for the federal government to enforce. The sixth change, pertaining to the government development banks, serves both purposes. The six components are:

1. A renunciation, and ensuing removal from the federal budget for 2000, of the Executive's power for discretionary transfer. Naturally, this policy proved uncontroversial with the opposition-dominated Congress.
2. The abolition of the *mandatos*. This left the states and their creditors to make their own *fideicomiso* arrangements for the collateralization of debt with *participaciones* or other revenue flows, assuming the legal risks involved and without recourse to the federation.
3. The elimination of the so-called *régimen de excepción* for borrower concentration limits. Now the regular rules apply also to subnational debt, limiting the extent of financial-sector damage that one single state can cause and signaling that state debt must be evaluated on a basis similar to other debt.
4. The establishment of a link between the capital risk weighting of bank loans to subnational governments and those governments' credit ratings. In particular, two, current, published, global-scale, local-currency credit ratings performed by internationally reputable credit rating agencies are to be used by bank regulators to assign capital risk weightings (between 20 and 115 percent) to loans given to states and municipalities. The rules for assigning these weights are fully specified by regulation.

    This innovative scheme, which is in line with the Basle Committee's recommendations of June 1999, is based on the distance between the rating obtained by the subnational borrower in question and the rating of the local-currency debt of the federal government. To control for agency shopping, two ratings are called for by the regulation and, in case of large discrepancies (more than two grades of distance), the capital weighting of the worse rating applies.

    The purpose of these regulations is, of course, to make the pricing of bank loans a function of the underlying risk of the subnational borrower, especially in the new framework of no federal intervention. Financially weaker states are likely to be priced or rationed out of the market (and become conditional clients of the development banks; see below), while stronger states would see the price of loans fall.
5. Registration of subnational loans with the federal government was made conditional upon the borrowing state or municipality being current on its publication of debt and associated fiscal statistics from the preceding year's final accounts, and on its debt service obligations toward the government's development banks. At the same time, and to make that registration appealing, unregistered loans are automatically risk-weighted by the regulators at 150 percent. This additional incentive to transparency has the purpose of ensuring that private contracting between the subnational borrowing and the credit rating agencies does not lead to the withholding of a minimum of quanti-

tative information on the borrower finances. Ultimately the discipline on these governments will come most effectively if voters and opposition parties have access to full information about the fiscal behavior of the administration in office.

6. Finally, and as a matter of corporate policy, federally owned development banks are to make new loans to states and municipalities (and their *organismos descentralizados*) only when the loan in question qualifies for registration and its capital risk-weighting is less than 100 percent. This policy, coupled with the conditions for registration mentioned above, makes the development banks part of the rigor of the new regulatory scheme, rather than potential loopholes to it.

Lending to weaker subnationals, however, is not forbidden. It is, after all, these clients whom the development banks have a mandate to assist. Instead, subnational loans with risk weightings of more than 100 percent are allowed if the loan package contains a technical assistance component funded by an international development bank. This latter arrangement conveys the signal that, when the loan is particularly risky (and correspondingly expensive), its origination and supervision are subject to a neutral, independent party.

Assuring Success: Key Implementation Issues

Mexico's new regulatory arrangement for subnational borrowing is a novel and promising start in putting local finances on a sustainable path. It is likely to generate momentum for further reform, notably in the distribution of tax and expenditure responsibilities among the three levels of government (currently embedded in the *Pacto Fiscal*). Because of the weak association between their access to bank credit and their creditworthiness, states and municipalities previously had no incentive to pay the political cost of raising local taxes or rationalizing local expenditures. With that association now firmly in place, subnational government will now take a more proactive and conservative approach to their finances.

This will benefit the country as a whole. But, for those benefits to occur, several elements will need to converge, most of which are within the control of the federal authorities. Among those that federation can control are the continuing application of the new rules to the development banks and the continuing commitment to renounce to discretionary budget powers. These factors would become all the more important if, in July 2000, a single party both won the presidential election and gained control of Congress.

Also within the policymakers' control will be the quality and enforcement of rules for the definition of bank capital, especially the new and sounder rules enacted in September 1999. The implementation of these rules will be critical if higher capital risk weightings for riskier borrowers are to be translated into more expensive loans, rather than fictitious capital allocations (like deferred taxes) without true opportunity cost to the bank owners.

Similarly, while capital risk-weightings will be a function of rating distances (from the federation), it will be up to the regulators to require that the ratings are performed and posted on a global scale. This will increase the reputational exposure of the credit rating agencies involved, and assure more thorough initial and follow-up analyses.

Finally, and beyond the policymakers' control, the level of competition in the market for nonlending bank services to subnational government will play a role in how differential capital risk-weightings are passed through and reflected on lending interest rates. If states and municipalities have plenty of alternative providers of the agency services that they contract from banks (for example, payroll payments and cash management), the latter may be reluctant in their loan price calculations to account fully for the higher capital allocations that subnational loans may require in the new regulatory framework.

Notes

N A to end

Overview

1. In the late 1990s some states have shown interest in complementing the Fiscal Pact by piggybacking state taxes on the federal income tax or value added tax.

2. A ramo is a section of the budget.

3. However, the primary purpose of these transfers between 1995 and 1998 was to bail out overindebted states.

4. For the Federal District, the federal Congress approves both the annual budget and borrowing.

5. The agreements are often used, in effect, to commit local governments to administer the property tax. Formation and updating of the fiscal cadastre are often—but not always—the responsibility of the state government.

6. Comités de Planeación para el Desarrollo del Estado (COPLADEs) and Comités de Planeación para el Desarrollo Municipal (COPLADEMUNs) should serve the purposes of intersectoral and public-private coordination at the state and municipal levels. However, these are predominantly spending mechanisms that are not usually concerned with fiscal responsibility or with balancing the revenue and spending columns of the fiscal equation. As a result, they are not effective for mobilizing additional local and regional resources.

7. Sector fragmentation of the budgets also discourages intersectoral coordination within one level of government (not to mention intergovernmental and intersectoral coordination) for allocating resources in a specified region or subregion.

8. A cadastre is an official record of property holdings and values.

9. Tax efficiency is measured as the ratio of tax revenue to the cost of tax administration.

10. If the federal government were simply to cede power to the states to levy a given tax, the "typical" state rate would be the rate previously levied by the federal government.

11. Excessive indebtedness of states may have equity implications. In Mexico, there is a clear positive correlation between state indebtedness and state per capita GDP. Therefore, debt bailouts tend to be highly regressive because the poorer states end up paying for the financial relief of richer states.

12. This calculation was for 16 states plus the Federal District, which employ about half of the total state employees.

13. This link between credit ratings and regulatory standards is in line with a recent consultative paper issued by the Basel Committee on Banking Supervision ("A New Capital Adequacy Framework," Basel Committee on Banking Supervision, Basel, June 1999). More generally, linking regulation to credit ratings is a common

practice in the financial sector of many countries (including Mexico), for example, in regulating corporate bond issues or insurance companies' investments (see Annex VI of IMF [1999] International Capital Markets—Developments, Prospects and Key Policy Issues, World Economic and Financial Surveys, at www.imf.org/external/pubs/ft/icm/1999/index.htm).

14. Banobras will be able to lend to a state with more risky credit ratings if the loans have an institutional development component funded by the Inter-American Development Bank, the World Bank, or other international development agencies because this may help improve the state's credit rating (especially among low-rated states).

15. By limiting the discretionary power of the federal authorities, the prevalence of rules will also directly support ongoing congressional efforts to grant more independence to subnational governments, including recent amendments to Article 115 of the Constitution.

Perspectiva General

1. De un tiempo a esta parte, los estados han mostrado más interés en complementar el Pacto Fiscal cargando los impuestos estatales al impuesto sobre la renta federal o al impuesto al valor agregado.

2. Un ramo es una sección del presupuesto.

3. Sin embargo, el propósito fundamental de esas transferencias entre 1995 y 1998 fue sacar de apuros a los estados que se habían endeudado de manera exagerada.

4. Para el Distrito Federal, el Congreso federal autoriza el presupuesto y el endeudamiento anual.

5. En efecto, a menudo se recurre a convenios para obligar a los gobiernos locales a que administren los impuestos prediales. La formación y actualización del catastro fiscal son a menudo—pero no siempre—responsabilidad del gobierno estatal.

6. Los Comités de Planeación para el Desarrollo del Estado y los Comités de Planeación para el Desarrollo Municipal deben servir para la coordinación pública–privada e intersectorial en los niveles estatal y municipal (COPLADEs y COPLADEMUNs, respectivamente). Sin embargo, se trata de mecanismos predominantemente de egresos que, por lo general, no se ocupan de la responsabilidad fiscal ni de equilibrar las columnas de gastos e ingresos de la ecuación fiscal. Por ende, no son eficaces para transferir recursos adicionales de carácter local y regional.

7. La fragmentación sectorial de los presupuestos también entorpece la coordinación intersectorial dentro de un nivel de gobierno para asignar recursos en una región o subregión específica (por no mencionar la coordinación intergubernamental e intersectorial).

8. El catastro es el registro oficial de la tenencia y valores de bienes raíces.

9. La eficiencia fiscal se mide como la proporción del ingreso fiscal con respecto al costo de la administración fiscal.

10. Si el gobierno federal simplemente fuera a delegar poder a los estados para gravar un determinado impuesto, la tasa estatal "típica" sería la tasa previamente fijada por el gobierno federal.

11. El endeudamiento excesivo de los estados puede tener repercusiones de equidad. En México, existe una evidente correlación positiva entre el endeu-

damiento estatal y el producto interno bruto per cápita de los estados. Por consiguiente, los rescates de deuda tienden a ser ligeramente regresivos porque los estados más pobres terminan pagando la ayuda financiera de los estados más ricos.

12. Este cálculo era para 16 estados más el Distrito Federal, que tiene contratados a cerca de la mitad de todos los trabajadores públicos estatales.

13. Este vínculo entre calificaciones de crédito y normas reguladoras va a la par con un reciente documento consultivo publicado por el Comité de Basilea para la Supervisión Bancaria (*Un Nuevo Marco de Suficiencia de Capital*, Comité de Basilea para la Supervisión Bancaria, Basilea, Junio 1999). En términos más generales, vincular la reglamentación a las calificaciones crediticias es una práctica normal en el sector financiero de muchos países (entre ellos México); por ejemplo, al regular las emisiones de bonos de empresas privadas o inversiones de compañías aseguradoras (consulte el Anexo VI del Fondo Monetario Internacional [1999], **International Capital Markets—Developments, Prospects and Key Policy Issues,** World Economic and Fiancial Surveys, en **www.imf.org/external/pubs/ft/icm/ 1999/index.htm.**

14. Banobras podrá otorgar préstamos a un estado con calificaciones crediticias más arriesgadas si los préstamos incluyen un factor de desarrollo institutional financiado por el Banco Interamericano de Desarrollo, el Banco Mundial o algún otro organismo internacional de fomento ya que esto puede ayudar a mejorar la calificación crediticia del estado en cuestión (sobre todo entre los que tengan una calificación baja).

15. Al limitar el poder discrecional de las autoridades federales, la preponderancia de reglas también apoyará de manera directa los esfuerzos que está realizando el Congreso para conceder más independencia a los gobiernos estatales, incluyendo las recientes enmiendas al Artículo 115 de la Constitución.

Chapter 1

1. Borrowing is efficient because it solves the problem of liquidity and allows local governments to match the timing of consumption with payment for those services. Having one generation of taxpayers pay for the capital equipment and then allow posterior generations to consume the services free of charge is unfair.

2. In general it seems that an origin-based sales tax would be more appropriate than a tax on commercial property because firms providing services generally have relatively little tangible property. But public services may be closely related to the existence of tangible property, especially real property, the base of most successful property taxation. It may appear that a source-based corporate income tax would also be appropriate in this case, but there are several problems with this reasoning. Services are presumably not provided only to corporations, and the value of such services is not likely to be closely related to profitability.

3. The result under a flat-rate surcharge on the base of the central government, as in some states of the United States, is very different from that under the Canadian system of imposing provincial surcharges on the tax liability to the national government. Since the national tax in Canada is levied at graduated rates, the provincial surcharge is also progressive, with the adverse effect already mentioned.

4. In addition, the retail sales tax provides some incentive for vertical integra-

tion. This is reduced by exempting goods bought for resale or direct use in production, for fuels, and for utilities; such exemptions vary from state to state.

5. By far the most important cause of tax exporting in the United States is the deduction for state and local income and property taxes that is allowed in computing liability for federal income tax, a provision that is hard to justify. Taxes are also exported to owners of firms that cannot shift taxes to others (customers, suppliers, or labor). Exporting to out-of-state customers is not likely to be important, because of pressures from untaxed competitors.

6. For more detailed descriptions, see McLure (1995), Martínez-Vásquez, McLure, and Wallace (1995), and Asian Development Bank (forthcoming). As explained there, the lack of *oblast* fiscal autonomy is much worse than suggested by the description in the text. Tax sharing commonly varies across taxes and between oblasts and is set to provide the revenue needed to finance a given level of expenditures. Where shared taxes do not provide adequate revenues, the central government provides subventions. Expenditure levels reflect a combination of norms, historical patterns, inflation adjustment, and negotiation. The German länder also rely heavily on shared taxes, particularly the value-added tax. In Canada the federal government collects the harmonized sales tax for itself and several of the poor Maritime Provinces, dividing the provincial share on the basis of estimated consumption in the various provinces.

7. The pervasiveness of revenue sharing conditions the applicability of this statement, since it implies that the federal government does not keep all the revenues from any tax that enters the coparticipation pool.

8. Under the state value added tax proposed in Chapter 4, interstate transactions would be zero-rated by the state of origin and subject to the compensating value added tax. Purchases by registered traders would be taxed by the state of destination on a deferred payment basis. It appears that the problem of assuring consistency of state taxation would be vastly more difficult in the absence of the compensating value added tax. The state of destination would have to rely on the federal government to see that the state of origin is not making zero-rated sales to households in its jurisdiction.

Chapter 2

1. Memorias de la Primera Convencion Nacional Fiscal, 1925, p.6.

Chapter 3

1. However, expenditure shares can be a misleading measure of decentralization. Subnational governments can have more resources pass through their budgets, but may not have more discretion over these expenditures.

2. These data are from the Ministry of Finance and Public Credit (SHCP). Data for total revenues available to the states for 1999 indicate much lower horizontal disparities across states (see Chapter 5). This may be because there was equalization in 1998 and 1999, or that the data sets are not consistent or comparable.

3. For the 23 states with complete data. The regression coefficient was statistically significant at the 1 percent confidence level, and the R-square was 0.57.

4. The degree of control actually exerted by the ministry depends on the state, in particular the governor and his team. One possible reason for the lack of decen-

tralization is that the ministry has not downsized significantly as a result of the National Agreement and federal employees have found it hard to change their roles.

5. This dual system existed for a number of years. Currently, even though the two systems have been formally integrated, they continue to be administered separately in many states.

6. The negotiations between the Ministry of Public Education and the national union are circumscribed by the budget allocation approved by Congress in the federal budget for federal teachers.

7. For example, parents in Zacatecas and Oaxaca complain that the absenteeism rate of teachers is very high (World Bank 1996).

8. The equity issue could be addressed by providing special scholarships for low-income students.

9. Any differences between decentralized and other states were mostly due to differences in initial conditions and not to decentralization per se (OCDE 1998).

10. However, wages and salaries are fixed at the national level through negotiations between the Ministry of Health and the national union.

11. INEGI (1998, p. 82) reports that the distribution of health transfers in the Fiscal Coordination Law is based on a capitation formula adjusted by mortality, poverty, and expenditure on health services. This is not described in the law itself. It could be that federal authorities plan to move toward this very desirable reform.

12. Despite increases in federal health expenditures and considerable investments in poorer states, until 1997 the Ministry of Health budget allocations per capita were inversely correlated with the poverty level of the state. Reportedly, the Ministry is using a new formula that takes into account demographic and epidemiological characteristics (OCDE 1998).

13. The average cost of transport to the nearest health center for treatment in Zacatecas is more than one month's earnings (World Bank 1996).

14. Per capita, risk-adjusted funding is more equitable and also more likely to contain costs (as opposed to payment for service rendered).

15. According to the Ministry of Health, the states manage 70 percent of all budget resources in health services, but 70 percent or more of these funds are for wages and salaries that are determined at the federal level.

16. Since 1990 the Irrigation District Authority has been transferred to producers themselves, and cost recovery has improved for those districts still administered by the National Water Authority.

17. For the most part, toll roads have not succeeded due to a combination of factors, including poor feasibility analysis, high tariffs, and the concessionary process.

18. Since 1985 the federal government has delivered funds for investment programs only when channeled through the COPLADE.

Chapter 4

1. This statement is not meant to imply that the base of the existing federal tax is optimal or even desirable. It may be that all payroll tax bases, including that of the federal tax, should be made to conform to the best of the state bases. The point is that all the bases should be the same. Uniformity of bases might be achieved by federal mandate or—perhaps more acceptable politically—by allowing credits for some portion of state taxes against a federal payroll tax, provided the states adopt

the federal base. The latter technique has been used to achieve uniformity of state taxes on transfers of real estate.

2. Mexican subnational governments accounts report "gross revenues" as the relevant measure of own revenue collection. That is not a correct measure of fiscal capacity because it includes borrowing, revenue sharing, and funds collected on behalf of other levels of government. Net tax revenues refers to revenues collected by a subnational government without borrowing, revenue sharing, and the so-called revenue "por cuenta de terceros." It is the sum of Impuestos, Derechos, Productos, and Aprovechamientos, which are the relevant tax and nontax revenues. All estimates in the tables are calculated as a percentage of net tax revenues.

3. If residence-based taxation were feasible, it might make more sense to reserve surcharges on the individual income tax for use by municipal governments, because of the scarcity of tax bases that are suitable for use by local governments. This is especially true if, as suggested below, state surcharges on the VAT are feasible.

4. A tax limited to a small portion of the population invites "tyranny of the majority." Whether this is more problematic for a federal or state tax is unclear.

5. These figures are calculated from state income distribution survey results released by 1999, but the raw data, which would produce a better analysis, could not be obtained from INEGI.

6. A long-run objective might be to merge the payroll and individual income tax systems, allocating to the states the capacity to levy flat rate income tax surcharges, while leaving the progressive element at the central level. This would necessitate unification of the two tax bases and the administration of the two taxes—a step that would presumably allow some savings in costs of compliance and administration. Whether this is a sensible objective from the point of tax assignment depends in part on one's view of the nature of the services provided by the states and the prevalence of commuting across state boundaries. If labor income is thought to be a reasonable proxy for the consumption of such services and if (a) most such services are provided where people work, rather than where they live, or (b) cross-boundary commuting is not overly important, it would be better to employ the (source-based) payroll tax to finance them, even in the long run. If total income (including nonlabor income) were thought to be a better proxy, if most services are provided where people live, or if cross-boundary commuting is important, unification of the income and payroll taxes into a single residence-based tax would be more appropriate, if it can be achieved.

7. One might think of the flat-rate state tax as being levied at the "basic" rate on virtually all income, with the graduated rates of the federal tax being levied only on income above a certain level.

8. Depending on the structure of personal deductions and credits, deductions and credits for personal expenditures, and other features of the individual income tax, the situation could be even worse. This cannot be assessed without a thorough examination of the structure of the individual income tax, which is beyond the scope of this paper.

9. Absent the constitutional requirement that taxes on hydrocarbons should be federal taxes, taxes on motor fuels could also usefully be assigned in part to the states to help cover the costs of highways and roads.

10. In the case of motor fuels the problem is more likely to take the form primarily of (a) households residing in high-tax states filling their cars in neighboring low-tax states, and (b) interstate truckers concentrating purchases of fuel in low-tax

states. The former abuse is difficult to prevent, but seems unlikely to be quantitatively significant, except in a few cases (for example, the Federal District and the State of Mexico). To prevent the latter abuse, if Mexico were to assign motor fuel excises to the states (following relaxation of the constitutional prohibition of state taxes on hydrocarbons), consideration might be given to the "base state" approach employed by all the states of the United States and some of the provinces of Canada. Under this approach, truckers pay the tax due where they purchase fuels. But they apportion road use, and thus consumption of fuel, among the states where they operate, based on mileage logs, and file returns with their "base state" (ordinarily the state or province where they have their primary place of business) showing tax liability to each state, based on estimated consumption and tax rates in the state. The taxpayer makes one payment to its base state if, on balance, the sum of residual tax due all states is positive (and receives a refund if the sum of residual liabilities is negative). Each base state then remits to (or receives from) an interstate clearinghouse the net balance due other states. Given Mexico's participation in the North American Free Trade Association with Canada and the United States, it seems appropriate for it to consider joining this arrangement, especially if its states are given the power to levy taxes on motor fuels.

11. The ease of smuggling from neighboring countries effectively limits the level of excises. Above a certain level, increases in excises are likely to produce less revenue, not more.

12. It is also generally inefficient to use "geographic separate accounting" for such a purpose, since such accounts generally are not needed for any other reason.

13. It is worth noting that over the past 25 years there has been a tendency for the states of the United States to shift from a formula that accords equal weight to the three factors to one that places double weight on sales (and even to formulas based entirely on sales), presumably to reduce the implicit burden on origin-based factors.

14. This discussion concentrates on sales to households and unregistered traders and those to registered traders. (It is assumed that sales to unregistered traders should be taxed, as a surrogate for taxing their sales.) It does not examine details such as the treatment of sales to and by governments and nonprofit institutions, because these are not central to the issues at hand.

15. The approach employed in the state RSTs levied by 45 states (and the District of Columbia) in the United States is to allow registered traders to purchase certain types of products by presenting "resale exemption certificates" to their suppliers. All states exempt purchases of goods to be resold without a change of condition and most purchases of goods to be incorporated in goods for resale. Beyond that, practice varies from state to state; some states exempt, *inter alia*, goods to be used directly in production, fuels, public utilities, agricultural implements, and seeds bought by farmers. For a more complete discussion, see Due and Mikesell (1994). It has been estimated that, on average, 40 percent of the state tax base involves sales to business, with wide variation around that average; see Ring (1989 and 1999). Thus Mexico should not emulate the typical RST levied by the American states, which deviates substantially from a pure consumption-based tax.

16. The usual problem with exemption systems is that they place the vendor in the unenviable position of determining whether each sale is taxable or legally exempt, and create an incentive for the vendor to "look the other way" when a household purchase masquerades as a business purchase. Under the Mexican pro-

666

posal it appears that the vendor need only ascertain that the purchaser has a valid VAT TIN.

17. If, contrary to the Mexican proposal, the state RST were to be implemented by the federal tax administration, costs of administration would be substantially lower than under state administration of the RST, and costs of compliance would be somewhat lower. The federal administration would determine for purposes of both the VAT and the RST whether a particular purchase was for business purposes, and thus eligible for VAT input credits and exemption from the RST. Taxpayers would need to deal with only one tax administration.

18. Much is made of the "cross-checking" that is made possible by the VAT—the fact that credits taken by registered purchasers must be shown on invoices issued by vendors, and thus subject to tax. This is probably less important than confirming that purchases are for legitimate business use.

19. If experience in other countries is any guide, taxpayers would not—as they should—be able simply to give state auditors photocopies of information provided to federal auditors.

20. This discussion refers only to the RST; the next subsection discusses the analogous problems under the VAT. Exemption of interstate sales to registered businesses by the state of origin would occur naturally under the RST, provided the state's tax administration respects the right of the out-of-state business purchaser to make exempt purchases.

21. Note that this discussion pertains directly only to "remote selling," sales of tangible products sent to the customer across state lines. It does not concern "cross-border shopping," in which the customer buys a product "across the counter" in a state where she or he does not live and takes it home for use there. It seems virtually inevitable that the latter transactions will bear tax at the rate prevailing in the state where the sale is made (the state of origin), and not that of the state of destination, except in rare cases, for example, where goods must be registered in the state to be used there, as in the case of automobiles (and perhaps boats and planes). This places revenues in the "wrong" state. People may engage in cross-border shopping in order to reduce taxes when two adjacent jurisdictions have markedly different tax rates. This abuse is inevitably difficult to prevent. It is, of course, important only where metropolitan areas straddle the boundaries of subnational jurisdictions, as in the case of Mexico City. Interstate sales of digital content over the Internet ("electronic commerce") could be handled in the same way as interstate sales of tangible products. The most difficult problems involve sales originating outside the country. Sales occurring within the country could, in principle if not in actuality, be monitored. It is difficult to tax a transaction in digital content between an unknown customer and a foreign seller (perhaps located in a tax haven), especially if payment is made in untraceable money. See McLure (1997 and 1999).

22.This may seem not to be an important problem in Mexico at the present time. It is certainly an important problem in the United States and Canada, and will grow in importance as the economy of Mexico develops. Part of the problem in both of Mexico's northern neighbors can be traced to constitutional restrictions on the taxing powers of the states and provinces. In the United States these restrictions were imposed on the states by the U.S. Supreme Court because of the overwhelming diversity of state and local tax laws; McLure (1999) describes the situation in the United States. There is no reason that Mexico need be bound by similar artificial restrictions.

23. In theory, each of the 32 states could rely on the tax administrations of the other 31 states to serve this purpose. Indeed, perhaps the "base state" approach described above in footnote 9 could be employed for the sales tax. The latter is one alternative being considered by the National Tax Association's Telecommunications and Electronic Commerce Tax Project, described in McLure (1999). One of the Project's concerns is that state tax administrators might not be diligent in auditing their own taxpayers on behalf of other states. This concern seems equally telling in Mexico. In any event, it would be feasible only if the tax base of the various states were essentially identical. With federal administration of the state RSTs, returns for all states would be filed with the federal administration. This would not relieve the most burdensome aspects of compliance, the need to distinguish the state of destination of remote sales.

24. Some technique such as this might be necessary in the case of electronic commerce in digital content, since the vendor may not know the location of the buyer. See McLure (1999).

25. See, for example, Boadway (1997) and (McLure) 1980a. Indeed, even sharing of revenues from a national tax has been thought to involve similar problems. See McLure (1995).

26. Much of this discussion is based on an excellent paper by Poddar (1990). It is assumed that international trade would be taxed under the destination principle, as is the virtually universal practice. Thus, exports would be zero-rated, and the full value of imported products would be subject to tax.

27. As above, it is assumed that unregistered traders are to be treated like households, since they are "outside the system," and thus not eligible for credits for tax paid on purchased inputs.

28. Even with uniform rates the value of goods crossing internal borders may be contentious. Values attached to such trade are a matter of indifference to taxpayers, but subnational governments would not be indifferent, because the valuation at the border would affect their tax bases. Thus taxpayers could be caught between tax authorities in the two jurisdictions.

29. The more affluent states of the south tax imports and the poorer states of the northeast rebate tax on exports. See Longo (1982). To ameliorate the resulting inequities, lower rates are applied to interstate sales than to intrastate sales, seriously complicating the system.

30. Poddar (1990, pp. 110–11) calls this a joint national-state VAT when imposed in the context of a two-tiered national/subnational VAT.

31. At the risk of excessive proliferation of labels, one might refer to the Quebec system as employing "unprotected zero-rating/deferred payment" and the CVAT system proposed below as involving "protected zero-rating/deferred payment."

32. It is worth noting that in this case the province administers both the federal and provincial VATs. The VAT in Mexico was administered by the states for some years prior to 1991, but the clearest effect of such measure was a drop in revenue, attributable probably to compliance problems. Thus, the federal component of any dual system employed in Mexico—and perhaps the state component—would presumably be administered by the federal tax authorities. In some countries there is a further issue: whether subnational governments trust the central government to deliver the revenue collected on their behalf.

33. In recent years there have been several proposals in Argentina and Brazil for a dual state/central VAT. In Argentina Libontti and Salinardi (1994) have proposed

state use of "unprotected" zero-rating and deferred payment. Drawing on a proposal originally made for Brazil by Varsano (1995), Gonzalez Cano (1996) and Fenochietto have proposed an "IVA compartido" or shared VAT that would combine zero rating/deferred payment with an additional "compensating" VAT on interstate sales to registered traders along the lines proposed below. See McLure (1998).

34. It should be noted that international trade poses no conceptual problem in this case. State tax is collected on imports and credit is allowed for the tax paid on imports. Similarly, exports are zero-rated for the state tax, as well as the federal tax.

35. This statement assumes that the price of power approximates the marginal long-run cost of producing it. If this is not true, marginal cost pricing should be introduced; taxation may be one way to do this.

36. In addition, Section IX of Article 117 provides that "the States may not in any case...levy duties on the production, storage, or sale of tobacco in a manner distinct from or with rates greater than those authorized by the Congress of the Union."

37. A common sense interpretation of the following article should not pose any problem: "Article 118. Nor shall the States, without the consent of the Congress of the Union...establish ship tonnage dues or any other port charges, or levy imposts or taxes on imports or exports." Sales taxes and excises levied on a destination basis include consumption of imported goods in their bases. While they may be collected at the point of importation, they are not taxes on imports.

Chapter 6

1. Total lending from commercial banks to subnational governments in early-1998 was only about 4 percent of their total portfolio.

2. It is not possible to compute the debt service ratio, because figures for interest *due* and amortization are not available. The available statistics on the fiscal/financial flows only show *cash* payments.

3. The impact of increased subnational government expenditure is bigger when they are financed with deficits, as is often the case in Mexico.

4. For a survey and a discussion of the relevant international experience see Ter-Minassian and Craig (1997) and Lane (1993).

Bibliography

Aguilar Villanueva, Luis F. 1996. "El federalismo mexicano: funcionamiento y tareas pendientes." In Hernández Chavez, Alicia, ed., ¿Hacia un Nuevo Federalismo? México: Fondo de Cultura Económica.

Alzati, Fausto. 1998. "The Political Economy of Growth in Mexico." Ph.D. Dissertation. Cambridge, MA: Harvard University.

Amieva-Huerta, Juan. 1997. "Mexico." In Ter-Minassian, ed., Fiscal Federalism in Theory and Practice. Washington, D.C.: International Monetary Fund.

Arellano Cadena, Rogelio, ed. 1996. México Hacia un Nuevo Federalismo Fiscal México: Fondo de Cultura Económica. Gobierno del Estado de Puebla.

Asian Development Bank. Forthcoming. Fiscal Transition in Kazakhstan. Manila: Asian Development Bank.

Bailey, John. 1994. "Centralism and Political Change in Mexico; The Case of National Solidarity." In Wayne Cornelius, Ann Craig and Jonathan Fox, eds., Transforming State Society Relations in Mexico: The National Solidarity Strategy. San Diego: Center for U.S.–Mexican Studies.

Barro, Robert, and Xavier Sala-i-Martin. 1991. "Convergence Across States and Regions." Brookings Papers on Economic Activity No. 1. Washington, D.C.

————. 1995. Economic Growth. New York: McGraw-Hill.

Basel Committee on Banking Supervision. 1999. "A New Capital Adequacy Framework." Basel, Switzerland. June.

Bird, Richard M., and Pierre Pascal Gendron. 1998. "Dual VATs and Cross-Border Trade: Two Problems, One Solution?" International Tax and Public Finance 5: 429–42.

Boadway, Robin. 1997. "Reforming the Fiscal Arrangements in Argentina: Lessons from Industrialized Federations." March 4. Processed.

————. 1998. "The Economics of Equalization: An Overview." In Robin Boadway and Paul Hobson, eds., Equalization: Its Contribution to Canada's Economic and Fiscal Process. Kingston, Ontario: Queen's University, John Deutsch Institute for the Study of Economic Policy.

Boadway, Robin, and Paul Hobson. 1993. *Intergovernmental Fiscal Relations in Canada*. Toronto: Canadian Tax Foundation.

Bonifaz Chapoy, Beatriz. 1992. *Finanzas Nacionales y Finanzas Estatales*. México: UNAM.

Bruhn, Katherine. 1996. *Social Spending and Political Support: The Lessons of the National Solidarity Program in Mexico World Politics*.

Burki, Javed, William Dillinger, Guillermo Perry, and others, 1999. *Beyond the Center: Decentralizing the State in Latin America*. Washington, D.C.: World Bank.

Cabrero, Enrique. 1995. *La nueva gestión municipal en Mexico*, Ed. Miguel Ángel Porrua-CIDE, México.

_____. Coordinador. 1996. *Los dilemas de la modernizacion municipal*, Ed. Miguel Ángel Porrua-CIDE, Mexico

Cabrero, E., L. Flamand, C. Santizo, and A. Vega. 1998. "Claroscuros del nuevo federalismo mexicano. Estrategias en la decentralización federal, y capacidades en la gestión local." *Gestión y Política Pública* (CIDE) 6(2).

CIDAC. 1998. "Fórmulas para la asignación de recursos del presupuesto de egresos de la federación a estados y municipios." Presentation to the Planning and Budget Committee, Mexican Chamber of Deputies. Mexico. Processed.

Commonwealth Grants Commission. 1999. *Report on General Revenue Grant Relativities: 1995 Update*. Canberra: Australian Government Publishing Services.

Courchene, Thomas J. 1984. *Equalization Payments: Past Present and Future*. Toronto: Ontario Economic Council.

_____. 1998. "Renegotiating Equalization: National Polity, Federal State, International Economy." *C. D. Howe Commentary* No. 113. Toronto: C. D. Howe Institute.

_____. 1999. "Subnational Budgetary and Stabilization Policies in Canada and Australia." In James Poterba and Jürgen von Hagen, eds., *Fiscal Institutions and Fiscal Performance: A National Bureau of Economic Research Conference Report*. Chicago: University of Chicago Press, 301–48.

Courchene, Thomas, and Colin R. Telmer. 1998. *From Heartland to North American Region State: The Social, Fiscal and Federal Evolution of Ontario*. Toronto: University of Toronto, Faculty of Management.

_____. 1998. "Revenue Redistribution and Federal-Provincial Fiscal Relations in Canada." In Robin Boadway and Paul Hobson, eds., *Equalization: Its Contribution to Canada's Economic and Fiscal Process*. Kingston, Ontario: Queen's University, John Deutsch Institute for the Study of Economic Policy.

Diaz Cayeros, Alberto. 1995. *Desarrollo Económico e Inequidad Regional: Hacia un Nuevo Pacto Federal en México*. México: M. A. Porrúa.

_____. 1997. "Asignación Política de Recursos dentro del Federalismo Mexicano: Incentivos y Limitaciones." *Perfiles Latinoamericanos* 10 (January-June): 35–73.

_____. 1997. "Political Responses to Regional Inequality: Taxation and Distribution in Mexico." Ph.D. Dissertation, Duke University.

Diaz Cayeros, Alberto. Forthcoming. "Diversidad regional, jurisdicciones concurrentes y desarrollo." In Jorge Javier Romero and Maria Amparo Casar, eds., *Federalismo Mexicano*. México: M. A. Porrúa.

Diaz Cayeros, Alberto, and Beatriz Magaloni. 1998. "Autoridad presupuestal del poder legislativo en México: una primera aproximación." *Política y Gobierno V*(2).

Diaz-Cayeros, and Martinez Uriarte. 1999. "Tensiones del Federalismo: Crecimiento y Pobreza en las Regiones." Presentation to the Campaign Team of Presidential Candidate Vicente Fox. Mexico: CIDAC. Processed.

Dillinger, William, and Steven B. Webb. 1999. "Fiscal Management in Federal Democracies: Argentina and Brazil." Policy Research Working Paper 2121. Washington, D.C.: World Bank.

Dillinger, William, Guillermo Perry, and Steven B. Webb. 2000. "Macroecnomic Management in Decentralized Democracies: The Quest for Hard Budget Constraints in Latin America." In Javed Burki and Guillermo Perry et al., eds., "Decentralization and Accountability of the Public Sector in Latin America." *Proceedings of Annual World Bank Conference on Development in Latin America*. 1999. Washington, D.C.: World Bank.

Dresser, Denise. 1991. "Neopopulist Solutions to Neoliberal Problems. Mexico's National Solidarity Program." La Jolla: Center for U.S.–Mexican Studies.

Due, John F., and John L. Mikesell. 1994. *Sales Taxation: State and Local Structure and Administration*. Second Edition. Washington, D.C.: Urban Institute Press.

Duncan, Harley T., and Charles E. McLure, Jr. 1997. "Tax Administration in the United States of America: A Decentralized System." *Bulletin for International Fiscal Documentation* 51(2): 74–85, February. Also forthcoming in Spanish translation in *Hacienda Publica Español*.

Fenochietto, Ricardo. (No date). "El IVA Compartido: Una Herramienta Útil para el Reemplazo del Impuesto sobre los Ingresos Brutos y la Descentralización de Tributos." Processed.

Garman, Christopher, Stephan Haggard, and Eliza Willis. 1999. "The Politics of Decentralization in Latin America." *Latin American Research Review* 34(1).

Gershberg, Alec, and Donald Winkler. 2000. "Education Decentralization in Latin America: The Effects on the Quality of Schooling." In Javed Burki and Guillermo Perry, et al., (eds.), "Decentralization and

Accountability of the Public Sector in Latin America." *Proceedings of the Annual World Bank Conference on Development in Latin America and the Caribbean 1999.* Washington, D.C.: World Bank.

Gonzalez Cano, Hugo. 1996. "La Reforma Tributaria de Brasil y Posible Aplicación del Nuevo IVA Federal y Estadual para el Reemplazo del Impuesto a los Ingresos Brutos." *Boletin de la DGI* 513: 1391–97, September.

Gonzalez Casanova, Pablo. 1965. *La democracia en Mexico.* Mexico, D.F.: Ediciones ERA.

Guerrero, Juan Pablo, et. al. 1998. "La Descentralización de los Fondos de Aportaciones Federales (Ramo 33): Análisis Preliminar de sus Efectos y Riesgos." México: CIDE.

Hobson, Paul. 1998. "Is there Too Much Revenue Redistribution through Canada's Fiscal Equalization Program?" In Robin Boadway and Paul Hobson, eds, *Equalization: Its Contribtution to Canada's Economic and Fiscal Progress.* Kingston, Ontario: Queen's University, The John Deutsch Institute for the Study of Economic Policy, 157-174.

International Monetary Fund (IMF). 1999. "International Capital Markets— Developments, Prospects and Key Policy Issues, Annex VI." *World Economic and Financial Surveys.* www.imf.org/external/pubs/ft/icm/1999/index.htm.

Instituto Nacional de Estadística Geografía e Informática (INEGI). 1998. "El ingreso y el gasto público en México: Diversas ediciones y poder ejecutivo federal." In *Cuarto informe de gobierno.* Mexico, D.F.

_____. 1996. *Encuesta Nacional de Ingresos y Gastos de los Hogares.* Mexico: INEGI.

_____. 1989. *Encuesta Nacional de Ingresos y Gastos de los Hogares.* Mexico: INEGI.

_____. 1999. *Encuesta del Estado de Campeche de Ingresos y Gastos de los Hogares 1996.* México: INEGI.

_____. 1999. *Encuesta del Estado de Coahuila de Ingresos y Gastos de los Hogares 1996.* México: INEGI.

_____. 1999. *Encuesta del Estado de Guanajuato de Ingresos y Gastos de los Hogares 1996.* México: INEGI.

_____. 1999. *Encuesta del Estado de Hidalgo de Ingresos y Gastos de los Hogares 1996.* México: INEGI.

_____. 1999. *Encuesta del Estado de Jalisco de Ingresos y Gastos de los Hogares 1996.* México: INEGI.

_____. 1999. *Encuesta del Estado de Oaxaca de Ingresos y Gastos de los Hogares 1996.* México: INEGI.

_____. 1999. *Encuesta del Estado de Tabaco de Ingresos y Gastos de los Hogares 1996.* México: INEGI.

_____. 1999. *Encuesta del Estado del Distrito Federal de Ingresos y Gastos de los Hogares 1996.* México: INEGI.

_____. 1999. *Encuesta del Estado del Estado de México de Ingresos y Gastos de los Hogares 1996*. México: INEGI.

_____. 1999. *Encuesta Ingreso Gasto de los Hogares*. México: INEGI.

Keen, Michael, and Stephen Smith. 1996. "The Future of the Value Added Tax in the European Union." *Economic Policy* 23: 373–420, October.

Lane, Timothy. 1993. "Market Discipline." International Monetary Fund Staff Paper. Washington, D.C.

Latapí, Pablo, and Manuel Ulloa. 1998. "Inconsistencias de la Fórmula de Distribución de los Recursos Federales para Educación y Propuesta de Alternativas." In *Comisión de Desarrollo Social Instrumentos de Distribución de los Recursos del Ramo 33*. México: Cámara de Diputados.

Levy, Santiago. 1998. "Análisis Metodológico de la Distribución de los Recursos en el Ramo 33." In *Comisión de Desarrollo Social Instrumentos de Distribución de los Recursos del Ramo 33*. México: Cámara de Diputados.

Libonatti, Oscar, and Mario Salinardi. 1994. *IVA Provincial: Una Propuesta para Su Implementación*. Buenos Aires.

Longo, Carlos. 1982. "Restricted Origin Principle under Triangular Trade Flows: Implications for Trade and Tax Revenues." *Journal of Development Economics* 10: 103–12.

Martínez Almazán, Raúl. 1980. "Las Relaciones Fiscales y Financieras Intergubernamentales en México." México: INAP.

Martínez Cabañas, Gustavo. 1985. "La Administración Estatal y Municipal en México." México: INAP.

Martinez-Vasquez, Jorge, Charles E. McLure, Jr., and Sally Wallace. 1995. "Subnational Fiscal Decentralization in Ukraine." In Richard M. Bird, Robert D. Ebel, and Christine I. Wallich, eds., *Decentralization of the Socialist State: Intergovernmental Finance in Transition Economies*. Washington, D.C.: World Bank, pp. 281–319.

McKinnon, Ronald I. 1997. "Monetary Regimes, Government Borrowing Constraints, and Market-Preserving Federalism: Implications for EMU." In Thomas J. Courchene, ed., *The Nation State in a Global/Information Era: Policy Challenges 5*. The Bell Canada Papers on Economic and Public Policy. Kingston, Ontario: John Deutsch Institute for the Study of Economic Policy, 101–142.

McKinnon, Ronald I. 1998. "Monetary Regimes, Government Borrowing Constraints, and Market-Preserving Federalism: Implications for the EMU." In Thomas J Courchene, ed., *The Nation State in a Global/Information Era: Policy Challenges*. Queen's University: The John Deutsch Institute for the Study of Economic Policy, 101-142.

McLure, Jr., Charles E. 1980a. "State and Federal Relations in the Taxation of Value Added." *Journal of Corporation Law* 6: 127–39.

_____. 1980b. "The State Corporate Income Tax: Lambs in Wolves' Clothing." In Henry J. Aaron and Michael J. Boskin, eds., *The*

Economics of Taxation. Washington, D.C.: The Brookings Institution, 327–346.

_____. "The Elusive Incidence of the Corporate Income Tax: The State Case." *Public Finance Quarterly* 9(4) :395–413, October.

_____. "Defining a Unitary Business: An Economist's View." In Charles E. McLure, Jr., ed., *The State Corporation Income Tax: Issues in Worldwide Unitary Combination*. Stanford, CA: Hoover Institution Press, 89–124.

_____. "The Sharing of Taxes on Natural Resources and the Future of the Russian Federation." In Christine Wallich, ed., *Russia and the Challenge of Fiscal Federalism*. Washington, D.C.: World Bank, 181–217.

_____. "Revenue Assignment and Intergovernmental Fiscal Relations in Russia." In Edward Lazear, ed., *Economic Reform in Eastern Europe and Russia: Realities of Reform*. Palo Alto, CA: Hoover Institution Press, 199–246.

_____. 1997. "Taxation of Electronic Commerce: Economic Objectives, Technological Constraints, and Tax Law." *Tax Law Review* 52 (Spring): 269-423.

_____. 1998. "Protecting Dual VATs from Evasion on Cross-Border Trade: An Addendum to Bird and Gendron." Processed. (Forthcoming.)

_____. 1999. "Electronic Commerce and the State Retail Sales Tax: A Challenge to American Federalism." *International Tax and Public Finance* 6(2): 193–224, May.

McLure, Charles E., Jr., Christine Wallich, and Jennie I. Litvack. 1995. "Special Issues in Russian Federal Finance: Ethnic Separatism and Natural Resources." In Richard M. Bird, Robert D. Ebel and Christine I. Wallich, eds., *Decentralization of the Socialist State: Intergovernmental Finance in Transition Economies*. Washington, D.C.: World Bank, 379–404.

Merino. M. Coordinador. 1994 *En busca de la democracia municipal*, Ed. Colmex, México

Merino, Gustavo. 1998. "Las transferencias federales para la educación en México: Una evaluación de sus criterios de equidad y eficiencia." *Gestión y Política Pública* (CIDE) 7(2).

Mieszkowski, Peter, and Eric Toder. 1983. "Taxation of Energy Resources." In Charles E. McLure, Jr. and Peter Mieszkowski, eds., *Fiscal Federalism and the Taxation of Natural Resources*. Cambridge: Lexington Books, 5–91.

Mogollón, Olivia. 1999. "Posibles influencias electorales y partidistas en la distribució de recursos del Fondo de Desarrollo Social Municipal." Washington, D.C.: The World Bank. Processed.

Molinar Horcasitas, Juan, and Jeff Weldon. 1994. "Electoral Determinants and Consequences of National Solidarity." In Wayne Cornelius, Ann Craig and Jonathan Fox, eds., *Transforming State Society Relations in*

Mexico: The National Solidarity Strategy. San Diego: Center for
U.S.–Mexican Studies.

Musgrave, Richard A. 1983. "Who Should Tax, Where, and What?" In
Charles E. McLure, Jr., ed., *Tax Assignment in Federal Countries*.
Canberra: Centre for Research on Federal Financial Relations, 2–19.

Navarrete, Juan. 1995. "Convergencia: Un Estudio para los Estados de la
República Mexicana." Documento de Trabajo del CIDE, División de
Economía, No. 42. México: CIDE.

Navarrete, Juan. 1995. "Convergencia: Un Estudio para los Estados de la
República Mexicana?" Documento de Trabajo del CIDE, División de
Economía No.42. México: CIDE.

Oates, Wallace E. 1972. *Fiscal Federalism*. New York: Harcourt Brace
Jovanovich, Inc.

———. 1983. "Tax Effectiveness and Tax Equity in Federal Countries:
Commentary." In Charles McLure, ed., *Tax Assignment in Federal
Countries*. Canberra: The Australian National University, Federalism
Research Centre.

———. 1994. "Federalism and Government Finance." In John M. Quigley
and Eugene Smolensky, eds., *Modern Public Finance*. Cambridge, MA:
Harvard University Press, 126–51.

Organización para la Cooperación y el Desarrollo Económico (OCDE).
1998. "Capítulo especial: Reforma del sistema de salud." Estudios
económicos de la OCDE. Paris.

Pani, Alberto. 1926. "Convocatoria." Primera Convención Nacional Fiscal
(1926) Memoria. México: Secretaria de Hacienda y Crédito Público.

Pineda, Sandra, and Marcela Gómez. 1999. "El Reparto Municipal del
Pronasol: Criterios de Asignación en Aguascalientes y Michoacán."
B.A. Thesis, ITAM, Mexico.

Poddar, Satya. 1990. "Value-Added Tax at the State Level." In Malcolm
Gillis, Carl S. Shoup and Gerardo P. Sicat, eds., *Value Added Taxation
in Developing Countries*. Washington, D.C.: World Bank, 104–12.

"Programa para un Nuevo Federalismo 1995–2000." 1997. México: *Diario
Oficial de la Federación*, 6 August. http://www.cedemun.gob.mx/
nuevofed.doc.

Retchkiman, Benjamín, and Gerardo Gil Valdívia. 1981. "El Federalismo y
la Coordinación Fiscal." México: UNAM.

Riker, William. 1964. *Federalism: Origin, Operation, Significance*. Boston:
Little Brown.

Ring, Raymond J., Jr. 1999. "Consumers' Share and Producers' Share of the
General Sales Tax." *National Tax Journal* 52(1) (March, 1999): 79–90.

Saucedo Sánchez, Alberto. 1998. "Hacia el Federalismo Fiscal. La Reforma
del Sistema de Asignación de Participaciones Federales a los Estados."
México: INAP.

Scott, Robert Edwin. 1959. *Mexican Government in Transition*. Urbana: University of Illinois Press.

Secretaría de Gobernación, CEDEMUN, and INEGI. 1995. *Censo nacional de desarrollo municipal*. Mexico, D.F.

Secretaria de Hacienda y Credito Publico (SHCP). 1973. *Primer Informe Sobre las Relaciones Fiscales Entre la Federacion y los Estados*. Mazatlan: SHCP.

Stepan, Alfred. 1997. "Toward a Comparative Theory of Federalism." All Souls College, Oxford University. Processed.

Ter-Minassian, Teresa, and Jon Craig. 1997. "Control of Subnational Government Borrowing." In Teresa Ter-Minassian, ed., *Fiscal Federalism in Theory and Practice: A Collection of Essays*. Washington, D.C.: International Monetary Fund.

Trejo, Guillermo, and Claudio Jones. 1998. "Poverty and Income Distribution." In Susan Kaufman and Luis Rubio, eds., *Mexico Under Zedillo*. Boulder: Lynne Rienner.

Varsano, Ricardo. 1995. "A Tributação do Comércio Interestadual: ICMS versus ICMS Partilhado." Texto para Discussão No. 382. Brasilia: Instituto de Pesquisa Econômica Aplicada, Setembro.

Walsh, Cliff. 1996. "Making a Mess of Tax Allocation: Australia, as a Case Study." In Paul Boothe, ed., *Reforming Fiscal Federalism for Global Competition: A Canada–Australia Comparison*. Calgary: Western Centre for Studies in Economic Policy.

Watson, W. G. 1986. "An Estimate of the Welfare Gains from Fiscal Equalization." *Canadian Journal of Economics* 19: 298–308.

Weingast, Barry. 1995. "The Economic Role of Political Institutions: Market-Preserving Federalism and Economic Development." *Journal of Law and Economics and Organization* 11: 1–31.

Wilkie, James. 1978. "La Revolución Mexicana. Gasto Federal y Cambio Social." México: Fondo de Cultura Económica.

Willis, Eliza, Christopher Garman, and Stephan Haggard. 1999. "The Politics of Decentralization in Latin America." *Latin American Research Review* 34(1).

World Bank. 1996. "Mexico: Poverty Reduction. The Unfinished Agenda." Report 15692ME. Washington, D.C., December.

_____. 1998a. "Mexico: Advancing Educational Equity in the Context of Decentralization." Phase I draft report. Washington, D.C., November.

_____. 1998b. "The Transport Sector in Mexico: An Evaluation." Report 18153. Washington, D.C., June 30.

Zedillo, Ernesto. Various years. *Informe de gobierno. Finanzas públicas estatales y municipales*. Mexico, D.F.

Ziccardi. A. Coordinador. 1995. *La tarea de gobernar*, Ed. Miguel Ángel Porrua-IISUNAM, México

Author Biographies

ENRIQUE CABRERO MENDOZA, a Mexican national, obtained his master's degree in public administration from the Centro de Investigación y Docencia Económicas (CIDE) in Mexico City and subsequently undertook his doctoral studies in public policy at the *Hautes Etudes Commerciales* (HEC) in France. For the past ten years Cabrero Mendoza has been a professor and researcher at CIDE, where he is also director of the public administration program and founder of the journal *Gestión y Política Pública*. He is a member of the National System of Researchers (SNI) in Mexico. In addition to a large number of articles and chapters, Cabrero Mendoza is author or editor of several major works, the most recent of which include *La nueva gestion municipal en México (1995); Los dilemas de la modernización municipal (1996); Las políticas descentralizadoras en México, 1983–1993 (1998);* and *Gerencia pública municipal (1999),* all published jointly by Editorial Miguel Angel Porrúa and CIDE.

THOMAS COURCHENE, a Canadian national, was educated at the University of Saskatchewan (Honours BA, 1962) and Princeton University (Ph.D., 1967). From 1965 to 1988 he was a Professor of Economics at the University of Western Ontario. Dr. Courchene spent the fall term of 1986 as a visiting Professor at Ecole nationale d'administration publique (Montreal). For the academic year 1987/88, he occupied the John P. Robarts Chair in Canadian Studies at York University. In 1988, he accepted the Directorship of Queen's new School of Policy Studies (1988–92). Currently, Courchene is the Jarislowsky-Deutsch Professor of Economic and Financial Policy at Queen's, is a member of the Department of Economics, the School of Policy Studies and the Faculty of Law, and is the Director of the John Deutsch Institute for the Study of Economic Policy. Dr. Courchene was Chair of the Ontario Economic Council of Canada from 1982 to 1985, has been a Senior Fellow of the C.D. Howe Institute since 1980, was a former member of the

Economic Council of Canada, is a Fellow of the Royal Society of Canada (elected 1981) and is a Past President (1991–92) of the Canadian Economics Association. He received an Honourary Doctorate of Laws from the University of Western Ontario in 1997. In April of 1999, Thomas Courchene was invested as an Officer in the Order of Canada. Recently, Thomas Courchene was awarded the 1999 Molson Prize from the Canada Council for the Arts.

ALBERTO DÍAZ-CAYEROS, a Mexican national, holds a Ph.D. and an M.A. in Political Science from Duke University, and a B.A. in Economics from the Instituto Tecnologico Autonomo de Mexico (ITAM). After working for many years at CIDAC, Centro de Investigacion para el Desarrollo, A.C. a think tank in Mexico City, he is now Assistant Professor in the Department of Political Science at the University of California, Los Angeles. While at CIDAC, he worked on policy projects related to technology, housing, the North American Free Trade Agreement, savings, federalism and munici-pal government. During the 1996–97 academic year he was a Fellow at Harvard University writing his dissertation, which won in 1998 the American Political Science Association Award for the best dissertation in the field of Political Economy. He has taught in Mexico at ITAM, in both the economics and the political science departments, at Duke and Stanford Universities in the United States, and at Humboldt Universitat in Berlin. He has published in the areas of federalism, regional development, and political economy of budgets. During the 1999–2000 academic year he was a Visiting Assistant Professor at Stanford University.

MARCELO GIUGALE, an Argentine/Italian national, holds a Ph.D. and an M.S. in Economics from the London School of Economics, and a B.A. in Economics from Universidad Catolica Argentina. After a spell in academia, he joined the World Bank in 1989 as an economist in its financial research department. From 1990 to 1994, he was a Senior Economist in the Middle East Operations Vice-presidency, supervising Egypt's structural adjustment program and leading the Bank's reconstruction work in post-war Lebanon. From 1994 to 1998, Mr. Giugale was a Principal Economist in the Eastern Europe and Central Asia Region, responsible for the Bank's lending and analytical economic work in Lithuania and Kazakhstan. In September 1998, he became the Lead Economist for the Mexico Department, the posi-tion he currently holds. He held teaching positions at the London School of Economics and the American University in Cairo, and has published in the areas of applied econometrics, finance, business economics and eco-nomic development. Over the last six months, he led the World Bank team that delivered the recently approved US$600 million Decentralization Adjustment Loan for Mexico.

FAUSTO HERNÁNDEZ TRILLO, a Mexican national, holds a Ph.D. and an MA in Economics from The Ohio State University, and a B.A. in Economics from the National University of México. He has written several academic articles and two books in the area of Financial Emerging Markets. He held teaching positions at The Ohio State University, Universidad de las Américas-Puebla and CIDE. He has been a consultant for the Inter American Development Bank and the World Bank. Recently, he obtained the first place in the Daniel Cosio Villegas Prize of Economics. Currently, he is the dean of the Economics College at CIDE.

JORGE MARTINEZ-VAZQUEZ, a Spanish national, holds a Ph.D. in Economics from Washington University in St. Louis, Missouri where he was a Fullbright Scholar. He also holds Lcdo degrees in Law and Economics from the University of Barcelona, and an Lcdo in Political Science from the University of Madrid. Dr. Martinez-Vazquez is now Professor of Economics and Director of the International Studies Program at the Andrew Young School of Policy Studies at Georgia State University in Atlanta. Dr. Martinez-Vazquez has worked on-site in thirty different countries on fiscal decentralization, tax policy, tax administration, social safety net, fiscal management and budgeting, and other economic development issues. He has been an advisor to many foreign governments and worked as a consultant for the World Bank, USAID, IMF, ADB, IDB and the UN. Dr. Martinez-Vazquez has published widely on public finance and fiscal reform issues, and is the author of several books, numerous articles in refereed journals, working papers and book chapters. Over the last two years, he has been the director of the Russia Fiscal Reform Project, a multimillion dollar and multi-year effort funded by USAID to advise Russia's federal government and six regions in the areas of intergovernmental fiscal relations, tax policy, and tax administration reform.

CHARLES E. MCLURE, JR. is a Senior Fellow at the Hoover Institution at Stanford University. Prior to joining the Hoover Institution he was Vice President of the National Bureau of Economic Research (1977–81) and Cline Professor of economics at Rice University (1965–77). As Deputy Assistant Secretary of the Treasury for Tax Analysis from 1983 to 1985, McLure was responsible for developing the Treasury Department's proposals to President Ronald Reagan that became the basis of the Tax Reform Act of 1986, the most comprehensive reform of the income tax since its introduction in 1913. He was also Staff Director of the Working Group on Worldwide Unitary Taxation appointed by Treasury Secretary Donald Regan at Reagan's request. McLure has served as a Senior Economist on the staff of the President's Council of Economic Advisers, as a consultant to various agencies of the U.S. government, and an adviser to several international organizations, including the World Bank, the United Nations, the International Monetary Fund, and the InterAmerican Development Bank. He holds degrees in economics from the University of Kansas (B.A., 1962) and Princeton (M.A., 1964; Ph.D., 1966).

VINH NGUYEN, a United States national, is the Chief of Staff in the Mexico Country Management Unit, helping coordinate and facilitate the various sectoral activities under the department's work program. Since joining the World Bank in 1991, he has spent his time equally between direct operational activities (mostly in the Human Development sector) and fiduciary and administrative areas such as quality enhancement, portfolio management, budget, and office administration. Except for a brief turn in the Europe and Central Asia region, he has been involved mostly with Mexico, Central America and parts of the Caribbean. He has an MBA from George Washington University and a BA from Amherst College.

JOÃO C. OLIVEIRA, a Brazilian national, holds a Ph.D. in Economics from University of Cambridge, England, an M.S. in Economics from The London School of Economics, England, and a B.A. in Economics from Universidade de São Paulo, Brazil. Intermittently, since 1972, he has taught economics at University of São Paulo, University of Campinas, and University of Brasilia (Brazil). He worked as policy researcher and adviser for the Brazilian Government since 1974, and was Deputy-Secretary of the Brazilian National Treasury from early 1996 to early 1998. He has published in the areas of agricultural policy, portfolio management, economic development, public finance and debt management, and subnational government finance. Mr. Oliveira joined the World Bank in 1989 as an economist at the World Bank Institute, and then moved to operations as a senior economist for Angola. During 1994 and 1995 he worked as a senior economist responsible for Mozambique at the IMF. Presently Mr. Oliveira is a senior economist at the ECSPE (Fiscal Decentralization) in the Eastern Europe and Central Asia Region.

FERNANDO ROJAS, Colombian national, lawyer, holds LL.M./ITP from Harvard Law School and M.P.A from Harvard University. He was an independent consultant on fiscal, financial and institutional decentralization issues for most Latin American countries from 1976 through 1996. Mr. Rojas has taught fiscal policy and state reform at several Colombian universities. He has held visiting professor and researcher positions at Stanford University, the University of Wisconsin, Harvard University, York University (Canada) the Institute of Social Studies and the University of Amsterdam (The Netherlands). Mr. Rojas joined the World Bank in 1998.

STEVEN B. WEBB, a United States national, holds a Ph.D. in Economics and an M.A. in History from the University of Chicago, and a B.A. in Economics from Yale University. He taught economics and economic history at the University of Michigan 1978–86 and then was a visiting senior economist at the U.S. Department of State. He published research primarily on German commercial and industrial policy in the 19th century and the hyperinflation in the 1920s. He joined the World Bank in 1988 as an economist in the Macroeconomics and Growth division of the Research Department. There he produced operational reports and published research on the political economy of policy reform and central bank independence. As a senior country economist he moved to the Caribbean country operations division in 1992. With the reorganization of 1997, he moved to the Poverty Reduction and Economic Management department of the Latin America region, where he has specialized in fiscal decentralization issues, for both research and operations.